GAUGUIN

GAUGUIN

A RETROSPECTIVE

Edited by Marla Prather

and Charles F. Stuckey

PARK LANE

New York

Copyright © 1987 by Hugh Lauter Levin Associates, Inc., New York
All rights reserved.

This 1989 edition is published by Park Lane,
distributed by Crown Publishers, Inc., 225 Park Avenue South, New York, New York 10003,
by arrangement with Hugh Lauter Levin Associates, Inc.

Printed and Bound in Singapore

Library of Congress Cataloging-in-Publication Data

Gauguin, Paul, 1848-1903.
    Gauguin: a retrospective / edited by Marla Prather and Charles F.
Stuckey.
      p.   cm.
    Includes index.
    ISBN 0-517-68612-0
    1. Gauguin, Paul, 1848-1903—Themes, motives. 2. Gauguin,
Paul,
    1848-1903—Criticism and interpretation. I. Prather, Marla.
    II. Stuckey, Charles F. III. Title.
    [ND553.G27A4 1989]
    759.4—dc20

                       89-32080
                       CIP

ISBN 0-517-68612-0
h g f e d c b a

Paul Gauguin, *Avant et Après* © 1923 by Les Editions G. Crès et Cie., Paris.

Jean de Rotonchamp, *Paul Gauguin* © 1925 by Les Editions G. Crès et Cie., Paris.

Joris-Karl Huysmans, "L'Exposition des Indépendants en 1881," *L'Art Moderne*, 1883, G. Charpentier, Paris.

Correspondance de Paul Gauguin, Documents Témoignages, edited by Victor Merlhès, 1984. Reprinted by permission of Fondation Singer-Polignac, Paris.

Gustave Kahn, "Gauguin," *L'Art et Les Artistes*, No. 61, November 1925, Paris.

Paul Gauguin, *Diverses Choses*, 1896–1898, from a manuscript in the Louvre Museum, Paris.

Paul Gauguin, "Notes Synthétiques," *Vers et Prose*, Introduction by Henri Mahaut, 1910, Paris.

A.S. Hartrick, *A Painter's Pilgrimage through Fifty Years* © 1939 by and reprinted with permission of Cambridge University Press, New York.

Emile Bernard, *Lettres de Paul Gauguin a Emile Bernard*.

The Complete Letters of Vincent van Gogh, reprinted by permission of Little, Brown and Company in conjunction with the New York Graphic Society. All rights reserved.

Douglas Cooper, *Paul Gauguin: 45 Lettres à Vincent, Théo et Jo van Gogh* © 1983 by Vincent van Gogh Foundation/National Museum Vincent van Gogh, Amsterdam.

Armand Séguin, "Paul Gauguin," *L'Occident*, March, April, May 1903.

Maurice Malingue, ed., *Paul Gauguin, Letters to His Wife and Friends*, translated by Henry J. Stenning © 1946 by The Saturn Press, London.

Charles Chassé, *Gauguin et le Groupe de Pont-Aven* © 1921 by H. Floury, Editeur, Paris.

Charles Morice, *Paul Gauguin* © 1919 by H. Floury, Editeur, Paris.

Jules Antoine, "Impressionnistes et Synthétistes," *Art et Critique*, No. 24, November 9, 1889.

Lettres à Odilon Redon, presented by Arï Redon © 1960 by Librairie José Corti, Paris.

Octave Mirbeau, *L'Echo de Paris*, February 16, 1891.

Octave Mirbeau, "Paul Gauguin," *Le Figaro*, February 18, 1891.

G.-Albert Aurier, "Le Symbolisme en Peinture: Paul Gauguin," *Mercure de France*, March 1891.

Felix Fénéon, "M. Gauguin," *Oeuvres Plus que Completes* © 1970 by Librairie Droz S.A., Geneva.

Jules Renard, *Journal*.

Paul Gauguin, *Noa Noa*, translated by O.F. Theis.

Jénot, "Le Premier Sejour de Gauguin à Tahiti," *Gazette des Beaux-Arts* © 1956 with the authorization of Gazette des Beaux-Arts, Paris.

Paul Gauguin, *Lettres de Paul Gauguin à Georges-Daniel de Monfreid* © 1918 by G. Crès et Cie., Paris.

Paul Gauguin, *Cahier Pour Aline*.

Thadée Natanson, *Peints à leur tour* © 1948 by Editions Albin Michel, Paris.

John Rewald with Lucien Pissarro, eds., *Camille Pissarro: Letters to his Son Lucien*, translated by Lionel Abel © 1943 by and reprinted with permission of Pantheon Books, Inc.

Charles Morice, Preface to *Exposition d'Oeuvres récentes de Paul Gauguin*, Galeries Durand-Ruel, November 1893, Paris.

François Thiébault-Sisson, "Les Petits Salons," *Le Temps*, December 2, 1893.

Charles Morice, "Paul Gauguin," *Mercure de France*, December 1893.

Thadée Natanson, "Oeuvres Récentes de Paul Gauguin," *La Revue Blanche*, December 1893.

Julien Leclercq, "Sur la Peinture," *Mercure de France*, May 1894.

István Genthon, *Rippl-Rónai, The Hungarian "Nabi"* © 1958 Corvina, Budapest.

Ambroise Vollard, *Recollections of a Picture Dealer*, translated by Violet M. MacDonald, English translation first published by Little, Brown and Company, Boston, 1936.

René Maurice, "Autour de Gauguin," *Nouvelle Revue de Bretagne*, November-December 1953.

Julien Leclercq, "Exposition Paul Gauguin," *Mercure de France*, January 1895.

Eugène Tardieu, "M. Paul Gauguin," reprinted in *Gauguin in the South Seas* by Bengt Danielsson, translated by Reginald Spink © 1965 by George Allen & Unwin Ltd., London.

Paul Gauguin, *Oviri: Ecrits d'un sauvage*.

Henry Lemasson, "Paul Gauguin vu par un de ses contemporains à Tahiti," *Encyclopédie de la France et d'Outre-Mer*, February 1950.

Gustave Geffroy, "Gauguin," *Le Journal*, November 20, 1898.

Thadée Natanson, "De M. Paul Gauguin," *La Revue Blanche*, December 1898.

André Fontainas, "Art Moderne," *Mercure de France*, May 1900.

Bengt Danielsson and Patrick O'Reilly, *Gauguin journaliste à Tahiti et ses articles des "Guêpes"* © 1966, Société des Océanistes, Paris.

Gustave Kahn, "Paul Gauguin," *L'Art et les Artistes*, November 1925.

Charles Chassé, "Les Démêlés de Gauguin avec les Gendarmes et l'Evéque des Iles Marquises," *Mercure de France*, 1938.

Bernard Villaret, "Les dernières Années de Gauguin," *La Revue de Paris*, February 1953.

Guillaume Le Bronnec, "La Vie de Gauguin aux Iles Marquises," *Bulletin de la Société des Etudes Océaniennes*, Papeete, March 1954.

Pierre Borel, "Les Dernières jours et la Mort Mysterieuse de Paul Gauguin," *Pro Arte et Libris*, Geneva, September 1942.

Charles Morice, "Paul Gauguin," *Mercure de France*, October 1903.

Charles Morice, "Quelques Opinions sur Paul Gauguin," *Mercure de France*, November 1903.

W. Somerset Maugham, *Purely for My Pleasure* © 1962 by A.P. Watt Ltd. on behalf of The Royal Literacy Fund and William Heinemann Ltd.

Charles Baudelaire, *Les Fleurs du Mal*, translated by Richard Howard (Boston: David R. Godine, 1983).

ACKNOWLEDGMENTS

It is our pleasure to thank the following colleagues, without whose help this volume could not have been prepared. First, for their valuable assistance in obtaining photographs, we are most grateful to Gilles Artur of the Musée Gauguin in Tahiti; B. de Boisseson of the Services Photographiques de la Réunion des Musées Nationaux, Paris; Julia Bernard of The Art Institute of Chicago; Jane Hankins of the Museum of Fine Arts, Boston; Ira Bartfield of the National Gallery of Art, Washington; Thomas Grischkowsky of the Museum of Modern Art, New York; and Daniel Malingue and Maurice Malingue. We also thank Sarah Kirshner, who helped coordinate research on photographic sources.

For their expertise with regard to special issues in Gauguin's life and art, we are indebted to our colleagues Carol Christensen, Darcy Gallucio, Nancy Iacomini, and Thomas McGill at the National Gallery of Art, Washington. Richard C. Bretell, Douglas Druick, Gloria Groom, and Peter Zegers of The Art Institute of Chicago; Charles Moffet of the Fine Arts Museums of San Francisco; Susan Alyson Stein of The Metropolitan Museum of Art, New York; Françoise Cachin and Claire Frèches of the Musée d'Orsay, Paris; and Bengt Danielsson, Linda Nochlin, Bogomila Welsh-Ovcharov, and, most of all, John Rewald deserve our great thanks.

For the editorial production of this book, we thank Maria Chiarino, Sheldon Paradis, and the staff of Harkavy Publishing Service for their commendable contribution—including the translations by Alexandra Bonfante-Warren, Chester Burnett, and Thomas Spear. Philip Grushkin created the book's handsome design.

Hugh L. Levin and Ellin Yassky deserve our sincerest thanks for their patience, support, and good humor from beginning to end.

MARLA PRATHER

CHARLES F. STUCKEY

CONTENTS

CHRONOLOGY

1848
7 JUNE. Birth of Eugène Henri Paul Gauguin at 52, rue Notre-Dame-de-Lorette, Paris, to Aline-Marie Chazal (1825–1867) and Clovis Gauguin (1814–1849).

1849
Family leaves France for Peru.
30 OCTOBER. Father dies from a ruptured blood vessel at Port-Famine on the coast of Patagonia.

1849–1855
Paul, his mother, and his older sister, Marie-Marcelline, live in Lima with Don Pio Tristan y Moscoso, the younger brother of Gauguin's grandfather, Don Mariano.

1855
Gauguin's mother returns to France with the children and lives in Orléans with Isidore-Fleury Gauguin (Zizi), Paul's paternal uncle.

1856–1859
Attends a private boarding school in Orléans as a day student.
His grand-uncle, Don Pio Tristan y Moscoso, dies.
In 1859 Paul becomes a boarding student at a seminary of the chapel Saint-Mesmin near Orléans, where he remains for the next three years.

1860
Mother moves to Paris, 33, rue de la Chaussée-d'Antin.

1862–64
Mother brings him to Paris, where he studies at a secondary school for boys and she works as a dressmaker.

1865
Mother retires to Village de l'Avenir and eventually to Saint-Cloud; appoints her neighbor Gustave Arosa, an art collector and photographer, legal guardian of her children.
7 DECEMBER. Boards a ship at Le Havre, the *Luzitano*, en route to Rio de Janeiro, as an apprentice in the merchant marine.

1866
29 OCTOBER. Begins a thirteen-and-a-half-month trip to South America aboard the *Chili*, already a second lieutenant.

1867
7 JULY. Mother, age forty-two, dies at Saint-Cloud.
14 DECEMBER. Gauguin disembarks at Le Havre from the *Chili*.

1868
22 JANUARY. Officially enlists in the military.
3 MARCH. Begins his military service as a sailor of the third class at Cherbourg aboard the *Jérôme-Napoléon*.

1871
23 APRIL. His military service completed, he disembarks from the *Desaix*, now a sailor of the first class. Goes to Saint-Cloud and discovers that his mother's house has been destroyed in the Franco-Prussian War.
Returns to Paris, where Gustave Arosa finds him a position in the brokerage firm of Paul Bertin, 1, rue Laffitte, as a "remisier," a middleman between stockbrokers and clients.

Probably begins sketching and painting with Arosa's daughter, Marguérite.

1872
Under Arosa's tutelage, becomes familiar with works of the Impressionists.
DECEMBER. Meets a Danish woman, Mette Sophie Gad, then twenty-two years old.
Meets Emile Schuffenecker (1851–1934) at Bertin's firm; goes with him to the Colarossi Academy, where they study painting together.

1873
22 NOVEMBER. Marries Mette Gad in a ceremony at the Evangelical Lutheran Church of Paris. They set up house at 28, Place Saint-Georges.

1874
31 AUGUST. Birth of his first son, Emil.
Probably meets Camille Pissarro (1830–1903), a friend of the Arosa family, who becomes his mentor and introduces him to his Impressionist colleagues.

1875
JANUARY. Family moves to 54, rue de Chaillot.

1876
Exhibits a painting for the only time at the Salon, the annual government-sponsored exhibition of contemporary art.

1877
Rents a studio at 74, rue des Fourneaux.
24 DECEMBER. Aline, his only daughter, is born.

Paul Gauguin, ca. 1871.
Roger Viollet, Paris.

1878

25 FEBRUARY. Sale of Gustave Arosa's collection at the Hôtel Drouot.

1879

Begins seriously to collect paintings by the Impressionists.

10 APRIL–11 MAY. Exhibits for the first time with the Impressionists, in their fourth group show at 28, avenue de l'Opéra, although his marble statue is evidently a last-minute addition and is not listed in the catalogue.

10 MAY. Birth of his son Clovis.

JULY. Working in banking for a M. Bourdon.

SUMMER. Paints with Pissarro in Pontoise.

1880

1–30 APRIL. Exhibits eight works with the Impressionists at 10, rue des Pyramides.

SUMMER. Employed at the Thomereau insurance agency. Mette goes to Denmark with Emil, who remains there after Mette returns to Rouen.

In August, rents a house at 8, rue Carcel.

Paints with Pissarro in Pontoise.

1881

2 APRIL–1 MAY. Places six works in the sixth Impressionist show at 35, boulevard des Capucines, including his first exhibited wooden sculptures.

12 APRIL. Birth of his fourth child, Jean-René.

SUMMER. Paints with Pissarro and Paul Cézanne in Pontoise.

1882

1 MARCH–2 APRIL. Exhibits in the seventh Impressionist show at 251, rue Saint-Honoré.

SUMMER. Paints in Pontoise.

1883

14 APRIL. Death of Gustave Arosa.

5 JUNE–5 JULY. Paints at Osny with Pissarro.

6 DECEMBER. Birth of his fifth child, Paul-Rollon (Pola). Around this time he leaves the insurance agency to devote himself entirely to painting.

1884

4 JANUARY. Moves his family to Rouen in the hopes of reducing living expenses. Takes occasional trips to Paris. Contributes to two exhibitions in Rouen, including the Murer collection.

SPRING. Goes to the Midi with Emile Bertaux (b. 1848) on a political mission for the Spanish Republicans.

END OF JULY. Mette moves to Copenhagen to explore possibilities of relocating the family.

AUTUMN. Sends three paintings to the Kunstudstillingen in Kristiania (Oslo), Norway.

EARLY NOVEMBER. Mette takes the children to Copenhagen, for it is decided that the entire family will move to Denmark.

EARLY DECEMBER. Becomes a salesman for a French canvas manufacturer, Dillies and Co. Joins family in Copenhagen.

1885

JANUARY. Settles with his family in a seven-room apartment in the Gammel Kongevej district of Copenhagen.

APRIL. Moves to 51 Norregad.

1 MAY. The Society of the Friends of Art in Copenhagen mounts an exhibition of his works, which is closed to the public after three days.

JUNE–JULY. Dislikes Denmark intensely; returns to Paris with his son Clovis.

SEPTEMBER. Travels to England for three weeks.

OCTOBER. Lives in Paris with Emile Schuffenecker at 29, rue Boulard, but eventually rents his own apartment at 10, rue Cail.

Works as a billposter for 5 francs a day.

1886

15 MAY–15 JUNE. Takes part in the eighth and final Impressionist exhibition at 1, rue Laffitte.

JUNE. Meets the printmaker Félix Bracquemond (1833–1914), who introduces him to the ceramicist Ernest Chaplet (1835–1909), with whom he makes his first ceramics.

JULY. Places Clovis in boarding school and leaves Paris for the artists' colony of Pont-Aven in Brittany in the hopes of cutting his expenses. Takes room and board at the hotel of Marie-

The Family of the Painter in the Garden of Rue Carcel. 1881. 34¼ × 44⅞″ (87 × 114 cm). Ny Carlsberg Glyptotek, Copenhagen.

Jeanne Gloanec. Rents a small studio, where he works on ceramics.

Participates in group exhibition of Impressionist painters in Nante.

AUGUST. Refuses to exhibit with Georges Seurat (1859–1891), Paul Signac (1863–1935), and other Neo-Impressionists at the Société des Artistes Indépendants.

Meets painter Emile Bernard (1868–1941).

13 NOVEMBER. Returns to Paris, lives at 257, rue Lecourbe.

Meets Vincent van Gogh (1853–1890) at the Galerie Boussod & Valadon, managed by Vincent's brother Theo.

END OF NOVEMBER–DECEMBER. Spends a month in the hospital because of heart problems.

1887

Mette visits Paul in Paris and takes Clovis back to Copenhagen with her.

9 APRIL. Leaves Paris with Charles Laval (1862–1894), a fellow Brittany painter; they travel steerage to Panama aboard a sailing ship.

Works long days as a navvy on the Panama Canal to earn money and subsequently has no time to paint.

JUNE. Leaves with Laval for Saint-Pierre, Martinique, which he finds far preferable to Panama.

Manages to paint twelve canvases despite a bad case of dysentery.

NOVEMBER. Returns to France as a crewman on a sailboat. Lives with Schuffenecker and paints in his studio. Schuffenecker introduces him to Georges-Daniel de Monfreid (1856–1929), who becomes a lifelong friend.

DECEMBER. Works included in a group show with Armand Guillaumin (1841–1927) and Pissarro at Boussod & Valadon.

1888

EARLY FEBRUARY. Leaves for Pont-Aven, where he paints in the company of Charles Laval, Paul Sérusier (1864–1927) and, by August, Emile Bernard.

SPRING. Works occasionally on view in Paris at Boussod & Valadon.

SUMMER. Works on view in group exhibition of French art in Copenhagen.

AUGUST. Theo van Gogh offers Gauguin 150 francs a year in exchange for twelve paintings. Vincent van Gogh invites Gauguin to join him in the Midi to create an artists' studio of the South.

OCTOBER. Theo sells 300 francs' worth of Gauguin's ceramics.

23 OCTOBER. After several postponements, finally leaves Pont-Aven for Arles, at the expense of Theo van Gogh, to paint with Vincent.

EARLY NOVEMBER. First one-man exhibition organized by Theo at Boussod & Valadon.

23 DECEMBER. After quarreling with Gauguin, Van Gogh cuts off part of his own ear. Gauguin returns to Paris three days later. Lives once again with Schuffenecker, but hopes to return to Martinique.

1889

JANUARY. Rents a studio at 25, rue de Montsouris. Meets Dutch painter Jacob Meyer de Haan (1852–1895) through Theo van Gogh.

FEBRUARY. Returns to Pont-Aven. Approximately twelve works, including Vision after the Sermon, exhibited in Brussels at the Salon des XX ("The Twenty"), an artists' cooperative devoted to contemporary art.

EARLY MAY. Returns to Paris to help Schuffenecker with preparations for the group exhibition of Impressionists and Synthetists at the Café Volpini, just outside the grounds of the Exposition Universelle.

Probably meets Charles Morice around this time.

6 MAY. Opening of the Exposition Universelle, a world's fair that includes a large, government-sponsored art exhibition, from which Gauguin and his friends are excluded. Gauguin visits the Far Eastern exhibits frequently, particularly the Javanese village.

LATE MAY. Café Volpini exhibition, which includes seventeen works by Gauguin, opens but leads to no sales and receives minimal critical response.

Returns to Pont-Aven with Paul Sérusier. Hopes for appointment to the Far East from the Colonial Department.

20 JUNE. Revolted by the commercial nature of Pont-Aven and its artistic community, Gauguin and Sérusier move to Le Pouldu, a small coastal village in southern Brittany.

JULY. Sérusier leaves and Gauguin remains alone to paint for a time, but eventually returns to Pont-Aven. Meets up with de Haan, who returns with him to Le Pouldu, where they lodge at Marie-Jeanne Henry's Buvette de la Plage.

LATE AUGUST. Returns to Pont-Aven, where he takes a new studio.

2 OCTOBER. Goes back to Le Pouldu with de Haan, who helps support him financially. Rents a studio in a large seaside villa. Together they decorate the dining room of the Buvette de la Plage, with assistance from Sérusier and Charles Filiger (1863–1928).

31 OCTOBER–11 NOVEMBER. Gauguin's art collection and several of his early works are included in the exhibition of French and Nordic Impressionists in Copenhagen.

1890

FEBRUARY. Shows ceramics in a room adjacent to an exhibition of Pissarro's paintings at Boussod & Valadon.

7 FEBRUARY. Returns to Paris; lives with Schuffenecker at 12, rue Alfred-Duvard-Claye until asked to leave. Takes room in a hotel in rue Delambre. Eventually moves to rue de la Grande-Chaumière.

SPRING. Request for foreign appointment rejected by the Colonial Department.

APRIL. Plans to go to Madagascar with Bernard, Van Gogh, de Haan, and Schuffenecker to create a studio in the tropics. Hopes to finance trip with a major sale to a Parisian doctor named Charlopin.

LATE JUNE. Returns to Le Pouldu.

14 JULY. Short stay in Pont-Aven.

29 JULY. Vincent van Gogh dies at Auvers-sur-Oise.

SUMMER. Receives letter from Bernard, who has just read Pierre Loti's The Marriage of Loti, the novel set in Tahiti, and who suggests this locale as a possible alternative to Madagascar for the studio in the tropics.

7 NOVEMBER. Returns to Paris, leaving his paintings with Marie-Jeanne Henry in Le Pouldu. Monfreid offers the use of his studio in the rue du Château.

Meets several members of the Symbolist literary circle, including G.-Albert Aurier (1865–1892).

1891

23 FEBRUARY. Successful sale of thirty paintings at the Hôtel Drouot.

Exhibits ceramics and sculpture at the Salon des XX in Brussels.

MARCH. Visits his family in Copenhagen, staying at Hôtel Dagmar. Fails to convince Mette to join him in the South Seas.

15 MARCH. In Paris, through the assistance of the poet

Paul Gauguin with his children Emil and Aline, Copenhagen. 1891. Photo courtesy of Musée Gauguin, Papeari, Tahiti.

Charles Morice (1861–1919), Gauguin requests an official artistic mission to paint in Tahiti from the Minister of Education and Director of the Academy. They agree to purchase a painting for 3,000 francs upon his return from Tahiti.

23 MARCH. Banquet in honor of Gauguin at the Café Voltaire, with poet Stéphane Mallarmé (1842–1898) presiding.

31 MARCH. Leaves Paris for Marseilles.

APRIL. Leaves for Tahiti as second-class passenger on the *Océanien*.

12 MAY. Arrives at Nouméa in New Caledonia.

20 MAY. Benefit performance in Paris at Théatre Libre for Gauguin and the poet Paul Verlaine.

21 MAY. Leaves for Tahiti aboard a naval transport, the *Vire*. Exhibits ceramics at the Salon de Champ de Mars.

9 JUNE. Arrives in Papeete, Tahiti. Immediately sees French Governor Lacascade and is given a room in a government building until he rents his own house.

16 JUNE. Funeral of King Pomare V, which Gauguin later describes in *Noa Noa*.

AUGUST. Stays thirteen miles outside of Papeete in the house of the schoolmaster, Gaston Pia.

SEPTEMBER. Returns to Papeete.

Tires of life in the city; moves to the district of Mataiea, forty-five kilometers south of the city, and rents a bamboo hut. Brings a native girl named Titi from Papeete to live with him, but eventually sends her back to the city.

DECEMBER. Contributes to exhibition at Le Barc de Boutteville.

1892

EARLY 1892. Requiring hospitalization and in need of funds, asks governor for vacant post of magistrate in the Marquesas Islands, which he is refused.

APRIL. Resorts to odd jobs for wealthy businessman and lawyer Auguste Goupil.

Sends first example of his Tahitian work to Boussod & Valadon to gauge response in Paris.

1 JUNE. Out of desperation, writes to the Director of the Academy in Paris asking to be repatriated to France.

SUMMER. Gauguin seeks out a new vahine and brings home Teha'amana, a thirteen-year-old native girl.

DECEMBER. Request for repatriation granted by French government, but Governor Lacascade refuses to provide him with passage. Gauguin is forced to reapply.

Sends eight paintings with Officer Audoye back to France.

1893

FEBRUARY. Learns that Maurice Joyant, who took over the Galerie Boussod & Valadon after Theo van Gogh's death, sold several of his paintings but that Morice failed to send him the proceeds.

26 MARCH. Fifty works exhibited in the Free Exhibition of Modern Art in Copenhagen. A second exhibition opens the same day in Copenhagen at the Kleis Gallery with seven paintings and six ceramics by Gauguin.

MAY. Moves into Papeete with Teha'amana.

Works included in group show at Le Barc de Boutteville in Paris.

25 MAY. The governor of Tahiti once again receives orders to repatriate Gauguin.

14 JUNE. Leaves Tahiti for Nouméa on the cruiser *Duchaffault*. Expenses for the voyage paid by the French government. Brings sixty-six paintings with him.

21 JUNE. Disembarks at Nouméa.

16 JULY. Leaves Nouméa aboard the *Armand Béhic*.

AUGUST. Lands at Marseilles on August 30. Goes to Paris after Sérusier sends him 250 francs. Lodges once again at 8, rue de la Grande-Chaumière. Speaks immediately to the Galerie Durand-Ruel, which promises him an exhibition. Asks Mette to come to Paris, but she declines.

AUTUMN. Two paintings included in the exhibition *Portraits du prochain siècle* at Le Barc de Boutteville.

In September, goes to Rouen upon the death of his paternal uncle, Isidore Gauguin.

4 NOVEMBER. Exhibition opens at Galerie Durand-Ruel with forty-six works, mostly paintings done in Tahiti. The catalogue carries an extensive preface by Charles Morice, and Gauguin receives an unprecedented amount of attention, mostly favorable, in the Parisian art press.

DECEMBER. Rents two large rooms at 6, rue Vercingétorix, which become a weekly gathering place for a bohemian coterie of painters, musicians, and writers. He lives there with

Annah, a Javanese woman introduced to him by Ambroise Vollard.

Around this time Gauguin drafts *Noa Noa*, an autobiography of his trip to Tahiti, in collaboration with Morice.

Exhibits one piece at Le Barc de Boutteville.

1894

FEBRUARY. Receives inheritance of 13,000 francs from his uncle Isidore. Sends 1,500 francs to Mette.

Travels to Belgium for six days for Exhibition of La Libre Esthétique, where five of his paintings are on view.

FEBRUARY–MARCH. Works included in group exhibition at Le Barc de Boutteville.

APRIL–MAY. Goes to Le Pouldu with Annah. Marie-Jeanne Henry refuses to relinquish paintings that Gauguin had left with her.

25 MAY. Breaks his leg during famous brawl in which he is assaulted by a group of local sailors in Concarneau. After recuperating for several weeks, he still walks with a cane and takes morphine for the pain.

23 AUGUST. Trial of Gauguin's assailants in Quimper, twenty miles from Pont-Aven. Though found guilty of assault, they are only fined 600 francs. Writes to his Parisian neighbor, the musician William Molard (1862–1936), of his plans to sell all his belongings and move to the South Seas with Armand Séguin (1869–1903) and Roderic O'Conor (1860–1940).

14 NOVEMBER. Loses his suit in Quimper to retrieve his paintings from Marie-Jeanne Henry. Returns immediately to Paris, where he discovers that Annah has cleaned out his apartment, but has left his paintings.

2–9 DECEMBER. Holds an exhibition including watercolors, woodcuts, and monotypes in his studio at 6, rue Vercingétorix.

1895

18 FEBRUARY. Auction of forty-nine works at the Hôtel Drouot.

SPRING. Controversy surrounds Gauguin's attempt to exhibit his sculpture *Oviri* at the Société Nationale des Beaux-Arts.

3 JULY. Boards the *Australian* in Marseilles en route to Tahiti. Leaves unsold paintings with two dealers who promise to forward funds to him.

5 AUGUST. Arrives in Sydney. Leaves for Auckland, New Zealand, where he remains until the 29th. Studies Maori art at the Auckland Museum.

9 SEPTEMBER. Arrives in Papeete aboard the *Richmond*. Lodges in a furnished bungalow. Disappointed by recent modernization in Tahiti, plans to leave for the Marquesas.

NOVEMBER. Changes plans and rents property in the district of Punaauia on the West coast of Tahiti. Builds a bamboo hut with the help of local natives.

1896

JANUARY. Begins to live with Pau'ura, his fourteen-year-old vahiné.

FEBRUARY. Experiencing severe leg pain, takes morphine and talks of suicide.

Exhibits a ceramic vase, which is purchased by Ernest Chaplet, in the exhibition of Les XX in Brussels.

MARCH 23. Exhibition of works opens in Paris at 11, rue de la Chausée d'Antin.

JULY. Sends paintings to Daniel de Monfreid.

6–18 JULY. In the hospital in Papeete.

AUGUST. Paints portrait of daughter of Auguste Goupil, who hires him as drawing instructor for his two daughters.

DECEMBER. Pau'ura has a baby, which dies shortly after birth. Receives 1,200 francs from a dealer in Paris.

Contributes to Exhibition of Mystical Arts in Paris. The Galerie Vollard exhibits several works.

1897

JANUARY. The French colonial who owns Gauguin's land dies and heirs sell the property. Forced to move, borrows 1,000 francs and builds a much larger wooden house with a connecting studio.

3 MARCH. Sends eight paintings to Daniel de Monfreid in Paris. Contributes to the Brussels exhibition of La Libre Esthétique, the successor to Les XX.

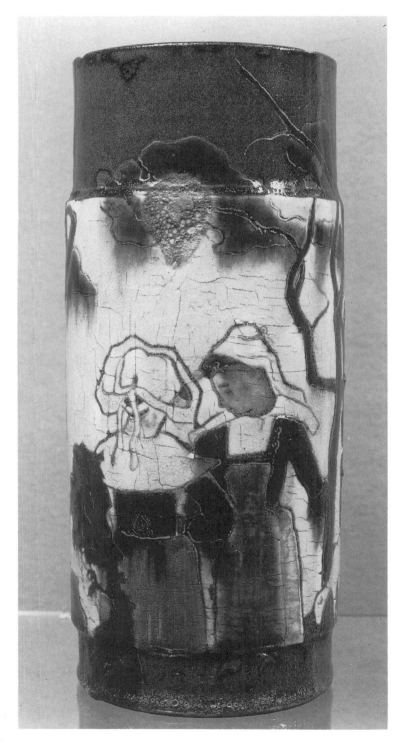

Vase decorated with Breton scenes. ca. 1887. Stoneware decorated with colored glazes, incised outlines, and lines in gold. Height: 11⅝″ (29.5 cm). Musées Royaux d'Art et d'Histoire, Brussels.

19 APRIL. Learns in a letter from Mette of the death, on 19 January, of his daughter Aline.

AUGUST. Has not painted for two months because of deteriorating health. Confined to bed because of ankle, begins to write *The Modern Spirit and Catholicism*.

FALL. Has a series of heart attacks.

OCTOBER–NOVEMBER. *Noa Noa* appears in *La Revue Blanche*.

DECEMBER. Completes magnum opus, *D'ou venons-nous?*. Contributes to exhibition of Impressionists and Symbolists at Le Barc de Boutteville.

1898

JANUARY. Attempts suicide by arsenic. Receives 700 francs from Chaudet.

MARCH–APRIL. Works as a draftsman for the Department of Public Works in Papeete for 6 francs a day.

SUMMER. Pau'ura steals some copra, a ring, and a coffee mill from Gauguin. She is fined 15 francs and sentenced to a week in jail.

AUGUST. Enters hospital for three weeks.

7 NOVEMBER–10 DECEMBER. Exhibition at Ambroise Vollard's gallery, 6, rue Laffitte, of ten works, including *D'ou venons-nous?* and eight related canvases.

1899

JANUARY. Quits position with Public Works. Returns to Punaauia and lives once again with Pau'ura.

19 APRIL. Birth of his son Emile.

JUNE. Contributes to satirical journal *Les Guêpes* (*The Wasps*) in Papeete. Maurice Denis writes to invite him to take part in a reunion exhibition of works by painters from the Café Volpini, but Gauguin declines.

21 AUGUST. First issue of *Le Sourire* (*The Smile*), Gauguin's mordant broadsheet, appears.

1900

FEBRUARY. Becomes editor-in-chief of *Les Guêpes*.

APRIL. *Le Sourire* ceases publication.

SPRING. At least one drawing included in an exhibition called "The Esoteric Group" at the Galerie Valéry in Paris.

MAY. Son Clovis dies. Gauguin, who has not corresponded with his wife since 1897, probably never finds out.

A single work is included in the Exposition Centennale.

23 SEPTEMBER. Speech against Chinese emigration delivered by Gauguin to the Catholic Party.

19 DECEMBER. Enters hospital at Papeete.

1901

WINTER. Through Morice's efforts, *Noa Noa* is published in book form.

Makes contractual arrangement with Vollard to send him twenty-five paintings a year, at 250 francs each, in return for an allowance of 350 francs a month.

2 FEBRUARY–23 MARCH. In and out of the hospital three times.

7 AUGUST. Sells his land in Tahiti for 4,500 francs.

10 SEPTEMBER. Leaves Tahiti for the Marquesas on the steamship *Croix du Sud*.

16 SEPTEMBER. Disembarks at Atuona on the island of Hivaoa in the Marquesas.

27 SEPTEMBER. Purchases plot of land in the center of the village from the Catholic Mission. Begins construction of his "House of Pleasure."

18 NOVEMBER. Takes new vahine, Marie-Rose Vaeoho.

1902

APRIL. Incurs wrath of Marquesan authorities by refusing to pay taxes and encouraging the natives to do likewise.

28 AUGUST. Charges brought against him.

14 SEPTEMBER. Birth of daughter, Tahiatikaomata. Sends *Racontars de Rapin* to Fontainas in the hopes of publishing it in the *Mercure de France*.

1903

27 MARCH. Summoned to appear before Judge Horville for accusations against the government. Fined 500 francs and sentenced to three months in prison, which he never serves.

2 APRIL. Appeals to the tribunal in Papeete. Asks Morice to incite opposition in France against the colonial authorities in the Marquesas.

8 MAY. Confined to bed and complaining of severe pain and fainting spells, sends for his friend Pastor Paul-Louis Vernier in the morning. Dies, presumably from cardiac failure, possibly from morphine overdose, around 11 A.M.

9 MAY. Buried in the Catholic cemetery on Hivaoa.

COLORPLATE 1. *Nude Study*. 1880. 45¼ × 31½″ (115 × 80 cm).
Ny Carlsberg Glyptotek, Copenhagen.

COLORPLATE 2. *Interior, Rue Carcel*. 1881. 51¼ × 64″ (130.5 × 162.5 cm).
Nasjonalgalleriet, Oslo. Photo: Jacques Lathion.

COLORPLATE 3. *The Sculptor Aubé and His Son.* 1882. 20⅞ × 28¼″ (53 × 72 cm).
Ville de Paris, Musée du Petit Palais, Paris. Photo: Bulloz.

COLORPLATE 4. *Rue Carcel in Snow*. 1883. 23⅝ × 19⅝″ (60 × 50 cm).
Private collection. Photo: Sotheby's, New York.

COLORPLATE 5. *Sleeping Boy*. 1884. 18⅛ × 22″ (46 × 55.5 cm).
Josefowitz Collection.

COLORPLATE 6. *Still Life in an Interior*. 1885. 23⅝ × 29 1/16″ (60 × 74 cm).
Private collection, Switzerland.

COLORPLATE 7. *Still Life with Peonies and Mandolin.* 1885. 24 × 20″ (61 × 51 cm).
Musée d'Orsay, Paris.

COLORPLATE 8. *Edge of the Pond.* 1885. 31⅞ × 25½″ (81 × 65 cm).
Civica Galleria d'Arte Moderna, Milan; Raccolta Grassi. Photo: Foto Saporetti.

INTRODUCTION

Although Paul Gauguin's controversial art career was relatively short, in just thirty years he created highly original masterpieces in a wide range of styles and mediums. Starting with his own unique version of Impressionist painting, he quickly moved on to a powerful, rather crude form of wood sculpture, to wildly unorthodox and fantastical ceramic objects, to Cloissonist painting, with its firm outlines, to Synthetist painting, with its broadly generalized forms, to Symbolist painting, with its mysterious contrasts. His evolution reflects his rapacious intellect, which absorbed the stylistic principles of a wide variety of art traditions: folk art, caricature, medieval sculpture and stained glass, Japanese printmaking and decorative arts, Persian manuscripts and textiles, Far Eastern sculpture, and the so-called primitive arts of the South Seas. Yet he seldom lost sight of the full range of Old Master conventions, epitomized for him by such diverse models as Botticelli, Holbein, Rembrandt, Quentin de la Tour, Delacroix, and Ingres. His eclecticism was apparently motivated by the desire to create a timeless, universal art language that could express, in addition to the physical facts of the visible world, the invisible emotional verities of thought, dream, and superstition.

Despite this rich complexity, Gauguin's extraordinary life has always intrigued his admirers at least as much as his art, and sometimes more. Global in scope, his life was shaped by noble, if heartless and often unnecessary, gestures of self-righteous sacrifice and defiance for the sake of art. No less willing to hurt others than himself to fulfill his destiny as an artist, Gauguin abandoned a business career and a wife and five children, and he manipulated friends and colleagues relentlessly, as he sought freedom from mundane responsibilities that interfered with his single-minded passion. Boasting of what he described as his half-savage temperament, Gauguin sought attention and admiration by posing as a restless maverick, always ready to accept poverty and suffering as he turned heel to escape compromise, leaving Paris for Rouen, Rouen for Copenhagen, Copenhagen for Brittany, Brittany for Martinique, and so on, until death overtook him on the remote South Pacific island of Hivaoa in 1903.

Of course, in the final analysis it is debatable whether Gauguin's peregrinations bought time for his art or lost it, but his unorthodox pilgrimage did startle and polarize the avant-garde art community in France. The purpose of this anthology of writings by the artist, his colleagues, and his adversaries is to enable modern readers to reconsider how the legend surrounding Gauguin came into being. Chosen for the revelations they present about the events in Gauguin's life and his principal theories about art, the majority of these selections first appeared before his death or shortly afterwards. Taken as a whole, they amount to a fascinating case study of how some modern artists have been able to obtain respect and understanding by manipulating public opinion. Apparently modeling himself on the outspoken James McNeill Whistler, who dared to speak out for his artistic views rather than rely exclusively on journalists and historians, Gauguin actively promoted his own cause by writing throughout his career, thus contributing to a trend that has continued with our own century's self-styled artist–celebrities, such as Max Ernst, Marcel Duchamp, Salvador Dali, or Andy Warhol. In a letter to Maurice Denis in 1895, Gauguin congratulated his young disciple for writing art criticism: " . . . it pleases me to see painters take care of their own interests. . . . For some time, most of all since [I formulated] my project to bury myself in the islands of the Pacific, I have felt this obligation with which young painters are imposed, to write about art topics in a reasonable fashion."[1]

Beginning in the summer of 1890, after Gauguin had decided to set off for Tahiti, he badgered such colleagues as Emile Bernard, Meyer de Haan, Camille Pissarro, and Charles Morice to use their influence with critics who were in a position to champion his works. Judging from the extensive essay that, by early 1891, Octave Mirbeau agreed to write, Gauguin himself must have dictated his colorful life in detail to the journalist, even while insisting that he welcomed obscurity, out of distrust for publicity. Mirbeau's highly romanticized account, reprinted as the preface to the catalogue for a fund-raising auction of Gauguin's works on 23 February 1891, subsequently influenced all of the artist's biographers, who tended to explore the same issues. In addition to Mirbeau, G.-Albert Aurier, a poet and critic dedicated to the new Symbolist movement in literature, agreed to write an extended explanation of Gauguin's work; this, too, became a touchstone for future authors. Signed on 9 February but not published until March, slightly too late to arouse interest in the auction, Aurier's analysis, with its detailed discussion of *The Vision after the Sermon*, articulates the theoretical tenets of Gauguin's art so comprehensively that, as with Mirbeau's essay, it seems that the artist must have helped to write the text. The parallels between Aurier's own ideas about Symbolist literature and Gauguin's art theories cannot by themselves account for Aurier's decision to stress certain, special issues. In particular, the passion of Aurier's conclusion, in which he proclaims that Gauguin should become a great mural painter, suggests that the artist himself or one of his closest associates must have supplied information, for otherwise Aurier, who claimed that his own personal acquaintance with Gauguin was strictly limited, could hardly have guessed that Gauguin aspired to such a career.

However, as editor-in-chief of *Le Moderniste*, the polemical and influential little periodical in which Gauguin made his debut as a critic, Aurier should have been aware of the artist's on-again, off-again ambition to write art criticism himself. Writers' genes were in Gauguin's blood. His maternal grandmother, Flora Tristan, a pioneering feminist and utopianist, published a novel, her memoirs, and several sociological texts; his father was a radical political journalist by trade. The first evidence of Gauguin's desire to write about art is contained in a letter to his mentor, Camille Pissarro, written just after the appearance of Joris-Karl Huysmans' 1883 article in *L'Art Moderne*, which included the first detailed discussion to be published of any of Gauguin's works. Disappointed with Huysmans' critical premises, Gauguin confided, "If only I were a man of letters! I should like to do this—there is something to be done here."[2] By 1885, Gauguin had begun to draft theoretical texts in the spirit of the writings of Eugène Delacroix, whose ideas about color intrigued Gauguin no less than they intrigued his chief rival, Georges Seurat. The present anthology includes the earliest of these drafts, entitled "Synthetic Notes," as well as the curious text about painting, alleged to have been written by one Vehbi Mani Zunbul-Zadi, that Gauguin showed to Seurat around this time. Since no source for this translation in the spirit of *1001 Nights* has yet come to light, it has been suggested instead that Gauguin may have composed it in the spirit of a fanciful literary forgery.[3]

[1]Maurice Malingue, ed., *Lettres de Gauguin à sa femme et à ses amis.* (Paris: Bernard Grasset, 1946), p. 267.

[2]Quoted in John Rewald, "Foreword," in *Paul Gauguin: A Sketchbook.* (New York: Hammer Galleries, 1962), p. 49. For related material, see Jean Loize, "Un Inédit de Gauguin: Huysmans et Redon," *Les Nouvelles littéraires*, May 7, 1953.

[3]H. R. Rookmaaker, *Synthetist Art Theories: Genesis and Nature of the Ideas on Art of Gauguin and His Circle.* (Amsterdam: Swets & Zeitlinger, 1959), pp. 314–315.

As the already cited letter from Gauguin to Denis makes clear, however, the former's serious efforts as a writer began around 1891, when he first sought exile in Tahiti. Three important texts by Gauguin must have been started at least as rough drafts by the time he returned to France two years later, although it is uncertain exactly when Gauguin neatly copied them into albums that, illustrated with watercolors, are reminiscent to some extent of picture books for children and, moreover, of illuminated medieval or Persian manuscripts. It is not known whether Gauguin intended to profit from the publication of all these texts as printed books or expensive facsimile editions. His direct source of inspiration for the visual format seems to have been Delacroix's magnificent album of notes and watercolors describing his visit to North Africa and Spain in 1832. This elaborate notebook was obtained by the Louvre in 1891, and Gauguin may have seen it either before his departure in June of that year or during his return visit to France from 1893 to 1895.

The first of Gauguin's illuminated manuscripts to have been completed was probably *Ancien Culte Mahorie*, a poetical account of native Tahitian religious beliefs. Adapted, and even plagiarized in parts, from an ambitious, early ethnographical study published in 1837 by Jacques-Antoine Moerenhout, this rambling gospel of exotic paganism has since served specialists as a subtext to the symbolism of Gauguin's early Tahitian paintings and sculptures, though it contains no information about modern Tahiti or what Gauguin did there. What was evidently Gauguin's second illuminated book, inscribed 1893 on the cover and entitled *Cahier pour Aline* in honor of his only daughter, is for the most part an anthology of short texts by Gauguin's favorite authors, including Edgar Allan Poe, Richard Wagner, and Paul Verlaine. But this manuscript does include several anecdotes from Gauguin's previous travels, as well as an exegesis of one of his most important 1892 paintings, *Manao Tupapau*. As if to contrast his own self-critical text in *Cahier pour Aline* with the efforts of professional journalists, Gauguin subsequently clipped all the newspaper reviews of his November 1893 exhibition in Paris and pasted them onto the blank pages of this same notebook.

The genesis of *Noa Noa*, Gauguin's most important literary account of his first trip to Tahiti, is too complicated to detail here, but it too was probably begun before his return to France at the end of August 1893.[4] In October of the same year Gauguin explained in a letter to his wife that he was busy with this book, which begins in diaristic fashion with Gauguin's arrival in Papeete, the capital, and goes on to describe the phases of his acclimatization to the Tahitian way of life that inspired him as an artist. As has often been pointed out, the ending of *Noa Noa*, with Gauguin's young Tahitian concubine watching his ship depart, so closely recalls the conclusion of a well-known book by Pierre Loti, *Le Mariage de Loti* (1882), that Gauguin's motivation to write *Noa Noa* can be presumed to have been at least partly financial. But that *Noa Noa* is foremost a highly romanticized autobiography indicates that Gauguin was most of all determined to create his own legend with this book. Coincidentally, between 1893 and 1895 Delacroix's *Journal* was published.

Although Gauguin had prepared a suite of ten magnificent woodblock prints to illustrate *Noa Noa*, these were not included when the text was ultimately published in 1897. The delay was mostly the result of Gauguin's decision to take advantage of the editorial skills of Morice, who offered to supplement the artist's own commentaries with poems as well as short sections of prose. Gauguin later claimed that he had been pleased at first with the notion that in such a collaborative undertaking

[4]The best accounts of the different manuscript versions of *Noa Noa* are: René Huyghe, "Présentation de l'Ancien Culte Mahorie/La Clef de *Noa Noa*," in Paul Gauguin, *Ancien Culte Mahorie*. (Paris: Pierre Berès, 1951); Jean Loize, "Gauguin sous le masque ou cinquante ans d'erreur autour de *Noa Noa*," in Paul Gauguin, *Noa Noa*. (Paris: André Balland, 1966); and Nicholas Wadley, ed., *Noa Noa: Gauguin's Tahiti*. (Oxford: Phaidon, 1935).

his own unpolished prose would seem "primitive" in contrast to Morice's more refined contributions. Morice felt at liberty to change Gauguin's texts, however, and diminished the intended contrast. Gauguin's "primitive" version is preserved only in an early draft of *Noa Noa* that was not published until 1954. But since the elaborately illustrated manuscript version of *Noa Noa* that Gauguin completed after his return to Tahiti corresponds rather closely to the text edited by Morice and published in 1897, it seems that Gauguin must have accepted the poet's changes. We have therefore included excerpts from this version, upon which the earliest biographers of Gauguin based their accounts of his life in Tahiti. The intentionally modern, stream-of-consciousness style that Gauguin preferred when he began *Noa Noa* is exemplified by the autobiographical fragments that he entitled "Natures mortes" and "Sous deux Latitudes" when he published them in a little art magazine in 1893 and 1894. Compared with Gauguin's spontaneously written letters, some of which are also included here, such accounts for the press were quite obviously literary exercises for him.

Every later witness account of his years in France between the trips to Tahiti indicates that Gauguin entertained liberally, holding court in his unorthodox studio full of South Seas exotica, and that he paraded through Paris and Brittany in unconventional outfits designed to attract attention. It may have been his overextended schedule that prevented Gauguin from publishing any sequels to "Natures mortes" and "Sous deux Latitudes." But no matter how busy, he hardly neglected the public relations campaign that preceded his final departure from France. His most brilliant idea was to invite the controversial Swedish playwright, August Strindberg, to write an introduction for the catalogue of a second fund-raising auction on 18 February 1895. After Strindberg replied with a thoughtful letter to decline this proposition, Gauguin went ahead and used the letter, along with his own reply to the unwilling supporter, as the sale catalogue's preface. A few months later he arranged an interview to state his case in the press one more time. The full extent to which Gauguin influenced journalists will never be known, but it is suggestive that by June 1895 his former friend Bernard had already issued a public challenge to the accuracy of the accounts written by Julien Leclercq, one of Gauguin's most dedicated acolytes.[5]

Such efforts to achieve notoriety and financial security before returning to the South Seas fell far short of success. His auction raised very little. No less optimistic that fame and fortune would catch up with him in the months ahead than he was that *Noa Noa* would soon be published, Gauguin left his unsold works of art with dealers and friends he entitled to accept offers. His letters back to France record the collapse of this optimism, aggravated by his failing health and constant poverty. Already by the summer of 1896 he was openly discussing the possibility of suicide. When he was too unwell or depressed to make art, he turned again to writing, making additions to his manuscript copy of *Noa Noa* and compiling a miscellany of other reminiscences and opinions which he entitled *Diverses Choses* (*Miscellaneous Thoughts*). At this time he also began a lengthy, tendentious, and turgid book, *L'Esprit moderne et le Catholicisme* (*The Modern Spirit and Catholicism*), about the shortcomings and contradictions of Christian theology. Putting all these texts aside at the end of 1897, however, he threw himself into one last monumental painting designed as a comprehensive testament to his world view: *Where Do We Come From? Who Are We? Where Are We Going?* This was a prelude to his suicide attempt in January 1898, the only record of which, of course, is the letter describing his failure to his most trusted correspondent, Daniel de Monfreid.

Embittered by his inability to exert meaningful control over his for-

[5]Emile Bernard, "Lettre ouverte à M. Camille Mauclair," *Mercure de France*, June 1895, pp. 332–339.

tunes in France, Gauguin involved himself in local politics and, following in his father's footsteps, became a contributor to a monthly anti-administration newsletter entitled *Les Guêpes* (*The Wasps*).[6] Enjoying his new spoiler's role and the notoriety it brought him, in 1898 he went so far as to begin his own little four-page monthly pamphlet, a broadside entitled *Le Sourire* (*The Smile*). Although these political articles shed considerable light on Gauguin's disenchanted personality, since they do not concern his art career, we have chosen to omit them here, preferring to focus instead upon the growth of his legend back in France. Reacting to the news of his suicide attempt, his supporters there renewed their efforts to bring his art to the public's attention by organizing an exhibition in Paris at the end of 1898 with *Where Do We Come From?* as the centerpiece.

When Gauguin received copies of the press reviews of this exhibition, he immediately recovered his drive to assert his critical beliefs and entered into correspondence with the critic of *Mercure de France*, André Fontainas, whom he had never met. Eventually Gauguin appointed this stranger as his literary agent, sending him in September 1902 a rambling text entitled *Racontars de Rapin* (*Tales of a Young Painter*) with the hope that *Mercure de France* would publish it. When it was refused, Gauguin, undeterred, sent Fontainas a long book in manuscript, full of disconnected anecdotes about his childhood, his tumultuous friendship with Van Gogh, his trials in the South Seas, and his ultimate opinions on criticism and aesthetics. Based in part on *Diverses Choses*, this final autobiography, which he entitled *Avant et Après* (*Before and After*), amounts to a sequel to *Noa Noa,* and he urged Fontainas to find a publisher.

Meanwhile, probably without Gauguin's knowledge, his former colleague Armand Séguin began to publish three important articles about the artist, whose works by now were in such demand that the murals he had painted at an inn in Brittany in 1889 had now been removed by speculators. Following Gauguin's death on 8 May 1903, news of which arrived in France in August, obituaries and biographies began to mushroom. Although *Avant et Après* would not appear in its entirety until 1918, Fontainas put this crucial autobiographical material into the hands of Morice, who used extensive excerpts for the biography that he raced to prepare for the October issue of *Mercure de France*.

With the help of Fontainas, Gauguin's widow, and Monfreid, Jean Brouillon, who had first met Gauguin in the company of Monfreid around the end of 1887, undertook the first official full-length biography. This appeared in 1906 under his *nom de plume* of Jean de Rotonchamp and included information from the missionary, Paul Vernier, who had cared for the dying Gauguin in Atuona, as well as from the writer Victor Ségalen, who had visited Atuona a few months after the artist's death and who subsequently attended the sale of Gauguin's possessions in Tahiti in September 1903. Upon his return to France, Ségalen met Monfreid and collaborated in the project—realized in 1918—to publish Gauguin's moving letters to his fellow artist. The first phase of the history of Gauguin's biography came to an end with the publication of Morice's long monograph in 1919. And as this brief introduction has tried to show, with few exceptions all the information in these early accounts was supplied directly or indirectly by Gauguin himself.

Some of the blanks in the story have been filled thanks to the ingenious, meticulous, and persevering scholarship of Merete Bodelsen, Charles Chassé, Jean Loize, Maurice Malingue, Ursula Marks-Vandenbroucke, and John Rewald, all of whom sought out documentary accounts from individuals who knew Gauguin or from their descendents.[7]

[6]Bengt Danielsson and Patrick O'Reilly, *Gauguin journaliste à Tahiti et ses articles des "Guêpes."* (Paris: Musée de l'Homme, 1966).

[7]For the best bibliography of writings by and about Gauguin, consult John Rewald, *Post-Impressionism from Van Gogh to Gauguin*, third ed. (New York: The Museum of Modern Art, 1978).

We have inserted some of this newer material into our unfolding chronological sequence of selections. With all of the material it has been our goal to keep the translations very literal (including misspelled names), even if the kind of prose favored by Gauguin's contemporaries sometimes seems stilted by today's standards.

It should be pointed out that the story is still far from complete. Although by now a full edition of Gauguin's correspondence has begun to appear and most of his important manuscripts have been published in facsimile editions—the major exceptions are *Diverses Choses* and *L'Esprit moderne et le Catholicisme*—many of the existing catalogues of his works in various mediums need serious revision, and there has still been no attempt at a comprehensive study of his drawings. Although Bengt Danielsson has written[8] and periodically revised a first-rate biography of Gauguin's years in Tahiti, the earlier part of his career has never been systematically studied. Until more information comes to light, Gauguin's own instincts about what to say and what to leave unsaid will continue to be the shaping force in how we see this last, great figure among the artists of the nineteenth century.

MARLA PRATHER

CHARLES F. STUCKEY

---

[8]Bengt Danielsson, *Gauguin à Tahiti et aux Iles marquises*, rev. ed., (Papeete: Editions du Pacifique, 1975).

Paul Gauguin

AVANT ET APRES

On His Family and His Early Life

January–February 1903

My grandmother was an odd old lady. Her name was Flora Tristan. Proudhon used to say that she had genius. Knowing nothing of the matter, I trust Proudhon.

She came up with a lot of Socialist intrigues, among other things, the Workers' Union. The grateful workers erected a monument to her in the Bordeaux cemetery.

She probably couldn't cook. A blue-stocking Socialist Anarchist. There is attributed to her, along with Père Enfantin of the Workers' Guild, the founding of a certain religion, the Mapa religion, of which Enfantin would have been the God Ma, and she, the goddess Pa.

I wouldn't know how to sort out the Truth and the Fable, and I give

Pierre Joseph Proudhon (1809–1865), prolific Socialist polemicist who was a staunch advocate of Gustave Courbet and of Realism in art.

Barthélemy Prosper Enfantin (1796–1864), French Socialist who, after the 1830 July Revolution, headed a group of followers of Saint Simonism. Known as "Père" to his disciples, his controversial stance on free love led to a rupture with this group, and he eventually founded his own experimental community.

Portrait of Flora Tristan (1803–1844), grandmother of Paul Gauguin. Lithograph by Jules Laure. Photo courtesy of Musée Gauguin, Papeari, Tahiti.

31

The Mother of the Artist. (Aline Marie Chazal.) 1890. Canvas. 16 1/8 × 13" (41 × 33 cm). Staatsgalerie, Stuttgart.

you all this for what it's worth. She died in 1844: many delegations followed her coffin.

What I can affirm, however, is that Flora Tristan was an extremely pretty and noble lady. She was a close friend of Mme. Desbordes-Valmore. I also know that she used all her fortune in the workers' cause, traveling constantly; in the meantime, she went to Peru to see her uncle, the citizen Don Pio de Tristan de Moscoso (a family from Aragon).

Her daughter, who was my mother, was raised entirely in a boarding school, the Bascans boarding school, an essentially republican establishment.

It was there that my father, Clovis Gauguin, made her acquaintance. My father was, at that time, a political reporter for Thiers and Armand Marast's newspaper, *Le National*.

Did my father, after the events of '48 (I was born 7 June '48), foresee the coup d'état of 1852? I don't know; in any case, he was taken with the notion of leaving for Lima, intending to start a newspaper there. The young family had some assets.

He had the bad luck to be stuck with a dreadful captain, which caused him to be atrociously ill, since he was in a very advanced stage of heart disease. Therefore, when he wanted to go ashore in Port-Famine, in the Strait of Magellan, he collapsed in the lifeboat. He was dead of a burst aneurism.

This is not a book, nor are these memoirs, and if I tell you of this, it is only incidentally, since I have in my head at this moment a lot of childhood memories.

Louis Adolphe Thiers (1797-1877), French historian, statesman, and key radical figure in the 1830 Revolution who served in various government ministries from 1832 to 1836. Known for his ten-volume Histoire de la Revolution française, *completed in 1827.*

The old, quite old uncle, Don Pio, fell head over heels in love with his niece, so pretty and bearing such a strong resemblance to his beloved brother, Don Mariano. Don Pio remarried at the age of 80, and had several children from the new marriage, among others Etchenique, who was for a long time president of the Republic of Peru.

All this made for a large family, and my mother, in the midst of it, was a truly spoiled child.

I have an outstanding visual memory, and I remember that period, our house, and lots of incidents; the monument to the Presidency, the church whose dome, all carved of wood, was added later.

I still see our little Negro girl, the one who, according to the rule, had to carry the small rug to the church for us to pray on. I also see our Chinese servant who knew how to iron our clothes so well. He is also the one who found me in a grocery store, where I was sitting between two barrels of molasses sucking on sugar cane while my mother was tearfully imploring people to look everywhere for me. I have always had that kind of whimsical tendency to run away, for at Orléans, at the age of nine, I had the idea of running away into the Bondy forest with a handkerchief full of sand at the end of a stick that I carried over my shoulder.

It was an image that had fascinated me, showing a traveler, his stick, and his bundle on his shoulder. Beware of pictures. Fortunately, the butcher took me by the hand on the road and led me back to the maternal home, calling me a rascal. Having the attributes of a very noble Spanish lady, my mother was violent, and I received a few slaps from a little hand supple as rubber. It is true that a few minutes later my mother, crying, was hugging and caressing me.

But let us not get ahead of ourselves, and return to our city of Lima. In Lima at that time, that delightful country where it never rains, the roof was a terrace, and the owners had madness imposed upon them, that is, on the terrace there was a madman attached by a chain to a ring, and the owner or tenant had to feed him with certain very basic food. I remember that one day my sister, the little Negro girl, and I, sleeping in a room whose open door looked out onto an interior courtyard, were awakened and were able to glimpse the madman climbing down the ladder. The moon lit the courtyard. Not one of us dared to say a word; I saw and I still see the madman coming into our room, looking at us, then tranquilly going back up to his terrace.

Another time, I was awakened during the night and I saw the magnificent portrait of our uncle, which hung in the room. With staring eyes, he was watching us, and he moved.

It was an earthquake.

No matter how brave, or even how cunning one is, one quakes along with an earthquake. That is a sensation common to everyone and that no one denies having felt.

I knew this later when I saw, in the Iquique anchorage, a part of the city collapse and the sea play with the ships like balls lobbed about by a racquet.

I have never wanted to be a Freemason, because I didn't want to belong to any society, either from an instinct for liberty or a lack of sociability. Nevertheless, I recognize the usefulness of that institution as regards sailors, for in that same Iquique anchorage, I saw a merchant brig, dragged by a very strong tidal wave, forced to break up on the rocks. It hoisted its Freemason pennant to the top of its masts, and immediately a large number of the ships in the anchorage sent boats to tow it with a bowline. As a result, it was saved.

*　*　*

How graceful and pretty my mother was when she wore the costume of a Lima woman, the silk mantilla covering her face, revealing only one eye: that eye so gentle and imperious, so pure and mild.

I still see our street, where the turkeys came to eat the garbage. Because Lima was not what it is today, a great, sumptuous city.

Four years slipped by thus, when one fine day pressing letters arrived from France. We had to go back to settle my paternal grandfather's estate. My mother, so impractical in business affairs, returned to France, to Orléans. She made a mistake, for the following year, 1856, the old uncle, tired from having successfully teased Mme. Death let himself be taken by surprise.

Don Pio de Tristan de Moscoso was no more. He was 113 years old. In memory of his beloved brother, he had settled on my mother an annuity of 5,000 hard piasters, which came to a little more than 25,000 francs. At his deathbed, the family circumvented the old man's wishes, and seized that immense fortune, which was swallowed up in Paris in extravagant expenditures. Only one cousin is left in Lima, still lives, very wealthy, in a mummified state. The mummies of Peru are famous.

Etchenique came the following year to propose an arrangement to my mother, who, proud as ever, replied: "All or nothing." It was nothing.

Although, aside from the wretched poverty, things were thereafter very simple.

Much later, in 1880, I believe, Etchenique returned to Paris as ambassador, charged with arranging the guarantee for the Peruvian loan with the Discount Bank (Guano business).

He stayed with his sister, who had a splendid mansion in rue de Chaillot, and, prudent ambassador that he was, he told them that all was going well. My cousin, a gambler, like all Peruvian women, made haste to speculate on a rise in the Peruvian loan at Dreyfus.

The opposite happened, for, a few days later, Peru was unsaleable. She took a bath for a few million.

"Caro mio!" she said to me, "I am ruined; I have nothing left now but eight horses in the stable. What will become of me?"

She had two wonderfully beautiful daughters. I remember one of them, a child my age, whom I had—it appears—tried to rape. I was, at the time, six years old. The rape could not have been very vicious, and we probably both thought it was an innocent game.

As one can see, my life has always been hurlyburly, very unsettled. There are, in me, many mixtures. A vulgar sailor, agreed: But there is some culture, or, to put it better, two cultures.

I could avoid writing that, but on the other hand, why shouldn't I write it: For no other reason than to amuse myself.

*   *   *

A little later, I was carving with a knife and sculpting dagger handles without the daggers; a lot of little dreams incomprehensible to grownups. A little old lady, a friend of ours, exclaimed with admiration: "He will be a great sculptor." Unfortunately, that woman was no prophet.

I was sent as a day student to a boarding school in Orléans. The teacher said: "That child will be either a cretin or a man of genius." I have become neither one nor the other.

I came back one day with a few colored glass marbles. My mother, furious, asked me where I had gotten those marbles. I lowered my head and I said that I had exchanged them for my rubber ball.

"What? You, my son, you engage in trade."

That word "trade" to my mother's way of thinking became a contemptuous thing. My poor mother! She was wrong and right in the sense that, even as a child, I intuited that there are lots of things that aren't for sale.

At eleven, I went into secondary school, where I made very rapid progress.

Jean de Rotonchamp

PAUL GAUGUIN

On Gauguin as a Young Man

1906

Jean de Rotonchamp was the pen name of Louis Brouillon (b. 1848), a poet and painter friend of Daniel de Monfreid who met Gauguin around 1887.

Madame Clovis Gauguin came back to France in 1855 in order to receive her father-in-law's inheritance and so that her son, who was seven years old at the time, could begin school. Up until then he had only spoken Spanish.

He began as an off-campus student in a boarding school in Orléans, then, at age eleven, he moved to a Catholic secondary school in that city, until finishing his last year as a boarding student at the lycée. This was how he did his primary and secondary study, which constituted all the literary and scientific knowledge he was to acquire.

The goal he set himself, therefore—due to the memory of his recent and precocious navigations—was to become a sailor. The family dreamed of him attending the naval academy, but the task was so arduous that when the hour of the exam arrived, the schoolboy, more in love with freedom than with work, was not in any state to participate advantageously.

They thus resolved to enter young Paul in the merchant marine.

For him, this solution was as good as the other, his desire being above all to sail.

At the age of seventeen, in 1865, the one-time Catholic schoolboy embarked as an apprentice in the merchant marine.

* * *

His mother, who had retired to Saint-Cloud, died there before he reached legal adulthood. She had established a close friendship with the Arosa family, who had a very pretty country house in the same little village neighboring her own. At her death, Gustave Arosa, who had developed a great affection for Madame Gauguin's young children, was asked by the family to become the guardian of the orphans, and, having accepted the responsibility, henceforth looked after them with the greatest consideration.

With his benevolent recommendation, Paul was employed, when he returned from his maritime service, at Bertin, a stock brokerage in the rue Laffitte, and there began his career in finance. He stayed with this company for eleven straight years. The banker Calzado, Gustave Arosa's son-in-law, was never other than a friend to him.

Having from then on an assured position, Paul Gauguin was married in Paris on 22 November 1873 at the city hall in the ninth arrondissement and at the temple in the rue Chauchat, to a young Dane of the Lutheran religion, Mlle. Mette-Sophie Gad. She came from a very honorable Copenhagen family. One of her sisters married M. Horst, a member of the Nobel committee of the Norwegian parliament, and another of them became the wife of Fritz Thaulow, the painter.

The latter's family (which Jacques Blanche, in a canvas that was acquired by the Luxembourg Museum, depicted grouped around a painting that was in the process of being executed) is the product of another marriage and has nothing to do with the Gad family.

Gustave Arosa (1818–1883), photographer of art and collector attentive to the affairs of the children of friend and neighbor Aline Chazel Gauguin after her death in 1867. Arosa found Gauguin a Paris Stock Exchange job in 1871. An early supporter of such Impressionists as Monet, Pissarro, and Sisley, he owned seventeen Delacroix works and several each by Courbet, Corot, and Daumier, a collection that presumably first stimulated Gauguin's interest in art.

Fritz Thaulow (1847–1906), Norwegian artist who married the sister of Gauguin's wife and settled in Paris around 1874. He was chosen to be godfather to Emil Gauguin in that year.

Sleeping Child. (Aline Gauguin.) 1881. 21¼ × 28¾" (54 × 73 cm). Ordrupgaardsamlingen, Copenhagen. Photo: Ole Woldbye.

Paul and Mette Gad Gauguin, Copenhagen. ca. 1874. Photo courtesy of Musée Gauguin, Papeari, Tahiti.

At Bertin, Gauguin served as a liquidator and quickly learned the mechanics of the operation of the stock market, as he did everything he studied, and made a veritable fortune in good speculations. According to one of his fellow workers, Emile Schuffenecker, in one year alone he made a profit of about 40,000 francs. This was the period of splendor.

The beginnings of his artistic career were, to some extent, an accident, because before his marriage it does not appear that Gauguin was ever interested in painting. While he was at Bertin he got the idea of buying some paints and brushes and trying a few pictures in order to occupy his Sunday leisure time. These attempts were, from the outset, very encouraging.

Perhaps as a child in his guardian's house—though it is superfluous, in his case, to call something that is obviously predestination an unsuspected fact—he acquired a latent love for the painted work, a rudimen-

Charles-Emile Schuffenecker (1851–1906) met Gauguin in 1872 when both worked for the Bertin firm on the Stock Exchange. An art student in his spare time, he probably interested Gauguin in the Impressionists. He suggested to Bernard that he seek out Gauguin and often gave the latter lodging, a studio, and storage space. While Gauguin was away, Schuffenecker sought buyers for his works and forwarded him money in advance of sales. In the 1890s, out of sympathy for Gauguin's wife, his role in his old friend's business affairs diminished.

Clovis and Pola. 1885. Pastel on paper. 27¾ × 25½″ (70.5 × 65 cm). Mr. and Mrs. David Lloyd Kreeger. Photo: Raymond Schwartz.

Bust of Mette Gauguin. 1877. White marble. Height: 13¼″ (34 cm). Courtauld Institute Galleries, London; Courtauld Collection.

COLORPLATE 94

Philippe Colarossi, a sculptor who exhibited at the Salons from 1882 and established, at 10, rue de la Grande Chaumière around 1884, an open studio where students worked from models. Gauguin evidently taught a painting course here around 1890 or 1891. Jules Bouillot exhibited at the Salon from 1888 to 1895. Gauguin lived at this address from 1877 to 1880.

tary technical education, because Gustave Arosa was far from a stranger to artistic matters. Blessed with a delicate taste from childhood, he gathered in his house a certain number of paintings of the modern school and made a hobby of copying them by photoengraving. In this way he engraved a series of the works of Delacroix, Courbet, Tassaert as well as other contemporary artists. His prints were of a gray tonality, done on rice paper and numbered.

"No one," Madame Gauguin wrote to us on 15 October 1905, "gave Paul the idea to paint. He painted because he could not do otherwise, and when we were married, I had no idea that he was inclined to the arts. As soon as we were married, he began painting every Sunday—sometimes going to the Colarossi studio—but without thinking of a teacher. . . ."

Whatever the causes that determined his sudden attraction to the arts, Gauguin was gifted, and from the beginning, produced works that were not without value. A child's head, among others, dated 1875, reveals, by the manner in which it is drawn, a hand that is no longer that of a novice.

He also undertook two small marble sculptures that he did in the studio of the sculptor's helper, Bouillot, who was the owner of the house in which Gauguin then lived at 74, rue des Fourneaux.

Paul Gauguin

AVANT ET APRES

On Reading

January–February 1903

I have written somewhere, and I am not sorry, that reading in Paris was not the same as reading in the woods.

In Paris, people are in a hurry. In the restaurant, eating, I couldn't read anything except the *Journal*. At the general delivery, I read the letters then and there, even though I may reread them later. On the train, on the expresses, I invariably read *The Three Musketeers*. At home, I read the dictionary. On the other hand, I never read the books of which I have previously read the reviews. As far as I'm concerned, advertising gets mixed up in there somehow.

It's already something if I taste Bornibus mustard because I had seen the posters for it. Here, I am lying to you shockingly, for I do not like mustard, but a man forewarned is forearmed.

Do not think of reading Edgar Poe anywhere but in a very comforting place. And though you may be very brave, if you were only a little so (as Verlaine said), you'd be cooked. And, above all, do not try to go to sleep after looking at an Odilon Redon.

Let me tell you a true story.

My wife and I were both reading in front of the fireplace. It was cold outside. My wife was reading "The Black Cat," by Edgar Poe, and I, "Happiness in Crime," by Barbey d'Aurevilly.

The fire was about to go out, and it was cold outside. Someone had to go get coal. My wife went down to the cellar of the little house we had sublet from Jobbé-Duval, the painter.

On the steps, a frightened black cat leapt: my wife, too. Nevertheless, after some hesitation, she kept on going. Two shovelfuls of coal, then a skull came loose from the coal pile. Overcome with fear, my wife left everything in the cellar and rushed back upstairs, finally fainting in

Jules Barbey d'Aurevilly (1808–1889), critic, Romantic novelist, and crime-fiction writer heralded in Gauguin's Symbolist circle as a forerunner. Félix Jobbé-Duval (1821–1889), Brittany-born painter who rented Gauguin a house in the rue Carcel in 1880. In 1885 he helped Gauguin care for his son Clovis, and he apparently urged Gauguin to go to Pont-Aven and lodge at the Hôtel Gloanec.

Mette Gauguin and two of her children, Rouen, 1884. Photo courtesy of Musée Gauguin, Papeari, Tahiti.

the room. I went down next and, wanting to get more coal, I uncovered an entire skeleton.

All together, it was an old articulated skeleton used by Jobbé-Duval, the painter, who had thrown it into the cellar when it had fallen to pieces.

As you see, it is extremely simple; but the coincidence is nonetheless bizarre. Beware of Edgar Poe, and having taken up my reading once more, remembering the black cat, I found myself imagining the panther that acts as prelude to that extraordinary story that is "Happiness in Crime," by Barbey d'Aurevilly.

Indeed, one often recalls during that kind of reading an incident that is the same as the one the author tells.

Joris-Karl Huysmans

L'ART MODERNE

"The Exhibition of the Indépendants of 1881"

1883

Joris-Karl Huysmans (1848–1907), decadent Realist novelist with ultra-Catholic beliefs. His review of the 1881 Impressionist exhibition apparently did not appear until he published an anthology of critical commentaries as a book in 1883.

Last year M. Gauguin exhibited for the first time; he presented a series of landscapes, diluted versions of the still unresolved works of M. Pissarro; this year M. Gauguin is represented by a canvas that is totally his own, a canvas that reveals incontestably a modern painter's temperament.

It carries the title *Nude Study*; in the foreground there is a woman seen in profile seated on a couch and mending her blouse; behind her the floor, spread with a violet-colored carpet, recedes in the background and is intersected by an Algerian curtain.

I am not afraid to claim that among the contemporary painters who have worked with the nude, none has yet given such a passionate note of realism.

COLORPLATE 1

*   *   *

Here . . . we have a girl of our own time, a girl who does not pose for spectators, who is neither lewd nor affected, who very nicely busies herself with repairs to her old clothes.

And the flesh cries out; it is no longer that flat, smooth skin without marks or pores, that skin soaked uniformly in a tub of rose water and smoothed out with a tepid iron by all the painters; this is an epidermis that is flushed with blood and trembles underneath with nerves. What truthfulness, finally, in every part of the body, in this slightly flabby stomach falling on the thighs, in these wrinkles running beneath the dancing bosom, encircled in dark brown, in these slightly angular knee joints, in this jutting of the wrist bent over the blouse.

I am happy to praise a painter who has experienced no less than myself the imperious distaste for mannequins with pink, well-proportioned breasts and hard little stomachs, mannequins burdened with so-called good taste, drawn by formula like student copies after plaster casts.

Ah! the female nude! Who has painted it in its glory and reality, without some premeditated arrangement, without any falsification of the features and flesh? Who has made it possible to see in an undraped woman her nationality and the historical era in which she lives, her sta-

COLORPLATE 9. *Four Breton Women*. 1886. 28¼ × 35¾″ (72 × 91 cm).
Bayerische Staatsgemäldesammlungen, Munich. Photo: Artothek.

COLORPLATE 10. *Still Life with Profile of Charles Laval*. 1886. 18⅛ × 15″ (46 × 38 cm).
Josefowitz Collection.

COLORPLATE 11. *The White Bowl.* 1886. 23⅜ × 28¼ (59.5 × 72 cm).
Kunsthaus, Zurich

COLORPLATE 12. *Mangoes,* or *Gathering Fruit.* 1887. 35 × 41¾" (89 × 116 cm).
Vincent van Gogh Foundation/National Museum Vincent van Gogh, Amsterdam.

COLORPLATE 13. *The Bathers.* 1887 34½ × 27½ (87.5 × 69.5 cm).
Museo Nacional de Bellas Artes, Buenos Aires. Photo: Daniel Menassé.

COLORPLATE 14. *The First Flowers*. 1888. 27½ × 36¼″ (70 × 92 cm)
Kunsthaus, Zurich.

COLORPLATE 15. *Tropical Vegetation*. 1887. 41¾ × 35″ (116 × 89 cm).
National Gallery of Scotland, Edinburgh.

COLORPLATE 16. *Self-Portrait: "Les Misérables."* 1888. 17¾ × 21⅝″ (45 × 55 cm).
Vincent van Gogh Foundation/National Museum Vincent van Gogh, Amsterdam.

The Singer. 1880. Polychromed mahogany
and plaster. Diameter: 21″ (53 cm).
Ordrupgaardsamlingen, Copenhagen.
Photo: Ole Woldbye.

tus, her age, the virginal or deflowered state of her body? Who has
thrown her on a canvas, so alive, so true, that we dream of the sort of
life she leads, that we can almost search the marks of childbirth in her
limbs and reconstruct her sorrows and joys, identify ourselves with her
for a few minutes?

Despite his mythological titles and the bizarre costumes in which he
dressed his model, until today Rembrandt alone painted the nude. . . .
For want of an admirable painter such as this man of genius, it is to be
hoped that talented artists such as M. Gauguin will do for their time what
Rembrandt did for his.

* * *

Let me then repeat what I've said: M. Gauguin is the first in years to
have tried to represent the woman of our own time, and, despite the
heaviness of that shadow that falls from his model's face across her chest,
he has fully succeeded and created an intrepid and authentic canvas.

Over and above this work, he has presented a statuette in wood,
modern in the Gothic style, and a medallion in polychromed plaster, a
Head of a Singer, who recalls just a bit the type of woman adopted by
Rops; also an amusing chair full of flowers, with a sunny corner of a
garden, plus several views par excellence of that most familiar neighborhood—Vaugirard—a view of a garden and a view of the church, the
dark interior of which makes one think of a factory chapel, a splenetic
church, fit for an industrial city, that has strayed into this joyful and domestic corner of countryside; but although these paintings may have
some qualities, I will not spend my time with them, for the personality
of M. Gauguin, so resolute in his study of a nude, has with difficulty escaped, again, the grasp of his teacher, M. Pissarro.

Letter from Gauguin
to Emile Schuffenecker

On Painting

14 January 1885

For a long time, philosophers have been rationalizing the phenomena which seem supernatural to us and which we somehow *sense*. Everything is in this word. The Raphaels and others were people in whom sensation was formulated long before thought, which allowed them in their studies never to destroy this sensation and to remain artists. And, as for me, the great artist is the formulator of the greatest intelligence, to whom come the most delicate and consequently the most invisible feelings, or translations, of the mind. Look into nature's immense creation and see if there aren't any laws to create all the human feelings in all their varying and yet similar aspects. Look at a big spider or a tree trunk in a forest; without your realizing it, both of them produce an awesome sensation in you. Why are you disgusted by touching a rat and many similar things? There is no logical reason which applies to these feelings. All our five senses reach *the brain directly* imprinted with an infinity of things that no education can destroy. I conclude from this that there are lines that are noble, deceptive, etc. . . a straight line gives infinity, a curve limits creation without consideration for numerical fatality. The numbers three and seven have been discussed enough. Colors are even more explanatory although less multiple than lines because of their power over the eye. There are noble tones, others which are common, quiet, comforting harmonies, others which excite you with their boldness. In short, in the graphology you can see some characteristics of a sincere man and others of a liar, the reason why, for an appreciator, lines and colors do not also give us the more or less grandiose temperament of the artist. Look at Cézanne, who is not understood: an essentially mystical, Ori-

Hilly Road, Osny. 1883. 30 × 39¾″ (76.5 × 101 cm). Ny Carlsberg Glyptotek, Copenhagen.

ental nature (his face looks like that of an old man from the Levant; in form, he is fond of the mystery and the heavy tranquillity of a man lying down to dream; his color is solemn, like the Oriental personality; a man of the Midi, he spends entire days on mountain summits reading Virgil and looking at the sky; thus his horizons are very high, his blues very intense, and his red is stunningly vibrant. Like Virgil, who has several meanings that can be interpreted to your liking, the literature of his paintings has a two-sided parabolic meaning; its depths are imaginary as well as real. To sum up, when you see one of his paintings, you exclaim, "Strange, but it's crazy . . . mystically separated w r i t i n g . . . *drawing*, too. . . ." The more I advance, the more I give credence to this sense of translations of thought by something totally different from literature; we'll see who is right. . . . If I am wrong, why does not your whole Academy, which knows all the methods used by the ancient masters, make its own masterworks? Because it isn't composed of a nature, an intelligence, or a heart; because young Raphael intuited this, and in his paintings there are harmonies of line of which one is not aware, for it is the most intimate part of the soul that finds itself completely concealed. Look, even in the accessories of a landscape by Raphael, you will find the same feeling as in a head. We are pure in everything. A landscape by Carolus-Duran is as much a mess as a portrait. (It's hard to express, but I feel it). . . .

Gauguin demonstrates here his fascination with theories of graphology popularized by such authors as Jean-Hippolyte Michon (1806–1881), who believed that the intuitive, mystical Eastern races use a noncursive script (in which letters are not joined), whereas the rational, positivistic European and American peoples employ a cursive script.

Carolus-Duran, pseudonym adopted by Charles-Emile-Auguste Durand (1837–1917), a highly successful Salon artist and portraitist whose style reflects his obsessive admiration for Velázquez.

Anonymous. *Portrait of Paul Gauguin Carving a Wooden Sculpture*. ca. 1880. 11⅞ × 9¼" (29.5 × 23.3 cm). Nationalmuseum, Stockholm. Photo: Statens Konstmuseer.

Letter from Gauguin to Camille Pissarro

On His Life in Copenhagen

May 1885

At the moment, I'm at the end of my courage and resources. Misery in a foreign town! No credit and no money; each day I wonder if it wouldn't be better to go to the attic and put a rope around my neck. What holds me back is painting; this is my stumbling block. Wife, family, everybody, hangs this cursed painting over me, claiming that it's a shame not to earn one's living. But a man's capacities cannot satisfy two things and I *can only do one thing*: paint. I'm terrible at everything else. To paint, I don't have anything to buy colors with, so I've limited myself to drawing—it's less expensive. The German colors sold here are awful; they don't dry easily and after a while, some places are still oily while others are completely dry. And I can't sell anything—neither a drawing nor a painting, not even for ten francs. In a short time, I will send a few things to Paris; ask Durand-Ruel to take something *at any price* so that I can buy some colors. . . .

Besides, in two months, either I will have disappeared from the face

Skaters in Fredriksburg Park. 1885. 25½ × 21¼″ (65 × 54 cm). Ny Carlsberg Glyptotek, Copenhagen.

of the earth, or I will come back to Paris to live as a vagabond, a *laborer*, anything rather than suffer in this dirty country. The Danes! you have to have come here, as I have, to know them. The most complete slavery. . . .

Letter from Gauguin to His Wife, Mette
On Family Matters
29 December 1885

Let's not hurl accusations, it serves no purpose; after all, we have to be fair: it serves us right. As to being reunited some day, I don't think so, because I don't see how I would be able financially. I don't feel that, without capital, I have the required ability to assure you of the luxury

Portrait of Clovis. ca. 1886. 22¼ × 16″ (56.5 × 41 cm). The Newark Museum; Gift of Mrs. L. B. Wescott, 1960.

you need. Clovis is in bed today with a slight fever from a cold, but it's not serious. The only problem is that I'm forced to be outside while he is alone in the house. He is very reasonable and has understood that his father is poor; he therefore never asks for cakes, he who loved them so much. He grows before your very eyes, maybe that's what tires him: in any event, don't worry about him because he's always cheerful and has become very talkative lately, surprising everyone with his endless questions, which are sometimes embarrassing to answer. . . .

Gustave Kahn

L'ART ET LES ARTISTES

"Paul Gauguin"

November 1925

Gustave Kahn (1859–1936), one of the earliest proponents of free verse, helped to found and edit several important Symbolist periodicals—La Vogue, Le Symboliste, and La Revue Indépéndante. As a critic, he was the foremost supporter of Seurat and the Neo-Impressionists.

Amid the success of the exhibition, the Neo-Impressionists received the greatest part of the praise and blame. They were treated as confetti makers, but they were spoken of with regard to their talent and the novel look of their works, and the rue Laffitte exhibition truly became their exhibition.

The successful exhibition Kahn refers to is the eighth and last Impressionist exhibition of 1886.

When Pissarro had the idea of celebrating the success of the exhibition with a small dinner to which would be invited a few critic friends, Degas abstained, so it would have been a meeting composed entirely of Neo-Impressionists had Gauguin not attended. He joined the group somewhat confused by the exhibition and the new technique, and not at all in order to join in with this technique; but certainly the method interested him, attracted him, repulsed him at one point, attracted him at another.

The formula for luminous radiance, in the most brilliant solar clarity, that Seurat produced did not at all conform to Gauguin's search for harmonies of color which were oriented from that time on (his Brittany landscapes) toward rich, deep colorings presented in areas of gradation. He was looking for some kind of pictorial resonance in a solidity and beauty of harmonies similar to that of Oriental carpets.

Seurat had already spoken to me, when Gauguin was not in Paris, of what was referred to in Impressionism as Gauguin's "paper." There was no other way to name this text. For a long time, Gauguin carried it with him in his pocket, and sometimes he showed it to his friends. Most probably, it was the translation of some Oriental text regarding the distribution of color tones in the manufacture of Oriental carpets. Undoubtedly, this text forms the basis for Gauguin's odd note about the aesthetics of Professor Mani-Vehni-Zunbul-Zadi [sic] on pages 247–250 of M. de Rotonchamp's book. Gauguin was, therefore, drawn toward an entirely different conception of a painting's harmony.

Georges Seurat (1859–1891), along with Signac, developed a method of applying paint in small, uniform dots of carefully articulated colors to maximize brightness. Although they had formed the Société des Artistes Indépendants to exhibit these controversial works, beginning in December 1884, both participated in the last Impressionist group show in 1886. In June that same year, Seurat became Gauguin's adversary by trying to prevent him from using Signac's studio; this undermined Gauguin's longstanding friendship with Pissarro, who had begun to emulate Seurat's technique.

But, in Seurat's art, and in the search for contour and involuntary abstraction of figures at which Seurat arrived, Gauguin found certain echoes of his own preoccupations; and he showed a great liking for the Neo-Impressionists who, moreover, appreciated his decorative power.

I think it was Gauguin who chose the place for the meal: the Château-Rouge, overlooking Belleville. It was a Saturday, a day for business and wedding parties; it would be picturesque! Once this matter was settled, Camille Pissarro wanted all of us to arrive together at the Château-Rouge, and he told how it would be done. An omnibus—one only—went to Lac St.-Fargeau, an old double-decker omnibus with stirrups hooked

Women Bathing. 1885. 15 × 18¼" (38.1 × 46.2 cm). National Museum of Western Art, Tokyo; Matsukata Collection.

on rods on the side for climbing into the upper seats; it left from the Square des Arts-et-Métiers. We agreed to take one of these vehicles together and so arrived at the Arts-et-Métiers stop from all corners of Paris: Montmartre, the Latin Quarter, Vaugirard—except for Pissarro and his son Lucien, who lived, if I remember correctly, in the rue Paradis-Poissonnière. We took over the upper seats, and Gauguin was very cheerful. The dinner was great fun; the dessert was brightened by the Bengal lights that people from weddings lit in the woods. It was a kind of Parisian Arcadia, well-suited to the Impressionist aesthetic, while passing by us and brushing against us during the long courses of coffee and after-dinner liqueurs were young couples in love, bridegrooms, best men and bridesmaids, and little girls fascinated with Camille Pissarro's long white beard and handsome face like the Heavenly Father's. Afterwards, we took the vehicle back to Paris and dispersed into the cafés on the large boulevards. Naturally, we chatted of aesthetics and especially about painting. Pointillism was going to conquer the world. Gauguin kept to himself; he announced to Pissarro plans for long and faraway journeys. The impression discernible from Gauguin's remarks—brief sentences which would burst out of his private meditation—was that he did not believe that absolute pictorial truth had been found and that there was room for further research. He was undoubtedly anxious, concerned with discovering his own originality within himself.

He was anxious through reasoning, temperament, and, one would guess, heredity. In his inner nature he was a primitive, and in outward fact a learned autodidact. His past gave him an inclination for long reveries. If the reason he left for faraway islands was, as it was said, because he believed one can live for very little money in the colonies, it is plausible that his sailor's past was probably a stronger reason, with nostalgia for warmer settings and more colorful lands. One single journey, although interrupted, gilded with sun the art of a Baudelaire, who could find but few elements for his art in traveling. What then could have given life to Gauguin in new countries, countries to whose charm he had been subjected when young without being able to give shape to his joy and admiration? He wrote somewhere (regarding his difficulties with Van Gogh):

I never had the cerebral powers that others find, without torment, at the tip of their brush. They are the ones who get off a train, pick up their palette, and in no time at all sketch you an impression of sunlight. When it's dry, it goes to the Luxembourg Palace and is signed Carolus-Duran; I don't admire the painting. I who am so uncertain and so anxious admire the man who is so sure of himself, so calm!

He seems to say that he doesn't like to change his surroundings. But, in his return to tropical countries, he did not entirely expatriate himself; in reality he repatriated himself: he went to find his memories once again, the impressions from childhood and youth. He returned to his heredity.

*   *   *

Nonetheless, he was able to leave for the West Indies in 1887. He stopped off in Martinique.

What he exhibited upon his return in 1888 disappointed his admirers and critics; they expected new conquests of color and more radiant and more violent sunshine. In these paintings, with heavy and warm shadows, shapes appeared in violet and black. He simplified his colors and contrasted them violently. Pissarro defended him and explained him. In those warm countries where shapes were eaten away by light, nuance didn't exist, so one wouldn't dream of rendering it, but would pursue it by means of violent oppositions. Nevertheless, it was not a success; the few Gauguin collectors were disconcerted. This wasn't Pointillism, or even optical mixture, and this painting clearly did not break completely with Impressionist habits; the evolution which was beginning wasn't understood and, moreover, wasn't expressed with vigor; Gauguin had had difficulty with the climate. He began to paint again in Paris. This year-long journey had been for him of great aesthetic use, however. Now, very clearly, he could be differentiated from the others.

*   *   *

It is completely logical that he became differentiated because, far away from his friends, he had recaptured the points of originality in his beginnings. He had never been equal to the Impressionist masters in the art of making light play on surfaces, of capturing precious moments of nature, of offering all the fresh vibration of a landscape under dappled and varied streams of light. But, among this group, he was one of those with a fine sense of composition. His vision had grown larger since he had painted other things besides the Ile-de-France and Brittany, with their sweet clarities and iridescent grays. He had painted creatures of color, of strong builds, and of copper or ebony tones on whom light plays not with the nuances that it does on white people, but with harsh contrasts of shadow and light. He had been modified to the core. In addition, he had sought an originality, a mastery, because, since Seurat had revealed himself as the leader of the group, the desire of all the Impressionists of the second period was to find a system and become leaders of a school of thought. This was a keen desire for Gauguin, much younger than those of the first publicizing of the Impressionists and older than those of the second group, the "Neos." But his ambition here was mixed with a concern for realistic art. It was no longer in tonal division or in optical mixture that Gauguin saw the pictorial future. The qualities of the sculptor acted upon those of the painter. All things said, he was an Impressionist no longer. He was therefore welcomed as a master among the new young artists who, while having been influenced enough by Impressionism to not be attracted by any academicism, were looking for something else, something lateral or more definitive.

*   *   *

Paul Gauguin

DIVERSES CHOSES

On the Theories of Professor Mani-Vehbi-Zunbul-Zadi

ca. 1885

It was during the time of Tamerlan, I believe, in the year x before or after Jesus Christ. What does it matter? Precision often damages dreams, decharacterizes fables. Out there, from the place where the sun rises, which caused that land to be called the Levant, in a fragrant grove, a few young people, swarthy but long-haired, contrary to the customs of the barrack-room crowd, and a clue to their future profession, found themselves gathered. They were listening, I don't know how respectfully, to the great Professor Mani-Vehbi-Zunbul-Zadi, the painter, giver of precepts. If you are curious to know what that artist of barbaric times could be saying, listen:

He was saying:

Always use colors of the same origin. Indigo is the best base; when treated with spirits of niter, it becomes yellow, with vinegar, red. Druggists always carry it. Keep to these three colorations. With patience, you will thereby learn to make up all the colors. Let your paper itself lighten your colors and be your white, but never leave it absolutely bare. One must paint linen and flesh only if one has the secret of the art. Who says that light vermilion is flesh and that linen is shaded with gray? Place a white fabric beside a cabbage or a bunch of roses, and you will see whether it will be tinted gray.

Spurn black, and that blend of black and white that they call gray. Nothing is black, nothing is gray. What seems gray is a compound of light shades that a practiced eye discerns. The task of he who paints is not like the mason's, that is, to build, compass and square in hand, according to the blueprint provided by the architect. It is good for the young to have a model, but let them draw the curtains on it while they paint. It is best to paint from memory; in that way, your [work] will be your own; your feelings, your intelligence, and your soul will then survive the amateur's eye. He goes to his stable when he wants to count his donkey's hairs to see how many he has in each ear and to determine the place of each one.

Who says that one must seek contrasting colors?

What is sweeter to the artist than to allow the tint of each flower to be distinguished in a bouquet? Two similar flowers would therefore never be identical, petal for petal.

Seek harmony and not contrast, agreement and not conflict. It is the eye of ignorance that assigns a fixed and immutable color to every object; I have told you, be on guard against that danger. Practice painting it coupled or shaded, that is near or placed behind the screen of objects of other or like colors. That way, you will please by your variety and your truth—your own. Go from light to dark, and not from dark to light. Your work

"Tamerlan" was Timur, known as Tamerlane (1336–1405), Mongol warlord.

can never be too luminous; the eye seeks diversion in your labor, give it pleasure and not grief. It is for the sign painter to copy the work of others. If you reproduce what another has done, you are merely a painter of miscellany: you blunt your sensibility and immobilize your richness of color. Let everything you do breathe the soul's calm and peace. Also, avoid the pose in motion. Each of your figures must be in the static state. When Umra portrayed the torture of Ocrai, he did not raise the executioner's saber, lend the Khakhan a gesture of menace, or twist the condemned man's mother into convulsions. The sultan, seated upon his throne, wrinkles the crease of anger on his brow; the executioner, standing, looks at Ocrai as at a prey that inspires him with pity; the mother, leaning against a column for support, shows her hopeless suffering in the dejection of her strength and body. So that an hour passes effortlessly in front of this scene, more tragic in its calm than if an unsustainable pose had elicited a scornful smile after the first minute.

Apply yourselves to each object's outline; the sharpness of the contour is a prerogative of the hand that no hesitancy of will weakens. Why embellish without cause and set purpose? That is how the truth, the scent of every person, flower, man, or tree, disappears; everything fades into a same note of prettiness that lifts the connoisseur's heart. This is not to say that one must banish the graceful subject, but it is preferable to render it just as you see, rather than pour your paint and your drawing into the mold of a theory prepared beforehand in your mind.

A few murmurs are heard in the grove; if the wind had not borne them away, one could have heard a few offensive words: Naturalist! . . . Conventionalist! . . . but the wind bore them away. Meanwhile, Mani frowned, called his students anarchists, then continued:

Do not polish too much: an impression is not so enduring that the search for the infinite detail, done after the fact, will not harm the first impetus; by so doing you cool its lava and make stone from boiling blood. Were it a ruby, cast it far away from you.

I will not tell you what brush you must prefer, what paper you will take, and in what orientation you will place yourselves. Those are things that young women with long hair and small minds ask, that place our art at the level of that of embroidering slippers or making succulent cakes.

Gravely, Mani went away.
Gaily, youth took flight.
All this happened in the year ten.

Paul Gauguin

"Synthetic Notes"

1884–1885

One will, I think, read with interest the following notes, extracts from a sketchbook of the great Tahitian painter.

This notebook, in pages sixteen-and-a-half centimeters high, covered in heavy, gray cloth that is rather stained, contains beyond these notes sixty or so pages of drawings done in pen and ink, charcoal and colored pencil. It was brought back from the Marquesas—where Gauguin lived at the end of his life and where he died— by a colonial administrator who was a friend of the artist there and, when needed, his defender throughout all the harassment that he was never spared by the missions, the constabulary, or the courts.

Judging from the choice of subjects, the drawings clearly date from the Brittany period at Pont-Aven, and exhibit an elegant charm and a delicate freshness.

Because of their overall literary nature, the quality of their enthusiastic conviction, and also the quite justifiably pious sentiment that characterizes everything Gauguin did, these notebooks seemed to me worthy of publication. We can only believe that these notes are new material: since the death of their author the notebook that contained them has passed through so few hands!

Henri Mahaut
[1910]

Gauguin's text was first published in 1910 in Vers et Prose *with this introduction by Henri Mahaut.*

Painting is the most beautiful of all the arts; in it all feelings are summed up, looking at it each one can, through his imagination, create a novel; one single glance can engulf the soul in the most profound memories, a slight effort of memory and everything is summed up instantly. A complete art that sums up all the other arts and completes them. Like music, it acts on the soul through the intermediary of the senses, harmonious hues correspond to harmonious sounds; but in painting one obtains a unity that is impossible in music, where the chords come one after the other and one's judgment is tried by an incessant fatigue if it wishes to unite the beginning and the end. Finally, hearing is an inferior sense compared to that of the eye. Hearing can only cope with one sound at a time, whereas sight embraces everything and at the same time simplifies it according to taste.

As in literature, the art of painting tells the story it wants to, but with the advantage that the viewer immediately knows the prologue, the mise en scène, and the denouement. Literature and music demand the use of the memory to appreciate the whole. The former art is the most incomplete and the least powerful.

You are able to dream freely while listening to music, just as when viewing a painting. When reading a book you are a slave to the author's thoughts.

The writer is obliged to address the intellect before striking the heart, and heaven knows a reasoned sensation is not very powerful.

Only sight produces an instantaneous impulse.

But also writers are the only art critics; they alone defend themselves to the public. Their preface is always the defense of their work, as though a truly good work of art isn't its own best defense.

These men flit about the world like bats flapping their wings at dusk, their somber masses appearing from all sides. Animals unhappy with their lot, with bodies too heavy to soar upward. Throw a handkerchief filled with sand and they stupidly scrap over it.

They must be heard judging all the works of man. God made man in his image, obviously that flatters man. This work is to my liking and done exactly as I myself would have conceived it. Therein lies the whole of art criticism. To be accepted by the public, to attempt a work in its image. Yes, men of letters, you are not capable of critiquing art without making of it a work of literature. Because as judges you are already corrupt; you have a preconceived notion, that of the literary man, and you find it too valuable to consider the thoughts of another. You do not like blue, because you condemn every blue painting. Sensitive and melancholy poet, you want all pieces in a minor key. So-and-so likes graceful things, he does everything this way. Another likes gaiety, he would never conceive a sonata.

To judge a book one needs intelligence and instruction. To judge painting and music one needs something beyond intelligence and artistic knowledge, special sensations from nature; one must be, in a word, born an artist, and though many are called, few are chosen. Every idea formulates itself; it is not the same with feelings from the heart. What of efforts to master fear with a moment of inspiration; isn't love often instantaneous and almost always blind? And to say that thought calls itself spirit, while instincts, nerves, the heart are part of the material self. What an irony!

The vaguest, most undefinable, the most varied is exactly that, the material self. Thought is a slave to feelings.

Above man is nature.

Literature is human thought described in words.

Whatever talent you may have for describing to me how Othello, his heart devoured by jealousy, comes to kill Desdemona, my soul will never be as moved as when I see with my own eyes the stormy-browed Othello as he advances across the bedchamber. You also need theater to complete your work.

You can describe a storm with utmost talent but you will never make me feel it.

Instrumental music is, like numbers, based on a unit. The whole musical system proceeds from this principle and the ear becomes accustomed to these divisions, but you can take another foundation and the tones, half-tones, semi-tones, and quarter-tones would still follow. Leave the foundation and the notes fall into disarray. The eye is less used than the ear to sensing these discordances, but the divisions are also more frequent, and for greater complication you have several units.

With an instrument you begin with a single tone. In painting you begin with several. In this way, you begin with black and divide it until you reach white—first unit—it is the easiest and the most frequently used and so the best understood. But take as many units as there are colors in the rainbow, add those made by composite colors, and you arrive at a very respectable number of units. What an accumulation of numbers, a veritable Chinese puzzle; it is not surprising that the colorist's science is rarely enhanced by painters and little understood by the public. But also what a wealth of means to develop an intimate relationship with nature.

We are criticized for using unmixed colors placed next to each other. In this regard we cannot help but win, strongly supported by nature itself, which does not proceed otherwise.

A green next to a red does not yield reddish-brown as mixing them would, but two distinct, vibrating tones. Next to this red put a chrome yellow and you get three notes enriching each other and augmenting the intensity of the first tone: the green.

In place of the yellow put blue, you will find three different tones but with each vibrating against the other.

In place of the blue put violet, again you will have a unique tone but one that is composed, entering into the reds.

The combinations are unlimited. The mixing of these colors creates

Breton Girl Seated. 1886. Charcoal with watercolor. 12 × 16⅝″ (30.5 × 42.2 cm). Musées des Arts Africains et Océaniens, Paris.

a muddy tone. One color by itself is raw and does not exist in nature. They are only found in a visible rainbow, but how rightly rich nature was in carefully showing them to you one next to the other in a deliberate and immutable order, as though each color were born from another.

Now, you have fewer means than nature and you condemn yourself to being deprived of all she puts in front of you. Could you ever have as much light as nature, as much heat as the sun? And you speak of exaggeration, but how could you exaggerate when you always fall short of nature?

Ah! If by exaggeration you mean works that are poorly balanced, then, in that sense, you would be correct, but I would ask you to remember that, no matter how pale and timid your work, it will be accused of exaggeration when there is a flawed harmony.

Is there then a science of harmony? Yes.

And in this regard the sense of the colorist is, in fact, natural harmony. Like singers, painters sometimes sing off-key, their eye does not have the harmony.

Later, through study comes a whole method of harmony, unless one pays no attention to it, as in the academies and in most of the ateliers. In effect, painting has been divided into two categories. One learns to draw and later to paint, which brings us back to the fact that one is reduced to coloring between prepared outlines, much like painting a statue.

I hold that until now I've only understood one thing from this exercise, that color is no more than an accessory. It is necessary, sir, to draw properly before painting, and this is said in a professorial tone; for that matter, the greatest inanities are always said in this way.

Do slippers disguise themselves as gloves? Can you really expect me to believe that drawing does not come from color and vice-versa? And as proof I would show you that I can make a drawing larger or smaller just by the color with which I fill it in. Or try to draw, in exactly the same proportions, a Rembrandt head but use the coloring of Rubens; you will see how formless it would become, and at the same time the color will have become disharmonious.

For the last century we have spent large sums of money for the propagation of drawing and so increased the number of painters without making any advancement. Who are the painters we admire now? All the ones who disapproved of the schools, all the ones who have derived their knowledge from their personal observation of nature. Not one. . . .

A. S. Hartrick

A PAINTER'S PILGRIMAGE
THROUGH FIFTY YEARS

1939

Archibald Standish Hartrick (1864–1950), Scottish painter who had joined Cormon's studio by early 1886, thus meeting Van Gogh, Toulouse-Lautrec, Anquetin, and Bernard before spending the summer in 1886 at Pont-Aven, where he met Gauguin.

No one who ever saw Gauguin in his prime is likely to forget him. More than once I have been asked to describe my personal recollections of this formidable though creative personality; so here they are, inadequate though they may be.

I never knew him in the way I came to know Van Gogh, and doubt, after considering the man, if that would have been possible.

To begin with, I was but a somewhat green youth, an art student and a foreigner, while he was a man of the world, nearly forty years of age, the first time I saw him in Pont-Aven during the summer of 1886. Why Pont-Aven became a great resort of painters I cannot say. The landscape round about the village is not very attractive or varied. But Le Pouldu, at the mouth of the Quimper river, about fifteen miles away, where Gauguin went after his return from Martinique, is another story.

For dramatic strangeness, that was a wonder of a place; at any rate, such is the impression of it that remains with me of those days before the hotel was built, and before it had become famous among artists.

Imagine a country of gigantic sand dunes, like the mountainous waves of a solid sea, between which appeared glimpses of the Bay of Biscay and the Atlantic rollers. All this, peopled by a savage-looking race, who seemed to do nothing but search for driftwood, or to collect seaweed, with strange sledges drawn by shaggy ponies; and with women in black dresses, who wore the great black "coif" (like a huge black sun-bonnet). Gauguin has given us the exact spirit of the place in that strange picture he called "Le Calvaire"; a carved group of primitive nun-like women (probably the three Maries) supporting the figure of Christ beneath the cross; in the foreground a Breton woman in black with a black sheep; behind, the mountainous sand hills and a peep of the bay beyond.

In this picture of 1888 or 1889 all the characteristics of his later Tahiti pictures are already worked out, and good-bye said to realism and impressionism as we knew it.

Although, as I have said, I never knew Gauguin intimately, I saw him daily at the Auberge Gloannec [sic] for three or four months, and heard him talk. At the same time, I knew fairly well Charles Laval, the man who went with him to Martinique in 1887, and also P., a young Frenchman of means who became his pupil.

Charles Laval (1862-1894), a student, with Anquetin and Toulouse-Lautrec, at Cormon's. He met Gauguin at Pont-Aven in 1886, became his disciple, and accompanied him to Panama and Martinique in 1887. "P." evidently refers to Ferdinand Puigaudeau (1864–1930), an aspiring painter.

From these two I gathered, vicariously, perhaps more about him than I should probably have arrived at on my own.

For one thing I learnt what may now be considered strange, that in spite of his later reputation for amorous adventures, Gauguin's one cry then was "pas de femmes," and I well remember how sardonic and sarcastic he could be about some transitory attachments of the kind which were noticeable at the time. For instance, when he described the fatter mistress of a fat painter as his "slop-bucket."

"Pas de femmes": no women.

I doubt myself if women, certainly no educated women, ever got on well with him. In his *Intimate Journals* (called *Avant et Après* in French) he himself says definitely on this subject: "As you perceive, I do not know love. To say 'I love you' would break all my teeth . . . women, who are shrewd, divine this, and for this reason I repel them."

Charles Laval. *Self-Portrait*. 1888. Canvas.
19¾ × 23⅝″ (50 × 60 cm). Vincent van
Gogh Foundation/National Museum
Vincent van Gogh, Amsterdam.

Tall, dark-haired and swarthy of skin, heavy of eyelid and with handsome features, all combined with a powerful figure, Gauguin at this time was indeed a fine figure of a man. Later on, his low forehead, with its suggestion of a *crétin*, was a source of grave disappointment for Van Gogh, to Gauguin's vast amusement! He dressed like a Breton fisherman in a blue jersey, and wore a beret jauntily on the side of his head. His general appearance, walk and all, was rather that of a well-to-do Biscayan skipper of a coasting schooner; nothing could be farther from madness or decadence.

In a manner he was self-contained and confident, silent and almost dour, though he could unbend and be quite charming when he liked.

I can well believe what his son writes of him: "All his life my father shocked smugly respectable people deliberately, and for the same impish reason that impelled him to hang on his wall that obscene picture he tells about in these journals." Most people were rather afraid of him, and the most reckless took no liberties with his person. "C'est un malin" was the sort of general verdict.

"C'est un malin": "He's a bad one."

He was distinctly athletic in his tastes and had the reputation for being a formidable swordsman. I believe it was truly earned; anyway it added to the caution with which he was usually approached, for he was treated as a person to be placated rather than aroused.

Perhaps the most vivid memory I have of him is of a blazing hot day when I was painting, some distance down the river Rance, and I saw a boat rowed by two Bretons coming slowly up the river; it contained his pupil P., Madame X., her five small children with their maid, and, just astern, Gauguin, naked save for a pair of slips, holding on to a rope, was being towed along on his back, like a dead porpoise, but evidently enjoying himself hugely. He passed about ten feet below me and about fifteen yards away.

At this time he was still painting under the influence of Pissarro, or perhaps rather experimenting with the color theories of Monet or even of Seurat and Signac. I remember he painted a panel for the dining room of the auberge, an autumn landscape, which appeared to most of

Paul Signac (1863–1935), with Seurat, champion of the Neo-Impressionist style of painting in dots of carefully calculated colors.

us who fed there as being very extreme in its crude exaggeration of purple and gold, though of course it was nothing compared with that to which we were soon to become accustomed.

I well recall, too, the attack made on him by V., a Dutch painter, who, on the strength of a medal in the Salon, was more or less cock-of-the-walk among the painters then in Pont-Aven. He swaggered about the village, with long carroty locks, on the top of which was set a green velvet cap of Rembrandt pattern, and laid down the law on everything to everybody. Gauguin, shortly after his arrival, a stranger to most, came back for déjeuner one day and passed through the crowd at the door of the auberge. He was carrying a canvas on which he had been painting some boys bathing on a weir, painted brilliantly with spots of pure color in the usual impressionist manner.

V. started by asking, in the rudest way, what game was this he was playing, going on to quote Rembrandt, Bastien-Lepage, and himself as witnesses of its futility, while the majority crowded round to enjoy the fun of the newcomer being baited. Gauguin, however, only smiled grimly, and elbowing his way through went about his business without explanation or retort.

The sequel to all this was really funny. Within a fortnight V.'s special pupil, P., went off to Gauguin for instruction, leaving V. altogether. He invited his new master to share a studio he had taken at les Avens, and there Gauguin worked in comfort for the rest of his time at Pont-Aven.

Within a month V. was secretly consulting his former pupil on Gau-

"V" refers to Hubert Vos (b. 1855), who won a medal at the 1886 Salon.

Jules Bastien-Lepage (1848–1884) received acclaim for his large Realist paintings of peasant life.

The Pension Gloanec, Pont-Aven. ca. 1890. Roger Viollet, Paris.

COLORPLATE 17. *Still Life, Fête Gloanec.* 1888. 15 × 21″ (38 × 53 cm).
Musée des Beaux-Arts, Orléans.

COLORPLATE 18. *The Vision after the Sermon,* or *Jacob Wrestling with the Angel.* 1888.
28¾ × 36¼″ (73 × 92 cm). National Gallery of Scotland, Edinburgh.

COLORPLATE 19. *Dancing a Round in the Haystacks*. 1888. 28¾ × 36½″ (73 × 92.7 cm).
National Gallery of Art, Washington, D.C.; Collection of Mr. and Mrs. Paul Mellon.

COLORPLATE 20. *The Turkeys*. 1888. 28¾ × 36¼″ (92 × 73 cm).
Private collection. Photo: Galerie Daniel Malingue, Paris.

COLORPLATE 21. *Little Breton Shepherd.* 1888. 35 × 47″ (89.3 × 116.6 cm).
National Museum of Western Art, Tokyo; Matsukata Collection.

COLORPLATE 22. *Madame Roulin.* 1888. 19¼ × 25" (50 × 63 cm).
The Saint Louis Art Museum; Gift of Mrs. Mark C. Steinberg.

COLORPLATE 23. *Van Gogh Painting Sunflowers*. 1888. 28¾ × 36¼″ (73 × 92 cm).
Vincent van Gogh Foundation/National Museum Vincent van Gogh, Amsterdam.

COLORPLATE 24. *Still Life with Three Puppies.* 1888. Oil on wood. 36⅛ × 24⅝″ (91.8 × 62.6 cm).
The Museum of Modern Art, New York; Mrs. Simon Guggenheim Fund.

guin's methods and theories; finally, he went over a large picture he had just completed, taking out the blacks in the shadows and substituting spots of pure color in their place.

Six months later he wrote to Cormon, whose pupil he had been, bumptiously congratulating his master that he, the pupil, had been awarded a gold medal for this picture at Amsterdam, and also announcing that he had turned "intransigent," as the "spot" painters at that time were labelled. I heard Cormon himself tell the story to his pupils at the studio. He spoke with much amusement and some contempt. Yet Gauguin did nothing in the matter himself; though I fancy he knew all about it, and enjoyed the situation in his silent way.

One final coincidence that is decidedly odd. This same painter, V., later went to America and there married the Princess X., daughter of the last King of Hawaii; fate thus bringing his life into touch with the Pacific and its peoples from quite another angle!

In art, Gauguin's greatest contempt was reserved for the schools and academic art generally. This, of course, is now all "vieux jeu." But I had one conversation with him, illustrating this side of him in a very unexpected way.

He had been making some drawings of geese which he showed me. He then produced one of Caldecott's colored books, in which some geese were depicted in that artist's very characteristic way. These he praised, almost extravagantly as it seemed to me then. "That," he said, "was the true spirit of drawing."

Gauguin would never allow that he owed anything in art, or anything at all for that matter, to anybody but himself. Self-determination was his god.

This spirit in later years led to much bitterness and recrimination with his early friends—Bernard especially, but there were others—as to who should be called the founder of the new School.

Personally, I believe that Gauguin had by far the best brains of them all. Like everybody of sense, he took much from what was going on round about him, but in my opinion the crucial change in his style came out of his study of stained glass. At Le Pouldu, he was in touch with Maurice Denis and others who were specially interested in Church art and Symbolism, though the latter was a phase he rather despised.

Round about 1888, too, quite a number of artists in France were painting the glass in the interiors of Chartres and other cathedrals. In 1889, I know that Gauguin, who noted everything, was in the Clichy quarter of Paris experimenting with glass design and pottery.

So it was from thirteenth- and fourteenth-century glass, I believe, that he got an idea of design and color which exactly suited him; and he then proceeded to translate it into an art of his own, using oil paint as a vehicle. The result was something as near originality as anyone is likely to get. Perhaps the most striking piece of evidence in this direction will be found in his celebrated picture called "The Yellow Christ".

To paint a "Christ" chrome yellow appears on the face of it a deliberate eccentricity, or worse; but when one remembers the magnificent effects obtained by the use of yellow stain in early glass in precisely similar subjects, the matter no longer appears so very arbitrary provided that one has the wit to see it. Gauguin noted the facts and promptly made use of them for his own purposes.

To Cézanne, too, he must be said to be indebted—indeed, Cézanne complained "il a chipé ma petite sensation." And we do know that he owned pictures by that painter at the time he himself was an amateur, and that a still life was one of the most precious of his possessions and the last to be parted with in evil times. It will be found painted in the background of one of his pictures of 1890—a portrait of a young woman. Indeed, he was one of the first to appreciate the significance of Cézanne's aims in art.

Cormon, pseudonym of Fernand Piestre (1845–1924), Salon painter whose studio school attracted many of the outstanding artists emergent in the 1880s, such as Anquetin, Bernard, Van Gogh and Toulouse-Lautrec.

"Vieux jeu": old hat.

Randolph Caldecott (1846–1886), children's books illustrator for whom the Caldecott Award was named. Gauguin probably learned of the artist in 1883 through discussions of children's art by Huysmans in L'Art Moderne. *Caldecott was also the subject of an illustrated* Gazette des Beaux-Arts *article in April 1886.*

Emile Bernard (1868–1941) was a precocious art student under Cormon before meeting Gauguin in Pont-Aven during a walking tour of Brittany. Friend of Vincent van Gogh and Aurier, Bernard had by 1888 developed a style that juxtaposed large areas of unmodulated color. Bernard later resented assumptions that Gauguin had influenced him, rather than vice-versa. In 1904, he gave eloquent support to the aging Cézanne. Maurice Denis (1870-1943), painter and theorist who learned of Gauguin through fellow-student Paul Sérusier. With Pierre Bonnard and others, he formed a Symbolist art group, the Nabis.

COLORPLATE 36

"Il a chipé ma petite sensation": "He stole my little sensation." Cézanne, distrustful of Gauguin's emulation, said this about him around 1881.

COLORPLATE 48

Emile Bernard. *Self-Portrait*. 1888.
Canvas. 18⅛ × 21⅝ (46 × 55 cm).
Vincent van Gogh Foundation/National
Museum Vincent van Gogh, Amsterdam.

In the last phase of all, however, Gauguin had worked round the full circle, and, in spite of his protest against the perfection of Greek art, his design especially is static and leans heavily toward the methods of the primitive Greek rather than the Gothic.

Degas was perhaps the only artist among his contemporaries whom he allowed to be "hors concours," and Gauguin's appreciation of the man and his work is one of the finest and most whole-hearted of all his writings on art.

In the final time of exile and sickness in the Marquesas, he delighted to think that Degas was reported to compete for his work at auction.

Paul Gauguin

AVANT ET APRES

On Self-Defense

January–February 1903

During my stay in Pont-Aven, there was a port-master and fish warden, a local Breton, retired sailor, fencing master, certified by the famous School of Joinville-le-Pont. In an agreement with him, we set up a small fencing school, which despite the low fees, provided him with small profits with which he was satisfied. He was, moreover, a good sort, a fairly good fencer, but unintelligent as a fencer and as an instructor. He understood nothing of fencing skills. All that had been pounded into him by persistence and drilling.

From the first day, I saw that the poor fellow had very short legs, so, big and strong-legged as I am, I amused myself by cheating on the distances, so that despite his quickness of hand he was always a few centimeters short of the target. I spoke to him about it, and it might as well have been in Hebrew. Fortunately, the poor fellow was not proud, and for a while I became his instructor in many things. For example, I had him give lessons by doing as I said above, that is, by frustrating the student taking the lesson with parries other than the one announced.

*　　*　　*

My first boxing lessons do not go back to my first youth. My instructor was an amateur, a painter named Bouffard, in Pont-Aven. Though an amateur, he was fairly strong: I continued for a while and it stood me in good stead a few times, even if it was only to give me self-confidence. But it was English boxing, whereas at Joinville-le-Pont they do what is called French boxing, or, to be more precise, Savate. Having been a sailor, I had done some Savate, but for fun.

Charlemont junior, today the great French boxing champion, devised a true boxing, not exclusively Savate. Far indeed from that was the School of Joinville-le-Pont.

Because it is imperfect, the English school is better.

Joinville-le-Pont boxing is only worthwhile for a very agile man, an acrobat, one very fit: in top condition. Otherwise it is truly dangerous, placing you quickly at the mercy of a very mediocre English boxer.

There you have my whole boxing lesson, which consists of warning you against the School of Joinville, and if you should take a fancy to devoting yourself to it, have agile legs, practice every day, give up reading anything, and become a *brute*.

Letter from Gauguin to His Wife, Mette

On His Arrival at Colón, Panama

12 May 1887

I have lots to tell you; it's all quite confused in my head. Our trip was as stupidly undertaken as possible, and we are mired now, as they say, "in the soup." To hell with all these people who misdirect travelers! We had layovers in Guadeloupe and Martinique—beautiful countries where there is work for an artist, where life is cheap and easy, and where people are friendly. That's where we should have gone; it would have cost half as much for the trip, and we wouldn't have lost any time. Unfortunately, we have come to Panama. My stupid brother-in-law has a store here which doesn't seem to prosper at all; he couldn't even spare 100 sous to welcome us; it was, in short, as rotten as possible. In anger, I stole a 35-franc shirt from him which has got to be barterable for 15 francs. Another inconvenience, the *cheapest* hotel is 15 francs a day, that is, 30 francs for the two of us, so we have spent 400 francs without having been able

By the Sea (I). 1887. 21¼ × 35½" (54 × 90 cm). Ny Carlsberg Glyptotek, Copenhagen.

to do anything. Since the canal was begun, these stupid Colombians won't give you a bit of land for less than 6 francs per meter. It's totally uncultivated, while everything sprouts; in spite of this it's impossible to build a hut and to live off fruits: instead, they jump on you and treat you as a thief. For having pissed in a filthy hole filled with broken bottles and feces, they made me cross over all of Panama, which took half an hour, escorted by two gendarmes, and they finally made me pay one piastre. Impossible to say no. I felt like taking it out on the gendarmes, but the cops here are expedient; They follow five steps behind you and if you move, they put a bullet in your head. Well, the mistake was made; it had to be paid for. I'm going to wield a shovel tomorrow in the cutting of the canal through the isthmus at some 150 piastres a month, and when I have put 150 piastres aside, that is, 600 francs (it will take two months), I will leave for Martinique. Laval, that's another story, he can earn enough money for a while doing portraits; it pays very well here—500 francs, as much as you could want (there is no competition)—but they have to be made in a very special and *very bad* style, something that I cannot do.

Don't complain of work. Here, I have to shovel earth from *5:30 in the morning to 6 in the evening* under the tropical sun and daily rain. At night, eaten up by mosquitos.

As for mortality, it isn't as frightening as one says in Europe; nine out of twelve of the Negroes who do the tough work die, but for the others, its an even ratio.

To get back to Martinique; there's a good life. If I could only get an outlet in France for 8,000 francs worth of paintings, the whole family could live as happily as possible, and I think you could even give lessons. People are so friendly and cheerful (true, it's a French colony). . . .

Letter from Gauguin to His Wife, Mette

On St.-Pierre, Martinique

20 June 1887

Brush holder. 1887. Bamboo with designs burned with hot iron. Height: 8″ (20 cm). Photo: Courtesy Galerie St. Etienne, New York.

I'm writing you this time from Martinique—I'd planned on coming here much later. Bad luck has been against me for a long time, and I don't do what I want. I had been working for two weeks for the Société when orders from Paris came to suspend much of the work, and the same day 90 employees were fired, and so on; naturally, I was listed as a newcomer. I took my trunks, and I came here. It's not a bad thing; Laval had just come down with a bout of yellow fever that I eased with homeopathy. Anyway, all's well that ends well.

For the time being, both of us are living in a Negroes' cabin, and it's a paradise near the isthmus. Below us, the sea bordered by coconut trees, overhead every sort of fruit tree, 25 minutes from town. Negro men and women walk by all day long with their Creole songs and endless chattering; not that it's monotonous, on the contrary it's quite varied. I couldn't describe for you my enthusiasm for life in the *French* colonies, and I'm sure that you'd feel the same. Nature at its richest, a hot climate, but with intermittent cool spells. With only a little money, there's enough to be happy. But one does need a certain amount. Thus, today with *30,000 francs*, you could buy property that would bring in a yearly income of 8,000 to 10,000 francs and live off of it as well, that is, eat like a gourmand.

The only work would be watching over a few Negroes who pick fruits and vegetables without having to cultivate them.

We started working, and I hope to send some interesting paintings from here soon. In any event, in the next few months we will need a little money—that's the only black spot on the horizon. I would like to hear from you and with all these upheavals I haven't gotten a letter. One more holiday (7 June) that goes by without *anyone* mentioning it. Well!! . . . .

Jean de Rotonchamp

PAUL GAUGUIN

On His Life in Paris

1906

Gauguin disembarked in Paris in the first days of 1888, haggard, thin, his eyes lifeless, his face tan from the climate of the Antilles. With neither a place to stay nor sufficient means to meet the periodic requirements of his new environment, when he arrived he knocked on the door of his old comrade from his days at Bertin, Schuffenecker, at whose house he had left a few paintings by friends that were his whole fortune.

Schuffenecker, like Gauguin, had quit the stock market with the cry of release: *"Anch'io sono pittore."*

* * *

With the stolidness of someone who is never surprised, he lived easily and—this will not surprise anyone who knew him—saw himself not just as a distinguished guest, in the face of whose caprices it was best to acquiesce, but the veritable master of the house.

In the studio next door was scattered a recent series of studies done by Schuffenecker, who, beginning in 1884, had definitively evolved toward intransigence and, not without success, had become one of the most ardent champions of Neo-Impressionism. At that time he employed divided tones and diagonal strokes, among which a reddish-pink, Veronese green, and cadmium yellow dominated the flesh tones. On an easel was a small study of a dancer in a spangled skirt, reminiscent of Degas.

And Gauguin, when an unexpected friend would pay a visit, would tour the room silently, taking up about thirty size 15 and 20 canvases brought back from his trip, and set them one after the other on a country easel, giving laconic explanations on their subject when he felt it was necessary.

Gauguin had no consideration for anyone, not even for those who put themselves at his disposal, unless he knew that they had beaks and claws and were inclined to use them. It was always very hard for Schuffenecker. Two events that the latter will never excuse sufficiently demonstrate the lack of tact in these actions when the question of art begins to get mixed up with that of friendship.

One day, Jean Dolent, who had come to say hello to Gauguin, admired one of Schuffenecker's paintings. Gauguin turned to the poet with such a sidelong glance, maintaining such a charged, stormy silence, that he believed he had committed an irreparable blunder.

And another day when Theodorus van Gogh, brother of Vincent, came to ask Gauguin, who was staying with Schuffenecker and being fed by him, to show him his recent paintings, Gauguin went with the visitor into Schuffenecker's studio and closed the door purely and simply in the face of his host, who was left outside, smoldering.

* * *

Gauguin, who had lived in solitude for almost fifteen years, absorbed by his daily work, began in 1890 to frequent certain literary circles. A few young writers, interested in him and in his talent, two of whom, Albert Aurier and Julien Leclercq, are now dead, recognized his rapport with the Symbolist pleiad which had just sounded the knell of the Naturalist and Parnassian schools.

Every Monday, at about nine in the evening, at the Café Voltaire, 1 Place de l'Odéon, there was a full meeting of all those who took part in this intellectual movement, or who were simply interested in it. In a decor of high, white walls appeared Verlaine, sickly, his neck wrapped in a twisted muffler and leaning pathetically on a heavy cane; Charles Morice, chief-designate of the younger school; Jean Moréas; Albert Aurier, with the dull complexion and the long, black hair of an Italian Renaissance poet; Julien Leclercq, with frizzy brown hair, seemingly plucked from a Jean Bellin set; Edouard Dubus; Adolphe Retté; Dauphin Meunier. Some painters came, like Gauguin and Carrière, some sculptors, since one sometimes saw Rodin, some entertainers, like the designer Cazals, who, dressed in a frock coat from 1830, completed this anachronism by borrowing the mask of Delacroix; finally the simply curious, such as Maurice Barrès.

* * *

Gauguin, who had a special admiration for Manet's *Olympia*, attempted to make a copy of it. Overcoming his horror of bureaucratic formality, he took the necessary steps to get authorization to work in the galleries of the Luxembourg museum. He did not resign himself to this

Jean Dolent (1835–1910), pseudonym for the poet Antoine Fournier.

Theo van Gogh (1854–1891), Vincent's devoted younger brother, began working for Goupil's branch gallery in 1873 and transferred to the Paris branch in 1878, where he developed a clientele for Impressionism and Post-Impressionism. He organized the first one-man exhibition of Gauguin's art in 1888. See John Rewald, "Theo van Gogh, Goupil, and the Impressionists," Gazette des Beaux Arts (January and February 1973).

Albert Aurier (1865–1892), critic, poet, and Sunday painter who met Bernard in spring 1888 at Saint Briac and, through him, Gauguin and Van Gogh. Julien Leclercq (1865–1901), eccentric poet and critic who met Gauguin through Van Gogh and Bernard and once was Gauguin's second in a duel.

Paul Verlaine (1844–1896), relatively poor and obscure lyric poet who frequented Paris cafés for literary debates. His sensual, mystical poems were among Gauguin's favorites.

Charles Morice (1861–1919); Jean Moréas, pseudonymn for Jean Papadiamantopoulos (1856–1910); Edouard Dubus (1863–1894); Adolphe Retté (1863–1930); Dauphin Meunier (1865–1924); Frédéric-Auguste Cazals (1865–1941); Maurice Barrès (1862–1923): Symbolists that frequented the Café Voltaire. Eugène Carrière (1849–1906), unorthodox painter whose dark, monochromatic paintings and working-class subjects appealed to many in this group.

without a feeling of disgust. Outside the monument he groaned as he passed in front of the shocking collection of bronze statues in burlesque poses that lined the facade facing the garden, which he picturesquely described as, "a group of clowns parading in front of the joint."

The copy of *Olympia*, which he worked on in front of the original for about eight days, was finished in his studio from memory, which explains why he reproduced Manet's work with an approximate fidelity. Nauseated by the throng of visitors and the thankless job of the copyist, he made haste to leave.

*   *   *

During his years in Paris, when Gauguin lived encamped in a hotel room and worked in borrowed studios, satisfying his material needs was far from easy. He took his meals, often alone, in the small, popular restaurants, and then, hardly full, would sit in some café in Faubourg, usually the brasserie Gangloff in the rue de la Gaîté. A half-dozen billiard tables took up the center of this immense hall, incessantly shaken by the blowing of the pipe organ, which noisily poured out Chabrier's *L'España*, an aria from *Carmen*, and the overture from *William Tell*.

With a cigarette in his mouth, Gauguin would distractedly pour a nearly full decanter of adulterated cognac into his coffee, scan the news-

Reference to Manet's controversial painting of a reclining nude, entitled Olympia *(1863), which Gauguin copied shortly after it was put on view at the Musée du Luxembourg in Paris in 1890.*

Emmanuel Chabrier (1841–1894), French composer and friend of the Impressionists who formed an important collection of their painting.

Base and lid for a "Fontaine." Wood, stained brown. Height: 17″ (43 cm). Musée d'Orsay, Paris.

paper and, more happily, chat with whatever friends happened by. Art was his habitual topic of conversation. What original observations, what sound insights must have deserved to have been preciously saved! He said to us one day:

> In nature, there are no "holes." All tones, even gaudy ones, are based on an invariable harmony. There are only "holes" in paintings. It is the "values" in these paintings that destroy the harmony of the tones by introducing foreign elements into the color and heightening the chiaroscuro.

This explains, with precise reasoning, the deliberate absence of relief that can be noted in most of the painter's work. The more colored a work, the less it takes from chiaroscuro. By the same token, the more a work presents an opposition of light and shade, the less it is colored.

Gauguin had in mind, and justifiably so in relation to his theory, the marvelous harmony of Asian tapestry, with its powerful and sumptuous tones, and the dazzling but not clashing richness of the textiles and ceramics of the Far East.

Another time, he gave us a complete exposé of the way colors mix optically, of the opposition of tones and the effect of complementaries, principles that had served as a foundation for his first works and of which he had retained only those that had a bearing on the association and separation of tones in terms of the harmonic elements of the pictorial ensemble.

Emile Bernard

LETTRES DE PAUL GAUGUIN A EMILE BERNARD

Preface

ca. 1911

It was in 1888; I had just spent three months in Saint-Briac whence I had pulled out of my studies, and I was on my way to Pont-Aven. Gauguin was there, in his clogs, with Charles Laval, his friend who rarely left him and who was also returning from Martinique, where he had followed him. I approached Gauguin, who this time greeted me cordially. He came to my house to see what I had brought back from Saint-Briac and looked at it carefully. In it, he found a lot of character, appreciating the rich coloring and the simple execution. He then took me to his studio, which had been installed in Mme. Gloannec's [sic] garret. I found a style that was more and more defined in his work; the division of tones, to which he remained faithful, destroyed their coloration, gave the whole a rather sickly feeling. I said this to him politely, only trying to express my esteem for his talent. A little while later there was a festival at Pont-Aven; I painted, with sketches, the "Bretons dressed in black sitting in a meadow deliberately of yellow-green." Gauguin was very impressed with this painting, which demonstrated more or less what I had said to him about his colors, and which only followed my own studies of coloration. "The more one divides the tone," I said to him, "the more it loses its intensity, it becomes gray or muddy"; he wanted to demonstrate it to him-

The Pension Gloanec, Pont-Aven. Roger Viollet, Paris.

COLORPLATE 18

self and borrowed some of the colors I had used, like Prussian blue, banished from the Impressionist palette, which he did not have. And so he made the painting, *The Vision after the Sermon*, for which he earned the title "creator of Symbolism." Here he did not just put into action the color theory that I had spoken of, but the very style of my *Breton Women in the Meadow*, after having established a willfully red background, as opposed to the yellow-green that I used. In the foreground he put the same large figures in their monumental lady's headdresses. He was so happy with this painting that he continued in the path it opened to him thereafter and definitively abandoned the Divisionism he had taken from Pissarro.

Not far from Pont-Aven, in Nizon, there was a small, very old church with a cemetery where we often went to admire an old, granite cross. We did not get there by the main roads, but through chestnut groves and fields of buckwheat, and by traversing the ruins of the château Rustéphan. The church deserved the cross: romanesquely arched, austere and granite, it had a heavy, feudal quality, inhabited by primitive, even grotesque, saints carved in wood and highlighted in ocher. The unstable roof was held up by wooden beams that were carved with bizarre monsters. Gauguin wanted to hang his painting, which was also simplistic, grotesque, and naive, in this ancestral setting. He signed his name and added in blue on the white border: "A gift of Don Tristan de Moscoso." It seems that, because of his grandmother, Flora Tristan, he valued this Peruvian nobility.

Laval and I had carried the painting; when we arrived in Nizon the church was open, and Gauguin himself picked out the place to hang his work. We lifted it there and he judged the effect. I went to find the priest in the presbytery, to let him know about the gift of great worth that he was receiving. He rejoiced at what I told him and walked faster and faster. We entered the ancient sanctuary. Gauguin came respectfully before the old priest, pointing with his extended hand to the work, which was resting on a bench. He read the title of the noble who donated it; it seemed somewhat Romanesque to him, then he looked at the painting, which terrified him. He must have been suspicious of some artist's caricature, since Pont-Aven had that reputation. It was obviously different from the usual trappings of the faith. The first words he spoke were those of polite refusal. Gauguin insisted, speaking of the relationship between his art and the old church's wooden saints, which seemed to call the parish priest to witness. Then the priest inquired as to the subject and declared the interpretation nonreligious and uninteresting for the faithful.

We brought the painting back to Pont-Aven, extremely upset, and this for the future glory of Gauguin, because it was this painting that made it possible for him to be named head of the pictorial Symbolists in Paris. I lived with him a lot during that season of 1888; we were hardly ever apart. Our works, therefore, were done together. I was, however, the only one to found them on logical and new reasons, and it was always I who showed the most daring and the most innovation; my extreme youth (I was twenty years old) fed my independence, liberty, and impassioned will, always pushing me further.

Letter from Vincent van Gogh to Gauguin

On Gauguin's Joining Van Gogh in Provence

6 June 1888

I have thought of you very often, and the reason why I did not write sooner is that I did not want to write empty phrases. The deal with Russell has not come off yet, but for all that Russell has bought some Impressionists, e.g. Guillaumin and Bernard, so bide your time—he will come to it of his own accord, but after two refusals I could not possibly insist any longer, as the refusals also contained a promise for the future.

I wanted to let you know that I have just rented a four-room house here in Arles.

And that it would seem to me that if I could find another painter inclined to work in the South, and who, like myself, would be sufficiently absorbed in his work to be able to resign himself to living like a monk who goes to the brothel once a fortnight—who for the rest is tied up in

John Peter Russell (1858–1931), Australian painter who studied at Cormon's studio starting in early 1885. He formed a boxing club in Paris and met Van Gogh there. Armand Guillaumin (1841–1927), dedicated to outdoor landscape painting by the early 1860s when he befriended Pissarro and Cézanne, was a founder of the Impressionists' cooperative. A participant in many of their famous shows, in late 1887 he was included in a Galerie Boussod & Valadon exhibition along with Gauguin and Pissarro.

The Yellow House in Arles. ca. 1940. Postcard. Vincent van Gogh Foundation/ National Museum Vincent van Gogh, Amsterdam.

his work, and not very willing to waste his time, it might be a good job. Being all alone, I am suffering a little under this isolation.

So I have often thought of telling you so frankly.

You know that my brother and I greatly appreciate your painting, and that we are most anxious to see you quietly settled down.

Now the fact is that my brother cannot send you money in Brittany and at the same time send me money in Provence. But are you willing to share with me here? If we combine, there may be enough for both of us, I am sure of it, in fact. Once having attacked the South, I don't see any reason to drop it.

I was ill when I came here, but now I am feeling better, and as a matter of fact, I am greatly attracted by the South, where working out-of-doors is possible nearly all the year round.

However, it seems to me that life is more expensive here, but on the other hand the chances of getting more pictures done are better. However this may be, if my brother were to send 250 francs a month for us both, we might share, should you care to come. Only in this case it would be necessary to have our meals at home as much as possible; we might engage some kind of charwoman for a few hours a day, so as to avoid all the expense of going to an inn.

And you would give my brother one picture a month; you could do what you like with the rest of your work.

Well, the two of us would immediately start exhibiting at Marseilles, thus clearing the way for other Impressionists as much as for ourselves. You must not forget that now there would be the cost of moving and of buying a bed, which would also have to be paid for in pictures.

Of course you are free to exchange views with my brother about this business, however I must warn you that in all probability he will decline responsibility for it. He will only assure you that up to the present the only means we have found of coming to your aid in a more practical way is this combining, if it should appeal to you. We have thought it over carefully. It seems to me that what your health requires above all is quiet. If I should be mistaken, and if the heat of the South should be too strong for you—well, then we must try to find another solution. As for myself, I am feeling quite well in this climate. I want to tell you a great many other things—but business must come first Send us both your answer at your earliest convenience.

Letter from Gauguin to Vincent van Gogh

On Painting

ca. 7–9 September 1888

I got your letter just when I was going to write you. Forgive me if I write so seldom and so little. I am terribly bored and I have stomach problems; we constantly have rain. I work and I don't do anything, in the sense that I draw with my hand, my head, and my heart with an eye toward what I want to do later. Yes, you're right to want painting with coloring suggestive of poetic ideas, and in this sense I agree with you, with one difference. I don't know any *poetic ideas*; it's probably a sense I'm lacking. I find *Everything* poetic, and it's in the corners of my heart, which are sometimes mysterious, that I perceive poetry. Led harmoniously, forms and colors in themselves produce poetry. Without letting myself be surprised by the motif, I feel a sensation in front of someone else's painting that brings me to a poetic state, depending on the painter's intellectual forces, which emanate from it. Useless to go on about this, we'll talk at length about it another time. On this matter, I'm quite sad to be held here in Pont-Aven; each day my debts increase and make my trip more and more unlikely. What a long calvary an artist's life is! And that's perhaps what makes us go on living. Passion gives life, and we die when it's no longer nourishing. Let's abandon these paths lined with thorny bushes, although they have their savage poetry. . . .

Letter from Gauguin to Vincent van Gogh
On Current Work and Future Plans
ca. 22 September 1888

It has taken me a long time to answer you: What do you expect? My sickly state and sorrow often leave me in a state of prostration, when I lock myself up in inaction. If you knew my life, you'd understand that after having struggled so much (in every way), I am just now catching my breath, and at this moment I am dormant. Your exchange project to which I haven't yet answered smiles at me, and I will do the portrait you want, though not *yet*. I am not up to doing it, seeing as it is not a copy of a face that you want but a portrait, as I understand a portrait to be. I watch little Bernard, and I don't yet possess him. I will perhaps do it from memory; in any case, it will be an abstraction. Maybe tomorrow, I don't know, it will come to me all at once. Right now, we're having a spell of good weather which leads both of us to try many things. I just did a religious painting, very poorly done, but which was interesting to do and which pleases me. I wanted to give it to the church at Pont-Aven. Naturally, they don't want it.

COLORPLATE 18

Groups of Brittany women pray, very intense black costumes. Very bright yellow-white headdresses. The two headdresses on the right are like monstrous helmets. A dark purple apple tree crosses through the painting, with foliage drawn in masses like emerald green clouds with intervals of yellow-green sunlight. The (pure vermilion) land. At the church it slopes down and becomes red-brown.

The angel is dressed in violent ultramarine blue and Jacob bottle-green. The angel's wings of pure chromium yellow one. The angel's hair chromium two and orange flesh-colored feet. I think I've succeeded in creating a great rustic and *superstitious* simplicity in the faces. The whole thing very severe. The cow under the tree is very small compared to life and rears up. In this painting I find that the landscape and the fight exist only in the imagination of the people who pray after the sermon— that's why there is a contrast between the life-sized people and the unnatural and disproportionate fight in its landscape. In your letter you seem *angry* at our laziness in regard to the portrait, and that makes me sad; *friends* don't get mad (at a distance words cannot be interpreted in their true value).

Another thing. You twist the dagger in the wound when you insist upon proving to me that I've got to come south, knowing I suffer by not being there right now. When you invited me to come there with your scheme, I formally wrote you one last *affirmative* letter, happy with your brother's offer. There is no way I can form a studio in the north, since every day I hope to sell something which would allow me to get out of here. The people who feed me here, the doctor who cured me, did it on credit and would never take a painting or scrap of clothing from me and are splendid toward me. I cannot let them down without committing a *misdeed*, which would bother me very much. If they were either rich or thieves, it wouldn't matter to me. I will wait, then. For example, if that day came, and you were in a different frame of mind and had to tell me "Too late" . . . I'd prefer that you do it right away. I'm afraid that your brother, who loves my talent, will price it too high. If he finds a collector or a speculator who is tempted by *low prices*, let him do it. I am a man of sacrifices, and I would like him to understand that I approve of whatever he does.

Little Bernard will bring several of my paintings to Paris with him shortly.

Laval plans to meet me in the Midi sometime in February. He found someone who will pay him 150 francs per month for a year.

Now it seems to me, my dear Vincent, that you count badly. I know the prices in the south; besides the restaurant, I am responsible for a house of three people for 200 francs per month, including food. I've kept up my household and I know how to get along—even more so with four.

As for housing; besides yours, Laval and Bernard could have a small furnished bedroom nearby. I like the layout of your dream house and the idea of seeing it makes my mouth water.

Well! as much as possible, I do not want to think about the promised fruit. Let's wait for better days; unless I rid myself of this foul existence that weighs down upon me so horribly outside of work.

Letter from Gauguin to Emile Schuffenecker

On Painting

8 October 1888

I made a painting for a church; naturally, it was refused, so I'm sending it back to Van Gogh. Useless to describe it to you—you'll see it. This year I sacrificed everything—execution, color—for style, wanting to force

Seaweed Gatherers. 1889. 34½ × 48½″ (87.5 × 123 cm). Museum Folkwang, Essen.

The family of Emile Schuffenecker. ca. 1886. Photo courtesy of Musée Gauguin, Papeari, Tahiti. See colorplate 30.

COLORPLATE 16

myself to do something other than what I know how to do. I think it's a transformation which hasn't borne fruit but which will. I made a portrait of myself for Vincent, who asked me for it. I think it's one of my best things; so abstract that it's absolutely incomprehensible (I suppose). A bandit's head at first sight, a Jean Valjean (*Les Misérables*) also personifying an Impressionist painter, run down and bearing the chains of the world. Its drawing is very special (complete abstraction). Eyes, mouth, and nose are like flowers of Persian carpets which also embody the symbolic aspect. The color is rather far from nature; it reminds you vaguely of my pottery gone lopsided because of a hot kiln. All the reds, the violets slashed through with fiery sparks, like a furnace shining in the eyes, the seat of the painter's struggling thoughts—everything on a pure chromium background sprinkled with childish bouquets—pure little girl's room. . . .

Letter from Gauguin
to Emile Schuffenecker

On His Artistic Career

16 October 1888

You speak to me of my *formidable* mysticism. Be an Impressionist to the end and do not be frightened of anything. Obviously, this Symbolist road is full of pitfalls and I have only just taken the first step, but it is in the depths of my nature and one must always follow his temperament. I well know that people will understand me *less and less*. What does it matter if I distance myself from others? For most I will be a puzzle, for a few I will be a poet, and sooner or later what's good will earn its place—no matter what, I tell you, I will end up doing things of *the first order*; I feel it and we will see. You well know that in art I am always right in the end. Be aware that right now there is a current among *the artists* that is highly favorable *to me*; I know of it because of certain indiscretions; don't worry, as much as Van Gogh loves me, he would not undertake to feed me in the Midi for my beautiful eyes. He studied the lay of the land like a cool Dutchman and intends to push things as much as possible, exclusively. I asked him to lower the prices to attract buyers. He replied that he intended, on the contrary, to raise them. Always the optimist, this time I am certainly walking on solid ground. . . .

Paul Gauguin

AVANT ET APRES

On Vincent van Gogh

January–February 1903

For a long time I have wished to write about Van Gogh, and I will certainly do so one fine day when I am in the mood: for the moment, I intend to recount about him—or, better, about us—certain things that are apt to correct an error that has circulated in certain circles.

It is surely chance that in the course of my existence several men who have spent time in my company and with whom I've enjoyed discussions have gone mad.

This was the case with the two Van Gogh brothers, and some, from evil intentions, and others, from naiveté, have attributed their madness to my doing. Certainly, some people may have more or less of an influence over their friends, but that is a far cry from provoking madness. Well after the catastrophe, Vincent wrote me from the mental asylum where he was being treated:

"How fortunate you are to be in Paris! This is still where one can find the leading authorities, and certainly you should consult a specialist in order to cure you of madness." Aren't we all a little mad? The advice was good, that is why I did not follow it, from contrariness, no doubt.

The readers of the *Mercure* were able to see, in a letter of Vincent's published a few years ago, how insistent he was that I come to Arles to found, according to his idea, an atelier of which I would be the director.

I was working at the time at Pont-Aven, in Brittany, and whether because the studies I had undertaken bound me to that place, or because by some vague instinct I foresaw something abnormal, I resisted for a long time, until the day when, won over by Vincent's sincere flights of friendship, I set out.

I arrived at Arles toward the end of night and awaited daybreak in an all-night café. The owner looked at me and cried out: "It's you, his pal, I recognize you."

A self-portrait that I had sent to Vincent suffices to explain this proprietor's exclamation. While showing him my portrait, Vincent had explained that it was of a pal who was to arrive soon.

Neither too early, nor too late, I went to awaken Vincent. The day was devoted to my settling in, to much chatting, to a bit of strolling to admire the beauties of Arles and the Arlésiennes (for whom, incidentally, I was unable to work up any enthusiasm).

Beginning the following day, we were at work, he continuing, and I, starting fresh. You should know that I have never had the cerebral facility that others, without any trouble, find at the tip of their brushes. Those others get off the train, pick up their palette, and in no time at all set you down a sunlight effect. When it's dry, it goes to the Luxembourg and it's signed: Carolus-Duran.

I do not admire such painting, but I admire the man: he so sure, so tranquil!—I so uncertain, so restless!

In every country, I need a period of incubation to learn each time the essence of the plants, the trees, of all of nature, in short—so varied and so capricious, never wanting to let itself be divined or revealed.

So it was several weeks before I clearly sensed the sharp flavor of Arles and its environs. That did not prevent our working steadily, especially Vincent. Between the two beings, he and I, the one entirely a volcano and the other, boiling as well, but inside. Some sort of struggle was bound to occur.

First of all, I was shocked to find a disorder everywhere and in every respect. His box of colors barely sufficed to contain all those squeezed tubes, which were never closed up, and despite all this disorder, all this mess, everything glowed on the canvas—and in his words as well. Daudet, de Goncourt, the Bible fueled the brain of this Dutchman. At Arles, the quays, the bridges, the boats, the whole Midi became another Holland for him. He even forgot how to write in Dutch and, as one could see from the publication of his letters to his brother, he always wrote in French only, and did so admirably, with no end of phrases like *tant que* and *quant á*.

Despite all my efforts to disentangle from that disordered brain a logical reasoning behind his critical opinions, I could not explain to myself the complete contradiction between his painting and his opinions. So that, for example, he had an unlimited admiration for Meissonier and a profound hatred for Ingres. Degas was his despair and Cézanne was nothing but a fraud. When thinking of Monticelli, he wept.

What angered him was to be forced to admit that I had great intelligence, although my forehead was too small, a sign of imbecility. In the midst of all this, a great tenderness, or rather, the altruism of the Gospel.

From the very first month, I saw our common finances taking on the same appearance of disorder. What to do? The situation was delicate as the cash box being filled, only modestly, by his brother employed at Goupil's, and, for my part, through the exchange of paintings. I was obliged to speak, and to come up against that great sensitivity of his. It was thus only with many precautions and quite a bit of coaxing hardly

Bernard published a selection of Van Gogh's letters in the Mercure de France *in April and August 1893.*

COLORPLATE 16

Alphonse Daudet (1840–1897), Provençal author; Edmond (1822–1896) and Jules (1830–1870) de Goncourt, naturalist novelists. Their works were admired by Van Gogh.

Jean-Louis Meissonier (1815–1891), acclaimed for his detailed Napoleonic battle scenes, which were the antithesis of Impressionism. Jean Dominique Ingres (1780–1867), leading Classical painter and portraitist whose advocacy of refined drawing dominated the official nineteenth-century art schools. Adolphe Monticelli (1824–1886), Provençal painter whose decorative style, fanciful themes, and rich impasto influenced Van Gogh.

COLORPLATE 25. *Les Alyscamps.* 1888. 36¼ × 28¾″ (92 × 73 cm).
Musée d'Orsay, Paris.

COLORPLATE 26. *Café at Arles*. 1888. 28⅜ × 36¼″ (72 × 92 cm).
The Pushkin Museum, Moscow.

COLORPLATE 27. *Old Women at Arles*. 1888. 28¾ × 36¼″ (73 × 92 cm).
The Art Institute of Chicago; Mr. and Mrs. Lewis Larned Coburn Memorial Collection.

COLORPLATE 28. *Landscape in Arles.* 1888. 28⅜ × 36¼″ (72 × 92 cm).
Nationalmuseum, Stockholm.

COLORPLATE 29. *The Harvest at Arles*, or *Human Miseries*. 1888. 28¾ × 36¼″ (73 × 92 cm).
Ordrupgaardsamlingen, Copenhagen.

COLORPLATE 30. *The Schuffenecker Family.* 1889. 28¾ × 36¼″ (73 × 92 cm).
Musée d'Orsay, Paris.

COLORPLATE 31. *Portrait of Two Children*. (Paul and Jean Schuffenecker.) ca. 1889. 18 × 24″ (46 × 61 cm). Ny Carlsberg Glyptotek, Copenhagen.

COLORPLATE 32. *La Belle Angèle*. 1889. 36¼ × 28¾″ (92 × 73 cm).
Musée d'Orsay, Paris.

compatible with my character that I approached the question. I must confess, I succeeded far more easily than I had supposed.

In a box, so much for nightly outings and hygiene, so much for tobacco, so much, too, for unforeseen expenses, including the rent. On top of it all, a piece of paper and a pencil to inscribe honestly what each took from this till. In another box, the balance of the sum, divided into four parts, for the cost of food each week. Our little restaurant was given up and, with the aid of a little gas stove, I did the cooking while Vincent, without going very far from the house, did the shopping. Once, however, Vincent wanted to make a soup, but I don't know how he mixed it—no doubt like the colors on his paintings—in any event, we couldn't eat it. And my Vincent exclaimed in laughter: "Tarasçon! La casquette au père Daudet!"

On the wall, with chalk, he wrote:

Je suis Saint Esprit.
Je suis sain d'esprit!

How long did we remain together? I couldn't say, having entirely forgotten. Despite the rapidity with which the catastrophe arrived, despite the fever of working that had overtaken me, that whole time seemed like a century.

Without the public having any suspicion, two men had done there a colossal work, useful to them both—perhaps to others. Certain things bear fruit.

Vincent, at the moment when I arrived in Arles, was fully immersed in the Neo-Impressionist school, and he was floundering considerably, which caused him to suffer; the point is not that this school, like all schools, was bad, but that it did not correspond to his nature, which was so far from patient and so independent.

With all these yellows on violets, all this work in complementary colors—disordered work on his part—he only arrived at subdued, incomplete, and monotonous harmonies; the sound of the clarion was missing.

I undertook the task of enlightening him, which was easy for me, for I found a rich and fertile soil. Like all natures that are original and marked with the stamp of personality, Vincent had no fear of his neighbor and was not stubborn.

From that day on, my Van Gogh made astonishing progress: he seemed to catch a glimpse of all that was within him, and hence that whole series of suns on suns in full sunlight.

Have you seen the portrait of the poet?

1. The face and hair, chrome yellow.

2. The clothing, chrome yellow.

3. The tie, chrome yellow. With an emerald, green-emerald pin.

4. On a background of chrome yellow.

This is what an Italian painter said to me and he added:

"Shit, shit, everything is yellow: I don't know what *painting* is any longer!"

It would be idle to go into details of technique here. This is said only to inform you that Van Gogh, without losing one inch of his originality, gained a fruitful lesson from me. And each day he would thank me for it. And that is what he means when he writes to M. Aurier that he owes much to Paul Gauguin.

When I arrived in Arles, Vincent was trying to find his way, whereas I, much older, was a mature man. I do owe something to Vincent; namely, in the awareness of having been useful to him, the *affirmation* of my ear-

"Tarasçon! La casquette au père Daudet!": *This nonsense phrase about the aging writer's hat seems to refer to an episode on bad cooking in one of his novels.*

Je suis Saint Esprit.
Je suis sain d'esprit!: *I am the Holy Spirit. I am of sound mind!*

lier ideas about painting. Moreover, for the recollection at difficult moments that there are those unhappier than oneself.

When I read this passage: "Gauguin's drawing somewhat recalls that of Van Gogh," I smile.

During the latter part of my stay, Vincent became excessively brusque and noisy, then silent. Several nights I surprised Vincent who, having risen, was standing over my bed.

To what can I attribute my awakening just at that moment?

Invariably it sufficed for me to say to him very gravely:

"What's the matter, Vincent?" for him to go back to bed without a word and to fall into a deep sleep.

COLORPLATE 23

I came upon the idea of doing his portrait while he painted the still life that he so loved—some sunflowers. And, the portrait finished, he said to me: "That's me all right, but me gone mad."

That same evening, we went to the café: he took a light absinthe.

Suddenly he threw the glass and its contents at my head. I avoided the blow and, taking him bodily in my arms, left the café and crossed the Place Victor Hugo; some minutes later, Vincent found himself in bed, where he fell asleep in a few seconds, not to awaken again until morning.

When he awoke, he said to me very calmly:

"My dear Gauguin, I have a vague memory of having offended you last evening."

"I gladly forgive you with all my heart, but yesterday's scene could happen again, and if I were struck I might lose control of myself and strangle you. So permit me to write your brother and announce my return."

My God, what a day!

When evening had arrived and I had quickly eaten my dinner, I felt the need to go out alone and take in the air, scented with flowering laurels. I had already almost crossed the Place Victor Hugo, when I heard behind me a familiar short footstep, rapid and irregular. I turned just at the moment when Vincent rushed towards me, an open razor in his hand. My look at that moment must have been powerful indeed, for he stopped, and lowering his head, took off running in the direction of the house.

Was I lax at that moment, and oughtn't I to have disarmed him and sought to calm him down? Often I have questioned my conscience, but I do not reproach myself at all.

Let him who will cast the stone at me.

Only a short stretch, and I was in a good hotel in Arles, where, after asking the time, I took a room and went to bed.

Very agitated, I could not fall asleep until about three in the morning, and I awoke rather late, about seven-thirty.

Upon arriving at the square, I saw a large crowd assembled. Near our house, some gendarmes and a little gentleman in a bowler hat, who was the police commissioner.

Here is what had happened.

Van Gogh returned to the house and, immediately, cut off his ear close to the head. He must have taken some time in stopping the hemorrhage, for the next day there were many wet towels scattered about on the floor tiles of the two rooms downstairs.

The blood had stained the two rooms and the little staircase that led up to our bedroom.

When he was in good enough condition to go out, his head covered up by a Basque beret pulled all the way down, he went straight to a house where, for want of a fellow-countrywoman, one can find a chance acquaintance, and gave the "sentry" his ear, carefully washed and enclosed in an envelope. "Here," he said, "a remembrance of me." Then he fled and returned home, where he went to bed and slept. He took the

Vincent van Gogh. *Gauguin's Chair*. 1888. 35⅞ × 28⅜″ (90.5 × 72 cm). Vincent van Gogh Foundation/National Museum Vincent van Gogh, Amsterdam.

trouble, however, to close the shutters and to set a lighted lamp on a table near the window.

Ten minutes later, the whole street given over to the *filles de joie* was in commotion and chattering about the event.

I had not the slightest inkling of all this when I appeared on the threshold of our house and the gentleman with the bowler hat said to me point-blank, in a more than severe tone:

"What have you done, sir, to your comrade?"—"I don't know."—"Oh, yes, . . . you know very well, . . . he is dead."

I would not wish anyone such a moment, and it took me a few long minutes to be able to think clearly and to repress the beating of my heart.

Anger, indignation, and grief as well, and the shame of all those gazes that were tearing my entire being to pieces suffocated me, and I stuttered when I said, "Allright, sir, let us go upstairs, and we can explain ourselves up there." In the bed, Vincent lay completely enveloped in the sheets, curled up like a gun hammer; he appeared lifeless. Gently, very gently, I touched the body, whose warmth surely announced life. For me it was as if I had regained all my powers of thought and energy.

Almost in a whisper, I said to the commissioner of police:

"Be so kind, sir, as to awaken this man with great care and, if he asks for me, tell him that I have left for Paris. The sight of me could be fatal to him."

I must avow that from this moment on the commissioner of police was as reasonable as possible and intelligently sent for a doctor and a carriage.

Once awake, Vincent asked for his comrade, his pipe, and his tobacco, and he even thought of asking for the box that was downstairs containing our money. A suspicion, without a doubt, that barely touched me, having already armed myself against all suffering.

Vincent was taken to the hospital where, upon arrival, his brain began to wander about again.

All the rest of it is known to everyone that it could be of interest to, and it would be useless to speak of it, were it not for the extreme suffering of a man who, cared for in a madhouse, at monthly intervals, regained his reason sufficiently to understand his condition and furiously paint the admirable paintings that we know.

The last letter that I had from him was dated Auvers, near Pontoise. He told me that he had hoped to recover enough to come to visit me in Brittany, but that now he was obliged to recognize the impossibility of a cure.

"Dear master (the only time that he had used this word), after having known you and caused you pain, it is more dignified to die in a good state of mind than in a degraded state."

And he put a pistol shot in his stomach, and it was not until a few hours later, lying in his bed and smoking his pipe, that he died having complete lucidity of mind, with love for his art, and without hatred for others.

In *Les Monstres*, Jean Dolent writes:

"When Gauguin says 'Vincent,' his voice is gentle."

Without knowing it, but having guessed it, Jean Dolent is right.

One knows why. . . .

Armand Séguin

L'OCCIDENT

"Paul Gauguin"

March, April, May 1903

Armand Séguin (1869–1903), who met Gauguin in Le Pouldu in 1891, died shortly after the publication of three articles, reprinted together here, that were to be part of a larger study on the art of Pont-Aven and Le Pouldu. Gauguin wrote a review of Séguin's one-man exhibition, which he helped to arrange in 1895 at Le Barc de Boutteville.

Poor old friend, his face will forever remain in my memory, even when I will no longer have the pleasure of seeing it ever again. It's a sweet hope that I've kept for seven years. I'd like it to be realized—certainly in preference to other hopes that each morning gives us, born of various passions and different desires that dictate necessities to us like conceits. It's true that I can draw his wide forehead, his blue eyes, his nose whose shape is reminiscent of an eagle's beak. His fine mouth under his already gray moustache. I can hear the way he speaks: sweet, bitter, caressing, willful, always evocative, and no one who knew him could forget his laugh that to this day still rings in my ears: a cheerfully resonant laugh, the laugh of an artist happy with life, taken by greatness and beauty, and the sarcastic laugh as well, yet without the least bit of jealousy, which bit, battled, revolted, and fought for his Art.

He invented everything. He had invented his easel. He had invented a way to prepare his canvases. He had invented a method to reproduce watercolors. In the same way as a majestic ship that was never built still had to avoid shipwrecks. In this way he'd invented his odd suitcoat, the Persian cap, and the huge, deep blue cloak held together with precious

Séguin could have seen Gauguin making his first monotypes, a printmaking method that involves transferring an image to paper without the use of incised lines to create a new, unique image, in the summer of 1894 in Pont-Aven.

carved ornaments and under which he seemed to the Parisians to be some splendid and gigantic Magyar, a Rembrandt of 1635, when he slowly and solemnly walked, with his white-gloved hand encircled with silver leaning on the cane he'd decorated.

If he invented everything, he decorated everything in an amusing, artistic way—always with style. At that time, which seems distant to me today, when we did our good work, our cans of color, our easels, our straw hats and our wooden shoes were, in accordance with our modesty, true marvels. But he easily triumphed in this contest and we whole-heartedly declared him the winner, since he was always the perfect dec-orator. It's in this sense that he proves himself to be a great master. When he wants it to, his line becomes docile, supple, and caressing to please him; at his command, the colors sing out their individual values in a pleasing harmony celebrating the passion he feels for them. I can see his Tahitian hut, if he realized his dreams; it is very beautiful, held up by thick columns, sculpted and painted; in it is arranged the furniture that he had promised to make for himself, as he must have done for all the objects of his daily life. I can imagine paintings of joy and of sun on the walls.

How vivid the suffering of this artist would be were he to come back from so far away to be among us! He would be incredibly furious to see our cafés, our posters, and the window displays of our merchants. Loot-ers have stolen from him, at first for the glory of "l'art nouveau," then for recognition, and, to obviate his status as an individual in this happy time, they've denied the power his work has had for us in engraving and in painting.

*   *   *

That, for such snobs! He had an inkling of this fact and perhaps it made him smile, on those golden shores, just as he laughed on Le Pouldu beach, draped in his vivid red Tahitian *paréo*, predicting all the causes of this downfall, since his spirit foresaw the ignorant and success-starved people who, by fashion or taste, wanted to make our findings more beautiful. While he spoke like this, his very beautiful hands constructed huge bas-reliefs in the sand.

Maurice Denis wrote eight years ago, in an article that he was kind enough to dedicate to me, that the Pont-Aven school would one day be as famous as that of Fontainebleau. Today I rate it as having even more importance; its role was of a different potency and of a greater, prouder scope. One has only to think how it not only brought painting to the eternal and immutable logic of its art—after having had the force to abandon the sterile theories of the Impressionists—but it also gave its formulas to foreign nations, renovated forgotten and perhaps scorned processes, and changed modern decoration completely. The greatest naiveté could not reproach us for the flock of technicians who followed us, ignorant of our research, of mathematical laws of proportion and of human wisdom, and whose taste recalls that of Gounod when he tried to poeticize Bach. Their genius, in spite of all my predictions, made me prefer the mahogany armoire that our fathers cherished to the pieces of furniture that they produced. I'm sorry to be unable to recall the terri-ble thoughts of Wagner concerning them that were inscribed in emerald green on the walls of the inn at Le Pouldu, threatening with frightful prayers for eternity all those who prostituted the art that God had granted them. Gauguin was superb, straight as a great tree, sneering like the angel who was condemned for his pride when he recited these words after having cited Besnard's name. He easily pardoned Bougereau.

*   *   *

Paul Gauguin has not painted from nature since the trip to Marti-nique that gave us, at Boussod and Valadon's, the series of paintings in

Charles François Gounod (1818–1893), French composer of sacred music and the opera Faust, *a great success in the 1860s. Richard Wagner (1813–1883), German opera composer lauded by the Symbolists as the master of "correspondences" between music and poetry. See Morice's "Paul Gauguin" of December 1893 in this volume.*

Albert Besnard (1849–1934), successful mural painter whose style was much derived from Impressionism. William Bougereau (1825–1905), celebrated painter whose highly finished oils were anathema to the Impressionists. He opposed hanging their art in the Salon, where he was a juror. For Gauguin's view of him, see Tardieu's "M. Paul Gauguin" in this volume.

which all the qualities of a rare artist converged, in which the line maintains a pleasing gentleness, tapers with so much grace, that one is reminded on seeing it as much of Hokusai as of Tanagra. We can observe it in his first album of lithographs, in the *Grasshoppers* print. He loved, in Brittany, to catch the movement of human life unawares, the peasant's toil in the struggle he carries on each day with the earth, and it happened that, in covering his notebooks with drawings, he captured the synthesis of the country around him. The race, its ways, its costume became familiar to him. He knew the anatomy of the animals, the flight of the goose, which he reworked a thousand times, the spreading of headdresses in the ocean's breeze. All these formulas remain to his credit. No one was more able than he to find, without exaggeration, the ever-perfect decoration in all things. By contemplating the emotions he felt, he perceived in rocks, in trees, in all of nature, the arabesque that thrills or charms you, the line that characterizes the undulation of a plain or fixes the expression of a face. From principles he goes to consequences, from causes to effects. A bucket of onions scattered on a table inspires him to decorate the ceiling that shelters him. Can I write that he no longer draws visually, but reflectively, giving each line all its value, emphasizing its clarity, lengthening it, shortening it, curving it, starting it over many times, so as to bring it back to its norm and express the impression of an action or a shape that his eye or his mind seeks to translate? His vision embraces the region and registers the synthesis of Brittany: behind the low stone wall, the black and white cow that the farm's servant girl tends as she spins; the farm rises in the distance on the hill and displays its ochre patch beneath the ultramarine of its roof and beneath the darkness of the oaks. Just as Leonardo da Vinci sought in marble the harmoniously formed vein, so does Gauguin amuse himself by following the undulations of the clouds chasing each other in the skies and detailing them with elegant lines. The sea gives him its silver embroidery and white collar, which Monet was often to repeat. His words teach us to think about what one wants to represent; to achieve a result of acts and ideas; to simplify in order to intensify; to study the elements of strength, of flight, of suppleness that nature possesses. She gives herself to him who has so loved her, and he condenses her onto a canvas; more rarely he recesses her in a sweeping arabesque, that keystone that every painting requires and whose importance he knew so well.

* * *

The painters at Le Pouldu look at heraldry and at the Japanese, who teach them the direction and symbolism of colors. Red looks vertical to them: it is the blood that streams from the wound; it is generosity and ardor; and it is also boldness and love. Blue, in its horizontal, expresses calm, gentleness, dreams, the heavenly rest to which we must aspire, perfect bliss. Its glad song of a desirable serenity and of goodness has always attracted me, has often moved me; my praises go to it for the joys that it has given me; is it not to be preferred to all its brothers, when we acknowledge that its harmony is more delicately determined? From right to left runs green as fresh and spruce as one of Watteau's libertines, who would play truant, dawdling, laughing, stopping here and there, kissing whom he meets and making friends with everyone, cordial and without hatred for anyone. It is violet's friend, forms an alliance with red and charms orange, caresses the ultramarine and yellow from which it is descended. The latter is adored by Bernard and Sérusier; it is the image of the sun, of life, of gold and its power, as some believe, while for others it seems to be, in its slanting movement, depraved, hypocritical, evil, and egotistic—as the common people have observed and translated by the figure of speech "he laughed yellow" when they talk about a cruel or sly person.

Tearing his students from the theories they enjoyed discussing, but

Hokusai (1760–1849), popular, prolific Japanese artist whose woodblock prints had a revolutionary impact on many Western artists in the latter nineteenth century. Tanagra figurines are small ancient Greek terracotta sculptures.

Gauguin painted the inn's ceiling at Le Pouldu in 1889 with a motif of geese and onions. This heretofore unknown work was presented by Robert P. Welsh in "Le plafond peint par Gauguin dans l'auberge de Marie Henry, au Pouldu," in Le Chemin de Gauguin *(a catalogue of the Musée Départemental du Prieuré, Saint-Germain-en-Laye, 1986).*

Paul Sérusier (1864–1927) met Gauguin in Pont-Aven in 1888 and promulgated Gauguin's theories among Parisian friends such as Denis, Vuillard, and Bonnard, artists in the Nabis group. Sérusier, in close contact with Gauguin over the next three years, probably encouraged him in mystical, philosophical, and theological studies.

Flowers and a Bowl of Fruit on a Table.
1889. 16⅞ × 24¾″ (42.8 × 62.9 cm).
Museum of Fine Arts, Boston; Bequest of
John T. Spaulding.

which de Haan did not understand and with which de Chamaillard was little concerned, Gauguin, in analyzing the work of Leonardo da Vinci, specifies the importance of rhythmic shading with the exterior line. Michelangelo had gently, step by step, guided him onto this path. By making rapid sketches from the works of the Sistine, showing himself to be like Rubens in this, or like Delacroix, who observed the latter, he had come to know [mural] and balanced decoration through the contour of swelling muscles, he had learned the envelopment of the human body in a supple and harmonious line, the containment of the composition in the arabesque produced by windswept, heavy draperies with nearly parallel folds. Only the laws of synthetic relation between light and dark still failed him: he adopted them with less difficulty than others suffered when they sought the same objective, not only because his spirit easily assimilates the beauty of all things, but also because his sculpture, which he did not abandon during this period and which required the study of different planes, was very helpful to him in this research. He saw that, when light moves with the passing of time, its modeling takes on new effects, and his intelligence was able to recognize that the shadow, according to its position, fixes the impression that the drawing had already sought to set down. Floating beneath the eyes, or inscribed over the arch of the eyebrows, shading off the corners of the mouth, hiding beneath the lip, receding here, caressing one place to soften or becoming violent elsewhere, it makes the smile laugh, eases melancholy, reveals mystery, accentuates lechery, authority, weakness, the most various and subtle sensations that our souls grant us. La Gioconda teaches these truths. Gauguin, in interpreting them each day, from those models whom he chose as most representative of the Breton race in its ugliness as well as in its nobility, its vigor as well as its indolence, would have foreshadowed the theory of temperaments later formulated by Gary de Lacroze, had his spirit, like that of Emile Bernard, wished to explore all the problems that artistic education and philosophy have posed for us.

When he paints, how will he address the differences in the values that slide timidly and listlessly or fasten tenaciously on nature? By darkening the overall tone with certain proportions of black? Certainly not! That would be to fall from the heights of his endeavor and accept the process that was so dear to the students of the Ecole, those devotees of bitumen whom we despise as deservedly as they hate us. Rest assured, those ignoramuses rested quite peacefully in their laziness and daily pondered

Jacob Isaac Meyer de Haan (1852–1895), Dutch painter who stayed with Theo van Gogh a few months in 1888 and 1889 before meeting Gauguin in Pont-Aven. In Le Pouldu, he helped support Gauguin, on whose style he based his own. Henri-Ernest Ponthier de Chamaillard (ca. 1865–1930), Breton member of Gauguin's circle in Pont-Aven and Le Pouldu.

La Gioconda *refers to Leonardo da Vinci's* Mona Lisa.

the academic teachings. Placidly, beneath a pundit's eyes, they thinned their paints with that hideous *sauce de Judée*. They were utterly unconcerned with harmony. Why should they have bothered themselves about it? The same daily process spared them any dissonance. Like nightmarish witches—and more terrible than Macbeth's, to be sure!—they routinely drowned, in that hideous mixture, in that repellent pitch, their pure and luminous colors—so fresh on the palette, the joy of our eyes—that tried to please their gaze by vainly appealing for mercy. Should we be amazed that the poor fellows become furious when Gauguin shook their sleep by saying this:

> Have you not noticed, then, the splendor of the flesh, its beauty, its delicacy, and its pearly radiance? Light, smitten with it, takes pleasure in enveloping it, caressing it; it wraps it in Iris's veil, strokes it with its thousand hues, embraces it continually, because it is in love with it; it falls asleep on it, happy. Can you not feel the terrible ugliness of your demarcation? The peasant, whose spirit on the subject is as simple as it is critically correct, would think, as he looked at it, of those diseases which it ill befits us to name to you. See how the shadow is not *in* the figure, but simply brushes against it, just as the black butterfly gathers nectar from or teases the pink flower. Learn that, shimmering, wavering, transparent, it recalls the green of the leaves, the blue of the sky, the red of the drapery; the stream, a thin, brilliant thread, that meanders through the Veronese green of the meadow. You, gentlemen, would have to take a lesson from Renoir, the worthy painter you ignore, who is acknowledged by those you hail at the Louvre, whose canvases smile to us and please us amid the soberness of the masters: Clouet, Watteau, Fragonard, Boucher. And perhaps you would have to consult the English school that shared our concern, as Reynolds, Lawrence, and Gainsborough said so well after seeing the portrait of the *Young Girl with Hat* that Rubens signed.

I mean that he spoke very well and that he was easily understood by his students, even though the realization of his aims was not very easily come by. Relatively, the harmony of two values, in the overall coloration, presents itself as a puerile task: but it is not within everyone's scope to work it out for one's own design. His talent and the memory of Delacroix, who had, to a particular degree, this gift and this science—the study of warm tones contrasting with cold tones—helped him to cross this new pass. The Ecole cried out, shrugged its shoulders, uttered a few witty words, I have no doubt, and, so as to dream of terrible retributions, fell back asleep into its eternal slumber, which even the trumpets of the Last Judgment cannot hope to interrupt.

When I think of the researches of Le Pouldu that I have attempted to explain, I can be amazed even now. A system of symbols has been created: it has placed on solid footing three laws: those of synthesis, of the characteristic, of Cloisonism; it has established formulas of decorative harmony through line and color. Having called on past centuries for their various canons of beauty, and having summarized them, he is, in a sense, a traditionalist; he awakens the Institute's torpor, brings a precious knowledge to whomever seeks the truth. But will it not be said that Gauguin and his students have scorned value, black contrasting with white, penumbras, all that singing range whose power is great? By what eccentricity, for what reason? Not, certainly, from ignorance. Their hands leafed over the Temptation of Saint Anthony and the homage to Goya by Odilon Redon.

* * *

Sauce de Judée, *or Jew's lampblack, is bitumen, a nondrying pigment favored by nineteenth-century academic painters.*

Temptation of St. Anthony (*1888*) *and* Homage to Goya (*1885*) *are albums of lithographic prints by Symbolist artist Odilon Redon.*

It is therefore inappropriate to consider the inn at Le Pouldu an austere temple. On winter nights, their roaring discussions would sometimes frighten the sailor, who would cross himself in his boat. The master, in the prime of life, and the young people who surrounded the good giant would, like big children, wake up after studying with ringing laughter heard well above the roar of the waves. These artists knew how to reap the happiness that life offers, ignoring the pretensions of that time: the fatalism and snobby attitudes of decadent poets. No one would have been able to judge them in their presence. Upon sight of them, the stranger would have taken them to be awful rogues and would have been justifiably frightened. Callot would have engraved them lovingly. Draped in his overcoat of rough serge and capped with a beret, the leader directed his faithful flock through the land. Red, windblown hair, Brittany vest on his chest, barefooted in his straw-filled wooden shoes, Sérusier would repeat Bach's chorale to the Ocean. Emile Bernard dreamed, Laval gamboled about, de Chamaillard yelled, Filiger philosophized, de Haan listened. The sun would reach the horizon and the shadows of these short and tall, slim and heavy-set men of picturesque gait would slide in an odd manner up the beach, climb up the rocks, spread out over the ground, scale the walls, reach the plowed fields, and disappear into the distance where they would terrify the girl returning home.

To exhaust their passion and to bring a new freshness to their vision, they would run in every which direction through their conquered domain. Easygoing and of cheerful moods, they had no fear of being badly received since they were well-regarded and like family with everyone, entertaining the waiters and the timid waitresses whom they caused to blush, the young as well as the immobile old folks who rekindled their lives at the hearth and who observed them with benevolent malice. At the farm where the wheat is chafed, they would help the workers, taste the season's cider, dance on wedding days, mix into the life of the peasant as into that of the sailor. If a quarrel arose at times, it would be immediately silenced by the imposingly tall stature of Gauguin, who would stand up. They liked force. On the sand, in the ancient tradition, they held brotherly combats: Sérusier throws the javelin with great agility; the discus replaced by a flattened pebble. When they tired of these games, they would saunter back to the road to return. At this time of the day, their thoughts would regain all their powers as the windows would light up in the solitary inn where they looked for the paths leading to true beauty.

* * *

Except for the remembrance we have of it, nothing remains of their past or of the interior they had decorated for their own amusement and to soothe the eye; everything has been taken away, piece by piece. The door panels were sawn off and the paintings cut out, just as were also taken the chimney they sculpted, the boxes they decorated, and the sketches and the watercolors that so gaily stood out from the walls. Where are: *Bonjour, Monsieur Gauguin*, that beautiful painting, the face of a peasant woman which Sérusier painted, the Saint Jean of Filiger, or the farmyard which de Haan signed? In which boxes lie all the sketches which they abandoned for travelers to steal? All of them, however, have produced a sufficient number of great works to keep us from grieving over these barbaric acts, but we will never again be able to see the cradle of symbolic art. Were he to come back from exile for our happiness, the gentle master would be brought to tears at the sight of the modern cabaret which has replaced his good inn of the days and the joyous hours of the past that I've tried to evoke for the glory of his name and of his good, dear, and paternal image that will forever be present in my thoughts.

Letter from Gauguin to His Wife, Mette

On Work and Family Matters

1889

Yes, you have not heard from me for over six months; but it is more than six months since I received news of the children. It seems there must be a serious accident before I do hear, which scarcely disposes me to cheerfulness, although you say all danger is now over.

*   *   *

What is it you want of me? Above all, what have you ever wanted of me? Whether in the Indies or elsewhere, I am, it appears, to be a beast of *burden* for wife and children whom I *must not see.* By way of return for my homeless existence, I am *to be loved if I love,* I am to be *written to if* I write. You know me. Either I weigh matters (and weigh them well) or I do not. Heart in hand, eyes front, and I fight with uncovered breast. Your powerful sister has not abdicated her authority over you, but, in return, where is the protection she promised you?

Very well then, I accept the role that has been assigned to me, and then I must calculate—not to lose the substance for the shadow—(the shadow being the role of an employee). If I should get a job at 2,000 or 4,000 francs—your brothers' figures—there would be no complaint to make against me, and yet we should both be practically in the same position. As to the future, no one ever gives a thought to it.

I determined, despite the certitude which my conscience gave me, to consult others (men who also count) to ascertain if I was doing my duty. All are of my opinion, that art is my business, my capital, the future of my children, the honor of the name I have given them—all things which will be useful to them one day. When they have to make their way in the world, a famous father many prove a valuable asset.

You will retort that this will be a long time ahead, but what do you want me to do about it? Is it my fault? I am the first to suffer from it. I can assure you that if those who know about such things had said that I have no talent and that I am wasting my time, I would have abandoned the attempt long ago. Can it be said that Millet failed in his duty and bequeathed a wretched future to his children?

You want my news?

I am in a fisherman's inn at the seaside, near a village of 150 inhabitants. I live here like a peasant, and work every day in canvas trousers (all those of five years ago are worn out). I spend a franc a day on my food and two pence on tobacco. So no one can say I am extravagant. I speak to nobody, and I have no news of the children. Only—only this—I am exhibiting my works at Goupil's in Paris, and they are creating a great sensation; but it is difficult to sell them. When this is going to happen, I cannot tell you, but what I can tell you is that today I am one of the artists who arouse the greatest astonishment. You have exhibited some old things of mine at Copenhagen. My opinion might have been sought first of all.

The 7th June, '89, passed without one of the children thinking of it. Anyhow, all's well that ends well. I am making inquiries through influential friends about a situation in Tonkin, where I hope I should be able to live for some time and await better times. As such posts are paid, you could have part of the pictures sold at Goupil's. As for the present I have nothing. I rather anticipate the sale of a wood carving. As soon as I have

Jean-François Millet (1814–1875), leading Realist painter whose pious portrayals of French peasant laborers were an inspiration to Pissarro and Van Gogh.

COLORPLATE 41

Mette Gauguin and her five children, Copenhagen. ca. 1888. Photo courtesy of Musée Gauguin, Papeari, Tahiti.

the proceeds I will send you 300 francs—you can rely upon getting them; it is only a question of time. I am writing to Paris to try to push the sale.

At the Universal Exhibition this year I have exhibited in a *Café Chantant*; perhaps some Danes will have seen it and told you about it. In any case, nearly all Norwegians see at Goupil's what I do and Philipsen, whom I met in Paris, has also seen them.

Once for all do not end your letters with that dry phrase "Your wife, Mette"; I should prefer you to say plainly what you think. I have spoken to you about it before, but you have not wanted to understand. . . .

Letter from Gauguin to Theo van Gogh

On Painting

ca. 20 November 1889

I feel somewhat hesistant to respond to your letter. Should I answer to Van Gogh the art dealer or to Van Gogh Vincent's friend and brother? It's easy in words, more difficult by letter—however, I have to talk. But frankly speaking, I have to stop for a moment before I decide to answer the friend and thus express all my thoughts. For a month, I have been going over with de Haan the many facets of the tempest which arose over my latest paintings.

Everything has a beginning for want of an end. Are you listening directly to me, Van Gogh, with your mind and your heart?

1. This summer we created a distinct trend which was badly exhibited but was given exposure, the art of Bernard and me with some fol-

Learning that wall mirrors for a M. Volpini's Café des Arts would not arrive in time for the 1889 Exposition Universelle opening, Schuffenecker convinced him to let the Groupe Impressioniste et Synthétiste exhibit on the walls. The opening date in late May or early June is not precisely known. This important exhibition's catalogue, from around early July, lists works by Gauguin, Laval, Fauché, Schuffenecker, Anquetin, Daniel, Bernard, Roy, and Nemo. Theodore Philipsen (1840–1920), a Danish painter who met Gauguin in Copenhagen in 1884, helped to organize a loan exhibition of his works there in 1893.

lowers. Be assured, Degas and others understood it well. There is a wolf in the fold! Impressionist, Synthetist, symbolic, all in *ist* and *ic*, etc. Well then, is art locked up in each period in the thoughts of a few, the powerful, with *their methods*—or else is it a direct personal emanation to come from the thoughts of those in existence? Those who suffered because they didn't follow the norm were enraged that the powerful ones at the Ecole did not want to understand them. Today they are somewhat satisfied, and they want to be the *authority* that is doing the injustice to others that had been done to them and about which they complain. Petty humanity.

Well then, we young people ourselves are seeking and will always seek. So down with them. Those are my exact thoughts from the point of *departure*. It has been said—they want to walk in a path that is not ours, well then we are waiting for them; we will see if they are strong enough.

Today you seem to feel that my latest works are stronger than my previous ones. Be logical and draw the conclusion—that the artist has not lowered himself and has worked more for *art* than for *his business*. New quests are more useful to the new generation than no searching at all; since what has been done was done more *forcefully* than anything modern. A Dutch man says that I resemble Bernard this year. I don't resemble him more than he resembles me, but we both are doing *different* research toward the same goal. A goal about which I have been thinking for a long time but which I have only recently formulated. I must sleep, this Dutch man says, but in sleep there is dreaming and you don't want dreaming. One does not yet know his God, adds the same Dutch man. But I don't know him yet myself: being infinite, my entire life isn't enough to arrive there to find him, to define him. He is the complete opposite of Degas, continues this friendly Dutch man. And why not! If one wants to make art then one must be of the same opinion as Degas, as strong as he is.

He also writes to his friend de Haan before leaving for the Transvaal. Gauguin will do you wrong and you do the same to him. My God, what does all that mean? Forget it.

Now to enlighten you, my dear M. Van Gogh, I am going to give you an insight into my paintings. Examine them carefully, *the wood* at the same time as the ceramic. You will see that all this holds together. I am searching for and at the same time expressing a general state of mind rather than a unique thought, to have someone else's eye experience an indefinite, infinite impression. *To suggest* a suffering does not indicate what kind of suffering; purity in general and not what kind of purity. Literature is one (painting also). Consequently, suggested and not explained thought.

You ask me, or rather you tell me, that people do not at all understand the work I do in wood. It is, however, simple. There is a nude of a woman, a man, a fox, and an inscription. Is that all!

COLORPLATE 41

Since you want literature, I am going to give you some (for you only).

At the top the rotting city of Babylon. At the bottom, as though through a window, a view of fields, nature, with its flowers. Simple woman, whom a demon takes by the hand, who struggles despite the good advice of the tempting inscription. A fox (symbol of perversity among Indians). Several figures in this entourage who express the opposite of the advice ("you will be happy"), to show that it is fallacious. For those who want literature, there it is. But it is not for examination. The background of all this is sculptural art of *bas relief* forms and colors in the expression of the material. Between *the possible and the impossible*. The same for the painting of the three women of stone holding Christ.

Brittany, simple superstition and desolation.

The hill is guarded by a line of cows arranged up the hill. My intention in this painting is that everything should breathe passive belief, suffering, primitive religious style, and great nature with its cry. It's wrong

of me not to be strong enough to express it better—but I am not wrong
to think it.

Moreover, the rest of us poor devils without lodgings, without models,
we resemble virtuosos who play in a café on a tin-kettle piano. But Degas, he plays in complete silence, surrounded by brilliant company on an
Erard piano.

It is good to meticulously touch up the model from nature, but be
careful lest you smell its odor.

I think I said (in telegraph-style) what I wanted to say, perhaps with
bitterness—you have to admit that there is reason—but from the depths
of my heart and without any misunderstanding with you. You know that
I have an Indian—Inca—background, and everything I do is affected by
it. It is the depth of my personality. To rotten civilization, I aim to oppose something more natural, beginning with savageness. I would need
a lot of time and ink to explain my painting to you, but I hope, however, that you will feel its uncertainty with this letter.

You would like to see the gray and lugubrious sea of Le Pouldu with
us! Yes they evoke, in contrast, very nice visions. I will *also take you to the
visions evoked*. And for these visions evoked, doesn't one feel an instinctive modesty to show them only *veiled*?

De Haan the disciple meditates at the window with me, and he who
has not breathed any other air than that of the bedroom finds this harsh

aspect of the great, hardly Parisian sea to be grandiose. What a powerful and sad voice. He sends you his regards and will write soon.

Now let's talk business. Schuff [enecker] found a buyer for a 30-franc pastel. The buyer is not rich; I gave it away, but it doesn't matter—a more flattering than productive affair.

The price of my work in wood. I'm scratching my head. I do not evaluate its artistic value. But the work of a craftsman and the costs of wood shipment, etc. If I ask 2,000 francs, that's nothing for it, and de Haan agrees with me. And the buyers will scream that it's expensive. On this, do what you *can*. Poor devil—I have nothing to say and am obliged to be content with a glance. Look, Van Gogh, you see it like I do (it is impossible for me to continue the struggle as an artist) or to smile at the public with professional paintings—(and that I cannot do). The most dignified thing for a good-hearted man to do is what I asked you to do. To leave for Tonkin and I ask you to please speak about it especially to Manet.

Do you have any better news from Vincent? I am sorry that he can't be there near you sometimes, in order to guide a bit in painting. You hear too many different voices. A painter, myself, and stubborn, I would be confused.

Follow your first impression; it will be better than contradictory reasonings of people who have a calculated interest.

Charles Chassé

GAUGUIN ET LE GROUPE DE PONT-AVEN

1921

Charles Chassé (1883–1965), one of the most important early scholars of Gauguin's Brittany period.

It was probably during the Pont-Aven period immediately preceding the departure for Le Pouldu that Gauguin did the portrait of Mme. Satre, whose husband, now deceased, was to become mayor of Pont-Aven. It is the painting well known as *La Belle Angèle*. "Degas became its owner at the Hôtel Drouot auction in 1891," M. de Monfreid wrote me. "It had been painted the year before or, at the earliest, in 1889." However, Mme. Satre, unable to confirm the exact date, told me that this portrait of her had been done before Gauguin left for Le Pouldu. She told me:

COLORPLATE 32

Gauguin was very sweet and very poor, and we were very fond of him. However, at that time, his painting was a little frightening. He kept saying to my husband that he wanted to do my portrait, and finally, one day, he started doing it. But while he was working, he never wanted to let me look at his canvas, because he said that one cannot understand anything while the painting is in progress; he always covered it after each session. When he had finished, he first showed it to other painters, and I heard that they had laughed at it; so, when he came to bring it to me, I was already ill-disposed; my mother had told me: "I've heard that some painters had a fight last night about your portrait. What things they're saying about you!" As for Gauguin, he arrived most contentedly and walked through our house looking for the best place to hang it. But when he showed it to me, I told him, "How horrible!" and that he might just as well take it back with him, because I would never want

such a thing in my house. Just think! at that time, and in such a small town as this one! Especially since I hardly knew anything about painting! Gauguin was very sad and said with great disappointment that he had never succeeded in painting a portrait as well as this. Since then, of course, we have been on bad terms with each other, and I have hardly seen him. I have learned since that, at the Degas auction, my portrait, which I had refused as a gift, was sold for tens of thousands of francs.

As I reminded her that in her home she had, nevertheless, agreed to keep a seascape by Moret, the friend and disciple of Gauguin, she said: "Yes, but it was a seascape, whereas a portrait! . . ."

It must have been around that time, too, that Gauguin offered his large painting depicting the struggle of Jacob and the Angel to the parish priest of Pont-Aven; Gauguin would have liked it to decorate his church, but the priest refused. "We then left for Nizon, carrying the painting we wanted to offer to the priest of that parish," M. Sérusier told me. "But he knew that Gauguin had already met with a refusal in Pont-Aven and he, too, refused."

Nizon is the large village which lies on a hill just across from Pont-Aven; I have been told that the church had an old and very interesting Christ which might have given Gauguin the idea for his *Yellow Christ*. But I have never been able to confirm this information.

* * *

Gauguin spent more than a year in Le Pouldu; the register at Mlle. Marie Henry's inn tells us that, at her place at least, he stayed from 2 October 1889 to 7 November 1890. It was a very important period of his life, during which the painter de Haan was one of his closest friends. Le Pouldu was not then the seaside resort it is now. The inn Gauguin stayed in did not, as it does today, form part of a long road of quaint houses leading down to the beach; it was an isolated inn right next to the sea and surrounded by fields.

Mlle. Marie Henry (today Mme. Mothéré) was the amiable hostess. I asked her to have the kindness to tell me about the long year that Gauguin and his friends spent at her place.

M. Mothéré, a very cultivated man, amiably put himself at my dis-

Henry Moret (1856–1913), Impressionist painter who worked with Gauguin and his colleagues at Pont-Aven and Le Pouldu.

COLORPLATE 18

COLORPLATE 36

posal, to supply me with all the information that he possessed and that he had learned not only from his wife but also from the friends of Gauguin he had been able to meet. I copy exactly all the details he kindly included in his letter:

... *Impressions.* Paul Gauguin arrived in Le Pouldu in 1889, accompanied by the painter Meyer de Haan. At the beginning of the summer, they were all boarding at the Destais Inn, situated at the intersection of the roads leading, one to Quimperlé, the other to Pont-Aven, on the heights overlooking the Grands-Sables. They came from Pont-Aven, where they had been disturbed by the crowd of bathers, to find peace and to live cheaply.

Meyer de Haan had met Gauguin through the elder Pissarro. He was a Dutchman who had begun an industrial career in Amsterdam. Having founded a very prosperous cookie factory there, he passed it on to his brothers in exchange for a monthly income of 300 francs in order to be able to devote himself to painting and cultivating the fine arts. This deal was always perfectly maintained.

He started by doing academic and classical painting, for which he quickly received recognition. When he left his country, his family was negotiating with the Amsterdam Museum for the sale of a historical painting, for which they asked 100,000 francs.

But Meyer de Haan had seen an exhibition of Impressionist paintings, and he was won over by this new ideal. He immediately went to London to solicit Pissarro's advice; Pissarro sent him to Gauguin, of whom he became the enthusiastic student and generous patron. Seeing all the financial, artistic, and social difficulties with which the master was struggling, he offered to share his income with him. This proposal was enthusiastically accepted, and its realization led the two artists successively to Pont-Aven, then to the Destais Inn at Le Pouldu.

Pont-Aven was already becoming popular, and crowds of American and English people were attracted to it during the summer peak season. Their artistic pretensions hardly agreed with the credo of our two pilgrims; the foreigners' mundane comings and goings would upset the painters' concentration. In fact, Gauguin was never able to produce in the midst of the tumult and uncertainties of bohemian life, of which only the passionate freedom appealed to him, while the other elements he repudiated. He needed to feel around him a minimum of stability and security, a certain amount of freedom. Temporary living and frequent moves put a damper on his inspiration. The only places where he created works of any worth were those where he had first set up his interior space according to his tastes. Driven by this desire, he and his companion went looking for a more deserted place and went to Le Pouldu. First housed at the Destais's, it was not long before they encountered the same problems as in Pont-Aven. For this reason, they finally migrated to a small inn situated a kilometer down the hill, right next to the sea, owned by Mlle. Marie Henry. They then completed their appointments by renting, for a studio, the attic of the one and only villa in the region, the Mauduit villa, just a few steps from their new home. They gave it up in the spring of 1890 to move their easels to a little wooden shed that leaned against one end of their inn and had served, until that time, for storage and as a stable. Cleaned, floored, and with a window put in on the north side, it became the practical shelter where they gave in to

COLORPLATE 33. *Self-Portrait*. 1889. Oil on wood. 31½ × 20½″ (79.2 × 51.3 cm).
National Gallery of Art, Washington, D.C.; Chester Dale Collection.

COLORPLATE 34. *"Nirvana"—Portrait of Meyer de Haan.* ca. 1890. Essence on silk. 8 × 11½" (20 × 29 cm).
Wadsworth Atheneum, Hartford; The Ella Gallup Sumner and Mary Catlin Sumner Collection.

COLORPLATE 35. Self-Portrait Cup. ca. 1889. Stoneware decorated with colored glaze. Height: 9½″ (24 cm). Konstindustrimuseet, Copenhagen. Photo: Ole Woldbye.

COLORPLATE 36. *The Yellow Christ*. 1889. 36½ × 28⅞″ (92 × 73.5 cm).
Albright-Knox Art Gallery, Buffalo, New York; General Purchase Funds, 1946.

COLORPLATE 37. *Christ in the Garden of Olives*, or *Agony in the Garden*. 1889. 28¾ × 36¼″ (73 × 92 cm).
Norton Gallery and School of Art, West Palm Beach, Florida.

COLORPLATE 38. *Bonjour, Monsieur Gauguin*. 1889. 36½ × 29″ (92.5 × 74 cm).
Národni Gallery, Prague.

COLORPLATE 39. *Woman in the Waves,* or *Ondine.* 1889. 36½ × 28⁵/₁₆″ (92 × 72 cm).
The Cleveland Museum of Art; Gift of Mr. and Mrs. William Powell Jones.

COLORPLATE 40. *The Coast of Bellangenay.* ca. 1890. 28¾ × 36¼″ (73 × 92 cm).
Museum of Fine Arts, Springfield, Massachusetts.

Portrait bust of Meyer de Haan.
1889–1890. Carved oak wood with
touches of color. 23 × 11¾ × 9″ (58.4 ×
29.9 × 22.8 cm). The National Gallery of
Canada, Ottawa.

their ardor for work without any worry of being interrupted or
disturbed. Thus, the artistic solitude dreamed of by Gauguin
first became a reality. Le Pouldu was the first of his "Tahitis,"
his "French Tahiti."

The register of the inn shows Gauguin was 42 at the time.
In the prime of life and with his health still intact, he stood upright, with a tanned face, dark and rather long hair, aquiline
nose, big green eyes, a light beard around his chin, and a short
moustache. He had a serious and imposing look, a calm and
thoughtful demeanor which would sometimes become ironic in
front of philistines, and a great muscular vigor which he did not
like to use. His slow gait, his sober gestures, his severe facial
expression gave him much natural dignity and held unknown
and foreign people at bay. Behind this mask of impassive coldness were concealed ardent senses and a sensuous temperament
always in search of new sensations. Having never finished
school, he was unable to understand Latin and Greek writers,
whom he despised because he had not studied them. From his
sailor's wanderings, he had brought back some precepts of a

Portrait of Meyer de Haan. 1889. Oil on panel. 31⅜ × 20⅜″ (80 × 52 cm). David Rockefeller Collection.

rudimentary pragmatism he summed up in a formula inscribed many times in his works or on the ordinary objects he liked to decorate: "Long live wine, love, and tobacco!" "Wine" for him fortunately never went beyond a few small and rare glasses of cognac, which he did not abuse and was served to him more for appearance's sake than for its taste. But "love and tobacco" were dear to his heart. This last item was supplied to him, like everything else, by his student. De Haan would buy huge one-pound packages of it that he would put in a ceramic vase especially used for this purpose. Gauguin would help himself to it according to his needs. When the receptacle was empty, out of discretion he would refrain from asking that it be refilled. But he became sad, quiet, somber. We would then wonder what was upsetting the master; we went to the vase, took off its lid, and immediately discovered the state of want that tormented him. Upon which discovery the provision was renewed and the great man's face would regain its accustomed serenity. As for "love," it was his great passion, the one whose domination possessed him all his life and, at first contained and repressed, that became from day to day more despotic and burning. . . . During the period in le Pouldu, he was still repressing it into a relatively strict discipline. But he openly regretted not having participated in the free life of the Latin Quarter when he was young and, perhaps in compensation for this loss, he already dreamed of emigrating to Tahiti, to which he had made plans to bring de Haan and M. Emile Bernard.

Thus, there was in him a great thirst for sensations. On the other hand, he had a penury of feelings. The basis of his character was a ferocious egoism, the egoism of a genius who considers the whole world his prey, devoted to the glorification of his power, and as raw material for his personal creations. Not the least charity, pity, tenderness, or altruism.

But the very exaggeration of this unrestrained egoism kept the artist, who was gifted because of it and who remained a heroic figure, from turning into a banal bourgeois or local bum. Gauguin had sacrificed to his ideal everything around him in which he could have taken part—men, animals, and people. He had begun by renouncing for himself the various elements that make up human happiness. Home, family, children, wealth, friendships, well-being, security, esteem, leisure—he had voluntarily destroyed or abandoned all these and many other things. And why? For the sole hope of being able, for the rest of his life, to give form to the splendid and rare visions of his imagination. And, by an unconscious extension of this principle, he did not understand that a human being could refuse to follow his example and to give himself as a burnt offering to the minotaur that Gauguin himself adored.

No doubt he did conceive painting as a devouring, frightening god to whom everything, absolutely everything, had to yield. The individual, gifted with genius in this art, certainly appeared to him as a priest, imbued with an august and fearsome function: that of creating pictorial beauty. For this lamentably privileged person, this was an imperious obligation that he had to obey without hesitation or reserve, and that authorized him, additionally, to commit any act, provided that it be useful to the superior goal at which he was aiming.

If he had been allowed to create the universe, he obviously would have given the human species the organization of a huge convent where the painter would have occupied the summit of the hierarchy and all the others would occupy different levels according to the importance of the services they could render the master in the completion of his work. And when Meyer de Haan's friendship allowed him to realize his secret aspirations, it was exactly this sort of brotherhood that he created at Le Pouldu, kept in modest proportions because of the minimal resources of his student. Minimal, but assuredly, that was the point of it. Gauguin spent his entire life searching for this simple capacity: to be able to work in complete independence, beyond any servile obligation to the trends of the day, those of fashion, of merchants, and of clients. He joyfully accepted the bleakest physical misery—bread and water—as long as he was left free to produce with all the ardor and exuberance of his creative temperament.

It was this magnificent abnegation which had seduced Meyer

de Haan to the point that he took on the responsibility of making it possible by sharing it. For him as well, talent and genius imposed a sort of divinely ordered mission upon the artist to which he had to devote himself body and soul. However, while Gauguin incorporated into the ranks of his victims all his friends and acquaintances with all their ins and outs, his student remained a bit more human and maintained some scruples. He would not allow the artist to infringe upon the domain of a personality other than his own. Gauguin's tyranny reached its limits at the frontiers of his own being.

Free from any care, the two painters arranged for themselves the laborious monkish existence of an artistic laity in this long-chosen setting. They got up very early and came downstairs from their bedrooms around 7 o'clock. Having finished their breakfast of café au lait and bread and butter, they went to work outside in the country with their painting apparatus or sketchbooks, depending upon the daylight. They came back around 11:30 for lunch at noon. At about 1:30 or 2:00, they would go back to work until 5:00, unless someone came visiting, which was exceptional. At 7:00, dinner. The interval between getting home and the meal was used to chat or to visit in the studio. They went to bed very early, around 9 o'clock in the evening, but not without having played a game of lotto or checkers. Gauguin's checkerboard, drawn on an old advertisement with a small, decorative border, is still at the house. Also, they often drew by lamplight.

They read nothing, neither books nor newspapers. De Haan's enormous, antique Dutch Bible is still, undoubtedly, stored in our attic. But it is unlikely he would have used such a cumbersome text very much. It weighs at least twenty pounds. One would have needed a pulley in order to look through it, and its owner was a small, stunted, deformed, sickly being— almost an invalid.

On the other hand, music was a favorite pastime for them. But Meyer de Haan liked to listen to it without ever playing any, although he liked to say that he knew how. As for Gauguin, he played the mandolin and the piano. He had learned the latter instrument very late, as an adult; he could hardly play more than a few pieces, and at a rather slow rhythm. He lacked the "agility" of experienced pianists. His repertory included some Schumann—the *Berceuse* and the *Rêverie*—and some Handel. Once, some foreign musicians, unknown at the house, came to play the violin.

They seldom worked in their studio and were almost constantly outside, except, of course, when sculpting. Their method consisted of spending a long time contemplating the points of view they wanted to paint—studying its lines, harmonies, colors, and light until they were satiated—and taking abundant notes, pencil in hand. Gauguin liked to say that a work of art has to be entirely completed in the painter's mind before he begins his canvas. When this meticulous and painstaking preparation was complete, when he knew the planned painting in advance by heart, so to speak, he watched for his lighting. Finally the precious morning came that gave the dearly cherished and desired effect. The artist would then jump to his brushes, and face to face with nature, in one sitting he would draw the poem out of his dream. He began by tracing the composition in a line of Prussian blue, thick, clear, bold, precise, expressive, and nuanced, so to speak, with upstrokes and downstrokes. Then, in the spaces rigorously drawn out, he would apply colors with

vertical or oblique strokes, barely covering the canvas, brushing
with a velvety, supple, and feline gesture. "It looked like a cat
playing with a mouse." The whole thing, in one swoop, without
hesitation or starting over. "In one session," he would often recommend. "Otherwise it's a failure, because it's better to start a
painting over than to touch it up later." This method, whose
basis rested on the intimate and incessant contemplation of
nature, had the practical advantage of sparing the costs of a
model. They hardly ever hired any. Gauguin only once used the
services of Madeleine Delorme, a girl of the region, and those
of Captain, an old beggar of a particularly picturesque nobility.
In reality, their true models were all the people of the region;
passersby, peasants working, seaweed fishermen and fisher-
women, ship's-boys prowling the shore, woman bathers lying on
the beach, housewives near their cottages and compost heaps,
shepherds and shepherdesses leading their animals to the fields,
etc., etc. With a quick and inquiring line, they would draw in
their notebooks the gestures, attitudes, gatherings, and poses of
animals and people. This whole first sketch, without which they
did not conceive of creating, served as nourishment to the work
when it was resumed later.

* * *

On 23 July, M. Filiger made his entry into this little circle, where his influence soon became considerable. So much so that in the middle of the summer of 1890, the poor little household of Le Pouldu sheltered under its roof Meyer de Haan in the big bedroom, Gauguin in the bedroom overlooking the yard, M. Sérusier in the bedroom overlooking the street, M. Filiger in the studio, the propietress in the bathroom, and the maid in the pantry. Gauguin took advantage of the fact that the kitchen roof, just beneath his window, gave him a short path to get up at night and fraternize with the maid in the pantry and pass a few joyous moments with her. There the former squadron helmsman would repeat the scenario of his "revels" as a sailor; the stopovers, the country maid, and the bottle. "Long live wine, love, and tobacco!"

* * *

Gauguin also exposed the principles of his pictorial credo to his friends and students. He would repeat to them the axioms that were dear to him, such as "Line is color"—a striking image which proves that Gauguin had as much respect for drawing as Ingres and also distinguishes between the type of drawing a colorist must cultivate and the type he must avoid. He also said: "A square centimeter of green in the middle of a billiard table is greener than a square centimeter of green seen by itself." Thus he summed up in a few syllables a whole part of his professional study, pursued at length in the most novel directions: the variation of tones and the painting of atmosphere.

He who hated to begin a conversation with hostile, foreign, and unknown people, on the other hand, enjoyed explaining himself as soon as he felt that he was in friendly surroundings. He was animated by no more than a noble passion for art, and nothing would have been further from his intentions than to try to monopolize the fruits of his studies. He much preferred to show the precedence that his age, experience, and talent conferred upon him. In Le Pouldu, he was always listened to with respect, and his young colleagues made a great deal of his precious advice. He was endlessly railing against the overly docile students of the Ecole, the "Americans" who would shut themselves up for hours in a closed studio to work with models instead of bravely attacking nature through direct observation. Such a genesis could give birth only to cold, false, and dead works. He also reproached them for the lack of any logic in their methods; he laughed at their strange way of beginning a painting in one corner, which they would work in depth while all the rest of the painting's surface would remain blank; he would also condemn the method of composing a work out of bits and pieces, like a mosaic of assembled fragments.

Also, more than once, he expressed the desire to see the success of color photography, at that time discovered yet hardly born; its realization, he hoped, would open academic painters' eyes and prove to what point Impressionism remains faithful to nature (while interpreting it to its whim), whereas painted zinc trompe-l'oeil works of his adversaries would ridiculously betray nature even when pretending servilely to copy it.

He little admired the Greeks and Romans, whom he considered decadent in comparison to the Egyptians, Indians, and Orientals. Although seductive, he confessed, their masterpieces represented, according to his very pure and haughty criterion, merely the abandonment of the noble and sublime stylizations of their predecessors. Near the Javanese pavillion of the World's

Fair, he found a fragment of a frieze depicting a dancing woman and piously hung it in the main room in Le Pouldu. He took inspiration from it to sculpt out of brown earth a small statuette keepsake holder that still exists here with us, though broken into several pieces. His audacious genius operated in the most extremely fantastic regions, where nothing more than the instinctive assurance of an impeccable, innate, and unlearned taste either guided or sustained him. It mattered little to him to be deprived of help—it was useless to him—as long as he could gain in this way an extra bit of freedom, independence, and power. "Between a flop and a masterpiece," he said, "there is only the difference of a millimeter." An imperceptible and capital error he felt strong enough never to commit. Style, nourished by the intimate study of nature, which he wanted to know deeply, in order to recreate it within himself after imposing his mark on it, was the essence of art in his eyes. To free himself from an order which was narrow, banal, and petrified in inert matter in order to raise himself up to another order—more grandiose, more intently expressed, entirely original, mobile, and variable, but always present—constituted his primary need, his constant preoccupation, and the general inclination of his character.

If, in the field of fine arts, these gifts of splendid initiative would open infinite and endlessly renewing perspectives for him, they carried him into political, social, and religious regions and into more controversial ideas. This instinct for simplification, which made him concentrate all the aspects of the physical world into superior harmonies, also made unbearable for him the complex paths that civilization took. Whence his hatred of the bourgeoisie, marriage, family, civil servants, and judges. He violently condemned their hypocritical egoism, which was sheltered behind laws in order to substitute it for a cynical egoism; he rejected all constraints, whose merits and advantages are difficult to perceive, and which, to impartial minds, seem six of one, half a dozen of the other.

In any case, in Le Pouldu, Gauguin would continually praise the charms of the savage life. He strongly urged Meyer de Haan and his other friends to follow him in a definitive emigration to those lands innocent of all culture. First, because this savage life appeared more beautiful to him. Light more radiant, colors more lively, lines more sensual, the lack of ugly and distorting veils hiding the human body, a more rational development of muscles and bodies, and everywhere the more elegant and supple rhythm of movements and postures—in short, the thousand attractions that seduce the gazing European in these lands of sun, along with their lively newness, gave them a great aesthetic superiority in his opinion. Furthermore, in terms of social matters, this life, more in conformity with natural needs, favored their satisfaction, whereas, in our inclement latitudes, everything worked against or aggravated them. Finally, he promised, life in the tropics was much cheaper. . . . Be that as it may, his impassioned dithyrambs converted first Meyer de Haan and then M. Emile Bernard to his ideas and plans. Both of them intended to accompany him in his exodus to Tahiti. . . .

* * *

Meanwhile, the quartet was busy with music. Gauguin took his guitar, Filiger his mandolin, and they would go sit in the sand in a nook in the rocks; a Schumann melody sweetly rose up from the mandolin, which Filiger played with much feeling; it

Here Chassé reprints a letter to him from Paul-Emile Colin containing a memoir of Gauguin at Le Pouldu.

was an almost imperceptible sound, though—he played only
for himself.

* * *

I can still see Gauguin swimming at Le Pouldu beach with his
eagle's-beak nose, his clear sailor's eyes, his black, slightly long
hair, his beret, his swimming trunks, his forty-year-old man's
belly; he made you think of a buffoon, a troubador, and
a pirate, all at once. He had the greatest admiration for Vautrin, the character in the *Comédie Humane,* and the idea would
enter your mind that, in other times and circumstances, and
bereft of his love of art, he could have been Vautrin's brother.
Tremendous energy sprung forth from his whole being; he
seemed to be hatching a huge work. He had read much: the
Bible, Shakespeare, and Balzac seemed to have the premier
place in his admiration.

* * *

M. Paul Sérusier told me about a trip he took with Gauguin from Le
Pouldu to Lorient. Gauguin, who by that time had earned a little money,
decided that they would go to Lorient by coach. When they were in Lor-
ient, Gauguin, who had seen a piano, decided to rent it and move it to
Le Pouldu. "You mean you know how to play the piano?" Sérusier asked.
"Oh! no," Gauguin answered, "but with a bit of intuition! . . ."

"Gauguin was amazingly intuitive," M. Sérusier told me. "When I
played the accordion, I tried to see how the instrument was made, how
it functioned, and what sounds one could get out of it. What Gauguin
looked for, however, was to begin from a tune he already knew; but very
quickly it would become another tune; he added his own improvisa-
tions. When he painted, it was the same thing. He told me, 'Here is a
study on which I will work for several weeks,' and then he would get all
fired up; all of a sudden, a head would appear in a corner of his painting, then another, and by evening, his painting was finished. In Tahiti,
however, he was to paint with more steadiness, more application."

*Chassé's researches also led him to
Sérusier, Gauguin's Pont-Aven
companion, who provided this
reminiscence.*

Charles Morice

PAUL GAUGUIN

On Morice's First Meeting with Gauguin

1919

It was in 1889, in a little restaurant near the Odéon where some of those
poets still indiscriminately called Symbolist, though, by then, sometimes
Decadent, would meet. The owner left them the mezzanine of his establishment—or perhaps their resounding discussions of aesthetics little by
little chased the rest of the clientele from this small, low room that was
quickly filled with the smoke of their inextinguishable pipes.

This particular night, arriving late at the Côte d'Or, I noticed a new
face in the group of my friends, a large, bony, solid face with a narrow
forehead, a nose neither curved nor hooked but that might have been
broken, a straight, thin-lipped mouth, heavy eyelids that opened lazily
over slightly bulging, bluish eyes that rotated in their sockets to look to
the left and right almost without the body or the head having to take the
trouble to move.

This stranger had little charm; however, he attracted one with his

*Charles Morice (1861–1919), whose
survey of literary theory* (Littérature à
tout à l'heure, *1889) became a keystone
for the emerging Symbolist movement,
staunchly supported Gauguin before he
left for Tahiti in 1891 and upon his
return to France in 1893. He collaborated with Gauguin on* Noa Noa, *writing
short prose and verse pieces to accompany
the artist's autobiography. Gauguin's
unaccompanied text finally appeared in
1897, edited by Morice; the full book did
not appear until 1901. Many Gauguin
biographers complain that Morice's editing
was excessive. In 1901 Morice tried
unsuccessfully to organize a purchase of*
Where Do We Come From? *for the
State. His 1919 Gauguin biography
remains a major one.*

very personal expression, a mixture of an obviously naive, noble haughtiness and a simplicity that bordered on triviality; one quickly perceived that this mixture signified strength: aristocracy gaining strength through the people. And if grace was lacking, the smile, which, moreover, was not well suited to his overly straight and thin lips—when loosening into a smile, they seemed to regret it, as if it were a confession of weakness in gaiety—the smile of Gauguin had, nonetheless, a strangely ingenuous gentleness. Above all, that face became very beautiful when grave; when it lit up, giving in to the heat of the discussion, rays of suddenly intense blue light shot out of his eyes.

When I saw Gauguin for the first time that night, he was indeed in one of these moments. Though there were other strangers in a group of which he was the center, I saw only him, and, coming closer, I remained standing for a long time near the table where a dozen or so poets and artists listened, listening myself after distractedly shaking the hands of my friends when they extended them to me.

In a somber, slightly hoarse voice, he said:

> Primitive art comes from the spirit and uses nature. So-called refined art comes from sensuality and serves nature. Nature is the servant of the first and the mistress of the second. But the servant cannot forget her origins, she degrades the artist by allowing him to adore her. This is how we fall into the abominable error of Naturalism. Naturalism begins with the Greece of Pericles. Since then, there have been no more or less great artists except those who have somehow reacted against this error; but their reactions have been no more than leaps of memory, glimmers of good sense within a movement of decadence, in the end, uninterrupted for centuries. Truth is purely cerebral art, this is primitive art—the most learned of all—this was Egypt. There is the principle. In our present misery, there can be no salvation without a rational and sincere return to the principle. And this return is the necessary action of Symbolism in poetry and art. . . .

That is what he said, approximately; and I listened, delighted, to these words that harmonized with my own thought and clarified it.

Suddenly a heated voice rang out—and I recognized it as that of Jean Moréas:

"Monsieur Gauguin, have you read Ronsard?"

It was with Moréas that Gauguin was arguing in the silence of the gallery around them. Moréas, who already carried the Romanesque school in his soul and was beginning to recruit for it, was certainly as diametrically opposed as one can imagine to this doctrine of reasoned Primitivism. Later, nevertheless, his thought would broaden, passing the horizon of the Renaissance in order to climb all the way to the simplicity of the veritable Hellenic spirit, that is to say, to the poems of Homer— these reflections, already, of an art even simpler than their own, and therefore, greater—Moréas was well aware of what was true and fecund in Gauguin's theories. Without wholeheartedly subscribing to them on his part, he only spoke of them with respect.

I notice that the poets still show, with rare exceptions, a spontaneous and profound deference to Gauguin, both to his person and his art. This is logically explained by the predilection the artist showed in his work for poetic thought, that is to say, "literary" thought. But we will come back to this point.

During this first encounter (since it was Gauguin's first contact with the literary professionals) there were, nevertheless, no clashes, but on the contrary, and this is worse, vague gestures of retreat, noisy objections, and silences. The attitude of this painter, who had just taught us, in one

Pierre de Ronsard (1524–1585), French Renaissance court poet.

lump with art, about poetry, its laws and its obligations, offended some. And the man's personality, which was so distinct, the breadth of both his theories and his shoulders, the incisive intuition of his gaze, the savory impropriety of his speech, in which the slang of the sailor and that of the studio strangely cloaked ideas of purity, of an absolute nobility, everything about him clashed with what the eye was used to and with the spirit of the writers who, despite their sincere desire to get to the truth—how they searched for it—of literary art and did so at the risk and at the price of a revolution, remained accountable to the immediate tradition and, moreover, maintained some of the superficial prejudices of propriety. Gauguin, without meaning to, imposed a sort of effacement on them, he ousted them from the forefront. Also involuntarily they too, without a doubt, attempted to regain the advantage from him through the privilege of their knowledge, richer and more precise, at least in literature, than his.

There followed an ill-at-ease feeling, which he was the first to sense. He let the controversy drop, asked to hear Moréas's poetry, and, while he listened, I studied him, now immobile. Yes, that strength, that was indeed the principal characteristic imprinted on his whole being, a noble force which justified a visible pretension to tyranny. Meanwhile, the short chin, the nose with the delicate nostrils that flared incessantly, the bitter expression of the mouth acknowledged, I told myself, possible abrupt relaxations of the will, moments of weakness or of despair, jealously hidden—and these traits contradicted to some extent his general expression, all energy, calm and conscious. . . .

Never again, afterwards, in our meetings of artists and poets, did he take up the discussion in that doctoral, professorial tone of the first day. He had understood.

Jules Antoine

ART ET CRITIQUE

"Impressionists and Synthetists"

9 November 1889

It is so easy to crush the young with the past, and this means has been used so often to block the way to artists today recognized as masters that I avoid letting myself be influenced by the often modest, sometimes ridiculous appearances that the small exhibitions manifest. So, not wishing to emulate the great critics who ignore, or pretend to ignore, any effort that does not emanate from a certain quarter, I have tried to see, as well as the necessarily defective installation permitted me to, the hundred or so works that Messieurs Gauguin, Schuffenecker, Roy, Fauché, Laval, Daniel, Anquetin, Bernard, and Hemo [sic] have shown in a restaurant on the Champ de Mars.

* * *

Among those exhibiting who are vulgar Impressionists (they are wise men, if we compare them to M. Anquetin), there is one, M. Gauguin, who already enjoys a certain reputation, which I find deserved, with mild reservations.

It is certain that *Dancing a Round in the Hay, The Young Wrestlers—Brittany, The Model—Brittany, The Mangoes—Martinique*, etc. are the works of a painter, even though they include, here and there, deformations of

Louis Roy (1862–1907) met Gauguin in Pont-Aven and contributed to the Café Volpini exhibition. During Gauguin's 1893–1895 return visit to France, Roy printed an edition of the Noa Noa *woodblock prints. Compared with Gauguin's own printing, Roy's lacks subtlety because he applied the ink too heavily. Léon Fauché (b. 1868), friend of Toulouse-Lautrec who also met Gauguin in Pont-Aven and had works in the Café Volpini exhibition. Daniel was the name under which Gauguin's friend Daniel de Monfreid participated in the Café Volpini exhibition. Louis Anquetin (1861–1932), student at Cormon's with Toulouse-Lautrec, Van Gogh, and Bernard, and the creator of Cloisonism, according to Edouard Dujardin in the 1 March 1888* La Revue Indépendante. *Ludovic Nemo was Bernard's alias for his "peintures au pétrole" (gasoline paintings) in the Café Volpini exhibition.*

Letter to Van Gogh, dated 25 July 1888.
Vincent van Gogh Foundation/National
Museum Vincent van Gogh, Amsterdam.

drawing and falsifications of color values that bother me, and that, in ·
other works where these are excessive, manage to damage a great deal
M. Gauguin's indisputable talent.

For example, the exhibition catalogue includes a lithograph by him
entitled *The Haymakers*, which is a very poor thing. M. Gauguin knows
how to draw, and there is no aesthetic that justifies too-long arms, too-
narrow torsos, and a woman's head resembling that of a mouse.

A watercolor, called *Eve*, portrays a naked woman crouched at the
foot of a tree equipped with a serpent; beneath it, I read: "Don't listen—him . . . him . . . liar!" What document supports M. Gauguin's assumption that Eve talked pidgin? . . .

Unless I am mistaken, M. Gauguin, too, is a Synthetist!

Among the nine exhibitors, there are two who visibly copy M. Gauguin. One, M. Bernard, is a Synthetist; the other, M. Laval, purely and
simply imitates him very closely.

Letter from Gauguin to Vincent van Gogh

On His Plans for Madagascar

ca. 25 May 1890

Do you remember our former conversations in Arles, when we spoke of establishing the atelier of the Tropics? I am about to put this plan into effect if I can get the necessary bit of money together in order to create the establishment. I will then go to Madagascar with a small tribe of gentle people without money who live off the land. From several sources I have *very precise* information. Out of a small earth and wooden hut I will make a comfortable home with my ten fingers; by myself I will plant there all kinds of food, chickens, cows, etc. . . . and in a short time my material life there will be assured. Those who will want to come later will find there all the materials in order to work at a very small cost. And the atelier of the Tropics perhaps will become the Saint John the Baptist of the painting of the future, invigorated there by a more natural, more primitive, and, above all, less spoiled life.

Right now, I could easily give up all my paintings at 100 francs each to make my dream come true.

In Madagascar I'm sure that I'll have the calm necessary to work well.

Letter from Gauguin to Odilon Redon

On His Plans for Tahiti

September 1890

As a matter of fact, your silence surprised me, I have judged man by his Art, and then later for himself, and the only explanation for me was an error by the post office. In these conditions, your letter was a double pleasure and I am happy to see you in the *inner* conditions that make one relatively happy.

The reasons you give me for remaining in Europe are more flatteries than facts intended to convince me. I am set in my decision, and since I have been in Brittany I have modified it. Madagascar is still too near to the civilized world; I am going to go to Tahiti and I hope to finish my life there. I believe that my art, which you love, is only a seed and I hope that down there I can cultivate it for myself to a primitive and savage state.

For this, I need calm. What does it matter that the glory goes to others?

Gauguin is finished here, you will not see him anymore. You can see that I am selfish. I bring with me in photographs, drawings, a whole little world of friends who speak to me every day; I have a picture in my head of nearly all that you have done and *a star*; when seeing it, in my cabin in Tahiti, I will not, I promise you, dream of death, but on the contrary, of eternal life, not death in life but life in death. In Europe, this death with its snake's tail is conceivable, but in Tahiti, it has to be seen with roots that come back as flowers. I have not said farewell to the artists who are in harmony with me. I remember a line from Wagner that explains the way I think:

> I think that the disciples of great art will be glorified, and,
> enveloped in a celestial fabric of rays of light, of sweet aromas,
> of melodious music, they return to lose themselves in eternity,
> in the bosom of the divine source of all harmony.

Therefore, my dear Redon, we will see each other again.

I still do not know when I am leaving, considering that the business of which I spoke to you is still not done, and I am in Brittany waiting, which is making me completely nervous. . . .

Charles Morice

PAUL GAUGUIN

On Preparation for the Hôtel Drouot Sale

1919

It was upon his return from Le Pouldu that I had the honor of meeting Gauguin.

As always, with Paris still hostile to him, he proposed, as soon as he arrived, to leave again and this time to go as far as possible in order to return as late as possible.

Staying first with Emile Schuffenecker and then in a narrow, furnished room—and working at that time in the studio of a talented painter he got to know when he returned from Martinique, M. Daniel de Monfreid—he could not, despite the generosity of his friends, work in their studios the way he could in his own, fully independent. But how, moreover, to free himself from this congenial servitude while the dealers continued to resist him?

One night at the Café Voltaire, where on Saturdays a large group of poets and artists gathered around Verlaine, he confided to me his desire for a new exile.

"The experience that I had in Martinique," he said to me, "is decisive. Only there did I really feel like myself, and it is in what I brought back from there that one has to search if one wishes to find out who I am, more so than in my work from Brittany, because in Brittany I am now too well-known. . . . I have to talk, to discuss things and not get anything done. . . . These are the inconveniences of glory," he added with his bitter smile. "And really, I want to go to Tahiti, but I need money. About 10,000 francs. . . . I think that a properly prepared sale of about thirty works from Martinique, Brittany, and Arles could raise that much. But the preparation is tricky. I cannot imagine anything better than a resounding article in a large newspaper, an article which could then be used as the preface to the catalogue, but by whom?"

The next day I went to see Mallarmé.

Georges-Daniel de Monfreid (1856–1929), painter and sailing enthusiast whom Gauguin met after leaving Martinique in late 1887. They exhibited in 1889 at the Café Volpini. Monfreid, who placed his Paris studio at Gauguin's disposal in late 1890, received letters regularly from Gauguin in Tahiti; first published in 1918, they are highly revealing Gauguin documents, since Monfreid was an artistic, legal, even personal agent for him. See Jean Loize, Les Amitiés du peintre Georges-Daniel de Monfreid et ses reliques de Gauguin *(Paris, 1951).*

Paul Gauguin. 1891. Photo courtesy of Musée Gauguin, Papeari, Tahiti.

It is well-known that Mallarmé, for the writers of the Symbolist generation, was more than a master: an elder friend, an unraveler of the soul, almost a director of conscience. As for me, I had already worshiped him for a long time. In difficult times, it was always to him that I went for advice.

A few days earlier, I had taken Gauguin to Mallarmé's house. A spiritual intimacy quickly developed between the great poet and the great artist who had admired each other from a distance, regarding each others' work highly. I was, therefore, sure of finding the necessary information from Mallarmé. Without hesitating, he said:

"Go see Mirbeau."

I first shook my head yes, then no.

Mallarmé smiled.

"Or," he concluded, "I will see him."

At the end of the week, he wrote to me that M. Mirbeau was expecting us, Gauguin and me, at his house for lunch on such and such a day.

On 16 February 1891, in *L'Echo de Paris*, the desired article, the "resounding article," appeared.

Stéphane Mallarmé (1842–1898), Symbolist poet, critic, and, in the early 1870s, collaborator with Manet on illustrated editions of his poems and Poe translations. He became the father-figure for the next generation of poets and artists; Gauguin cherished his support, quoting him in a March 1899 letter to Fontainas: "In front of my Tahitian pictures Mallarmé was also heard to say: 'It is extraordinary that one can have so much mystery in such outbursts.'" Octave Mirbeau (1848–1917), novelist, critic, and amateur painter whose friends included Mallarmé, Monet, and Rodin.

It had exactly the effect that Gauguin had promised himself. For the first time, the art lovers seemed to suspect that he was alive. M. Mirbeau's article, reproduced in the catalogue of the sale, brought large crowds to the Hôtel Drouot.

Charles Morice

PAUL GAUGUIN

On the Tahiti Exhibition

1919

Then, months passed, during which Gauguin and I got to know each other, got to love each other.

We wasted no time before we began to use the informal *tu* with each other, a detail that is not without merit because the *tu* permits, while the *vous* ordinarily excludes, confidences. All the theories that he professed at Pont-Aven—the famous "Ecole" at Pont-Aven—he reasoned through them with me, often attempting to transpose them from the plastic to the poetic domain. But let us recall the artist at leisure. That is the man that I would like to present here.

We will go back to the Direction des Beaux-Arts, where thanks to the recommendation of Ary Renan, Gauguin, who was ready to go to Tahiti, obtained an artistic commission. I was happy about this event, and I spoke of it with joy. Gauguin was silent. I told him that the period of painful struggles was over for him, that he could finally go off and work freely. . . . Suddenly, having looked at him, I also became quiet, stupefied by the desolate expression on his face. His color, naturally leaden, had lightened to a morbid pallor, his features dissolved, the staring eye no longer looked anywhere except inwardly, and his step became hesitant. I gently took his arm. He started, and, pointing to some café, he said to me, "Let's go in there."

We sat in the darkest corner in the establishment, which was otherwise empty—it was morning—and Gauguin, leaning on the table with his head in his hands, cried. I was filled even more with terror than with pity: this man, this very man, crying!

"I have never been so unhappy," he murmured to me, finally sitting up again.

"But how! today, today justice begins, glory comes! . . ."

"Listen to me. . . . I did not know how to feed my family and my thoughts. . . . I did not even know, until now, how to feed just my thoughts. . . . And today when I can hope, I feel more awfully than ever the horror or of the sacrifice that I have made, which is irreparable."

And then he spoke to me at length of his wife, of his children, from whom he separated in order to concentrate all his strength, all his years, on the accomplishment of his work. How he loved them!

And all of a sudden, he got up:

"Let me leave, I need to be alone. And we will not see each other for a few days. . . . The time," he added with a heart-rending smile, "for you to forgive me for having cried in front of you."

I am sure that I have betrayed neither discretion nor his friendship by relating this scene. It shows the naked truth about a maligned heart.

Ary Renan (1857–1900), Salon painter and poet.

Octave Mirbeau

On Gauguin's Progress

16 February 1891

I have learned that M. Paul Gauguin is going to Tahiti. He intends to live there alone for several years, to build himself a hut and to begin work anew on those things that haunt him. The case of a man fleeing from civilization, voluntarily seeking obscurity and silence the better to understand himself, the better to listen to the inner voices that are suffocated by the clamor of our passions and disputes, seemed to me curious and touching. Paul Gauguin is a very exceptional artist, very disturbing, who rarely appears in public and of whom, consequently, the public knows little. I have many times promised myself to speak of him. Alas! I hardly know why, it seems to me one no longer has time for anything. And then, perhaps I retreated from such a task and the fear of not speaking well of a man for whom I profess the highest and most particular esteem. To capture in a few brief and rapid notes the significance of the art of Gauguin, so complicated and primitive, so clear and so obscure, so barbarous and so refined, is this not, perhaps, unrealizable—I mean to say beyond my capabilities? To make you understand such a man, there would need to be developments that would deny me the necessary brevity of a chronicle. Nevertheless, I believe that by beginning with the intellectual characteristics of Gauguin and then epitomizing, by means of a few characteristic traits, his strange and tortured life, the work will become clear by itself in a living light.

Paul Gauguin was born of parents who, if not extremely wealthy, at least knew a life of ease and sweetness. His father collaborated at Armand Marrast's *National* with Thiers and Degouve-Denunques. He died at sea in 1852 during a voyage to Peru that would, I think, have been an exile. He left the memory of a strong soul and a high intelligence. His mother, born in Peru, was the daughter of Flora Tristan, of the beautiful, fiery, energetic Flora Tristan, the author of many books on socialism and art, and who took such an active part in the phalansterian movement. I am familiar with one of her books, *Walks Through London*, in which one finds generous and admirable outbursts of compassion. Paul Gauguin had, then, from the crib, the example of these two highly moral forces forming and plunging him into the higher sensibilities: struggle and dreaming. His childhood was very sweet and loving. It developed happily in this familial atmosphere, run through as it was with the spiritual influence of that extraordinary man who was certainly the greatest of the century, in whom alone since Christ was the spirit of God truly incarnated: Fourier.

At the age of sixteen, he signed on as a sailor so that he could stop the studies that were costing his mother too dearly: the family fortune had disappeared with the death of his father. He traveled. He crossed unknown seas, sailed under new suns, made contact with primitive races and prodigious flora. He did not think—at least, he believed he did not— he thought of nothing but his difficult work, to which he devoted all the energy of a healthy, well-muscled young man. However, unconsciously, in the silence of the night watches, he developed a taste for dreaming and for the eternal; sometimes during free hours he would draw, though without any goal in mind, simply to "kill time." Moreover, these were small feelings and they had only weak repercussions on his intellectual self; brief glimpses of the shining, mysterious horizons of the interior world, quickly closed. He had not yet received the great shock; he had not yet felt the passion for art that would fall upon him and seize him

COLORPLATE 41. *Be in Love and You Will Be Happy.* 1889. Polychromed linden wood. 47 × 38″ (119 × 96.5 cm). Museum of Fine Arts, Boston; Arthur Tracy Cabot Fund.

COLORPLATE 42. *Brittany Landscape.* ca. 1889. 37¾ × 30½″ (96 × 77.5 cm).
Private collection.

COLORPLATE 43. *Fields by the Sea.* 1889. 28⁵⁄₁₆ × 35¾″ (72 × 91 cm).
Nationalmuseum, Stockholm. Photo: Statens Konstmuseer.

COLORPLATE 44. *The Yellow Haystacks,* or *The Golden Harvest.* 1889. 28⅞ × 36⅜″ (73.5 × 92.5 cm).
Musée d'Orsay, Paris.

COLORPLATE 45. *Haymaking in Brittany.* 1889. 36¼ × 28¾″ (92 × 73 cm).
Courtauld Institute Galleries, London; Courtauld Collection.

COLORPLATE 46. *Still Life with Fan*. 1889. 19⅝ × 24″ (50 × 61 cm).
Musée d'Orsay, Paris.

COLORPLATE 47. *Still Life with Ham*. 1889. 19⅝ × 22¾″ (50 × 58 cm).
The Phillips Collection, Washington, D.C.

COLORPLATE 48. *Portrait of a Seated Woman.* 1890. 25⅝ × 21⅝″ (65.3 × 54.9 cm).
The Art Institute of Chicago; The Joseph Winterbotham Collection.

wholly, body and soul, as far as suffering and torture. He did not yet have the awareness of the enormous, powerful, and varied impressions that through a latent and unfelt phenomenon of perception would enter and accumulate in his mind without his knowing so profoundly that later, when he returned to normal life, he would become nostalgically obsessed with those suns, those races, that flora, and with the Pacific Ocean where he was surprised to find the cradle of his own race, and which seems to have rocked him in bygone times with familiar lullabies.

He returned to Paris when his tour was finished. He had burdens; he had to support himself and his family. Gauguin entered into business. To the superficial observer, his entrance into the stock exchange as a runner at an outside-broker's may not be one of the less bizarre events in the unpredictable existence of this supreme artist. Far from crushing the dream that he had begun to form, the stock exchange helped to develop it and gave him a direction. For when it comes to higher natures, the stock exchange, for those who know how to watch it, is powerfully evocative of the mysteries of human nature. A great and tragic symbol lies there. Above the furious melee, that riot of screaming passions, of convulsed gestures and bewildering shadows, one could say the terror of an accursed cult rises and survives. I would not be surprised if Gauguin, by natural contrast, by a necessary spirit of revolt, found there the heart-rending love of Christ, a love that would later inspire his most beautiful creations.

While waiting, a new self rose up within him. The revelation was almost instantaneous. All the elements of his birth, of his travels, of his memories, of the life he was living at the time, combined to cause the explosion of his artistic faculties, which were all the stronger for having been so late and so slow to come about. Passion enveloped him, deluded him, and devoured him. He used all the spare time he had from work to paint. He painted with rage. Art became his only preoccupation. He lingered in the Louvre, consulted the contemporary masters. His instinct lead him to the metaphysical artists, to the great tamers of line, the great synthesizers of form. He fell in love with Puvis de Chavannes, Degas, Manet, Monet, Cézanne, the Japanese, known at that time only to a privileged few. It is a curious thing, though it can be explained by a burst of youthful enthusiasm and, even better, by his lack of experience at the profession that made him unskillful at the expression of dreams, that despite his intellectual wonderment and aesthetic predilections, his first attempts at painting were naturalistic. He strove to free himself from this restriction because he had a strong sense that naturalism was a supression of art, as it is the negation of poetry, that the source of all emotion, of all beauty, of all life, is not on the surface of things, but that they reside in the depths where the hook of the nocturnal rag picker no longer reaches.

But how to go about it? How to collect one's thoughts? At every minute he was halted in his impulses. The stock exchange was always there to take him back. One cannot simultaneously follow a dream and pay the rent, marvel in ideal visions and then fall back just as quickly from those heavens into the hell of stock liquidations and reports. Gauguin did not hesitate any longer. He abandoned the stock exchange that made his material life easy, and dedicated himself wholeheartedly to painting despite the threat of miserable tomorrows and their probable uncertainty. Years of struggle without thanks, tremendous efforts, desperation and drunkenness by turns. From this difficult period, when the artist was searching, date a series of landscapes that were, I believe, exhibited in the rue Laffitte with the Impressionists. Here already, despite the inevitable lapses, he asserted himself as a superior talent, vigorous and willful, almost savage, but charming in this, and sensitive because he was so very aware of light and the ideal quality that it can give to objects. His canvases, still too full of details, already showed, in their order, a sin-

In the 1870s, Mirbeau had a position in the Stock Exchange very much like Gauguin's.

gular decorative taste, a taste that Gauguin has since pushed to perfection in his recent paintings, his strangely styled pottery, and his wood sculpture, which make up so stunning a body of work.

In spite of his apparent moral heartiness, Gauguin was of a troubled nature, tormented by the infinite. Never satisfied by what he produced, he continually searched for something higher. He sensed that he had not given all he was able. Confused feelings arose in his soul; vague but strong aspirations pulled his spirit toward more abstract paths, more abstruse forms of expression. And his thoughts brought him back to the lands of light and mystery that he had once traversed. It seemed to him that there were there, sleeping, unviolated, elements of a new art that conformed to his dream. Then there is the solitude that he needed so much; he needed peace and silence so that he could listen better, so that he could better feel himself living. He left for Martinique. He stayed there two years, finally returning because of sickness; yellow fever of which he should have died and from which it took him months and months to recover. However, he brought with him a series of dazzling and severe canvases in which he had finally conquered his personality and which showed enormous progress, a rapid improvement toward the art he hoped for. The forms in these were no longer a representation solely of exterior appearance; they revealed the state of the spirit of the one who understood them and expressed them thus. There is in the undergrowth, in the vegetation, in the monstrous flowers, in the overwhelming washes of sunlight, an almost religious mystery, a sacred and Eden-like abundance. And the design is supple, amplified: he only tells us that which is essential, the thought. In the majesty of the contours, the dream drives it to a spiritual synthesis, to an eloquent and profound expression. Henceforth, Gauguin was to be his own master. His hand had become his slave, a docile instrument loyal to his brain. He would soon realize the *oeuvre* for which he had searched so long.

His work is strangely cerebral, passionate, still uneven but poignant and superb in that very inequality. The work is sad because to understand it, to truly feel its shock, one must oneself have known sadness and the irony of sadness, which is the threshold of mystery. Sometimes, his work raises itself to the height of a mystic act of faith; sometimes it seems to be scared and grimacing in the shadows of doubt. And always emanating from it is the bitter and violent smell of the poisons of the flesh. In this work, there is an unsettling and savory mingling of barbarian splendor, Catholic liturgy, Hindu meditation, Gothic imagery, and obscure and subtle symbolism. There are harsh realities and the desperate flights of poetry by which Gauguin creates an art that is absolutely personal and wholly new; an art of the painter and the poet, of the apostle and the devil, that anguishes.

In the completely yellow countryside, an agonizing yellow, atop a Breton hillock in full view, a cross rises, a cross of rough-hewn wood, rotting and coming apart, that extends its warped arms into the air. The Christ, a Papuan divinity summarily carved by a local artist into a tree trunk, the pitiful and barbarian Christ, is daubed yellow. At the foot of the cross, the peasant women are kneeling on the ground. Indifferent, their bodies sagging heavily on the ground, they have come there because it is the custom to do so on a Day of Pardon. But their eyes and their lips are devoid of prayers. They have no thought, no regard for His image, for the one who died for love of them. Already stepping over the hedges and fleeing beneath the red apple trees, other peasants are hastening toward their hovels, happy to have finished their devotions. And the melancholy of this wooden Christ is ineffable. His expression is that of horrible sadness; his wasted flesh may regret the ancient torture, and he seems to be saying to himself, as he looks down at the miserable humanity clustered at his feet that understands nothing, "And what if my martyrdom has been useless?"

COLORPLATE 36

146

Such is the work that begins Gauguin's series of symbolic canvases. Unfortunately, I cannot expound further on the art that would so please me to study in all its manifestations: sculpture, ceramics, painting. But I hope that this brief description will suffice to show the very special spirit of this artist, his high ambitions, his noble wishes.

It seems that Gauguin, having reached this lofty state of thought, this breadth of style, should attain a certain serenity, a tranquillity of spirit, a rest. But no. Dreams never rest in that keen mind; he grows and continues to exalt as he further defines himself. And so it is that he again becomes nostalgic for the lands from which his earliest dreams were plucked. He would like to live alone again for several years among the things that he left over there. Here, he was spared few tortures, and great sorrows overwhelmed him. He lost a friend whom he loved and admired dearly, poor Vincent van Gogh, one of the most magnificently spirited painters, one of the most beautiful souls of all the artists to whom we entrusted so much of our hope. And then, life has the most unrelenting demands. The same need of meditation, of absolute solitude, that drove him to Martinique this time takes him even farther, to Tahiti, where nature is better adapted to his dream, where he hopes that the Pacific Ocean will have for him caresses more tender, an old and true love of a regained ancestor.

Wherever he may go, Paul Gauguin can be assured that our devotion will go with him.

Octave Mirbeau

LE FIGARO

"Paul Gauguin"

18 February 1891

Monday at the Hôtel Drouot, a few canvases and pottery pieces by M. Paul Gauguin will be sold, and I am told that the state made a point, before the public sale, of securing the ownership of an altogether delightful painting, one of the master's landscapes, which portrays a corner of the beautiful Pont-Aven valley. I could not too heartily congratulate the state, in the person of M. Larroumet, on this choice, which indicates, at least, the laudable desire and the encouraging goodwill that it sometimes displays toward breaking free from acquired habits and the old, traditional routines. There exists there a certain courage, for, if M. Paul Gauguin has won admiration and well-deserved fame in the artists' special world because of his talent, he remains unknown, or nearly so, to the art public and critics because of his silent dream, his reticent dignity.

And yet he is a highly exceptional painter, one of the most interesting there is today, one of the rare ones upon whom many found great and enduring hopes for the future. I believe that they are not mistaken. As for myself, I have, for M. Gauguin and for the very noble, very strange, very refined, and very barbaric, for the passionately literary art that he practices, a high and ardent esteem. Let others laugh before these canvases, these most recent ones, some of which have the mystical and distant breadth of a cathedral's stained glass; laughter is more often than not the inability to feel beauty. Before these canvases, I myself sense a thinking brain and a suffering heart, and this moves me; I also see a

Gustave Larroumet (1852–1903), a critic and biographer, became Director of the Ministry of Fine Arts in 1888. Evidently a rumor spread in early 1891 that he had decided to purchase a work by Gauguin.

Pot in the form of a tree stump (left side) ornamented with two heads, an incised figure of a woman and birds (right side). ca. 1888. Stoneware. Height: 9″ (23 cm). Musée d'Orsay, Paris.

hand trained to all the secrets of drawing, to all the syntheses of line, and this charms me.

And I also experience a profound joy in holding in my hands, turning this way and that, one of his miraculous pottery pieces, one of his surprising firings: tangible poems, with their unexpected oxidations, their rich and muted colorations blending into one another, in flows of tawny gold, mineral red, poisonous green; vases, goblets, symbolic groups, hallucinatory statuettes, sexual flowers with their tempting convolutions, whose forms, so new, so bold, so harmoniously combined, bend to the whims of the imagination and dream of a poet who has seen everything, sung everything, mourned everything.

Pot in the shape of a fountain. Coffee-colored stoneware. Height: 6¾″ (17 cm). Musée d'Orsay, Paris.

Pot decorated with a figure of a woman under a tree. ca. 1887. Stoneware. Height: 5¼″ (13.5 cm). Musée d'Orsay, Paris.

But alas! we are in an age in which pure art calls down only suffering and disappointment upon those who worship it; and life has immediate, implacable demands. M. Gauguin, tired of struggling, and feeling a need for solitude and recollection, has made the choice of self-exile, for years, in lands that have long visited his dreams. He is leaving for Tahiti—glimpsed, once upon a time, during his sailor's voyages—as he once left for Martinique, from which he brought back a series of wonderful paintings. Out there, alone, he will build his cabin, and he will work, free of the cares among which, in civilized life, his flights of fancy crash and shatter. Nor is it altogether an exile; it is a return toward known skies and cherished things. His mother was born on the shores of the Pacific Ocean; his father died there. In that solitude, in the hours of inevitable sorrows and heavy surrenders, he will be able to hear voices dear to him, long silent; and his soul will once more be fortified by them.

And I wished, in this difficult moment of his life, to address all my sympathy to M. Paul Gauguin, as well as the sympathies of all the artistic and literary youth who love him and whose thoughts will accompany him out there.

G.-Albert Aurier

MERCURE DE FRANCE

"Symbolism in Painting: Paul Gauguin"

March 1891

In 1890 Aurier had co-founded the monthly Mercure de France, *which he inaugurated with a major article on Van Gogh. He was introduced by Bernard to Gauguin, whom he came to regard as the chief exponent of Symbolism in painting; this seminal article amounts to a manifesto of the Symbolist movement. Aurier's life was cut short at the age of twenty-seven by typhoid fever.*

How do you think he would answer if he were told that until then he has seen only ghosts, that now, before his eyes, are objects more real and closer to the truth? Would he not think that what he saw before was more real than what he is being shown?

Plato

Far, very far away, on a fabulous hill, where the earth seems to glow bright red, Jacob's Biblical struggle with the Angel is taking place.

While the two legendary giants—transformed by the distance into pygmies—fight their fearsome battle, a group of women are watching, interested and naive, uncertain, doubtless, about what is happening over there, on the fabulous crimsoned hill. They are peasant women. And by the breadth of their white headdresses, which spread like seagull wings, and by the typical array of colors in their scarves, and by the shapes of their gowns and jackets, they reveal their Breton origins. Their respectful manners and their wide-eyed faces are those of simple creatures listening to extraordinary and somewhat fantastic tales affirmed by some incontestable and revered mouth. They might be in church, so silently do they pay attention, so collected, so worshipful, so pious is their bearing; they might be in church, with a vague scent of incense and prayer fluttering amidst the white wings of their headdresses, and with the respected voice of an old priest soaring above their heads. . . . Yes, certainly, in a church, in some poor church in some poor Breton market-town. . . . But, if so, where are the moldy and green pillars? Where are the milk-white walls with their infinite multichromatic stations of the Cross? The pine pulpit? The old priest preaching, whose mumbling voice we hear, yes, to be sure, we hear? Where is it all? And

COLORPLATE 18

why, over there, far, very far away, the swell of that fabulous hill, whose earth seems to glow bright red?

Ah! The moldy and green pillars, and the milk-white walls, and the little multichromatic stations of the Cross, and the pine pulpit, and the old preaching priest vanished some minutes ago, no longer exist for the eyes and the souls of the good Breton peasant women! . . . What marvelously stirring intonation, what luminously vivid description, strangely appropriate to the rough ears of his lumpish congregation, has he found, this droning village hunchback? All the surrounding objects have dispersed into vapors, have disappeared; he himself, the evocator, has faded away, and it is his Voice, his poor old pitiful stammering Voice that has now become visible, imperiously visible, and it is his Voice that the white-coiffed peasant women contemplate, with naïve and pious attention, and it is his Voice, this rustically fantastic vision that has risen over there, far, very far away, his Voice, that fabulous hill with its earth the color of vermillion, land of a child's dream, where the two Biblical giants—transformed by the distance into pygmies—fight their arduous and imposing battle!

Now, before this marvelous canvas by Paul Gauguin which truly illuminates the riddle of the Poem, during primitive humanity's paradisiacal hours; which reveals the ineffable charms of dream, mystery, and the symbolic veils only half-lifted by the hands of the simple-hearted; which resolves, for the wise reader, the eternal psychological problem of the possibility of religions, politics, and sociologies; which, finally, shows the fierce primordial beast tamed by Chimera's magical philters; before this miraculous canvas, not just a certain fat and Prudhommesque banker, priding himself on a gallery full of Detailles (a sure thing) and Loustauneaus (an investment), but even a certain art enthusiast, known to be intelligent and sympathetic to youthful audacities to the point of accepting the Pointillists' harlequinesque vision, exclaimed:

"Oh, no! Absolutely not! . . . It's too much! . . . Ploërmel's head-dresses and scarves, Breton women, at the end of this century, in a painting entitled *Jacob Wrestling with the Angel*!! I am certainly no reactionary, I accept Impressionism, in fact, I only accept Impressionism, but. . . ."

"And who says, my dear sir, that this is Impressionism?"

In fact, it is perhaps time to clear up a troublesome misunderstanding, undoubtedly created by the word "Impressionism," which has been all too misused.

The public—I mean that tiny, more or less intelligent public that still cares about art, that useless anachronism—acknowledges only two categories of painters: academic painters, that is, those who, adequately educated, qualified, and licensed by the Art Faculty in the rue Bonaparte, deal, at Israelite prices, in official beauty, in the classical, modern, or other manner, certifiably backed by a government guarantee: and, on the other hand, the Impressionist painters, that is, all those who rebelled against the idiotic tastes of the boulevard critics and against the ignorant academic formulators, and who now allow themselves the presumptuous freedom of not copying someone else.

That would be fine, and the latter term would be as good as another. Unfortunately, however broadly the term is used, it implies a meaning, a precise meaning, in fact, that can confuse the public. The word "Impressionism," indeed, whether one wishes or not, suggests an entire aesthetic program based upon sensation. Impressionism is and can only be a variety of Realism, a sharpened, spiritualized, amateurized Realism, but Realism nonetheless. The desired goal is still the imitation of materiality—no longer, perhaps, in its own form or its own color, rather in its perceived form and its perceived color—and the translation of sensation, with all the unexpected qualities that arise from instantaneous notation, all the deformations that arise from rapid, subjective synthesis.

Monsieur Prudhomme, a fictional bourgeois created by Henry Monnier and depicted by Daumier. Edouard Detaille (1848–1912), Salon painter popular for French military scenes.

Louis Auguste Loustauneau (1864–1898), landscape and genre painter.

Ploërmel is a Breton village known for hemp and cloth production.

Although Messieurs Pissarro and Claude Monet without a doubt translate forms and colors differently than Courbet, nevertheless, in essence, like Courbet, even more than Courbet, they translate only form and color. The substratum and the ultimate goal of their art is the material subject, the real thing. Thus the public, in speaking the word "Impressionism," inevitably has the vague notion of a program of a special kind of Realism; they expect works that are but the faithful translation—*and nothing more*—of an *exclusively sensory impression*, of a sensation. So that, if there were, by chance, among the heterogeneous group of independent painters labeled with the title in question, a few artists pursuing different, even opposite paths, the good public, that eternal and blissful adorer of catalogues, would clearly be unable to make heads or tails of it, as they say, and—I can see it now—would shrug its omnipotent shoulders and sneer:

"This is absurd! . . . This Impressionist is painting impressions that no one can ever have felt! . . . "

Might this not, possibly, explain the similar tirade uttered before Gauguin's painting by the aforementioned "art enthusiast, known to be intelligent and sympathetic to youthful audacities to the point of accepting the Pontillists' harlequinesque vision?"

In any event, now that it is becoming evident that we are witnessing, in literature, the death-throes of Naturalism, even as we are seeing an idealist, even mystical reaction taking shape, it would be surprising if the plastic arts showed no tendency toward a similar evolution. *Jacob Wrestling with the Angel*, which I attempted to describe in the beginning of this piece, is evidence enough, I believe, of this tendency, and one must understand that it is entirely in the interest of the painters committed to this new path to be free of the absurd label of "Impressionists," which implies—and this bears repeating—a program diametrically opposed to their own. This quibbling over words may appear ridiculous, but it is, in my opinion, necessary; the public, the supreme judge where art is concerned, has the incurable habit, as we all know, of only judging things by their names. Therefore, let there be a new *-ist* word invented (there are already so many that it won't be noticed!) for the newcomers whom Gauguin leads: Synthetists, Idéistes, Symbolists, as you please, as long as this foolish general term "Impressionist" is abandoned, except as a specific title for those painters for whom art is only a translation of the artist's sensations and impressions.

Oh, how truly rare, among those who pride themselves on their "artistic aptitudes," how rare are those happy beings whose soul's eyelids are half-open and who can exclaim, with Swedenborg, that inspired hallucinator: "That very night, the eyes of the inner man were opened: they were made fit to look into the heavens, into the world of ideas and into the nether regions! . . . " And yet, is that not the necessary, prerequisite initiation that the true artist, the absolute artist must undergo? . . .

Paul Gauguin seems to me to be one of these sublime voyeurs. To me, he appears to be the pioneer of a new art, not in history, but at least in our time. Let us, therefore, analyze this art from the standpoint of a general aesthetic. This would amount, it seems to me, to studying the artist himself, and perhaps improving upon the superficial monograph consisting of the descriptions of some twenty canvases and ten flattering clichés that usually satisfies today's body of critics.

It is evident—and it is almost a platitude to say it—that there exist in the history of art two great and opposite tendencies that incontestably depend, the one, on blindness, the other, on the acumen of "man's inner eye," as Swedenborg says; the Realist tendency and the Idéiste tendency (I do not say Idealist, we shall see why).

Undoubtedly, Realist art, that art whose sole aim is the representation of the material exteriorities, of the perceptible appearances of things, constitutes an interesting aesthetic manifestation. It reveals to us, in some

Gustave Courbet (1819–1877), an unorthodox painter who advocated Realism and outspokenly challenged the Salon system, was an early supporter of Manet, Monet, and Pissarro, among others.

Emanuel Swedenborg (1688–1772), Swedish scientist, philosopher, and theologian whose diverse treatises were consulted by French Symbolists and other nineteenth-century writers. Especially popular was his notion that manifestations in the material realm have "correspondences" in the spiritual world.

way, by indirection, the worker's soul, since it shows us the deformations that the object underwent in passing through it. Furthermore, no one disputes that Realism, though it was the pretext for many hideous works, as impersonal and banal as photographs, has also produced, at times, some undeniable masterpieces that shine in the museums of all our memories. And yet it is no less indisputable that to whomever wishes to reflect honestly, it is Idéiste art that seems purer and nobler—purer and nobler by all the purity and nobility that divides matter from idea. One could even state that the highest art could only be Idéiste, since art is, by definition (as we intuit), only the representative materialization of what is noblest and most truly divine in the world, of what is, in the final analysis, the only living being, the Idea. Are not those who can neither see the Idea nor believe in it, worthy therefore of our compassion, as were, for free men, the poor, stupid prisoners of Plato's allegorical Cave?

And yet, with the exception of most of the Primitives and a few of the great Renaissance masters, the general tendency in painting, as we know, has, until now, been almost exclusively Realist. Indeed, many confess that they cannot understand how painting—the representational art par excellence, which can copy, to the point of illusionism, all the visible attributes of matter—can be anything but a faithful and exact reproduction of objectivity, an ingenious facsimile of the allegedly real world. The Idealists themselves (whom, I repeat, one must avoid confusing with the artists whom I choose to call "Idéistes") were more often than not, whatever they claim, only Realists; the aim of their art was only the direct representation of material forms. They were content to order objectivity according to certain conventional and preconceived notions of quality; they prided themselves on presenting us with objects that were beautiful, but that were beautiful considered as objects, the focus of their works residing always and still in the qualities of the form, that is, the qualities of reality. What they called ideal was never other than the artful cosmeticizing of ugly, tangible things. In short, they have painted a conventional objectivity, but an objectivity nonetheless and, to paraphrase the famous dictum of one of them, Gustave Boulanger, basically, the only difference between today's Idealists and Realists is the choice "between a hat and a cap"!

They, too, are poor, stupid prisoners of the allegorical Cave. Let us, therefore, leave them to grow more stupid as they contemplate the shadows that they take to be reality, and let us return to the men who, their chains broken, are entranced by the contemplation, far from their cruel native dungeon, of the radiant heaven of ideas.

The usual and ultimate goal of painting, as I have said, moreover that of all the arts, cannot be the direct representation of objects. Its finality is to express ideas by translating them into a special language.

Indeed, in the artist's eyes—that is, in the eyes of whomever must be the *evocator of the absolute beings*—objects—the relative beings that are but a translation, adjusted in proportion to our intellects, of the absolute and essential beings, of Ideas—can have no value only insofar as objects. They can only appear to him as *signs*. They are the letters of an immense alphabet that the man of genius alone can spell out.

To write his thought, his poem, with these signs, keeping in mind that the sign, as indispensable as it may be, is nothing in itself and that the idea alone is everything, appears therefore to be the task of the artist whose eye has known how to discern the essence of tangible objects. The first consequence of this principle, too obvious to belabor, is, one divines, a necessary simplification in the writing of the sign. If it were not so, in fact, would the painter not resemble the naive writer who believes that he is adding something to his work by polishing his penmanship and ornamenting it with useless flourishes?

But, if it is true that, in the world, ideas are the only real beings, if it is true that objects are but the outward forms that reveal those ideas, and thus are important insofar as they signify ideas, it is no less true that in our human eyes, that is, in the eyes of the arrogant *shadows of pure beings* that we are, shadows living in ignorance of their illusory condition and in the beloved falsity of the spectacle of a deceptive reality, it is no less true that in our myopic eyes objects appear most often to be objects, nothing but objects, independent of their symbolic significance—to the point that, at times, we cannot imagine them as signs despite our sincere efforts.

This vile propensity to consider, in our practical lives, an object to be only an object is obvious and, one might say, virtually universal. Only the superior man, enlightened by that supreme virtue that the Alexandrians so rightly called ecstasy, can persuade himself that he is but a sign, cast by some mysterious preordination amidst a numberless crowd of signs; he alone, tamer of the illusion-monster, can walk as master within this fantastic temple

> Where living pillars
> Let out, at times, confused words. . . .

whereas the idiot human herd, duped by appearances that lead it to deny the essential ideas, will ever blindly pass

> Through the forest of symbols
> That observe him with intimate gazes.

The work of art must not, even to the eye of the common cattle, lend itself to such an error. Indeed, the dilettante (who is not an artist and who therefore has no sense of symbolic correspondences) would find himself before it in a position similar to that of the crowd faced with natural objects. He would perceive its represented objects only as objects—and it is important to avoid this. Thus, the Idéiste work must not allow this confusion; thus, we must be allowed to know for certain that the objects in the painting have no value as objects, that they are but signs, words of no other importance in themselves.

Consequently, certain appropriate laws must govern pictorial imitation. The task of the artist will necessarily be to avoid carefully the paradox of all art: concrete truth, illusionism, *trompe l'oeil*, so as not to give, through one's painting, a deceptive impression of nature that would act upon the viewer as nature herself does, that is, without any possible suggestion, that is (if I may be forgiven the barbarous neologism), in an Idéiste manner.

It is logical to imagine him fleeing, so as to guard himself against the perils of concrete truth, the analysis of the object. Indeed, each detail is, in reality, only a partial symbol, more often than not useless with regard to the total significance of the object. The Idéiste painter's strict duty is, therefore, to make a reasoned selection among the multiple elements combined in objectivity, to use in the work only the general and distinguishing lines, forms, and colors that will help to write clearly the Idéiste significance of the object, plus those partial symbols that corroborate the overall symbol.

Indeed, as one may easily deduce, the artist will always have the right to exaggerate, attenuate, deform the directly signifying characters (forms, lines, colors, etc.) not only according to his individual vision, not only molding it by his personal subjectivity (as happens even in Realist art), but, further, to exaggerate, attenuate, deform them according to the requirements of the idea to be expressed.

Therefore, to sum up and conclude, a work of art, as I have chosen to evoke it logically will be:

1. *Idéiste*, since its unique ideal will be to express the idea;

2. *Symbolist*, since it will express the idea through forms;

3. *Synthetic*, since it will present these forms and signs in a commonly intelligible fashion;

4. *Subjective*, since the object will never, in the work of art, be considered as an object, but as the sign of an idea perceived by the subject;

5. (This is a consequence) *decorative*—for decorative painting, properly speaking, as the Egyptians and quite probably the Greeks and the Primitives understood it, is nothing other than a manifestation of art that is at once subjective, synthetic, symbolist, and idéiste.

Now, if one pauses to consider, decorative painting is, strictly speaking, the true art of painting. Painting could only have been invented to *decorate* with thoughts, dreams, and ideas the banal walls of human edifices. The easel painting is but an illogical refinement, invented to satisfy the whim or the commercial spirit of decadent civilizations. In primitive societies, the first pictorial attempts could not have been other than decorative.

The art that we have attempted to legitimize and to characterize with all the preceding deductions, the art that may have seemed complicated and that certain chroniclers will gladly call decadent art, thus becomes, in the final analysis, a return to the formula of simple, spontaneous, and primordial art. Therein lies the criterion for the soundness of the aesthetic arguments applied. Idéiste art—which had to be justified with abstract and complicated reasoning, so paradoxical does it seem to our decadent civilizations that have forgotten all the initial revelations—is thus, indisputably, the genuine and absolute art, since, it is not only legitimate from a theoretical standpoint, but it also happens to be fundamentally identical with Primitive art, with art as it was divined by the instinctive geniuses of humanity's first ages.

But is this all? Is there not a further element missing that would make art as we have understood it truly Art?

The man who, because of his native genius, because of his acquired qualities, can, in the face of nature, read the abstract significance, the primordial and underlying idea of every object, the man who, by his intelligence and his skill, knows how to use objects as a sublime alphabet to express the ideas that are revealed to him, would he truly be, by virtue of these qualities, a complete artist? Would he be the Artist?

Is he not, rather, an inspired scholar, a supreme formulator, who is able to write ideas as does a mathematician? Is he not in some sense an algebraist of ideas, and is his work not a marvelous equation, or, better, a page of ideographic writing that recalls the hieroglyphic texts of the obelisks of ancient Egypt?

Yes, to be sure, the artist who has not some further psychic gift will be nothing more, for he will be nothing more than an understanding evocator, and while understanding complemented by the power to express may be enough to make a scholar, it is not enough to make an artist.

To be really worthy of this fine title of nobility—so polluted in our industrialist present—he must join to the capacity to understand a still more sublime gift: I mean the gift of *emotivity*. Not, to be sure, the emotivity every man knows in the face of the illusory, passionate combinations of beings and objects, not the emotivity known to nightclub singers and chromo-print manufacturers—but that transcendental emotivity, so great and so precious, that causes the soul to shiver in the face of the undulating drama of abstractions. Oh, how rare are those whose bodies and hearts are stirred by the sublime sight of pure being and ideas! But that as well is the gift *sine qua non*, it is the spark that Pygmalion wanted for his Galatea, it is the illumination, the golden key, the Daimon, the Muse. . . .

With this gift, symbols, that is, ideas, rise from the darkness, animate, begin to live with a life that is no longer our contingent and relative life, a dazzling life that is the essential life, the life of art, the being of being.

With this gift, complete, perfect, absolute art exists at last.

Such is the art it is consoling to dream of, such is the art that I like to imagine, in my compulsory strolls amidst the miserable or base art trash that clutters our industrialist exhibitions. Such, too, I think—unless I have misinterpreted the thought in his work—is the art that Paul Gauguin, that great artist of genius with the soul of a primitive and, somewhat, of a savage, wanted to establish in our deplorable and rotten nation.

I can neither describe nor analyze his already marvelous work here. It is enough for me to have tried to characterize and legitimize the highly laudable aesthetic conception that seems to guide this great artist. Indeed, how can one suggest in words all that is inexpressible, the whole ocean of ideas that the clear-sighted eye can glimpse in those masterful works: *The Calvary*; *Jacob Wrestling with the Angel*; *The Yellow Christ*; in those marvelous landscapes of Martinique and Brittany, where each line, each form, each color is the word for an idea; in that sublime *Garden of Olives*, where an incarnadine-haired Christ, seated in a desolate place, seems to mourn the ineffable sorrows of dreams, the death-throes of Chimeras, the treason of chance, the vanity of the real, of life, and, perhaps, of the hereafter. . . . How can one relate the philosophy sculpted in the bas-relief that reads, ironically, *Be in love and you will be happy*, in which all lust, all the struggle of flesh and thought, all the sorrow of the sexual pleasures writhe and, so to speak, gnash their teeth? How to evoke that other wood sculpture: *Be mysterious*, which celebrates the pure joys of esotericism, the disturbing caresses of the riddle, the fantastic shadows of problem's forests? How to describe, finally, those strange, barbarous, and savage ceramics, into which he kneaded, sublime potter, more soul than clay?

COLORPLATE 37
COLORPLATE 18
COLORPLATE 36

COLORPLATE 41

And yet, if one thinks about it, as disturbing, as masterly, and as marvelous as this work may be, it is little enough, compared with what Gauguin could have produced, had he been placed in another civilization. Gauguin, it must be repeated, like all the Idéiste painters, is, above all, a decorator. His compositions find themselves confined by the limited field of the canvases. One would be tempted, at times, to take them for fragments of immense frescoes, and they nearly always seem ready to explode the frames that unduly limit them! . . .

So! We have in our dying century only one great decorator, two perhaps, counting Puvis de Chavannes, and our idiotic society of bankers and polytechnicians refuses to give this rare artist the least palace, the meanest national hovel wherein the sumptuous mantles of his dreams may hang!

The walls of our Pantheons of Stupidity are soiled by the ejaculations of the Tom, Dick, and Harrys of the Institute!

Ah, gentlemen, how posterity will curse you, mock you, and spit on you, if one day the meaning of art awakens in humanity's spirit! . . . Come now, a little common sense, you have among you a decorator of genius: walls! walls! give him some walls! . . .

Félix Fénéon

LE CHAT NOIR

"M. Gauguin"

23 May 1891

Félix Fénéon (1861–1944), brilliant critic who championed Seurat and the Neo-Impressionists. He was a co-founder of two important Symbolist periodicals, La Revue Indépendante *and* La Vogue.

Jens Ferdinand Willumsen (1863–1958), Danish painter and sculptor who met Gauguin at Le Pouldu in 1890 and exchanged works with him in Paris in 1891. Henri Gabriel Ibels (1867–1936), painter and caricaturist associated with the Nabis.

COLORPLATE 41

Long neglected, the tradition of Cézanne is today in full cultivation, thanks to Messieurs Sérusier, Willumsen, Bernard, Schuffenecker, Laval, Ibels, Filiger, Denis, etc. M. Paul Gauguin has not been a stranger to the blossoming of these talents. He has disciples and a public. In Oceania, a rapidly won glory ferments; in the meantime his finances prosper at the Vaudeville and, at the Salon of the Champ de Mars, the fame of his colored-wood bas-relief "Be in love: You will be happy" continues to grow.

Five years ago, at the rue Laffitte exhibition, his landscapes and his bathing women were somewhat thrown into disarray by the dazzling works of his companions in Impressionism and by the lucid works of a handful of newcomers. Was M. Gauguin to fail his destiny? About this time, he met in Brittany a young painter of adventurous spirit and fairly well-informed, M. Emile Bernard, who today may be his student, but who appears to have been his initiator: for M. Bernard was the first to paint, in saturated colors, wheeling Breton women outlined in the drawing like the leading of stained-glass windows, and enveloped in a setting with neither atmosphere nor values. The characteristics of that painting derived in part from the artist's choice, in part from the painter's awkwardness. When M. Gauguin returned from there, he was in full literary fervor, he who up until then had, with the most paradoxical obstinacy, ignored bookshops and ideas in general; and he excelled at M. Bernard's Breton women, but, being a skilled painter, he applied logic to their barbarousness, which, beneath fierce exteriors, was a very refined barbarousness. Later on, those Breton women and that literature were to combine their effectiveness. In 1887, he was able to see the Antilles with an astonished gaze, such as they might have appeared to the crew of the *Pinta*. From there, he brought back canvases of a maleficent luxuriance. It was then that he became the prey of the literary set: they asserted that he had the cure of souls, that he was entrusted with a mission (a similar fortune had befallen old Courbet). M. Gauguin terrorizes reality, recreates lines and tints, annuls the element of depth: he claims all license to express himself as he pleases. So be it, but one expected loftier mosaics, more hallucinatory arabesques, as well as more personality. (At the Hôtel Drouot, where thirty of his canvases were recently collected, to be dispersed at a sale, one recognized, there, some Japanese nudes; there, some of Monet's landscapes; there, some of Cézanne's trees; and his Arles canvases were pure Van Gogh.) Unquestionably, he has enriched the contemporary soul. But the asymmetry of his Christs cannot have helped him much in that respect. And why do his deformations always resolve themselves by greater ugliness? M. Gauguin, or M. Delaherche's workmen, or Takatori's ceramicists are able to incorporate moving tints into their stoneware. M. Gauguin extracts highly decorative effects in this way. He is more sculptor than painter, and one must admire his sculpture, but, from concession to concession, one will admire Zapotec funeral urns. And M. Emile Bernard? Well, he was exhibiting, last month at the Société des Artistes Indépendents, a painting of saintliness, with the fairly uncompromising title *Memory*. Memory of what? Of one of those monstrous *grainy* engravings,

Auguste Delaherche (1857–1940), sculptor and ceramicist whose Japanese-style vases at the 1889 Exposition Universelle Gauguin had admired while calling their shapes unimaginative. Judging from Morice's comments, Delaherche, who took over Ernst Chaplet's ceramic factory in 1887, may have fired some of Gauguin's pots. Takatori is a variety of Japanese ceramic noted for its brown and yellow glaze and naturalistic shape.

even earlier than wood engravings, and of which Holland and Germany argue over the birth certificates—the *engraving* known by the name *Christ in the Garden of Olives*. Some ideal.

Jules Renard
JOURNAL
15 April 1891

Jules Renard (1864–1910), playwright and diarist who co-founded La Mercure de France *in 1890.*

Daudet, in great form, tells us about Gauguin's departures: Gauguin, who would like to go to Tahiti in order to find no one there, never leaves. To such an extent that his best friends end up telling him: "You've got to go, my dear friend, you've got to go."

Paul Gauguin
NOA NOA
On His Arrival in Tahiti
1893–1895

> "Dites, qu'avez-vous vu?"
> CHARLES BAUDELAIRE

"Dites, qu'avez-vous vu?": "Tell me, what did you see?"; quoted from "Le Voyage" in Les Fleurs du Mal.

On the eighth of June, during the night, after a sixty-three days' voyage, sixty-three days of feverish expectancy, we perceived strange fires, moving zigzags on the sea. From the somber sky a black cone with jagged indentations became disengaged.

We turned Morea and had Tahiti before us.

Several hours later dawn appeared, and we gently approached the reefs, entered the channel, and anchored without accidents in the roadstead.

The first view of this part of the island discloses nothing very extraordinary; nothing, for instance, that could be compared with the magnificent bay of Rio de Janeiro.

It is the summit of a mountain submerged at the time of one of the ancient deluges. Only the very point rose above the waters. A family fled thither and founded a new race—and then the corals climbed up along it, surrounding the peak, and in the course of centuries built a new land. It is still extending, but retains its original character of solitude and isolation, which is only accentuated by the immense expanse of the ocean.

Toward ten o'clock I made my formal call on the governor, the negro Lacascade, who received me as though I had been an important personage.

Dr. Etienne Lacascade (1841–1906), governor of French colonies in Oceania from 1887 until 1893.

I owed this distinction to the mission with which the French government—I do not know why—had entrusted me. It was an *artistic* mission, it is true. But in the view of the negro, however, this word was only an official synonym for espionage, and I tried in vain to undeceive him.

158

Every one about him shared this belief, and when I said that I was receiving no pay for my mission no one would believe me.

Life at Papeete soon became a burden.

It was Europe—the Europe which I had thought to shake off—and that under the aggravating circumstances of colonial snobbism, and the imitation, grotesque even to the point of caricature, of our customs, fashions, vices, and absurdities of civilization.

Was I to have made this far journey, only to find the very thing which I had fled?

Nevertheless, there was a public event which interested me.

At the time King Pomare was mortally ill, and the end was daily expected.

Little by little the city had assumed a singular aspect.

All the Europeans, merchants, functionaries, officers, and soldiers, laughed and sang on the streets as usual, while the natives with grave mien and lowered voice held converse among themselves in the neighborhood of the palace. In the roadstead there was an abnormal movement of orange sails on the blue sea, and often the line of reefs shone in a sudden silvery gleam under the sun. The natives of neighboring islands were hastening hither to attend at the last moments of their king, and at the definite taking possession of their empire by France.

By signs from above they had had report of this, for whenever a king was about to die the mountains in certain places became covered with dark spots at the setting of the sun.

The king died, and lay in state in the palace in the uniform of an admiral.

There I saw the queen. Marau—such was her name—decorating the royal hall with flowers and materials. When the director of public works asked my advice about the *artistic* arrangements of the funeral, I pointed out the queen to him. With the beautiful instinct of her race she dispersed grace everywhere about her, and made everything she touched a work of art.

I understood her only imperfectly at this first meeting. Both the human beings and the objects were so different from those I had desired, that I was disappointed. I was disgusted by all this European triviality. I

Arearea (Amusements) (II). ca. 1892–1895. Watercolor on linen, fan-shaped. Maximum dimensions: 10¼ × 21¾" (26 × 55.3 cm). The Museum of Fine Arts, Houston; John A. and Audrey Jones Beck Collection.

Pomare V (1849–1891), alcoholic king of Tahiti, who became a mere figurehead when the French took complete charge of the island in 1880.

Marau (1860–1934), queen of Tahiti, widow of Pomare V. Like her mother, Marau was devoted to the documentation of ancient Tahitian legends.

Reverie. 1891. 37 × 26¾″ (73 × 92 cm).
The Nelson-Atkins Museum of Art,
Kansas City; Nelson Fund.

had disembarked too recently yet to distinguish how much of the nationality, fundamental realness, and primitive beauty still remained in this conquered race beneath the artificial and meretricious veneer of our importations. I was still in a manner blind. I saw in this queen, already somewhat mature in years, only a commonplace stout woman with traces of noble beauty. When I saw her again later, I revised my first judgment. I fell under the spell of her "Maori charm." Notwithstanding all the intermixture, the Tahitian type was still very pure in her. And then the memory of her ancestor, the great chief Tati, gave her as well as her brother and all her family an appearance of truly imposing grandeur. She had the majestic sculptural form of her race, ample and at the same time gracious. The arms were like the two columns of a temple, simple, straight; and the whole bodily form with the long horizontal line of the shoulder, and the vast height terminating above in a point, inevitably made me think of the Triangle of the Trinity. In her eyes there sometimes burned something like a vague presentiment of passions which flared up suddenly and set aflame all the life round about. Perhaps it is

COLORPLATE 49. *Still Life with Apples, a Pear, and a Ceramic.* 1889. Oil on cradled panel. 11 × 14¼″ (28 × 36 cm). The Harvard University Art Museums (Fogg Art Museum); Gift of Mr. Walter E. Sachs.

COLORPLATE 50. *The Red Cow*. 1889. 36¼ × 28¾″ (92 × 73 cm).
Los Angeles County Museum of Art; Mr. and Mrs. George Gard de Sylva Collection.

COLORPLATE 51. *Nostalgic Promenade.* 1889. 35½ × 28¼ (90 × 72 cm).
Private collection.

COLORPLATE 52. *Landscape at Le Pouldu.* 1890. 28¾ × 36¼" (73 × 92 cm).
National Gallery of Art, Washington, D.C.; Collection of Mr. and Mrs. Paul Mellon.

COLORPLATE 53. *Haystacks in Brittany.* 1890. Canvas. 29¼ × 36⅞″ (74.3 × 93.6 cm).
Gift of the W. Averell Harriman Foundation in memory of Marie N. Harriman,
National Gallery of Art, Washington.

COLORPLATE 54. *The Loss of Virginity.* 1890–1891. 35½ × 51½″ (89.5 × 130.2 cm).
The Chrysler Museum, Norfolk, Virginia; Gift of Walter P. Chrysler, Jr.

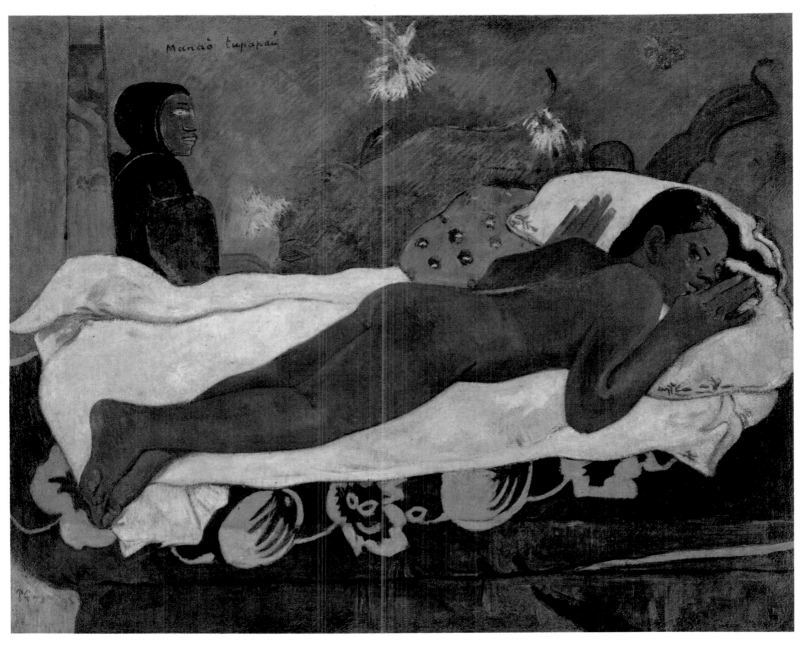

COLORPLATE 55. *Manao Tupapau (Spirit of the Dead Watching)*. 1892. 28½ × 36⅜″ (72.5 × 92.5 cm).
Albright-Knox Art Gallery, Buffalo, New York; A. Conger Goodyear Collection, 1965.

COLORPLATE 56. *Vahine No Te Tiare (Woman with a Flower)*. 1891. 27½ × 18″ (70 × 46 cm).
Ny Carlsberg Glyptotek, Copenhagen.

Tahitian woman. ca. 1890s. Photo by
Henry Lemasson. Photo courtesy of
Musée Gauguin, Papeari, Tahiti.

thus that the island itself once rose from the ocean, and that the plants
upon it burst into flower under the first ray of the sun . . .

All the Tahitians dressed in black, and for two days they sang dirges
of grief and laments for the dead. It seemed to me that I was listening
to the Sonata Pathétique.

Then came the day of the funeral.

At ten in the morning they left the palace. The troops and the authorities were in white helmet and black dress-coat, the natives in their
mourning costume. All the districts marched in order, and the leader of
each one bore a French flag.

*The Sonata Pathétique is Beethoven's
Sonata No. 8 in C minor, opus 13.*

* * *

It was only one king less.

With him disappeared the last vestiges of ancient traditions. With him
Maori history closed. It was at an end. Civilization, alas!—soldiers, trade,
officialdom—triumphed.

A profound sadness took possession of me. The cream which had brought me to Tahiti was brutally disappointed by the actuality. It was the Tahiti of former times which I loved. That of the present filled me with horror.

In view of the persistent physical beauty of the race, it seemed unbelievable that all its ancient grandeur, its personal and natural customs, its beliefs, and its legends had disappeared. But how was I, all by myself, to find the traces of this past if any such traces remained? How was I to recognize them without guidance? How to relight the fire the very ashes of which are scattered?

However depressed I may be I am not in the habit of giving up a project without having tried everything, even the "impossible," to gain my end.

My resolve was quickly taken. I would leave Papeete, and withdraw from this European center.

I felt that in living intimately with the natives in the wilderness I would by patience gradually gain the confidence of the Maoris and come to *know* them.

And one morning I set out in a carriage which one of the officers had graciously put at my disposal in search of "my hut."

My *vahiné*, Titi by name, accompanied me. She was of mixed English and Tahitian blood, and spoke some French. She had put on her very best dress for the journey. The *tiaré* was behind the ear; her hat of reeds was decorated above with ribbon, straw flowers, and a garniture of orange-colored shells, and her long black hair fell loose over the shoulders. She was proud to be in a carriage, proud to be so elegant, proud to be the *vahiné* of a man whom she believed important and rich. She was really handsome, and there was nothing ridiculous in her pride, for the majestic mien is becoming to this race. In memory of its long feudal history and its endless line of powerful chiefs it retains its superb strain of pride. I knew very well that her calculating love in the eyes of Parisians would not have had much more weight than the venial complaisance of a harlot. But the amorous passion of a Maori courtesan is something quite different from the passivity of a Parisian cocotte—something very different! There is a fire in her blood, which calls forth love as its essential nourishment; which exhales it like a fatal perfume. These eyes and this mouth cannot lie. Whether calculating or not, it is always love that speaks from them. . . .

The journey was soon accomplished—a few bits of inconsequential conversation, a rich, monotonous country. On the right there was always the sea, the coral-reefs and the sheets of water which sometimes scattered in spray when they came into too violent contact with the waves and the rocks. To the left was the wilderness with its perspective of great forests.

By noonday we had accomplished our forty-five kilometers, and had arrived at the district of Mataïea.

I made a search through the district and succeeded in finding a suitable enough hut, which the owner rented to me. He was building a new one nearby where he intended to dwell.

On the next evening when we returned to Papeete, Titi asked me whether I wished her to accompany me.

"Later, in a few days, when I have become settled," I said.

Titi had a terrible reputation at Papeete of having successively brought a number of lovers to their grave. But it was not this which made me put her aside. It was her half-white blood. In spite of traces of profoundly native and truly Maori characteristics, the many contacts had caused her to lose many of her distinctive racial "differences." I felt that she could not teach me any of the things I wished to know, that she had nothing to give of that special happiness which I sought.

I told myself that in the country I would find that which I was seeking; it would only be necessary to choose.

On one side [of my hut] was the sea; on the other, the mountain, a deeply fissured mountain; an enormous cleft closed by a huge mango leaning against the rocks.

Between the mountain and the sea stood my hut, made of the wood of the bourao tree. Close to the hut in which I dwelled was another, the *faré amu* (hut for eating).

It is morning.

On the sea close to the strand I see a pirogue, and in the pirogue a half-naked woman. On the shore is a man, also undressed. Beside the man is a diseased coconut tree with shriveled leaves. It resembles a huge parrot with golden tails hanging down, and holding in his claws a huge cluster of coconuts. With a harmonious gesture the man raises a heavy ax in his two hands. It leaves above a blue impression against the silvery sky, and below a rosy incision in the dead tree, where for an inflammatory moment the ardor stored up day by day throughout centuries will come to life again.

On the purple soil long serpentine leaves of a metallic yellow make me think of a mysterious sacred writing of the ancient Orient. They distinctly form the sacred word of Oceani origin, ATUA (God), and Taäta or Takata or Tathagata, who ruled throughout all the Indies. And there came to my mind like a mystic counsel, in harmony with my beautiful solitude and my beautiful poverty the words of the sage:

> In the eyes of Tathagata, the magnificence and splendor of kings and their ministers are no more than spittle and dust;
> In his eyes purity and impurity are like the dance of the six nagas;
> In his eyes the seeking for the sight of the Buddha is like unto flowers.

In the pirogue the woman was putting some nets in order.

The blue line of the sea was frequently broken by the green of the wave-crests falling on the breakwater of coral.

It is evening.

* * *

I raro te Oviri (Under the Pandanus). 1891. 29 × 37⅞″ (73.6 × 96.2 cm). The Minneapolis Institute of Arts; The William Hood Dunwoody Fund.

As they were to me, so was I to them, an object for observation, a cause of astonishment—one to whom everything was new, one who was ignorant of everything. For I knew neither their language, nor their customs, not even the simplest, most necessary manipulations. As each one of them was a savage to me, so was I a savage to each one of them.

And which of us two was wrong?

I tried to work, making all kinds of notes and sketches.

But the landscape with its violent, pure colors dazzled and blinded me. I was always uncertain; I was seeking, seeking. . . .

In the meantime, it was so simple to paint things as I saw them; to put without special calculation a red close to a blue. Golden figures in the brooks and on the seashore enchanted me. Why did I hesitate to put all this glory of the sun on my canvas?

Oh! the old European traditions! The timidities of expression of degenerate races!

In order to familiarize myself with the distinctive characteristics of the Tahitian face, I had wished for a long time to make a portrait of one of my neighbors, a young woman of pure Tahitian extraction.

One day she finally became emboldened enough to enter my hut, and to look at photographs of paintings which I had hung on one of the walls of my room. She regarded the *Olympia* for a long time and with special interest.

"What do you think of her?" I asked. I had learned a few Tahitian words during the two months since I had last spoken French.

My neighbor replied, "She is very beautiful!"

I smiled at this remark, and was touched by it. Had she then a sense of the beautiful? But what reply would the professors of the Academy of Fine Arts have made to this remark?

Then suddenly after a perceptible silence such as precedes the thinking out of a conclusion, she added,

"Is it your wife?"

"Yes."

I did not hesitate at this lie. I—*the tané of the beautiful Olympia!*

While she was curiously examining certain religious compositions of the Italian primitives, I hastened, without her noticing it, to sketch her portrait.

She saw it, and with a pout cried out abruptly, "*Aita* (no)!" and fled.

An hour later she returned, dressed in a beautiful robe with the *tiaré* behind the ear. Was it coquetry? Was it the pleasure of consenting of her own free will after having refused? Or was it simply the universal attraction of the forbidden fruit which one denies one's self? Or more probably still, was it merely a caprice without any other motive, a pure caprice of the kind to which the Maoris are so given?

Without delay I began work, without hesitation and all of a fever. I was aware that on my skill as painter would depend the physical and moral possession of the model, that it would be like an implied, urgent, irresistible invitation.

She was not at all handsome according to our aesthetic rules.

She was beautiful.

All her traits combined in a Raphaelesque harmony by the meeting of curves. Her mouth had been modeled by a sculptor who knew how to put into a single mobile line a mingling of all joy and all suffering.

I worked in haste and passionately, for I knew that the consent had not yet been definitely gained. I trembled to read certain things in these large eyes—fear and the desire for the unknown, the melancholy of bitter experience which lies at the root of all pleasure, the *involuntary and sovereign* feeling of being mistress of herself. Such creatures seem to submit to us when they give themselves to us; yet it is only to themselves that they submit. In them resides a force which has in it something superhuman—or perhaps something divinely animal.

Ta Matete (The Market). 1892. 28¾ × 35⅞" (73 × 91.5 cm). Kunstmuseum, Basel.

Almost nothing is known about the life of P. Jénot, a naval officer stationed in Tahiti when Gauguin arrived in 1891, yet his notes about their friendship during Gauguin's first stay on the island are a crucial source of information about the artist.

P. Jénot

GAZETTE DES BEAUX-ARTS

"Gauguin's First Stay in Tahiti"

January–April 1956

Also, I was surprised when one morning in June 1891—the *City of Papeete* having already come and gone—Brenner, my orderly (a Breton from Lower Brittany), came to alert me that the guard-ship of the Navy, *La Durance*, was en route from New Caledonia and that it had our captain aboard. I made haste to get to the quay but at a short distance from my house I met two strangers. One was a Marine Infantry Captain, to whom I introduced myself. It was indeed my new captain (Swaton) coming from a detachment at New Caledonia. M. Gauguin, a painter on a mission from France, embarked at Nouméa as his companion.

I brought the captain and M. Gauguin to my quarters to tell them the indispensable things anyone new to the island should know right away, and that was how I first met Gauguin.

Let us say right away that as soon as Gauguin disembarked he attracted the stares of the natives, provoked their surprise and also their jeers, above all from the women. Tall, erect, a forceful figure maintaining, despite his already awakened curiosity and, no doubt, anxiety about his future work, an air of profound disdain. He contrasted with his neighbor the captain, who was a little smaller with a slightly heavy figure, easy-going, and a little hunched over. They must have been about the same age, in their forties, but what focused attention on Gauguin above all was his long, salt and pepper hair falling in a sheet on his shoulders from beneath a vast, brown felt hat with a large brim, like a cowboy's. As far as the inhabitants could remember they had never seen a man with long hair on the island—except for the Chinese, who did not wear it the same way—also, that very day, Gauguin was renamed *taata vahiné* (man–woman), which the natives made up ironically, but which provoked such interest among the women and children that I had to chase them from the entrance to my cabin. At first, Gauguin laughed when told of this, but after a few weeks, with the help of the heat, he cut his hair in the same style as everyone else.

Head of a Tahitian Woman. 1891. Pencil. (31 × 24 cm). Cleveland Museum of Art; Mr. and Mrs. Louis B. Williams collection.

Mask of *Teha'amana*. Pua wood? Height: 9⅞″ (25 cm), Width: 8″ (20 cm). Musée d'Orsay, Paris.

Naturally, I had to spend this day with my two guests, attend to their first needs in Papeete, facilitate their search for room and board, help them set themselves up, direct them in their initial duties as new arrivals concerning the authorities, and finish this very full day at the Officer's Club, where they completed their acquaintance with the garrison and made contact with the vahinés, who crowned them with flowers.

Also, Gauguin was always aware of my attentions, and despite our age difference he always held an affection for me that did not diminish the many discussions we had shortly thereafter about the way he expressed himself in his paintings and, above all, in his drawings. Moreover he found my complete frankness on these subjects agreeable, and I could not doubt, when I saw him leaving sometime later, that the air of disdain and haughtiness that he showed when he arrived and that he took up again each time he met someone new, that he would keep up for a long time and sometimes never let down, was something he had to do, otherwise he would not be able to risk exposure at all.

Captain Swaton took the cabin that Captain Onfroy de la Rosière had given up, on the extreme western beach of Papeete, close to the old battery of the Uranie.

Gauguin chose to take a cabin at the foot of the mountain, at the very back of the town near the cathedral.

My own, being next to the Avenue Militaire des Casernes, naturally became the meeting place for the two men. These meetings, if they were not an everyday occurrence at the beginning of their stay, nevertheless became all the more frequent because Gauguin, who wanted to learn

Deep bowl. Tamanu wood. Perhaps 1891. Length: 17¼″ (44 cm); Width: 10¼″ (26 cm). Musée d'Orsay, Paris.

something of the Maori language, found out that I knew it well and began to count on me to help him. I tried little by little, with patience, to do my best, because this student had an infuriating propensity to forget, to mix up syllables or to invert them—after a certain age it is difficult for some tongues to learn a new language—even when it is simple, like Tahitian: still, one at least needs a memory. This is why Gauguin, even though he saw my name written many times, mostly by myself, was never able to spell it correctly and usually called me Gino, the sound that must have struck his ear when we first met.

* * *

As everywhere in the colony, it was near the end of the afternoon, which was sometimes heavy, either with the temperature or with work, that we most often met. Rarely would Gauguin arrive without a question to ask me, for information he needed, or where to find a model, since he was interested from the very beginning in everything that touched the lives of the natives and the country itself, as much in the present as the past. This is why I put him in touch with the government's official interpreter, M. Cadousteau, whose father was French and whose mother was Tahitian; the man who was most competent in Maori language and history and who knew the diverse dialects of the archipelago.

Not only was he looking for models, but also for potential buyers of his paintings. So I had to intercede to introduce him to the civil sector, colonial officials or not, through the mayor of Papeete, M. Cardella; M. Simonin, a businessman from Lorraine, like myself; my landlord, a lawyer named Langomasino (called Titipa, a Tahitian translation of Hégésippe, his first name); through my neighbor, M. Drollet, an ice cream producer; an old colonist, M. Goupil; and finally, a retired Marine doctor, a regular visitor of Queen Marau, Dr. Chassaniol; as well as others.

As soon as he was set up, Gauguin began to paint several small pieces, landscapes, figure studies, and nudes. But he did not paint any large canvases in Papeete. He simply made his eye and his hand discover the Tahiti that he wanted to understand and express. This is how he came to do the portraits that I now have of his neighbor's children, of Captain Swaton, and of Teuraheimate à Potoru.

He had brought with him from France enough material to work for at least a few months, counting on reprovisioning himself little by little as he needed. Along with a certain number of fine colors, he had a huge assortment of tubes of colors for decoration from Lefranc and Co. Beyond that, he had brought roles of canvas, one of which was a heavy canvas of thick hemp fiber, which he tried out on the children's portraits I mentioned above, and other finer ones like that which he used for the portrait of Captain Swaton. With the canvases, he also brought casein, glue, and Spanish white, with which to make the first, preparatory coat. Often this preparation took place at my house, and it came

Teuraheimate: a possible reference to Gauguin's vahiné Teha'amana.

about much later that, lacking the glue and the casein, Gauguin asked me if I did not think he could replace these products with the ripe [*uru*] or rotten [*pu*] fruit of the breadfruit tree, which in those conditions has the consistency, and to some extent the smell, of very ripe Marolle cheese. I thought not, fearing that a vegetable material without other preparation would have a tendency to mildew. But Gauguin said necessity would rule, and he used the *uru* not only for trial paintings, but also for some large canvases that he finished. All the while, if he was using it, it was only temporary, and he could restock himself from France or San Francisco through the captains of the mailboat.

Beyond his painting material, Gauguin brought with him an assortment of gouges and chisels for wood sculpture. He asked me if the natives I knew could find him the kind of wood they used to make their tableware, some examples of which I owned. One of them appears in a painting Gauguin did that is reproduced in the Gauguin collection of Braun and Company's *Collection de Maitres* (no. 33, *le repas*, Tahiti; 1891; private collection), it is a *popoi* (soup) bowl, sort of an oval cup with a handle at each end, one of which has a canal that lets the liquid pour through when the other is lifted. I was able to help him procure several pieces of guava wood, which is similar to pear, but which is flawed in tending to be eaten by worms and soon crumbling into dust. But his attention was drawn to my wooden plates, which were indeed made from very beautiful material, and in particular to the popoi bowl. Then one morning he came to my house with some tools and asked me if I would allow him to cut into the wood. I acquiesced and, happy, Gauguin took the object, examined it, turned it around and around, and suddenly, without preparation, chose an implement and began cutting into it. I watched him do it, but without saying anything, for when he was working Gauguin was mute and even deaf. He sculpted in this way for a long while, until lunchtime, during the course of which he asked me if he could find figures sculpted in wood or stone in Tahiti and was surprised when I replied that, to the best of my knowledge, nothing like that existed on the island or in the archipelago, that I had seen reproductions of stone sculptures from Easter Island, but that this island was very far

The Meal. 1891. 28¾ × 36¼" (73 × 92 cm). Musée d'Orsay, Paris.

Three wooden sculptures by Gauguin: *Idol with a Shell, Idol with Pearl* (center), *The Moon and the Earth*. Photograph purportedly taken by Georges Chaudet, ca. 1895. Photo courtesy of Musée Gauguin, Papeari, Tahiti.

from Tahiti and undoubtedly not of the same ethnic group as our islands. In the same way, the sculpted figures of New Caledonia and New Zealand were unknown to the Papeete islanders. He then showed me photographs of Marquesans who were tattooed over fully half their bodies. He admired the designs and was surprised that the artists, capable of tattooing such figures, never thought of reproducing them in wood or stone. Then, full of the subject of our conversation, he again took up his work, reproducing several Marquesan designs with the gouge and the chisel. He left me the popoi bowl he had resculpted, and I still have it. Afterward, he bought similar utensils, and I was able to see in the retrospective exhibition of his work that took place at the Petit Palais in Paris in 1906, a popoi bowl identical to my own and sculpted in the same manner, by the same method.

My guava trunks took the form, one after the other, under his fingers, of bizarre gods and always with a strength of expression and an unexpected and impressive design.

In order to look for wood that he would find interesting, I took him up the mountain above the Valley of the Queen where an old Tahitian man lived in seclusion. He often came down to Papeete to sell various products in the market; cocoa, *feï* [plantains], fruit from the forest, but mostly the flowers from which he made crowns. His name was Téréa; he had the best disposition in the world and knew the secret of curing a certain number of illnesses, which assured him a widespread reputation among the natives. But the wood Gauguin was able to find this way was not dry, and he was sorry to see that most often the pieces he sculpted split irreparably.

Painting and sculpture were not the only occupations that Gauguin had envisioned for his stay in Tahiti.

He had packed two mandolins, a guitar, and even a hunting horn, as well as a certain number of collections of music, one of which was Schumann, another Schubert, and others. He gave me one of his mandolins and I energetically set myself to strumming it, so that I would be able to play duets with him.

Letter from Gauguin to
His Wife, Mette

On His Work in Tahiti

March 1892

For I am an artist and you are right, you are not mad, I am a great artist and I know it. It is because I am such that I have endured such sufferings. To do what I have done in any other circumstances would make me out as a ruffian. Which I am no doubt for many people. Anyhow, what does it matter? What distresses me most is not so much the poverty as the perpetual obstacles to my art, which I cannot practice as I feel it ought to be done and as I could do it if relieved of the poverty which ties my hands. You tell me that I am wrong to remain far away from the artistic center. No, I am right, I have known for a long time what I am doing, and why I do it. My artistic center is in my brain and not elsewhere and I am strong because I am never sidetracked by others, and do what is in me.

Beethoven was blind and deaf, he was isolated from everything, so his works are redolent of the artist living in a world of his own. You see what has happened to Pissarro, owing to his always wanting to be in the vanguard, abreast of everything; he has lost every atom of personality, and his whole work lacks unity. He has always followed the movement from Courbet and Millet up to these petty chemical persons who pile up little dots.

No, I have an aim and I am always pursuing it, building up material. There are transformations every year, it is true, but they always follow each other in the same direction. I alone am logical. Consequently, I find very few who follow me for long.

Poor Schuffenecker, who reproaches me for being wholehearted in my volitions! But if I did not behave in this manner, could I have endured the endless struggle I am waging for one year? My actions, my painting, etc., are criticized and repudiated every time, but in the end I am acknowledged to be right. I am always starting all over again. I believe I am doing my duty, and strong in this, I accept no advice and take no blame. The conditions in which I am working are unfavorable, and one must be a colossus to do what I am doing in these circumstances. . . .

Letter from Gauguin to
Daniel de Monfreid

On Illness and Work in Tahiti

11 March 1892

As a matter of fact, I was quite seriously ill. Imagine spitting blood, a quarter-liter a day. Impossible to suppress; mustard plasters on my legs, cupping-glasses on my chest, nothing worked. The doctor at the hospital was quite worried and thought I was done for. My lungs were undamaged and even quite sound, he said: it was my heart that was playing tricks on me. It has had so many rents that it is not surprising. Once I stopped vomiting blood, I followed a course of digitalis treatment and here I am, recovered without having noticed any setbacks. All the same, I'll have to be careful. My life is now that of a savage, naked except for the essential, which the women don't like to see (they say). I am working more and more, but so far only studies, or rather records that are piling up. If I don't use them later on, they will be useful to others. However, I have done one painting, a size 50 canvas. An angel with yellow wings points at two Tahitian women, Mary and Jesus are Tahitians as well—naked, dressed in the *paréo*, a sort of flowered cotton fabric attached as one pleases to one's belt. Very dark mountain background and flowering trees—deep violet path and emerald-green foreground; on the left some bananas. I'm quite satisfied with it. . . .

COLORPLATE 57

Paul Gauguin

NOA NOA

On His Early Life in Tahiti

1893–1895

My neighbors have become my friends. I dress like them, and partake of the same food as they. When I am not working, I share their life of indolence and joy, across which sometimes pass sudden movements of gravity.

In the evening they unite in groups at the foot of the tufted bushes which overtop the disheveled heads of the coconut trees, or men and women, old men and children intermingle. Some are from Tahiti, others from the Tongas, and still others from the Marquesas. The dull tones of their bodies form a lovely harmony with the velvet of the foliage. From their coppery breasts trembling melodies arise, and are faintly thrown back from the wrinkled trunks of the coconut trees. They are the Tahitian songs, the *iménés*.

A woman begins. Her voice rises like the flight of a bird, and from the first note reaches even to the highest of the scale; then by strong modulations it lowers again and remounts and finally soars, the while the voices of the other women about her, so to speak, take flight in their turn, and faithfully follow and accompany her. Finally all the men in a single guttural and barbarous cry close the song in a tonic chord.

Sometimes in order to sing or converse they assemble in a sort of communal hut. They always begin with a prayer. An old man first recites it conscientiously, and then all those present take it up like a refrain. Then they sing, or tell humorous stories. The theme of these recitals is very tenuous, almost unseizable. It is the details, broidered into the woof and made subtle by their very naïveté, which amuse them.

COLORPLATE 65

More rarely, they discourse on serious questions or put forth wise proposals.

*   *   *

I have won a friend.

He came to me of his own accord, and I feel sure here that in his coming to me there was no element of self-interest.

He is one of my neighbors, a very simple and handsome young fellow.

My colored pictures and carvings in wood aroused his curiosity; my replies to his questions have instructed him. Not a day passes that he does not come to watch me paint or carve. . . .

Even after this long time I still take pleasure in remembering the *true* and *real* emotions in this *true* and *real* nature.

In the evening when I rested from my day's work, we talked. In his character of a wild young savage he asked many questions about European matters, particularly about the things of love, and more than once his questions embarrassed me.

But his replies were even more naive than his questions.

One day I put my tools in his hands and a piece of wood; I wanted him to try to carve. Nonplussed, he looked at me at first in silence, and then returned the wood and tools to me, saying with entire simplicity and sincerity that I was not like the others, that I could do things which other men were incapable of doing, and that I was *useful to others*.

I indeed believe Totefa is the first human being in the world who used such words toward me. It was the language of a savage or of a child, for one must be either one of these—must one not?—to imagine that an artist might be *a useful human being*.

It happened once that I had need of rosewood for my carving. I wanted a large strong trunk, and I consulted Totefa.

"We have to go into the mountains," he told me. "I know a certain spot where there are several beautiful trees. If you wish it I will lead you. We can then fell the tree which pleases you and together carry it here."

We set out early in the morning.

The footpaths in Tahiti are rather difficult for a European, and "to go into the mountains" demands even of the natives a degree of effort which they do not care to undertake unnecessarily.

Between two mountains, two high and steep walls of basalt, which it is impossible to ascend, there yawns a fissure in which the water winds among rocks. These blocks have been loosened from the flank of the mountain by infiltrations in order to form a passageway for a spring. The spring grew into a brook, which has thrust at them and jolted them, and then moved them a little further. Later the brook when it became a tor-

Te Burao (The Burao Tree). 1892. Canvas. 26¾ × 36¾" (68 × 90.7 cm). The Art Institute of Chicago; The Joseph Winterbotham Collection.

rent took them up, rolled them over and over, and carried them even to the sea. On each side of this brook, frequently interrupted by cascades, there is a sort of path. It leads through a confusion of trees—breadfruit, ironwood, pandanus, bouraos, coconut, hibiscus, guava, giant-ferns. It is a mad vegetation, growing always wilder, more entangled, denser, until, as we ascend toward the center of the island, it has become an almost impenetrable thicket.

Both of us went naked, the white and blue *paréo* around the loins, hatchet in hand. Countless times we crossed the brook for the sake of a short-cut. My guide seemed to follow the trail by smell rather than by sight, for the ground was covered by a splendid confusion of plants, leaves, and flowers which wholly took possession of space.

The silence was absolute but for the plaintive wailing of water among the rocks. It was a monotonous wail, a plaint so soft and low that it seemed an accompaniment of the silence.

And in this forest, this solitude, this silence were we two—he, a very young man, and I, almost an old man from whose soul many illusions had fallen and whose body was tired from countless efforts, upon whom lay the long and fatal heritage of the vices of a morally and physically corrupt society.

With the suppleness of an animal and the graceful litheness of an androgyne he walked a few paces in advance of me. And it seemed to me that I saw incarnated in him, palpitating and living, all the magnificent plant-life which surrounded us. From it in him, through him there became disengaged and emanated a powerful perfume of beauty.

Was it really a human being walking there ahead of me? Was it the naïve friend by whose combined simplicity and complexity I had been so attracted? Was it not rather the Forest itself, the living Forest, without sex—and yet alluring?

Among peoples that go naked, as among animals, the difference between the sexes is less accentuated than in our climates. Thanks to our cinctures and corsets we have succeeded in making an artificial being out of woman. She is an anomaly, and Nature herself, obedient to the laws of heredity, aids us in complicating and enervating her. We carefully keep her in a state of nervous weakness and muscular inferiority, and in guarding her from fatigue, we take away from her possibilities of development. Thus modeled on a bizarre ideal of slenderness to which, strangely enough, we continue to adhere, our women have nothing in common with us, and this, perhaps, may not be without grave moral and social disadvantages.

On Tahiti the breezes from forest and sea strengthen the lungs, they broaden the shoulders and hips. Neither men nor women are sheltered from the rays of the sun nor the pebbles of the seashore. Together they engage in the same tasks with the same activity or the same indolence. There is something virile in the women and something feminine in the men.

This similarity of the sexes make their relations the easier. Their continual state of nakedness has kept their minds free from the dangerous preoccupation with the "mystery" and from the excessive stress which among civilized people is laid upon the "happy accident" and the clandestine and sadistic colors of love. It has given their manners a natural innocence, a perfect purity. Man and woman are comrades, friends rather than lovers, dwelling together almost without cease, in pain as in pleasure, and even the very idea of vice is unknown to them.

In spite of all this lessening in sexual differences, why was it that there suddenly rose in the soul of a member of an old civilization a horrible thought? Why, in all this drunkenness of lights and perfumes with its enchantment of newness and unknown mystery?

The fever throbbed in my temples and my knees shook.

But we were at the end of the trail. In order to cross the brook my companion turned, and in this movement showed himself full-face. The androgyne had disappeared. It was an actual young man walking ahead of me. His calm eyes had the limpid clearness of waters.

Peace forthwith fell upon me again.

We made a moment's halt. I felt an infinite joy, a joy of the spirit rather than of the senses, as I plunged into the fresh water of the brook.

"*Toë, toë* (it is cold)," said Totefa.

"Oh, no!" I replied.

This exclamation seemed to me also a fitting conclusion to the struggle which I had just fought out within myself against the corruption of an entire civilization. It was the end in the battle of a soul that had chosen between truth and untruth. It awakened loud echoes in the forest. And I said to myself that Nature had seen me struggle, had heard me, and understood me, for now she replied with her clear voice to my cry of victory that she was willing after the ordeal to receive me as one of her children.

We took up our way again. I plunged eagerly and passionately into the wilderness, as if in the hope of thus penetrating into the very heart of this Nature, powerful and maternal, there to blend with her living elements.

With tranquil eyes and ever uniform pace my companion went on. He was wholly without suspicion; I alone was bearing the burden of an evil conscience.

We arrived at our destination.

The steep sides of the mountain had by degrees spread out, and behind a dense curtain of trees, there extended a sort of plateau, well-concealed. Totefa, however, knew the place, and with astonishing sureness led me thither.

A dozen rosewood trees extended their vast branches.

We attacked the finest of these with the ax. We had to sacrifice the entire tree to obtain a branch suitable for my project.

I struck out with joy. My hands became stained with blood in my wild rage, my intense joy of satiating within me I know not what divine brutality. It was not the tree I was striking, it was not it which I sought to overcome. And yet gladly would I have heard the sound of my ax against other trunks when this one was already lying on the ground.

And here is what my ax seemed to say to me in the cadence of its sounding blows:

> Strike down to the root the forest entire!
> Destroy all the forest of evil,
> Whose seeds were once sowed within thee by the
> breathings of death!
> Destroy in thee all love of the self!
> Destroy and tear out all evil, as in the autumn we cut
> with the hand the flower of the lotus.

Yes, wholly destroyed, finished, dead, is from now on the old civilization within me. I was reborn; or rather another man, purer and stronger, came to life within me.

This cruel assault was the supreme farewell to civilization, to evil. This last evidence of the depraved instincts which sleep at the bottom of all decadent souls, by very contrast exalted the healthy simplicity of the life at which I had already made a beginning into a feeling of inexpressible happiness. By the trial within my soul mastery had been won. Avidly I inhaled the splendid purity of the light. I was, indeed, a new man, from now on I was a true savage, a real Maori.

Totefa and I returned to Mateïea, carefully and peacefully bearing our heavy load of rosewood—*noa, noa!*

The sun had not yet set when, very tired out, we arrived before my hut.

Totefa said to me,

"*Païa?*"

"Yes!" I replied.

And from the bottom of my heart I repeated this "yes" to myself.

I have never made a single cut with the knife into this branch of rosewood that I did not each time more powerfully breathe in the perfume of victory and rejuvenation: *noa, noa!*

* * *

I left the road which follows the edge of the sea, and took up a narrow path leading through a dense thicket. This path led so far into the mountains that at the end of several hours I reached a little valley where the inhabitants still lived in the ancient Maori manner.

They are happy and undisturbed. They dream, they love, they sleep, they sing, they pray, and it seems that Christianity has not yet penetrated to this place. Before me I can clearly see the statues of their divinities, though actually they have long since disappeared; especially the statue of Hina, and the feasts in honor of the moon-goddess. The idol of a single block of stone measures ten feet from shoulder to shoulder and forty feet in height. On the head she wears in the manner of a hood a huge stone of reddish color. Around her they dance according to ancient rite, the *matamua,* and the *vivo* varies its note from lightness and gaiety to somberness and melancholy according to the color of the hour. . . .

I continue my way.

At Taravao, the district farthest from Mataïea at the other extremity of the island, a gendarme lends me his horse, and I range along the east coast, which is little frequented by Europeans.

At Faone, a tiny district which precedes the more important one of Itia, I hear a native calling out to me,

"Halloa! Man who makes human beings!" He knows that I am a painter. "*Haëre maï ta maha* (come and eat with us)." This is the Tahitian formula of hospitality.

No persuasion is required, for the smile accompanying the invitation is engaging and gentle.

I dismount from the horse. My host takes the animal by the bridle and ties it to a branch, simply and skillfully, without a trace of servility.

Together we enter a hut where men and women are sitting together on the ground talking and smoking. Around them children play and prattle.

"Where are you going?" asked a beautiful Maori woman of about forty.

"I am going to Itia."

"What for?"

I do not know what idea flitted across my mind. Perhaps I was only giving expression to the real purpose of my journey, which had hitherto been hidden even to myself.

"To find a wife," I replied.

"There are many pretty women at Faone. Do you want one?"

"Yes."

"Very well! If she pleases you, I will give her to you. She is my daughter."

"Is she young?"

"Yes."

"Is she pretty?"

"Yes."

"Is she in good health?"

"Yes."

"It is well. Go and bring her to me."

The woman went out.

IA ORANA MARIA

P. Gauguin 91

COLORPLATE 57. *Ia Orana Maria (Hail, Mary)*. 1891. 44¾ × 34½″ (113.7 × 87.7 cm).
The Metropolitan Museum of Art, New York; Bequest of Sam A. Lewisohn, 1951.

COLORPLATE 58. *Upaupa (Tahitian Dance)*. 1891. 28¾ × 36¼″ (73 × 92 cm).
The Israel Museum, Jerusalem.

COLORPLATE 59. *Idol with a Shell.* 1893. Toa (ironwood), mother of pearl aureola and pectoral, teeth, inlaid bone. Height: 10⅝″ (27 cm); Diameter: 5½″ (14 cm). Musée d'Orsay, Paris.

COLORPLATE 60. *Te Ra'au Rahi (The Large Tree)*. 1891. 29⅛ × 36⅜" (74 × 92.8 cm).
Jointly owned by The Cleveland Museum of Art and an anonymous collector.

COLORPLATE 61. *Te Faaturama (The Brooding Woman)*. 1891. 35⅞ × 27″ (91.2 × 68.7 cm).
Worcester Art Museum, Worcester, Massachusetts.

COLORPLATE 62. *The Black Pigs.* 1891. 35¾ × 28⅜" (91 × 72 cm).
Museum of Fine Arts, Budapest.

COLORPLATE 63. *Parahi te Marae (There Is the Temple)*. 1892. 28¾ × 35¾″ (68 × 91 cm).
Philadelphia Museum of Art; Gift of Mrs. Rodolphe Meyer de Schauensee.

COLORPLATE 64. *Vahine no te Miti (Woman by the Sea)*. 1892. 36⅝ × 29¼" (93 × 74.5 cm).
Museo Nacional de Bellas Artes, Buenos Aires. Photo: Daniel Menassé.

Haere Pape (Going Down to the Fresh Water). 1892. 35½ × 26⅜″ (90 × 67 cm). Photo copyright 1987. The Barnes Foundation, Merion Station, Pennsylvania.

A quarter of an hour later, as they were bringing on the meal, a truly Maori one of wild bananas and shellfish, she returned, followed by a young girl who held a small bundle in the hand.

Through her dress of almost transparent rose-colored muslin one could see the golden skin of her shoulders and arms. Two swelling buds rose on the breasts. She was a large child, slender, strong, of wonderful proportions. But in her beautiful face I failed to find the characteristics which hitherto I had found everywhere dominant on the island. Even her hair was exceptional, thick like a bush and a little crispy. In the sunlight it was all an orgy in chrome.

They told me that she was of Tonga origin.

I greeted her; she smiled and sat down beside me.

"Aren't you afraid of me?" I asked.

"*Aïta* (no)."

"Do you wish to live in my hut for always?"

"*Eha* (yes)."

"You have never been ill?"

"*Aïta!*"

That was all.

My heart beat, while the young girl on the ground before me was tranquilly arranging the food on a large banana leaf and offering it to me. I ate with good appetite, but I was preoccupied, profoundly troubled. This child of about thirteen years (the equivalent of eighteen or twenty in Europe) charmed me, made me timid, almost frightened me. What might be passing in her soul? And it was I, so old in contrast with her, who hesitated to sign a contract in which all the advantages were on my side, but which was entered into and concluded so hastily.

Perhaps, I thought, it is in obedience to her mother's command. Perhaps, it is an arrangement upon which they have agreed among themselves. . . .

I was reassured when I saw in the face of the young girl, in her gestures and attitude the distinct signs of independence and pride which are so characteristic of her race. And my faith was complete and unshakable when, after a deep study of her, I saw unmistakably the serene expression which in young beings always accompanies an honorable and laudable act. But the mocking line about her otherwise pretty, sensual, and tender mouth warned me that the real dangers of the adventure would be for me, not for her. . . .

I cannot deny that in crossing the threshold of the hut when leaving my heart was weighed down with a strange and very poignant anguish.

The hour of departure had come. I mounted the horse.

The girl followed behind. Her mother, a man, and two young women—her aunts, she said—also followed.

We returned to Taravao, nine kilometers from Faone.

After the first kilometer, they said:

"*Parahi téié* (here stop)."

I dismounted from my horse, and all six of us entered into a large hut, neatly kept, almost rich—with the riches of the earth, with beautiful straw-mats.

A still young and exceedingly gracious couple lived here. My bride sat down beside the woman, and introduced me.

"This is my mother."

Then in silence fresh water was poured into a goblet from which we

Te Raau Rahi (The Big Tree). 1891. 28¾ × 36″ (73 × 91.5 cm). The Art Institute of Chicago; Gift of Kate L. Brewster.

drank each in turn, gravely, as if we were engaged in some intimate religious rite.

After this the woman whom my bride had just designated as her mother said to me with a deeply moved look and moist lashes,

"You are good?"

I replied, not without difficulty, after having examined my conscience, "I hope so!"

"You will make my daughter happy?"

"Yes."

"In eight days she must return. If she is not happy she will leave you."

I assented with a gesture. Silence fell. It seemed as if no one dared to break it.

Finally we went out, and again on horseback I set out, always accompanied by my escort.

On the way we met several people who were acquainted with my new family. They were already informed of the happening, and in saluting the girl they said:

"Ah, and are you now really the *vahiné* of a Frenchman? Be happy!"

One point disturbed me. How did Tehura—this was my wife's name—come to have two mothers?

I asked the first one, the one who had offered her to me:

"Why did you lie to me?"

The mother of Tehura replied,

"I did not lie. The other one also is her mother, her nurse, foster-mother."

At Taravao, I returned the horse to the gendarme, and an unpleasant incident occurred there. His wife, a Frenchwoman, said to me, not maliciously, but tactlessly:

"What! You bring back with you such a hussy?"

And with her angry eyes she undressed the young girl, who met this insulting examination with complete indifference.

I looked for a moment at the symbolic spectacle which the two women offered. On the one side a fresh blossoming, faith and nature; on the other the season of barenness, law and artifice. Two races were face to face, and I was ashamed of mine. It hurt me to see it so petty and intolerant, so uncomprehending. I turned quickly to feel again the warmth and the joy coming from the glamor of the other, from this living gold which I already loved.

At Taravao the family took leave of us at the Chinaman's who sells everything—adulterated liqueurs and fruit, stuffs and weapons, men and women and beasts.

My wife and I took the stagecoach which left us twenty-five kilometers farther on at Mataïea, my home.

My wife is not very talkative; she is at the same time full of laughter and melancholy and above all given to mockery.

We did not cease studying each other, but she remained impenetrable to me, and I was soon vanquished in this struggle.

I had made a promise to keep a watch over myself, to remain master of myself, so that I might become a sure observer. My strength and resolutions were soon overcome. For Tehura I was in a very short time an open book.

In a way I experienced, at my expense and in my own person, the profound guilt which separates an Oceanian soul from a Latin soul, particularly a French soul. The soul of a Maori is not revealed immediately. It requires much patience and study to obtain a grasp of it. And even when you believe that you know it to the very bottom, it suddenly disconcerts you by its unforeseen "jumps." But, at first, it is enigma itself, or rather an infinite series of enigmas. At the moment you believe you have seized it, it is far away, inaccessible, incommunicable, enveloped in laughter and variability. Then of its own free will it reapproaches, only

Tehura: according to Bengt Danielsson, Gaugin and Morice may have simplified the name of Gauguin's thirteen-year-old vahiné Teha'amana (d. 1918) for the French readers of Noa Noa, *or they may simply have misspelled it.*

to slip away again as soon as you betray the slightest sign of certitude. And when confused by its externals you seek its inmost truth, it looks at you with tranquil assurance out of the depths of its never-ending smile and its easy lightheartedness. This tranquility is, perhaps, less real than it seems.

For my part I soon gave up all these conscious efforts which so interfered with the enjoyment of life. I let myself live simply, waiting confidently in the course of time for the revelations which the first moments had refused.

A week thus went by during which I had a feeling of "childlikeness," such as I had never before experienced.

I loved Tehura and told her so; it made her laugh—she knew it, very well.

She seemed to love me in return, but she never spoke of it—but sometimes at night the lightning graved furrows in the gold of the skin of Tehura. . . .

On the eighth day—to me it seemed as though we only for the first time had entered my hut—Tehura asked my permission to visit her mother at Faone. It was something that had been promised.

I sadly resigned myself. Tying several piastres in her handkerchief in order to defray the expenses of the journey and to buy some rum for her father, I led her to the stagecoach.

I had the feeling that it was a good-by forever.

The following days were full of torment. Solitude drove me from the hut and memories brought me back to it. I was unable to fix my thought upon any study. . . .

Another week passed, and Tehura returned.

Then a life filled to the full with happiness began. Happiness and work rose up together with the sun, radiant like it. The fold of Tehura's face flooded the interior of our hut and the landscape round about with joy and light. She no longer studied me, and I no longer studied her. She no longer concealed her love from me, and I no longer spoke to her of my love. We lived, both of us, in perfect simplicity.

How good it was in the morning to seek refreshment in the nearest brook, as did, I imagine, the first man and the first woman in Paradise.

Tahitian paradise, *navé navé fénua,*—land of delights!

And the Eve of this paradise became more and more docile, more loving. I was permeated with her fragrance—*noa noa*. She came into my life at the perfect hour. Earlier, I might, perhaps, not have understood her, and later it would have been too late. Today I understand how much I love her, and through her I enter into mysteries which hitherto remained inaccessible to me. But, for the moment, my intelligence does not yet reason out my discoveries; I do not classify them in my memory. It is to my emotions that Tehura confides all this that she tells me. It is in my emotions and impressions that I shall later find her words inscribed. By the daily telling of her life she leads me, more surely than it could have been done by any other way, to a full understanding of her race.

I am no longer conscious of days and hours, of good and evil. The happiness is so strange at times that it suppresses the very conception of it. I only know that all is good, because all is beautiful.

And Tehura never disturbs me when I work or when I dream. Instinctively she is then silent. She knows perfectly when she can speak without disturbing me. We talk of Europe and of Tahiti, and of God and of the gods. I instruct her. She in turn instructs me.

I had to go to Papeete for a day.

I had promised to return the same evening, but the coach which I took left me half way, and I had to do the rest on foot. It was one o'clock in the morning when I returned.

When I opened the door I saw with sinking heart that the light was extinguished. This in itself was not surprising, for at the moment we had

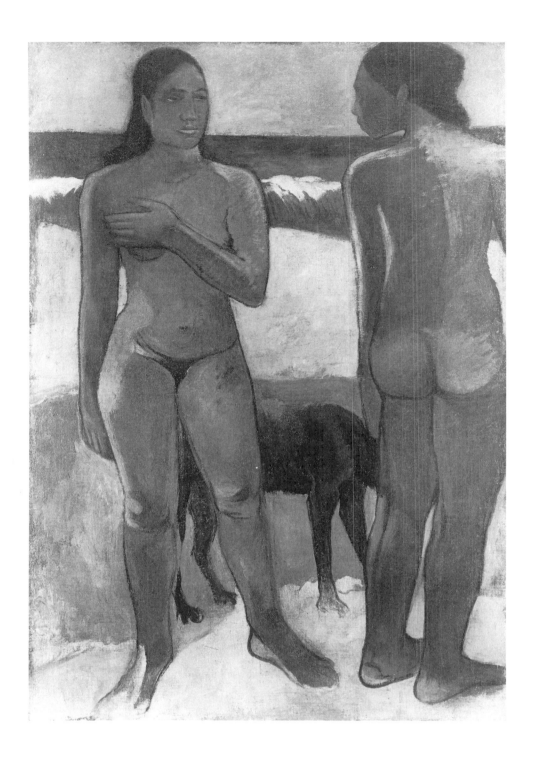

Two Tahitian Women on the Beach. ca.
1892. 35¾ × 25½″ (91 × 65 cm).
Honolulu Academy of Arts; Gift of Mrs.
Charles M. Cooke, 1933.

only very little light. The necessity of renewing our supply was one of the
reasons for my absence. But I trembled with a sudden feeling of appre-
hension and suspicion which I felt to be a presentiment—surely, the bird
had flown. . . .

Quickly, I struck a match, and I saw. . . .

Tehura, immobile, naked, lying face downward flat on the bed with
the eyes inordinately large with fear. She looked at me, and seemed not
to recognize me. As for myself I stood for some moments strangely uncertain. A contagion emanated from the terror of Tehura. I had the illusion that a phosphorescent light was streaming from her staring eyes.
Never had I seen her so beautiful, so tremulously beautiful. And then in
this half-light which was surely peopled for her with dangerous apparitions and terrifying suggestions, I was afraid to make any movement
which might increase the child's paroxysm of fright. How could I know
what at that moment I might seem to her? Might she not with my frightened face take me for one of the demons and specters, one of the Tu-
papaüs, with which the legends of her race people sleepless nights? Did
I really know who in truth she was herself? The intensity of fright which

COLORPLATE 55

had dominated her as the result of the physical and moral power of her superstitions had transformed her into a strange being, entirely different from anything I had known heretofore.

Finally she came to herself again, called me, and I did all I could to reason with her, to reassure her, to restore her confidence.

She listened sulkily to me, and with a voice in which sobs trembled she said, "Never leave me again so alone without light. . . . "

But fear scarcely slumbered, before jealousy awoke.

"What did you do in the city? You have been to see women, those who drink and dance on the marketplace, and who give themselves to officers, sailors, to all the world."

I would not quarrel with her, and the night was soft, soft and ardent, a night of the tropics. . . .

Tehura was sometimes very wise and affectionate, and then again quite filled with folly and frivolity. Two opposite beings, leaving out of account many others, infinitely varied, were mingled in one. They gave the lie, the one to the other; they succeeded one another suddenly with astonishing rapidity. She was not changeable; she was double, triple, multiple—the child of an ancient race.

One day, the eternal itinerant Jew, who ranges over islands as well as continents, arrived in the district with a box of trinkets of gilded copper.

He spread out his wares; everyone surrounded him.

A pair of earrings pass from hand to hand. The eyes of the women shine; all want to possess them.

Tehura knits her brows and looks at me. Her eyes speak very clearly. I pretend I do not understand.

She draws me aside in a corner.

"I want them."

I explain to her that in France those trifles have no value whatsoever, that *they are of copper*.

"I want them."

"But why? To pay twenty francs for such trash! It would be folly. No!"

"I want them."

And with passionate volubility, her eyes full of tears, she urges.

"What, would you not be ashamed to see the jewel in the ears of some other woman? Some one there is already speaking about selling his horse so that he may give the pair of earrings to his *vahiné*."

I will have nothing to do with this folly. For the second time I decline.

Tehura looks at me fixedly, and without saying another word begins to weep.

I go away, I return, and give the twenty francs to the Jew—and the sun reappears.

Two days later was Sunday. Tehura is dressing. The hair is washed with soap, then dried in the sun, and finally rubbed down with fragrant oil. In her best dress, one of my handkerchiefs in the hand, a flower behind the ear, the feet bare, she is going to the temple.

"And the earrings?" I ask.

With an expression of disdain, Tehura replies,

"They are of copper."

And laughing aloud she crosses the threshold of the hut, and suddenly becoming grave again continues her way.

At the hour of siesta, undressed, quite simple, we sleep on this day as on other days, side by side, or we dream. In her dream Tehura, perhaps, sees other earrings gleam.

I—I would forget all that I know and sleep always. . . .

Paul Gauguin

CAHIER POUR ALINE

"Genesis of a Painting"

1893

A young Kanaka girl is lying on her stomach, showing a part of her frightened face. She lies on a bed decorated with a blue *paréo* and a clear, chromium-yellow sheet. A violet purple background, sown with flowers like electric sparks; a rather strange figure stands next to the bed.

COLORPLATE 55

Seduced by a shape, a movement, I paint them with hardly any other concern than to do a nude piece. As is, the nude study is a bit indecent, nevertheless I want to make a chaste painting out of it which would render the Kanaka spirit, character, and tradition.

The *paréo* being intimately linked to the existence of a Kanaka, I use it as a bedcover. The sheet, of a fabric made from tree bark, must be yellow because when it is this color it inspires something unexpected in the spectator, because it suggests the lighting from a lamp, which spares me having to make a lamp-light effect. I've got to have a background which is a bit frightening. Violet is everywhere. That's the musical part of the painting which has been built up.

In this rather daring position, what can a young Kanaka girl be doing completely nude on a bed? Preparing herself for love? All of this is in her character, but it's indecent and I don't want it. To sleep! The love-making still indecent, will have been finished. I see only fear. What kind of fear? Certainly not the fear of a Susanna surprised by the elders. That doesn't exist in Oceania.

The *tùpapaù* (Spirit of the Dead) is all that's needed. For the Kanakas, it's a constant fear. At night, a lamp is always lit. No one walks out in the streets when there is no moon, unless someone has a lantern, and even then they go out in groups.

Once my *tùpapaù* is found I attach myself to it completely, and I make it the theme of my painting. The nude is relegated to the background.

What could a ghost be for a Kanaka woman? She doesn't know theater, doesn't read novels, and, when she thinks of a dead person, she necessarily thinks of someone she has already seen. My ghost can only be a small and very ordinary woman. Her hand reaches out as though to seize a prey.

The sense of the decorative leads me to sow the background with flowers. They are flowers of *tùpapaù*, phosphorescences, a sign that the ghost is taking care of you. Tahitian beliefs.

The title, *Manao tùpapaù,* has two meanings; either she thinks about the ghost, or the ghost thinks about her.

To recapitulate. The musical part: horizontal, wavy lines; harmonies of orange and blue, linked together with yellows and violets—their derivatives—lit up with greenish sparks. The literary part the Spirit of a living woman linked with the Spirit of the Dead. Night and Day.

This genesis is written for those who have always wanted to know the *whys* and *wherefores.*

Otherwise, it's simply a study of an Oceanian nude.

Paul Gauguin

NOA NOA

On Leaving Tahiti

1893–1895

I was compelled to return to France. Imperative family affairs called me back.

Farewell, hospitable land, land of delights, home of liberty and beauty!

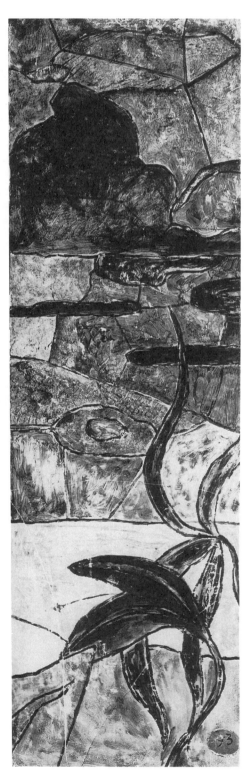

Tahitian Woman in a Landscape. 1893. Oil on glass. 45⅝ × 29½″ (116 × 75 cm). Musée d'Orsay, Paris.

I am leaving, older by two years, but twenty years younger; more *barbarian* than when I arrived, and yet much *wiser*.

Yes, indeed, the savages have taught many things to the man of an old civilization; these ignorant men have taught him much in the art of living and happiness.

Above all, they have taught me to know myself better; they have told me the deepest truth.

Was this thy secret, thou mysterious world? O, mysterious world of all light, thou hast made a light shine within me, and I have grown in admiration of thy antique beauty, which is the immemorial youth of nature. I have become better for having understood and having loved thy human soul—a flower which has ceased to bloom and whose fragrance no one henceforth will breathe.

As I left the quay, at the moment of going on board, I saw Tehura for the last time.

She had wept through many nights. Now she sat worn-out and sad, but calm, on a stone with her legs hanging down and her strong, little feet touching the soiled water.

The flower which she had put behind the ear in the morning had fallen wilted upon her knee.

Here and there were others like her, tired, silent, gloomy, watching without a thought the thick smoke of the ship which was bearing all of us—lovers of a day—far away, forever.

From the bridge of the ship as we were moving farther and farther away, it seemed to us that with the telescope we could still read on their lips these ancient Maori verses,

> Ye gentle breezes of the south and east
> That join in tender play above my head,
> Hasten to the neighboring isle.
> There you will find in the shadow of his favorite tree,
> Him who has abandoned me.
> Tell him that you have seen me weep.

Jean de Rotonchamp

PAUL GAUGUIN

On His Studio in Paris

1906

On 12 September 1893 the painter was called to Orléans for the settling of the will of one of his father's brothers, Isidore Gauguin, who had remained a bachelor. For his part, he inherited about 13,000 francs. Not a fortune, but it was some safety.

Thanks to this unexpected contribution, the artist was in a position to have his own home in Paris. He found an inexpensive apartment at 6, rue Vercingétorix, almost at the corner of the avenue—at that time the Chaussée du Maine—that seemed to satisfy his conditions of comfort and convenience.

Behind a large wall framing the door of a slaughterhouse was a large square courtyard, slightly shaded by a sickly tree and cluttered with blocks of stone and marble left over by hardworking sculptors' assistants. At the far end was a windowed shed made up of a ground floor

and then two floors above. At the top of the stairs and at the level of the
second floor was a balcony that connected with three studios. The third
and last of these, at the end of the balcony, was Gauguin's.

Many writers and painters visited it. All of them remember the small
entrance, the windows which were decorated with paintings by the master and offering this characteristic slogan: *"ici farùrù,"* (here there is love).
To the left of the entrance was a small room containing a fireplace and
a small, iron bed, which served as his bedroom. At the end of the ante-
chamber was the studio, the entrance to which was masked by a San
Germano door curtain.

This rather vast room, which was lit from the west through a lateral
window that had been completely painted over with chrome yellow—
no. 1 chrome—immediately gave one a sensation of the strange and the
unexpected. On the walls, which were covered with barbaric canvases,
were interlaced weapons of war: truncheons, boomerangs, axes, picks,
lances, all made from an unknown wood that was dark red, orange, and
black.

In fact, the only furniture one saw other than the tools of his profession, was a fairly good piano, which, moreover, the painter did not know
how to play, and a heavily used sofa, in the purest Louis-Philippe style.

In a corner there was an enormous, 18 × 24 format camera, mounted on legs. On the unused fireplace seashells and mineral samples were displayed.

At the fragile tinkling of a primitive bell, a superbly beautiful mulatto lady with burning eyes whom Gauguin had met in Paris, but who was of Javanese origin, appeared before the visitor. A shivering monkey was curled up among the easels and, in this exotic environment, recalling the pied-à-terre of the naval officer or the intermittent home of the explorer, one felt one was very far from Paris.

Friends and the curious flowed in and out incessantly. Gauguin, now an aristocrat, was having his day, just like an aspirant to the medal of honor. He gave parties, had teas, had little cakes handed around by the refined rival of Téhoura, who did so with a silent dignity. Among the regular visitors were Julien Leclercq, who was at that time infatuated with palmistry, Charles Morice, Paul Roinard, other people of letters more or less familiar at the house, Aristide Maillol, who at the time wove original decorative tapestries, and a certain number of young artists who were very impressed by Gauguin's powerful originality.

Thadée Natanson

PEINTS A LEUR TOUR

"Gauguin"

1948

Despite everything Paul Gauguin said, his easy style, his verve, and a kind of joviality added to his appeal. At the brasserie he tossed off his drink, which was often a double, as though he were drinking from a tankard, and I remember a gesture he once made, to give someone a light, that was broad enough for him to have brandished a torch. On Mallarmé's Tuesdays—he engraved a very agreeable portrait of Mallarmé—when he

COLORPLATE 86

Paul Roinard (1856–1910), Symbolist poet. Aristide Maillol (1861–1944), sculptor who was primarily a painter committed to decorative stylization when he received encouragement from Gauguin around 1893–1894.

Thadée Natanson (1868–1951), Polish-born journalist and art collector who, with his two brothers, founded the influential Revue Blanche *in 1891, presenting articles by such notable writers as Mallarmé, Proust, and Wilde.*

By no later than 1887, Mallarmé had begun to host gatherings of notable literary and artistic figures on Tuesday evenings.

put in an appearance there, he listened to himself a little and we listened to him a lot. We were so close to everything that happened to him that we were sorry to see that on his feet, in place of the all-too-ordinary slippers, he did not wear the hand-sculpted clogs we had learned he wore in Pont-Aven.

How much I prefer the image that remained with me of Gauguin, who years later came back to us from Tahiti. Was this because he had suffered so much there? But the man seemed so much wiser. And yet all the trials and the tribulations that he complained of seemed much more attributable to his own character than to the country's or to the natives'. That he went so far to find this illusion seems lamentable and his new-found wisdom seemed to diminish him. Nevertheless, he had submitted to his destiny. One never falls from paradise except by one's own fault, and the Adam that was banished remains much more compelling than the one who vegetated beatifically before the Fall. For Gauguin, who thought of nothing more than to regain what was his own, returned from the islands having gained much in naturalness and simplicity, and nothing was more touching than the attachment he maintained to the enchantment of those happy isles, the memory of which made his eyes shine, as did the hope they gave him. Moreover, his wisdom seemed much like maturity—despite the strangeness of the wooden sculptures and the engravings or the monotypes that he brought back from his voyages, and, similarly, despite the dictums and the maxims of the far-off isles that he liked to note and then comment upon. Paris was no more than a ladder on the route to a happy life that he never doubted he would recover. All the while, he lived more simply than anyone could have feared, and if he wore a fur vest it was because since returning from his trip to the Pacific countries he suffered from the cold of Montmartre. He maintained a swaggering yet melancholy air, and he acknowledged his poverty more naturally if not more easily than before, though there were many who would have been more than happy to help. The painter did not have less faith than that in the future, in the results that his friends hoped for from a sale they talked about all the time and that would unfortunately disappoint his entourage more than himself. And just before his departure one could hear him speak much more simply, almost carefully avoiding too-general ideas. His words, more precise, would fix objectives more exactly.

The memories of his long stay abroad, which I had the pleasure of hearing him recount, made the Polynesian villages seem similar to those of Finistère, and the huts on the islands did not seem so different from the cottages of Brittany. At least it seemed that he liked the residents of the two places for reasons not without similarity and for the ingenuousness they have in common. It did not seem that he was particularly aware of the difference in virtue, or, further, of the difference in their religions; Tahitians, both male and female, seeming to have none other than sensual love.

Paul Gauguin did not have to be persuaded to bring back to life the number of landscapes and small scenes of the paradise he abandoned but would regain. He seized any pretext for this, the way lovers always come back to the same goal. Generally, he began by laughing only to finish in a serious tone marked even with melancholy, when his voice could be heard trembling with nostalgia. In particular, I remember him repeating the story of an excursion into the mountains where he had followed this young native, who was strongly attached to him, to a very old, wild rosewood tree the youth had found, which would provide a denser and richer material for the sculptors than the trees of the plains. The story, without going into too much detail, of his climb up a narrow footpath in blazing sunlight behind the young man who often turned around to smile at his big, white friend, was much like a poem, even before the surprise of the rosewood tree, which was left to blossom in the end.

Without the storyteller stressing it at all, we were disturbed, indeed more than he, by the ambiguous sensuality that radiated from the brilliant back of the youth to the teeth of his smile, of which the painter only said that they were hardly different from the body and the smile of his companions of the same age. The exotic site, with almost nothing obvious, did not lack character. It is one of the most happy Gauguins from Tahiti that I remember.

Charles Merki

MERCURE DE FRANCE

"Apologia for Painting"

June 1893

This carnival of painting, with nothing more to recommend it, takes on another aspect with M. Gauguin. M. Gauguin represents Idéiste—or Symbolist, as one prefers—art. The color here is not two inches thick, but his brutality is perhaps more disconcerting. It has been said that M. Gauguin was imitating stained glass. That opinion is as good as another and hurts no one. Hyperbolic landscapes, of a savagery that no phenomenon of vision can excuse, are dotted with gingerbread men. Meaningful positions, plates of spinach, bad drawing, great ideas, Bob's doodles on his schoolbook covers. At present, M. Gauguin is devoting himself to painting negresses. We will find him again, one of these mornings, with a complete change of wonders, and we will then speak of him again. What we can say today about his *Jacob Wrestling with the Angel* is that, if Jacob and the angel are deformed in the Breton women's minds, the Breton women have been similarly deformed in the painter's mind, for they are as badly turned out as the rest.

Merki is referring to a recent group exhibition at Le Barc de Boutteville.

Charles Morice

PAUL GAUGUIN

On the Tahiti Exhibition

1919

I saw him again at the opening of his big exhibition of 1893, when he returned from his first trip to Tahiti.

Singularly complex was the Gauguin of this solemn hour, of this occasion that would irrevocably decide his future, the hour of his greatest hopes and greatest fears.

In the vast gallery where the walls were aflame with his vision in painting, he watched the people, he listened. Soon he had no doubt: nobody understood. It was the definitive separation between him and Paris; all his grand projects were ruined, and, perhaps the most cruel wound of all for this overly proud man, he had to acknowledge that he had devised his plans poorly. Had he not dreamed of being the prophet who, unappreciated by philistines incapable of understanding the genius at the moment, goes away in search of perspective and returns greater than ever? "That my flight be in defeat," he said, "so that my return will be a victory."

And the return aggravated the defeat of the departure, irremissibly.

Nothing can make one doubt the anguish that gnawed at his heart. Following an image of which he was naively fond, to which he willingly returned, he was the Indian who smiles throughout torture. Not for an instant, it must be said, in the midst of universal repudiation, did he doubt that he was right against the rest. And maybe, so as not to bend, he took refuge in this idea. Whatever the enormous error of the present, he had the future.

And from the moment he acquired this certainty that nobody wanted him, that nobody would even consent to discuss it, he showed an inalterable serenity, smiling so no one could see anything forced in his smile, asking his friends their opinions, discussing them with a completely open mind, gaily, without the slightest bitterness.

Near the end of this ill-fated day, going to the door with M. Degas, who spoke to him of his admiration, he did not respond to him; but as the illustrious old master was leaving:

"Monsieur Degas, you are forgetting your cane," said Gauguin, indeed handing him a cane, but a cane he had sculpted himself, that was on display there, and that he had just taken off the wall.

And I truly believe that, during the whole month the exhibition ran, he came every day and listened assiduously to the inept gibes of which he bore the pain, although the press, taking care not to leave him the least doubt, the least hope, pointed him out ironically, by minute descriptions of his person.

Charles Morice

EXPOSITION D'OEUVRES RECENTES DE PAUL GAUGUIN

Preface

November 1893

Hina said to Téfatou:
"Make man come back to life when he is dead."
The God of the earth answered the Goddess of the moon:
"No, I shall not make him live again. Man will die, vegetation will die, as will everything that lives from it; earth will die, earth will end, it will end never to live again."
Hina answered:
"Do as you please; as for me, I shall make the moon live again."
And what Hina possessed, continued to be; what Téfatou possessed, perished, and man had to die. . . .
From the luminous shores of Tahiti and from amongst this race of fishermen who, in the undeniable luxuriance of a very old and very young nature, dream only of terrible myths—received with resignation—of the immemorial past or the eternal becoming, Gauguin left for the island's interior. He arrived at the foot of the Aroral, the mountain which touches the sky, when he saw the voluptuous and beautiful moon rise, kissing the summit of the rough earth darkening in the dusk. Then the legend of this daily spectacle, born right then in dreamy souls, awak-

Hina Te Fatou (The Moon and the Earth).
1893. Oil on burlap. 45 × 24½" (114.3 ×
62.2 cm). The Museum of Modern Art,
New York; Lillie P. Bliss Collection.

ened in the painter's soul—a wild and deep soul as well. He heard Hina
say to Téfatou:

"Make man come back to life when he is dead."

He understood the female element's tricky counsel given to the male
element—the counsel of false sympathy that sterilizes—and he admired
the rebellious generosity of the fierce God because life only fertilizes it-

self in death and, for having refused to die, the moon became a pale, useless specter of life. And what he heard and understood is what the painter painted in this composition that he called *Hina and Téfatou*, excellently indicative of his talents and his intentions: a powerful head of God upon which nature has conferred all the conscious pride of its power, a glorious face of God, breaking the last lines of the horizon and on the threshold of the world. A caressing, frail woman gently seized the God by the hair and told him:

"Make man live again when he is dead . . . ," and the wrathful, yet not cruel, lips of the god are about to open to answer:

"No, I shall not make him live again. . . ." Man will die.

This painting, as I was saying, is indicative of the talents and intentions of this artist.

The poet Albert Aurier, speaking of Gauguin specifically, wrote; "the work of art will be *Idéiste* since its sole ideal will be the expression of Idea, *Symbolist* since it will express this idea through forms, *Synthetic* since it will inscribe these forms—these signs—according to a mode of general understanding, *subjective* since the idea therein will never be considered as an object as such but rather as a sign of the idea perceived by the subject, and *decorative*."

All of these characteristics essential to Gauguin's painting are borne out in a striking manner in the composition whose genesis I was speaking of earlier—and the elements of symbol, subjectivity, and decoration should be stressed. But this is not the place for subtle aesthetic ramblings. The work itself speaks loudly and clearly enough to your eyes, developing out of its proximity to paintings and commenting on itself with its own quite rich and frank eloquence—especially for those of us who did not know much about foliage other than that of Meudon Forest, because of its exotic, luxuriant enormity.

We were a bit amazed three years ago when Gauguin left France (by an instinctive predilection that I do not want to explain here) and chose a beautiful exile for himself in Tahiti. We were amazed that a painter—above all, a creator like him—looked outside of our customary landscape for the pretext of his creation. "Brittany and Provence are inexhaustible," a well-known artist said jokingly about this subject, "and the lone hill of Montmartre is enough for my dreams . . . ," and this was a bit scandalous, a big mistake.

Gauguin did not go there to find spiritual renewal through "new subjects." He would content himself, perhaps more than anyone else, with the indefiniteness of the same place or the same face, from which he knew, each time, how to make a rendering never before seen. But beside the qualities of personal and spiritual invention and the in-depth intuition that characterize his temperament, he has expansive, bountiful, and big-hearted faculties for which the narrow life and factitious splendor of our Western civilization is unsuitable.

He becomes irritated with our habits, our prejudices, our conventions in art and in everything else, and with our mimetic traditions, which particularly oppress painting. He wants to find, for himself, his own poetry and expression: He wants to be, according to a figure of speech which recently pleased me, "both the miner and the goldsmith of his gold."

This is why he took his quest so far away: to forget us and to find the sole concern for his artistic preferences. Add to this the fact that, regarding his ancestry, this late descendant of the Incas was somewhat justly intolerant of our vapid salon manners and the proper lines of our English gardens. Finally, let us not forget that, having once been a sailor for a long time, he kept in his Indian eyes the bedazzlement of the pit-

COLORPLATE 65. *Te Fare Hymenee (The House of Hymns)*. 1892. 19⅝ × 35⅝″ (50 × 90 cm).
Josefowitz Collection.

COLORPLATE 66. *Nafea Faa Ipoipo? (When Will You Marry?)*. 1892. 41¼ × 30½″ (105 × 77.5 cm).
Rudolf Staechelin Foundation, Basel. Photo: Hans Hinz.

COLORPLATE 67. *Two Women on the Beach.* 1891. 27⅛ × 36″ (69 × 91.5 cm).
Musée d'Orsay, Paris.

COLORPLATE 68. *Te Nave Nave Fenua (Delightful Land)*. 1892. 35¾ × 28¼″ (91 × 72 cm).
Ohara Museum of Art, Kurashiki, Japan.

COLORPLATE 69. *Parau na te Varua Ino (Words of the Devil)*. 1892. 36⅛ × 27″ (91.5 × 70 cm).
National Gallery of Art, Washington, D.C.; Gift of the W. Averell Harriman Foundation in memory of
Marie N. Harriman.

COLORPLATE 70. *Aha oe Feii? (What! Are You Jealous?).* 1892. 26 × 35″ (66 × 89 cm).
The Pushkin Museum, Moscow.

COLORPLATE 71. *Fatata te Miti (By the Sea)*. 1892. 26¾ × 36″ (68 × 92 cm).
National Gallery of Art, Washington, D.C.; Chester Dale Collection.

COLORPLATE 72. *Matamoe (Landscape with Peacocks)*. 1892. 45½ × 33¾″ (115 × 86 cm).
The Pushkin Museum, Moscow.

iless sun and of its lively, vegetal, animal, and human reflection. The flames of the tropical flowers, with beautiful human animals, strong, agile, and naive in their physical candor, lying under the opaque foliage, left in his memory a transporting enchantment that no other luxury could extinguish. The decorative painter remembered this unique decor: he brings it back to us.

He brings us a natural world and, in this vast countryside that is unified in spite of its variety, an entire, strange civilization—or so it seems, because it is foreign to ours—that we would readily call (would we not?) barbaric.

Black, feminine forms; the sun has burned them, but it has penetrated them as well! It lives in them, it radiates from them, and these shadowy forms conceal the most intense, luminous warmth. And how they harmonize with the boldness of these flowers and the vigor of these trees, with the complete drunkenness of this loving, prolific, crazy nature!

Really, this painting (the opportunity to be happy!) is like a rite in a religion of joy. Joy, often mysterious, sometimes altered with terror. Look at the painting *To Frighten*: someone is telling a chilling tale and, in the naiveté of one of the listeners, the legend takes shape; in her credulity she distorts nature horribly with enlarged, phosphorescent eyes. The soft night of Tahiti is populated with fearful, unknown, and unnamable beings, with ancient and fallen divinities, or with the ancient dead looking on.... The spirit of the dead! It inhabits and subtilizes this admirable composition; *The Spirit of the Dead Watching*, in which the very same eyes, lit with the phosphorous of fear, make the androgynous little girl lying there toss in her half-sleep; she can no longer rest peacefully because the dead return—dead lovers or dead gods.

COLORPLATE 55

Tahiti was calling both Gauguin the painter and poet, poet and sculptor; he found once again the land of his dreams. But he did not arrive there with a naked soul! The only land is that of thought, and the place which lets our thought most freely gambol about we call our homeland. For the reasons I have mentioned, Gauguin was able to choose the place of innocence, grandeur, splendor, and calm where he could best give his ambition a pretext for subjective decoration. But his work would be a bad guide to the *Island* if your soul were not kin to his. Do you think you would see Hina and Téfatou as he did? He brings you a race, a religion remote in its origins and developed to a point that, in effect, brings it to the dawn of Christianity—a race, a religion, a world—and an *oeuvre*! Where will you look for a point of comparison? Where will you find a point in common between his vision and yours?

I am mistaken.

This point in common exists: It is the general element (and all the more general because it is personal), which is the human element in Gauguin's work.

Remember how he interpreted Brittany. The black Calvary, the yellow Christ? What is left of this place, seen, breathed, listened-to, except for the atmosphere?

COLORPLATE 36

Nothing more, in fact, though it is enough sufficiently and precisely to name the poetic and pictorial reverie; that is why Gauguin—revealer of the meaning of things as seen in his eyes at a chosen site— is a great painter and a great poet. In the landscapes he traverses, he asks only for a pretext, an allusion to an episode in the perpetual drama that he contemplates: Now this is in its essence human, universal. It is up to you to take pleasure and to suffer deliciously from it.

His will, this time, was to express an infant yet virile race in an eternally youthful nature. For this, he made of himself a savage, a naturalized Maori—without ever ceasing to be himself, an artist. He said that his work was as much that of his friends over there as his own, and at the cost of such audacious divinations, such genial distortions! Let him look back and uncover for us—with a wonder of intelligence and art—the former Tahiti, the Tahiti before our terrible sailors and the fragrant bouquet of M. Pierre Loti, the Tahiti where the gods slept in the deep seas and, for the insult of an imprudent fisherman, would bring their heads to the peaceful ocean's surface and let loose the floods—or let him awaken the present life of this wisely lazy people; the pain taken is, more or less, the same. For this race of defiant antelopes, the present time is not easier to penetrate than the deep fogs of antiquity. Past and present, how far away they are for us! And for a man—even an artist—cradled in our lies, what an effort to penetrate these natural truths, so remote from us in space and time!

He wanted to confront these two civilizations—for which, yet again! a great artist was the link—in one of his most extraordinary compositions:

Two young women, two Tahitian women, their countenances marked by naive piety, contemplate this apparition with the sincere innocence that life itself will never touch, never deflower: a woman—another woman—of a slightly superhuman stature, yet carrying on her shoulder a child who, with a tender gesture, rests his head on the head of his mother. Around the two heads the divine halo is faintly visible. Behind the worshipping female spectators with clasped hands, an angel stands among the flowers, rich and calm, a flower himself:

Ia orana Maria: Ave Maria.

And the sun and the flora, all around, pray as well, powerfully, softly, odorously (*noa-noa*), subtle as the smile of the Virgin herself—a smile in which religion and pleasure coexist, the majesty and the mischievousness of goddess and woman, such as these natural souls could conceive them.

François Thiébault-Sisson

LE TEMPS

"Les Petits Salons"

2 December 1893

In the Tahitian scenes that M. Gauguin is exhibiting in the rue Laffitte, at M. Durand-Ruel's, scientific painting triumphs, but not a single landscape recedes, not a single figure exists in space. The backgrounds and foregrounds merge into one another, and the absence of atmosphere, in all the views of the country he shows us, is so clearly pronounced, so flagrant, that one feels, if one looks at them too long, an indefinable malaise.

Yet what artist would be more gifted if exclusively literary friendships did not cloud his judgment and paralyze the instinctive sense of painting that he has? If the lack of air and light in his canvases did not mute his color, one would keenly savor, here and there, certain delicate relations between tones, certain happy and full harmonies. If he consented to reproduce, instead of distorting, nature, what magnificent pieces he would paint! What magnificent pieces he has painted when he was content to observe his model without second thoughts and to translate simply what he saw! Why must we find, beside superlatively constructed and modeled pieces, like his young girls on the shore and his delectable portrait of a woman, such shapeless ones? Why has the artist so far forgotten himself as to see in the Tahitian woman of today, as in the Tahitian woman of old, only a female quadrumane?

Pierre Loti, pseudonym for Julien Viaud (1850–1923), a naval officer who spent a short time in Tahiti in 1872 and transformed his diary notes into a popular novel published as Rarahu *in 1880 and brought out subsequently, from 1882, as* The Marriage of Loti. *Vincent van Gogh may have brought it to Gauguin's attention in 1888; if not, Bernard had done so by early 1890.*

COLORPLATE 57

François Thiébault-Sisson (b. 1856), brilliant art critic for Le Temps, *who was an important innovator in the genre of the interview.*

COLORPLATE 70

Charles Morice

MERCURE DE FRANCE

"Paul Gauguin"

December 1893

Two artistic events of the greatest significance have just taken place simultaneously, harmonically: the day that Ibsen's *Enemy of the People* was performed on a Parisian stage, there opened the exhibition of the paintings and sculptures that Paul Gauguin brought back from Tahiti.

At the Oeuvre Theater and at Durand-Ruel's the same drama was being enacted.

With a new, simple dramatic form, in a new country—at least to us—Ibsen shows us a man suffering for the truth. Gauguin is at once the hero and the author of a wholly similar tragedy. He has chosen a country, a setting, a race unknown to the West to express his personal artistic truth. In this chosen environment, the artist speaks freely, with the natural splendor of his dream of beauty. The setting is even simpler than the playwright's, just as the liberties he takes are, it is true, bolder, more individual. And yet, in order to understand him, to follow him into the daring of his simplifications, need we make any effort other than to accept the total independence that is the painter's first right—as it is the poet's—and to forget, as we enter his space, the preferences, the habits of the greatest artists, as well as the irrational conventions of the least of them? This is the effort we were unwilling to make. And I am speaking here much less of the public—easily shaped and malleable despite their preconceptions—than of the special world of art, of the artists themselves, the critics, certain journalists, and the art-workers. Bad faith and foolishness have made a fine harmony there. Oh! what nonsense has been uttered, hypocritically or guilelessly, these last few days in rue Lafitte! Oh! what one reads, beneath the most diverse signatures in the most knowledgeable daily newspapers! Everything played a part, and because I had the honor to write the preface to the catalogue for Gauguin's exhibition, I was called, in *Libre Parole*, an "*Israelite*-aesthete!" One probably has to be Jewish to utter an opinion, even only in art, that is condemned by M. Dumont's [sic] coadjutors. Yet, I am not Jewish.

Will it be said that Gauguin's adventure—his denial by idiot justice or enlightened hostility—is the usual story of all true artists? That they were all long-opposed? That they all had to struggle against the official pontificators who were unwilling to make way for the newcomers? That the art critics, once they have established their positions, do not gladly consent to giving them up, and frown severely upon the innovators? Granted. But there is much more, something most particular, most personal. Gauguin is no beginner; his *oeuvre* is large, single in conception, multiple in form and matter—painter, sculptor, ceramist. His work has attracted attention for some time: anyone who is interested in matters of art has seen it, knows it. It has excited many antipathies without the artist's reaping the usual benefits from the din of battle. It has met with some sympathies, the most precious kind, the kind that have meant victory for others, for a Rodin, a Monet. Octave Mirbeau, for example, praised Gauguin enthusiastically, as he praised these two. But the same effort did not have the same success three times. Other critics, joining the bandwagon and out to be avant-garde, also proclaimed Gauguin's genius, in a first movement that they believed to be good and that would position them well. Soon they ran out of breath, and since they did not

Henrik Ibsen (1828–1906), Norwegian playwright whose An Enemy of the People *(1882), concerns a man of truth at odds with a polluted society.*

Edouard Drumont (1844–1917), publisher of the viciously anti-Semitic newspaper, La Parole Libre.

know why they liked Gauguin, they stopped liking him for the same reason—unless they were giving in to the badgering of those who thought they could benefit from the Master's absence, his three-year stay in Tahiti. Some of them maintained that they had introduced him, others, that they had surpassed him. Bad critics and spurious artists are made for one another.

Nevertheless, Gauguin had an unexpected moment of sadness on his return, when he found them so solidly united against him. He had worked so sincerely, so valiantly out there in the great solitude that his mind had become, among that ingenuous race and beneath the generous sun! Now that he was returning with his work completed, was he not entitled, however little, to expect a welcome as sincere as his endeavor? Would we not be grateful for this transposition of a dream from one hemisphere to the other, for this newly revealed nature, this unknown race, both of them penetrated by his gaze and recombined by his thought, this transposition that he added to the treasures of our ancient riches?

Naive man! In three years the "art world" had followed its bent, which is not toward the better. The trace that the departed had left, nonetheless, in people's minds, with his beliefs and his creations, had made easier the task of the clever, the cunning, those who do not seek on their own, but exploit the discoveries of others and declare them definitive—which is, in art, the most shameless of lies—and thus, with their detestable ingenuities, they close eyes that were beginning to open, minds that were about to understand. The artistic establishment, using any method, had also buttressed its strength, and tradesmen—the honorable M. Valadon, for example—were decorated in the name of the boldest art, so that they would become the establishment middlemen for establishment art. At the Luxembourg, Gauguin met again a certain Delaherche, his former cook—or his firer: he ran into him *with* the artists, and asked himself what the pottery trade was doing in a museum of painting and sculpture: why didn't M. Delaherche go parade his products at Bing's instead, and compete with the Japanese, whose lacquer he borrows?

Finally—and despite the legitimate, if exceptional glory of a few famous idealists who, after all, have only conquered the public's favor with a long run of masterpieces and years, or, if they are younger, have only a very small circle of admirers—the taste is hardly for high art, in these days of Naturalism's interminable death-throes. It is negative art that reigns, and sordid art, its natural substitute. I think the obscene song has not flung the filth of its refrains in everyone's memory in vain. Paris is an enormous café concert, to which the annual salons—with some necessary exceptions—provide very suitable surroundings. Sorry days.

And Gauguin melancholically remembers his happy life, in the great beyond, when he worked with the fine frenzy of a poet drunk with his poem—far from our decadence and its coteries, and its cabals.... Perhaps he will leave again. And it will be we who will have driven him away. He is already saying: "I would not like to see any more Europeans."

In the meantime, the liars and the thieves will continue their factitious but offensive triumphs. A great artist—that one!—used to say, smiling, of one of them: "He flies with our wings."

Oh! if it were always possible to smile!

And yet this much-discussed *oeuvre* will have been seen, this lover of truth will have been heard once more: and what matter if he is a martyr to his love? An artist's joy and victory, like his homeland, are in himself—his joy and victory, in the testimony he can bear to himself, his most severe judge, that he has expressed his dream, and his homeland in that dream. Nothing is in vain. Embattled, even denied, today, and whether he stays or goes, Gauguin will have largely contributed to the renewal, the recovery of contemporary art.

Around him or after him, the struggle will be less arduous for the sincere few who follow him—Sérusier, Ranson, Denis, Vuillard, etc. . . . Even for those who pursue a similar goal of personal creation, albeit along other paths and by other means, he will not have spoken in vain. Some noble alliances are possible . . .

The meaning of his words: to faithfully obey one's inner necessities, to sacrifice nothing to external necessities; not to be a slave to nature, but to conquer her, to use her only as a pretext for the creation of the feeling or thought that enchants; to see the perceptible world as an immense riddle whose word is within us, a multiple word, varied word, as human essences are multiple and varied; to break free, therefore, if one is a painter, from every convention of color and line, if one is a poet, from every common habit of thought and language; finally to possess matter without allowing oneself to be possessed by her. The painter has the right to make of lines and colors whatever he wishes, provided that he has a sense of the overall harmony and that his will is governed by a logical and individual conception. He has the right to deform, provided that he has the desire and the power to symbolize. To him, nature is the prey that he wants to conquer. But of what does the conquest consist? Of revelation. The painter and the poet are the revealers of their conception of the infinite. For this revelation, any means they deem appropriate are legitimate. Let us speak here only of the painters' means. Thoughts are cast with immeasurable speed from their minds into the sight—face or landscape—that they have before their eyes, and to find in it, to extract the thought from the sight, they clear away, simplify, synthesize, they brush aside everything that might obscure from them a clear vision of the object, they deform—that is, they correct everything that would divert them from the object's reality. Try to recognize in objective nature the landscape wherein Gauguin has seen only his thought! Go then to Tahiti, you photographers, with your most sensitive plates: it is to be feared that the sun will not reveal to you what it has to this painter . . .

A red earth, a blue tree, shadowless light. . . . Gauguin dared to do that: one is astonished . . .

He had dared to do it well before Tahiti, since Brittany, many years ago.

The Yellow Christ. From yellow moors there rises a cross, whereon a yellow Christ eternally dies. The land around it is rich, and the color of the sheaves that makes the painting harmonize. In this luxuriance, human brutes rest or move, indifferent or joyous. At the foot of the cross, but with their backs to it, slack, shabby women are sitting, animals tired of childbearing; in the background, some little girls gaily climb over a boundary wall: and everything is joyous or indifferent, save the yellow Christ who eternally dies on the cross. He could have not come! His death agony has not affected the luxuriance of the land, has not consoled the shabby ones tired of childbearing, has not interrupted the gay frolics, and joy, sadness, indifference; everything that comes after him is as it was before him.

Bonjour, Monsieur Gauguin. Storm clouds and, on the ground, as if in movement, a color like that of fixed lightning. A man, tempestuous according to the hour and the place, comes to the edge of the plain toward the gate that a woman is passing, apprehensive about the bad weather and visibly astonished by the passer-by who is unconcerned about it. And, half turned toward him, hesitating whether to approach or flee him, disconcerted by the man's hard and heavy gaze, she greets him with a pretty gesture: "Good day, monsieur Gauguin." How much more at home this wandering Breton is, in this stormy Brittany, than the little Breton herself hurrying home, he who will continue walking.

But we may say that the soul of this Peruvian, born in love with the sun, with strength, and with the simplicity that is tractable to all the spir-

COLORPLATE 36

COLORPLATE 19

221

itual desires, found its essential element in Tahiti. An instinct that did not deceive him called him there. He has been able to see, to speak the savage beauty, the natural nobility, not yet affected by the phosphorescence of our decay, of those distant races at whom our white vanity believes itself entitled to smile; he has been able to understand the often terrifying, often, also, profound naiveté of their legends; he has loved the vital openness of this existence in the open air; he shared it morally as well as physically.

Noa noa. Flowers, flowers, trees that are flowers, and the little ground one sees is made of flowering colors. The ardent tranquillity of a nature too proud of its richness to show it to anyone: for there is no human or even animal trace. A rivalization of bold and sumptuous joy among these infinitely varied essences. And this painting breathes the fresh and spiced scent of the whole island; *Noa noa*, fragrant.

Nave nave fenua. This is the same land, the delightful land. It is the Tahitian Eden. But here, the painter's eye, though it remains faithful to feeling, obeys a poetic thought, and the painting takes shape. A naked, powerful, and very gentle woman catches, with a timid gesture, flowers like the dazzling eyes of peacock feathers, flowers of pride. She is about to pluck them, and a winged monster, black with red wings, whispers the evil counsel in her ears.

COLORPLATE 68

Manao tupapau. The spirit watches. Beneath every manifestation of life lies a mystery. The noonday demon, the demon of the living, opens his eyes at the hour of sun and action. The midnight demon, the spirit of the dead, keeps vigil in the dream-hour. It is a tropical night. Stretched out on her stomach, on brilliantly colored cloths, a young woman, a maiden, an androgyne, is disturbed—by nothing, by the hour's sound— or by the great frightened and frightening eyes shining there, at the foot of the bed, which seem to see fearful apparitions from which the little girl is turning away. The spirit of the dead keeps vigil. The eyes are aware, with the first glance, of what this painting stands for, its technique, how it commands attention with its splendor of lines and colors, as much as the singular beauty of the poem that is concealed within it. It is perhaps the wonder of the exhibition. The painter has put into this naked woman's body all the luminous heat of the forest blazing with flowers, and all the languorous, innocent lewdness of this childlike and wise race; for whom pleasure is the only serious matter in life—and also the dread of some terrible secret that the dreamer would exorcise with caresses. These lines from Baudelaire offer the best commentary on *Manao tupapau*:

COLORPLATE 55

> Wilderness and desert haunt
> the tumult of your hair;
> without a word, your lips propose
> the riddle of the Sphinx;
>
> and when you move, the shifting scent—
> as if a censer swayed—
> prepares the advent of your flesh:
> the night is warm with you.
>
> *   *   *
>
> there is a throbbing intercourse
> between your breasts and thighs—
> the very cushions are enticed
> by your slow attitudes.

These verses are excerpted from Baudelaire's "Chanson d'après-midi" from Richard Howard's translation of Les Fleurs du Mal.

"This painting," a very astute critic said to me—

is at the extreme edge of literature: is that not its failing? By dint of dominating matter, of rekneading it and refashioning it

Evidently the astute critic to whom Morice refers was Gauguin, since these lines from Poe's Marginalia *are quoted at the opening of Gauguin's* Cahier pour Aline. *In 1897 Gauguin put these same passages into* Diverses Choses.

as he sees fit, does the artist not exempt himself somewhat arbitrarily from the providential laws of his art? does he not evade certain difficulties? I am well aware that E. Poe said: "It is this thorough harmony of an imaginative work which so often causes it to be undervalued by the thoughtless, through the character of *obviousness* which is superinduced." But he was speaking chiefly of imaginative literary works, and, in order to evoke conceptions of pure written poems, it seems that Gauguin resolved himself to an obstinate course of peculiarity that demands from us a too-complete submission . . .

The same E. Poe also said: "There is no exquisite Beauty which has not some strangeness in its proportions." And he said: "The clay is, in fact, the slave of the artist. It belongs to him." And also, "He is only the former [artist] who can carry his most shadowy precepts into successful application." I do not think that E. Poe had only written poetry in mind. These are the fundamental laws of art in general. The Primitives themselves—the great deformers, the great simplifiers—were not aware of them. To do as they did—consider nature as the subject of our thought, seek harmony only within the composed work and between its various parts, without concern for the objective exteriority that served as pretext for it—is not to imitate them. They imitated that nature that perpetuates its creation according to certain laws wherein we are often tempted to see only whims, that nature that deforms as it sees fit, multiplies monsters, only continually to reduce them to infinitely simplified lines. To imitate nature, to absorb her secrets, to steal her processes, to produce an incalculable detail subordinated to an invincible unity—that is the soul and foundation of all the arts. Nature harmonizes the colors of the animals' coats and of feathers, and those of trees and flowers, moving lines and motionless lines, the song of birds and the brilliance of light, the sound of water, which is not the same in the morning and in the evening, the dramas of hunger and love, which succeed each other in the forest with the instants of day and night: all at the same time, she is making painting, sculpture, music, and literature. The union of all the arts is the supreme wish of human genius, and it will, perhaps, be the work of the imagined being whom Stéphane Mallarmé calls "the supreme primitive man," that is, the man who has returned to and is retempered by the essential laws, the precepts that constitute life, but yet has lost nothing of the conquests amassed by the centuries. This is why every great painter is a great poet. This is why, too, the poets can, from the broad domain where they practice their art, consider more freely, I believe, than any other artist the more particular domains of the other arts, and like, for example, painters who are very different from one another: these differences resolve into harmony in the poet's conception.

And would it not be an excellent critical method, one that would consist of seeking correspondences between the art one practices and that which one studies? If a painter wishes to understand Flaubert, he will have to give himself over to great frescoes, but M. Daudet will evoke only a vignette, and M. Loti, only a chromo. All the same, Gauguin suggests to me great lyric poetry, the kind that breaks free of the apparent requirements of the craft, the too strict necessities for order, the small tricks of transition. He calls upon a feeling for vast compositions that fill the spirit with beautiful conceptions expressed in a vast setting. And I have just spoken the word that characterizes his *oeuvre*. Gauguin is a great decorator. Decorator of dreams that would gladly surpass our horizon. His eyes, with their penetrating, profound yet sideways, disconcerting, perhaps irritated, perhaps disenchanted gaze, his eyes of a man, as Van Gogh said of him, "who comes from the planet Mars," seem at times to seek the frame that could contain the immense decoration whose elements he bears within himself. "A dome," wrote Albert Aurier in these pages, in a piece on Gauguin, "let him be given a dome!"

These lines from Poe's Marginalia *also correspond to the transcriptions in French included in Gauguin's* Cahier pour Aline. *The first of these propositions—about the strangeness of beauty—was actually written by Francis Bacon (1561–1626), whom Poe was quoting.*

When he says "dome," Morice is misquoting the March 1891 article by Aurier (included in this anthology), which concludes, ". . . walls! walls! give him some walls!"

They will not be given him. No matter! an indication of a unique *oeuvre*, fragmented by life, is this not all the greatest can do? Gauguin did it and his indication is by no means complete. The consciousness of the noble duty done must be reward enough for him, and, as revenge for injustices suffered, he is satisfied to know that the unjust, too, bear their sentences within themselves.

I believe in the holiness of the spirit and in the truth of art one and indivisible. I believe that the source of this art is divine and that it lives in the hearts of all men illuminated by the heavenly light; I believe that, having tasted the sublime delights of that great art, one is inevitably consecrated to it; one cannot abjure it. I believe that, through its intercession, all may attain beatitude. I believe in a last judgement where they will be condemned to terrible punishments, all who in this world will have dared to traffic in sublime and chaste art, all who will have defiled and degraded it with their low feelings, their base cupidity for material possessions. I believe that, on the other hand, the faithful disciples of great art will be glorified and that, wrapped in a heavenly fabric of rays, of melodious chords, they will return, to lose themselves for eternity in the bosom of the divine source of all harmony.

Wagner's Credo

Gauguin copied Wagner's Credo into two of his manuscripts, and part of it was painted on the dining room wall of the inn at Le Pouldu by Paul Sérusier. The text was known to the artists from a French tranlation published in 1887; see Henri Dorra, "Le 'Texte Wagner' de Gauguin," Bulletin de la Société de l'Histoire de l'Art français (1984).

Thadée Natanson

LA REVUE BLANCHE

"Recent Works by Paul Gauguin"

December 1893

M. Gauguin brought back from a long exile in Tahiti some forty canvases and some pieces of wood that he has hollowed-out, chiseled, and decorated.

And it is not only the talent of the artist, the charm or the attraction of the paintings or of the wooden pieces that make this exhibition important. We were able to see on the whole a complete work of a homogeneous inspiration and, in a sense, uniform, which at the same time represents extensive work and expresses a very particular effort of intention.

From the sole faraway and unknown country that attracted him, where he went to escape both the constraints of an oppressive, crusty series of traditions and their well-known examples, where he would scarcely encounter even crude attempts at artistic expression, M. Gauguin wanted to bring back a representative work that would more freely reveal the art and the sensibility that he was liberating. These are not merely his impressions, translated to his liking, that he revitalized and of which we can take advantage, but also, he initiates us to what seemed to him to be the thought of the inhabitants as well as their attitudes, to what has evoked the history and the soul of this country whose landscape he traces.

Here, women whose indolence lingers in fixed positions look far away with their shining, black eyes and under their black braids show serious, brown faces; there, their coppery, glimmering bodies mix with the luminous splendor of the place or of the decor whose blues, yellows, creams, and pinks borrow their intensities from intimacies or imagination.

This one, naked on her bed, turns around towards the spirit that watches over her; the body of another, leaning on branches, expresses the charm of the sweet earth on which she lies; yet another bends toward the rough rock from which seeps the mysterious water that flows over the multicolored flowers; of this other one, sitting on the sand, you can see only the tanned back among the nearly symmetrical flowers that the froth embroiders on the waves.

One woman slowly wanders into the woods, disturbed by the words of the devil, whose face remains impassive. Not far away are the portraits of women in which the artist seems preoccupied only by the plastic quality of physiognomies and expressions: *the woman of the flower*, *the woman with the mango*.

Here, there are some in couples, one crouching down and speaking with another who lays back and whose black hair embellishes the ground and the pink carpet. And then, groups of women whose pastorals, ceremonies, or dances perhaps bring ancient time back to life.

In the sumptuousness of the landscape, a man stands near the tree that he has just cut down. Here, in the foreground, a man raises his axe while a slender woman's body bends behind him, in front of a background of dark, limpid water on which canoes float.

Numerous, always vivid landscapes with more or less simplified shapes speak of the luminous and luxurious attraction of the fairylike decors of this country of dreams and, with colors of dawn or of sunset, show houses, marshes, the prodigious richness of vegetation, of rivers and of little streams. Flowers, springs, pebbles and branches remain delicate and graceful in detail without diminishing the powerful richness of the ensemble.

Almost face to face in extremely ingenious compositions M. Gauguin shows, in one painting, the divinities of the native legend and, in another, the apparition of the Christian Virgin in this far-off land.

Hina, the goddess of the moon, leans her graceful and indolent, shining and coppery body against the somber, bluish bust of disquieting placidity of this Téfatou, who is Earth. The words that the serious woman whispers into the ear of the God leave him impassive as the stone from which he seems to be made; a deliciously delicate spring flows, its transparent, brilliant water illuminates and reddens the earth among the flowers.

In the friendly, clear plain among the trees, to two dreamy women appears another one, almost as simple as they except that she is higher and sweeter and crowned with a halo, carrying on her shoulder the Divine Child, who studies her face. The flowers and the bird feathers in a small tree suggest the celestial body of the Angel they represent.

At last there are the woods, whose charm surprises and delights. The very freely-chosen shapes simplify the positions, bodies and physiognomies of which only the essential and what is necessary to produce the effect of the ensemble remains. They dig and search in the woods for the mysterious scenes and troubling colloquia of a strange, hieratic charm. They evoke legends. Without analogies, these *tiis* make you think invincibly of the undoubtedly different decorated utensils that you find in Scandinavia, because of their express choice of simplified, almost abstract, motifs and their decorative taste.

But all this is only a literary description, all the more difficult and clumsy because we are in the presence of unknown locations and beings, postures and feelings, which the artist sought to render anew, essentially different, and without any relation to our own.

Truly it is only up to the individual taste—however little right one

COLORPLATE 55

COLORPLATE 79
COLORPLATE 64

COLORPLATE 69

COLORPLATE 56

COLORPLATE 70

COLORPLATE 74

COLORPLATE 72

COLORPLATE 57

COLORPLATE 59

may have to judge—to favor or disfavor the intentions and the plastic effect realized in M. Gauguin's paintings and works in wood.

One must at least give hommage to the prodigious delicacy and infinite grace of detail that never breaks up the honesty or audacity, even the crudity, of the whole. We can try to describe, for the paintings as well as for the works in wood, the hieratic meaning that is liberated and that so strongly marks his *oeuvre*; the charm and ingenuity of his compositions, after their troubling attractiveness; and the definitive decorative splendor of such enervating richness of coloration that it is almost too strong by day and needs artificial light to soften it. More than of the subjects, we should likewise speak of his preoccupation with juxtaposing the colors so vividly, or with refining and simplifying the drawing down to the symbol; moreover, we owe the charm of the work singularly to those properly plastic qualities that have loyally put down the lie that most often they merely depict, *trompe l'oeil*, a facial expression or some objects.

But before leaving such an interesting and touching scene, we should take into account a scruple that it has created.

Isn't it, above all, after the pleasure and the worry of having made freely beautiful or pretty paintings and captivating sculptures, the preoccupation with getting rid of traditions, with forgetting models and schools of thought, with freeing himself to gain more control over his work, and with creating something original that led M. Gauguin from us and made him search in a virgin country for subjects of his inspiration and motifs with which he could realize his aesthetic?

Well, one must admit, however, that, far from reassuring us on the value of originality and creation, all of these new things—if I may say so for the ease of expression—leave us wary and suspicious, making us rightly see that perhaps they surprise more than they carry away our admiration.

Undoubtedly, it is not important whether or not a memory preoccupied M. Gauguin when he created the woman whose name is the Olympia of Tahiti; the rider galloping through the woods as in a Grecian frieze; the foreshortening here, the woman's slender body stretched out there, this or that detail, this or that composition.

Undoubtedly, it is difficult to deny the spell of strangeness and mystery that he knew how to give to his work, which comes out of it. It is equally difficult to lessen the originality and newness of this spell.

Undoubtedly, he has the merit not to have yielded to the desire to reduce the character of the scene or to accommodate it to our taste and to have chosen his subjects far enough from us to be free of the influence of objects that would spoil the spectator's emotion and make him admire, for instance, a painting only because a woman who was represented therein looks desirable, or because a piece of furniture, clothing, or decor therein would look pretty.

But, besides the intrinsic grace and the particular charm that they can have, is the quality that we really admire in these works one that borrows its spark of novelty from the novelty of subject or from a motif unknown until now, or is it because they prove old formulas by way of new objects?

We could even fear that the preoccupation with making new things, if it is limited only to renewal of objects and motifs, does not end up leading the artist very far from any real novelty and from the true originality for which the most ordinary and frequently considered objects are sufficient.

Do we not in fact need, in order to bow before the mastery of a creator and to praise his originality—there are others that we can love or admire—do we not need to be in the presence of the temperament and taste of the artist who transformed the substance already expressed—even all eternity—which preceded him?

Julien Leclercq

MERCURE DE FRANCE

"On Painting"

May 1894

People who repudiate Gauguin have three grievances against him: his ignorance, his extravagance, and his barbarity.

His ignorance? Is it possible that he is an ignorant person, he who, *doing what he can and knowing what he wants*, brings into his work only elements which he chooses from among several others!

His extravagance? When you see his work in Brussels in the surroundings of the painters of *La Libre Esthétique*, in good conscience you could rescind this inappropriate judgment. His work is just as unextravagant as Poussin's; it is just as controlled, as stern; it shines with a similar dazzle of color.

His barbarity? No, I would rather describe this Tahitian landscape as full of peacefulness, joy, and grace.

In a light softened with dusk, in which the colors, without growing weak, become melancholy, a stream flows, decorated by the reflections of a remarkable sky, as though decorated with flowers; the flowers intertwine, harmoniously forming fanciful, carefree bouquets. On a purple plot of land enlivened with pink at the stream's bank, here are two young women crouched in the position of graceful she-monkeys. Nature surrounds them like an Oriental carpet. The one on the left, meditative, bending over, halved, isn't she a virgin whose wild purity is not threatened by the Evil One? But on her right, near to her, oh! this must certainly be the temptress of an oceanic Lesbos: a gourmand girl ready to eat the fruit she holds in her hand, doubtlessly wanting to share it. On the other side of the stream, which murmurs its simple melody as in a Bach fugue, two women, weakened by the sharpened pleasure of their senses, are chatting. Naked and sitting down, the first one delights in remembering while the other, standing and already dressed, seems to have forgotten. In a hollow surrounded by woods a little farther beyond, there are still more women, dancing and rocking their hips to the rhythms of invisible music in front of images of gods. Over there, in the background, the mountain sinks into night.

In a corner of the painting there are some enigmatic words: *Nave nave moe*—translated *délicieux mystère*.

Really, is he a barbarian?

M. Péladan thinks so.

The artists' group La Libre Esthétique succeeded the defunct Les XX in Brussels in 1894.

COLORPLATE 81

The Sâr Péladan was Joséphin Péladan (1859–1918), critic, novelist, self-proclaimed mystic, and leader of the Rosicrucian movement. He initiated annual Salons of the Rose + Croix in 1892.

Achille Delaroche

L'ERMITAGE

"Concerning the Painting of Paul Gauguin"

1894

Among these [recent painters], an exalted and solitary place must be reserved for Paul Gauguin, not only because of the precedence, but because of the innovation of his art. During the recent exhibition to which he invited us, we walked amid the enchantments of a fairyland of light. Light so dazzling that it seemed impossible, on leaving it, to see the canvases of our usual image-makers as other than contradictory shadows.

Gauguin is the painter of primitive natures: he loves and possesses their simplicity, their evocative hieratic quality, their somewhat awkward and angular naiveté. His characters partake of the unstudied spontaneity of the virgin flora. Thus it was logical that he exalt, for our visual rejoicing, the riches of those tropical vegetations in which there is lasciviousness, beneath happy stars, an Edenic and free life: translated here with marvelous color-magic, yet with no superfluous ornamentation, redundancy, or Italianism. It is sober, awe-inspiring, imposing. And how the serenity of these natives crushes the vanity of our insipid refinements, our childish agitations! All the mystery of the infinites is at work in the naive perversity of their eyes, open onto the newness of things.

I care little whether or not there is exact reproduction in the name of exotic reality. Gauguin used this unprecedented framework to localize his dream, and what setting could be more favorable than one yet unpolluted by our civilized lies! But from these human figures, these ardent flora, the unreal and the wondrous emerge as well or better than from the chimerae or mythological properties of certain others. It was the fashion at the time to split one's sides with laughter at the scandal of those overly simian, unlifelike figures! before those vertical landscapes that are not given sufficient breath by perspective. Could one so deform nature? And the usual harmonious proportion of Greek modeling, of Italian painting was irrelevantly invoked. But aside from the fact that it would be easy to cite Egyptian, Japanese, Gothic art, which little heeded those so-called imprescriptible laws, the Dutch school, in its full, Classical flowering, proved indisputably that the ugly could also be aesthetic. It would therefore behoove us to put aside the prejudices of our academies, with their conventional lines, their cliché settings, their rhetorical torsos, if we wish to evaluate this strange art correctly.

* * *

Gauguin, better than any other until now, seems to us to have understood the role of the evocative setting. He proceeds above all by abbreviating lines, by synthesizing impressions. Each of his paintings is a general idea, without, however, enough formal reality to induce verisimilitude. And in no work of art is the constant concordance of state of mind and landscape—so luminously formulated by Baudelaire—better manifested. If he shows us jealousy, it is with a conflagration of pinks and violets, in which all of nature seems to participate as a sentient and tacit being; if the mysterious water gushes for the thirsty lips of an unknown person, it will do so in a strangely tinted *cirque,* like the stream of a diabolical or divine potion—one knows not which. Elsewhere, an unreal or-

Gauguin was especially fond of this article by Achille Delaroche, about whom nothing is known. He pasted it into Cahier pour Aline *and copied it into* Diverses Choses *and* Avant et Après. *In an August 1899 letter to Fontainas, Gauguin singled out Delaroche as the only writer who understood his painting.*

COLORPLATE 70

COLORPLATE 79

chard offers its insidious flora to the desire of an Edenic Eve, whose arm reaches hesitantly to gather the flower of evil, while murmuring at her temples is the beating of the Chimera's red wings. Then there is the forest, luxuriant with life and springtime: Some passersby take shape, faraway, in the happy calm of their unconcern; there, fabulous peacocks make their sapphire and emerald plumes glow, but the fatal blow of the woodcutter who strikes the branches intervenes, and behind him a slender thread of smoke rises, which signals the transitory destiny of this rejoicing. There stands, in legendary landscapes, the idol, hieratic and formidable: and the vegetations' tribute flows forth in lavas of colors onto its brow, and idyllic children sing on the pastoral flute the infinite happiness of Edens, while at their feet, like evil spirits keeping vigil, the heraldic red dogs are charmed and grow still. Farther away, a stained glass window, luminous with rich plant and human flowers; her divine child on her shoulders, a haloed vision of woman, before whom two others join hands among the flowers, to the gesture of a seraph who, as if from a miraculous chalice, exhales the mystical words. Supernatural flora that pray, and flesh that flowers, on the wavering threshold of the conscious and the unconscious.

COLORPLATE 68

COLORPLATE 72

COLORPLATE 75

COLORPLATE 57

All these canvases, and the others too, about which the same comments may be made, denote fairly well, in Gauguin's work, the intimate correlation between theme and form. But the skillful harmonizing, especially of colors, is significant in them and completes the symbol. The tones intermingle or oppose one another in gradations that sing like a symphony with multiple and varied choirs and play their truly orchestral role. Treated in such a way, color, which is vibration, just like music, attains what is most general and, hence, most vague in nature: its inner strength. So it was logical, in the present state of the aesthetic sense, that it would little by little encroach upon the place of drawing, whose evocative usefulness henceforth recedes into the middle distance.

And here the goal to which the different arts tend, virtually the place where they meet, becomes specific: To build the future city of the spiritual life, of which poetry, which is mood, would be the organizing gesture; music, its atmosphere; and painting, the marvelous decor.

* * *

Among all others, painting is the art that will prepare the way by resolving the paradox of the sensory and intellectual worlds. And, in the presence of a body of work such as Gauguin's, one finds oneself imagining a Des Esseintes, not the senile maniac whom we know, collector of inane bibelots, purveyor of hysterias, or deviser of Chinese sonnets, but truly intellectual, who would build, from an unrestrained imagination, the high hurdles of his dreams. The luminous frescoes of a Gauguin would represent the mural landscape there, where the symphonies of a Beethoven or a Schumann would sing in mystery, while the sacred lyrical words would solemnly chant the spiritual legend of the human odyssey.

Des Esseintes is the reclusive, hedonistic hero of the Huysmans novel, Against the Grain *(1883).*

József Rippl-Rónai
EMLEKEZESEI

1911

József Rippl-Rónai (1861–1927), Hungarian painter who joined the Nabis in 1892 and met Gauguin in Paris the following year.

I went to see him one evening. Already in the passage I noticed several beautiful things, in particular a still life of fruit, painted earlier, in the manner of Cézanne. (He never denied that healthy influence.) Entering the studio, I could just discern several human figures in the dim light. A curly-headed man was playing the piano: it was Leclerque [sic]. Another long-haired fellow was lying on the floor: it was the poet Ruinard [sic]. In the middle of the room, a perpetually moving monkey was climbing up and down a rope that hung from the ceiling. Underneath, on the floor, sat a small woman with a yellowish-dark complexion, wearing a blue cotton frock, silently smiling: it was the artist's mistress. Gauguin himself was busy at the foot of the bed, reproducing one of his typical woodcuts. As soon as he had finished printing the block he was at work on, we shook hands, and the little dark woman offered me some tea; and when the pianist stopped playing, we began to talk. Gauguin complained of his lack of success. His pictures were at the time on exhibition at Durand-Ruel's, but they had found no buyers. The fact that not even the Musée de Luxembourg had acquired any of his works nearly drove him to despair; and all those who had any spiritual contact with him shared his feelings. The pictures were sent back to the studio, and, with the aid of some friends, some of them were sold, at a time when the best, most typical Gauguin paintings could be brought for 50 to 100 francs. He could not understand the reason for his lack of success, but sought to account for it by the white frames: so that as soon as the exhibition was over he painted them yellow, before hanging them up in his own studio. As an illustration of Gauguin's love of independence, it was rumored that Durand-Ruel had offered him an annuity of 10,000 francs in return for the exclusive right of selling his pictures, but that he had refused the offer. As a souvenir, he gave me three copies of his woodcuts, printed in a primitive way by using the foot of his bedstead as a press. I still have them.

COLORPLATE 86

Ambroise Vollard

RECOLLECTIONS OF A PICTURE DEALER

On Gauguin

1936

Ambroise Vollard (1868–1939) opened a gallery in Paris in 1893 that became a mecca for advocates of avant-garde painting when he presented Cézanne's works in late 1895. In late 1896 he bought three paintings by Gauguin from Chaudet; he eventually acquired most of the pictures Gauguin had left with Chaudet. At the end of 1896 Vollard organized an exhibition of Gauguin's Tahitian works. He wrote to Gauguin in 1897 to ask for other works to sell, and in late 1898 he staged an important Gauguin exhibition. In 1901 Gauguin and Vollard signed a contract.

To see him, with his great height and arrogant bearing, a fur cap on his head and a cloak thrown round his shoulders, followed by a little half-breed Indian girl dressed in brightly-colored finery, one would have taken Gauguin for some Oriental Prince. The story of this colored girl, straight from the Malayan Isles, is worth telling.

An opera singer, Mme. Nina Pack, was on friendly terms with a rich banker who had business relations with the traders of the Malayan Isles. The singer happened to say before the representative of one of these, "I would love to have a little negro girl." A few months later a policeman brought Mme. Nina Pack a young half-breed, half Indian, half Malayan, who had been found wandering about the Gare de Lyon. She had a label hung round her neck, with the inscription: *Mme Nina Pack, rue de la Rochefoucauld, à Paris. Envoi de Java.* She was given the name of Anna. Some time later, in consequence of a little domestic drama in which Anna was implicated, she was dismissed. She came to me, as I had known her at her employer's house, to ask me to find her a good situation. I judged her qualifications as a housemaid to be very middling, and thought she stood more chance of succeeding as a model. I told Gauguin about her.

"Send her to me. I'll try her," he said.

Anna pleased him, and he kept her. She was the cause of Gauguin's memorable battle with the Breton peasants, who threw stones at the poor girl, accusing her of being a witch. In the course of the fray the painter had his foot broken. He never got over this accident.

René Maurice

NOUVELLE REVUE DE BRETAGNE

"Concerning Gauguin"

November–December 1953

Sometime during April 1894, just after receiving an inheritance from an uncle who died in Orléans, Gauguin arrived in Brittany with his friend Annah the Javanese, whom he had met several weeks earlier through Ambroise Vollard, an art dealer who thought she might be a good model for him. He was hoping to be able to set himself up again in Le Pouldu at Mlle. Henry's inn, but it had gone out of business in November 1893. He stayed for several weeks with the Polish painter Slevinsky, who had a villa near the large beaches, then he went down to Pont-Aven, to the inn at Gloanec. On 25 May 1894, accompanied by Annah and the painter Séguin and his wife, he went to visit Concarneau and its old port.

It would be curious to know how Gauguin was dressed, since, for some, his dress was part of the cause of the scene that took place that day. Several writers, notably Charles Kunstler, want to see him dressed up as a cabaret performer, with an astrakhan cap, blue coat with mother-of-pearl buttons, putty colored pants, white gloves on his hands, a sculpted cane with real pearl inlays, a gray, Buffalo Bill–style felt hat with a sky-blue band, and, to complete the character, a monkey perched on his shoulder. . . .

Nothing suggests that he was in the habit of dressing like this in Brittany. Only Etienne Port, under the name Careil, wrote in an article that appeared in *Fureteur Breton* in November 1919, 25 years after the event, that that afternoon the painter went for a stroll with his Negress and his "exotic bird" (a green parrot). For some, this "green parrot" has become a young monkey. . . .

All the photographs that I have seen of Gauguin in Brittany, which are in the possession of Emile Bernard, and some of which have been reproduced in his *Memories of Pont-Aven and Le Pouldu*, show the painter of *La Belle Angèle* dressed like a Breton fisherman: beret, blue wool sweater, clogs. It seems, in fact, that Gauguin liked to dress in the costume of each country he lived in, one after the other. Thus, he later dressed in the Maori style.

For the study of this "news item," I want to keep strictly to the stories in the Breton newspapers of the period, leaving aside all the captions and "images d'Epinal." What did they say? They all wrote his name with an *e* where the *i* should be: Gauguen, evidently a confusion due to the common Breton name Guéguen, as M. Waquel [sic] judiciously writes. There is no question of the artist's eccentricity in dress, nor of the presence of an "exotic animal," but only of the presence of "Madame Gauguen" who "is of the black race" and who, for that alone, could have been the unintentional cause of the row.

Wladyslaw Slewinsky (1854–1918) met Gauguin in Paris in 1889 and soon became a disciple, painting with Gauguin in Le Pouldu.

Charles Kunstler (1887–1977) wrote a popular biography of Gauguin in 1934.

COLORPLATE 32

Henri Waquet (b.1887) authored scores of studies on Breton history and culture.

In the course of this afternoon of 25 May 1894, during the time when "these artists took a stroll on Quai Péneroff, accompanied by their ladies," some children, attracted by the presence of the Negress (undoubtedly they had never seen one in their lives), followed and threw stones at them. Séguin seized one of the rascals, the young Sauban, and pulled his ear. The people of the port immediately took the part of this scamp and began to insult the strangers grossly. A pilot from Concarneau, the child's father, René Sauban, ran toward them and punched Séguin in the face. He was so frightened that he dove into the water to escape his aggressor by swimming. Gauguin, intervening in turn to defend his friend, threw Sauban to the ground. But three fishermen who had been sitting at the tavern next door then came to the latter's aid. Gauguin defended himself courageously, but he was not able to avoid a blow that "fractured his right leg at the internal malleolus and dislocated his right foot." Mme. Séguin was also struck and suffered an "injured side."

Le Finistère, (a weekly Quimpérois newspaper run by Louis Hémon, a deputy and later a senator from Finistère, and the uncle of the author of *Maria Chapdelaine*) related the events in the Saturday, 29 May 1894 edition of his paper, filed from Concarneau, on page 3 as follows:

A brutal assault, without reasonable motive, took place last Friday in Concarneau.

M. Paul Gauguen, a painter living in Pont-Aven, went to Concarneau accompanied by his wife and some friends. Mme. Gauguen is of the Negro race. Nothing more was needed for several children to feel they had the right to throw stones at her and at the same time those who accompanied her. M. Gauguen's friends pulled the ear of one of these poorly raised children. Immediately, several people at the scene began to insult the strangers in the grossest possible manner.

On the Quai Péneroff, an individual ran toward them and struck one of M. Gauguen's friends, M. Séguin, in the face. M. Gauguen, therefore, pushed the aggressor and threw him to the ground. But he got up. Three others joined him and, all together, attacked M. Gauguen. He defended himself energetically but he could not avoid a blow that fractured his leg at the internal malleolus and dislocated his right foot.

These savages also struck Mme. Séguin and injured her side.

The principal author of this unspeakable and ridiculous assault is someone named Réne Sauban, age 44, pilot, living in the rue Duguay-Trouin.

The other individuals who took part are as yet unknown. It is to be hoped that the police and the gendarmerie, who are uniting their efforts to find the accomplices of Sauban, are successful in their investigation.

And here is the article that appeared in *L' Union Agricole et Maritime* of Quimperlé, in the 30 May 1894 edition, page 3, in the local news:

CONCARNEAU (by our correspondent). Last Friday, following an altercation between fishermen and painters vacationing at Concarneau, blows were exchanged. One of these men, named Gauguen, suffered a broken leg; the doctor who was called to treat this poor man filed a certificate declaring that the malleolus of his right leg was fractured and his foot dislocated and that rest in a cast for 40 to 45 days was critical.

Our populace was very much struck by this act of brutality, committed by one called Sauban, a pilot who, furious that anyone should pull the ear of his son, wished to avenge himself.

Here is more or less what happened:

COLORPLATE 73. *Tahitian Scene.* 1891–1893. Watercolor. 15¾ × 23¼″ (40 × 59 cm).
Thielska Galleriet, Stockholm.

COLORPLATE 74. *Tahitian Pastorals.* 1893. 33¾ × 44½" (86 × 113 cm).
The Hermitage, Leningrad.

COLORPLATE 75. *Arearea (Amusements)*. 1892. 29½ × 37″ (75 × 94 cm).
Musée d'Orsay, Paris.

COLORPLATE 76. *Merahi Metua no Tehamana (Tehamana Has Many Ancestors)*. 1893. 30 × 21¼"
(76.3 × 54.3 cm). The Art Institute of Chicago; Anonymous gift.

COLORPLATE 77. *Ea haere ia oe? (Where Are You Going?).* 1893. 36½ × 28¾″ (92 × 73 cm).
The Hermitage, Leningrad.

COLORPLATE 78. *Tahitian Landscape.* 1891. 26¹¹/₁₆ × 36⅜″ (67.8 × 92.4 cm).
The Minneapolis Institute of Arts; The Julius C. Eliel Memorial Fund.

COLORPLATE 79. *Pape Moe (Mysterious Water)*. 1893. 39 × 29½″ (99 × 75 cm).
Private collection, Switzerland. Photo: Walter Dräyer.

COLORPLATE 80. *Oviri (Savage)*. 1895. Stoneware, glazed. Height: 29″ (74 cm).
Musée d'Orsay, Paris.

These artists were strolling on the Quai Péneroff, accompanied by their ladies, one of whom was a Negress; the color of this one attracted the children, who followed them throwing stones. One of the men, tired of the pursuit, and above all of the scheming, was able to surprise one of the stone throwers, grab him, and pull his ear. There began the altercation, during which one lady who was vacationing with her husband at Le Pouldu also received a punch that injured her left side.

We should point out just how much this aggression can be prejudicial to the interests of our city. The fortune of Concarneau is due largely to the affluence of strangers who are attracted to the beauty of our port and its surroundings as well as the affability they find here. Now, it could take an act of savagery such as the one of which we have just spoken to set against us strangers who, fearing that they will not be safe in our town, may hesitate to come to our locality. It was, it is true, an isolated incident, and we are sure that nothing like it will happen again. But it is good to point out the harm that can result from such a thing, should it happen, for our city where, moreover, we have been unanimous in censuring Sauban's brutality.

During the fracas, Gauguin thus received a broken leg and the doctor who was called to treat him estimated that he would not be able to work for 40 to 45 days.

*   *   *

Following the investigation, two men from Concarneau, René-Yves Sauban, pilot, and Pierre-Joseph Monfort, fisherman, were served summonses to appear before the *Tribunal correctionel de Quimper*, in the session of 23 August 1894, to answer for having voluntarily struck and injured Paul Gauguen on 25 May 1894 with the result of malady or incapacity to work for more than twenty days.

*   *   *

Here follows the complete text of the court's findings:

Public Audience of the Tribunal of the first instance, in session at Quimper (Finistère) conducted 23 August 1894 by Messieurs Leray, chief justice, presiding judge; Lignier, judge; and Coquet, substitute judge, replacing M. Debled, president, on vacation.

Present: Messieurs Vidal, substitute for the Public Prosecutor, and Le Poussin, court clerk.

The Director of Public Prosecutions against:

1. SAUBAN, René-Yves, age 44, pilot, born in Concarneau 30 October 1849 of René Guénolé and of Alexandrine Rivonal, married to Marie Le Rose, five children, no. 3 of the quarter de Concarneau.

2. MONFORT, Pierre-Joseph, age 30, fisherman, born in Concarneau 21 November 1863 of Hervé and of Marie-Perrine Hervéet, married to Francine Allot, one child, no. 1214 of the quarter de Concarneau.

Both living in Concarneau.

At the reading of the charges, M. Vidal, substitute for the public prosecutor, pointed out that, with a summons from the minister of Morvan, the process server for Concarneau, on 17 August 1894, he cited the above-named to appear before the tribunal, in the present hearing, to answer the charges against them as follows: having on 25 May 1894, in Concarneau, together and willfully struck and injured one Gauguen Paul, committed on his person other violence or acts of violence, with the result that the injuries sustained constitute an illness or an incapacity to work for more than twenty days: and he requested, if it pleased the tribunal, the reading of the writ of dismissal in the court of summary jurisdiction, and to proceed in the hearing of witnesses and in the questioning of the accused.

The clerk read from said writ. Those witnesses cited appeared; they were heard orally and separately and, before they testified, they swore to tell the truth and nothing but the truth.

The accused were questioned.

The clerk noted the declarations of the witnesses who were heard and of the responses of the accused.

Through Messieurs. Marchadour and Le Chabre, lawyers, the accused presented their defense. After the hearing of the first witness, M. de Chamaillard, lawyer, read and proffered conclusions tending to be in sympathy with the plaintiff, one Gauguen and on the grounds therein deduced, concluded that he enter the plea that Monfort and Sauban be condemned to pay a fine of 10,000 francs in damages. The tribunal conferred to grant this action.

M. Vidal, substitute for the public prosecutor, resumed the proceedings and requested the application of the law against the accused.

The tribunal, after listening to the reading of the piece mentioned above, advised Messieurs Le Marchadour and de Chabre, on their means of defense, and M. Vidal, substitute for the public prosecutor, on the summary of the affair and his requisitions, and after having deliberated:

Considering that which concerns Monfort, Pierre-Joseph, that he is not established as having been the author of the fracture suffered by M. Gauguen, on these grounds he is exonerated without penalty or fine.

Concerning Sauban,
Considering the outcome of the debate that Sauban, René-Yves, did, on 25 May 1894, willingly commit violence and acts of violence on the person of M. Gauguen, but that it has not been established that the fracture of the leg of said Gauguen came of his actions; that, therefore, one cannot apply article 309 cited in the subpoena, but instead article 311 of the Penal Code which punishes the blows alone; on these grounds, the tribunal condemns Sauban, René-Yves to eight days' imprisonment and ruling on the pleas of the plaintiff, considering that it is not established that Sauban was directly responsible for the grave injury to M. Gauguen, but that it is certain that a grave responsibility is incumbent upon him in this affair. Considering that the indemnity of 10,000 francs claimed by the plaintiff seems exaggerated; condemns Sauban, René-Yves, to pay the sum of 600 francs in damages to M. Gauguen.

Condemns him, beyond this, by bodily labor to reimburse the expenses totaling 150 francs in this, not including the present trial. And in execution of article 9 of the law on 22 July 1867, fixes the duration of the bodily imprisonment at the minimum. Said that the plaintiff, having expenses, except those of the treasury, will have his recourse against the condemned.

The whole, by application of articles 311 and 52 of the penal code and 194 of the criminal code, the reading of which was done by the presiding judge and which are thusly conceived:

Thus pronounced and decreed in the aforesaid public hearing, at the Palais de Justice at Quimper.

Signed:
Leray, Lignier, de Coquet, Le Poussin

Gauguin wrote:

I was at the court of summary jurisdiction last Thursday. Despite all the lawyers' speeches, despite all the barbarous wrongs that were proven, only a laughable decision was handed down, and that because in these backwaters, justice only looks after the electoral party. I was given 600 francs in damages. And I have 475 francs in doctor's fees, 100 francs for the lawyer (would not, then, his friend Chamaillard have made a gesture of sympathy?), and all the expenses in the hotel that an illness drags out. This has completely ruined me. Despite that, the opposing party is appealing for a trial in Rennes, which would be much better for me. Then Leclercq would have to see Dolent to get to Geffroy, who could get an article in *Le Journal* or *L'Echo de Paris*, a severe article against the system of justice in Quimper, explaining my case. It would appear that in Rennes the judges are very sensitive to these articles. What?—one should have the right to murder or cripple an innocent man because he is a stranger to Concarneau; his illness, his suffering, the time he has lost would be nothing, because the bandits of Concarneau are the voters and my attacker is a friend of the republican authorities? I ask, then, as a favor, for an article in the Parisian papers.

Armand Séguin

L'OCCIDENT

"Paul Gauguin"

April 1903

The first attempts proved to Gauguin that it was absurd, as the goal he had chosen for himself, to adopt the theory of complementaries. Its falsity, at least in its general thrust, was visible to him at once, and he explained it in a spiritual fashion. Here, he said, on this white tablecloth, is a glass of red wine; if its shadow is green, the linen would become vermilion. If this transposition existed, the wine, in turn, would be Veronese green. What sharp outcries followed upon these sentences! Apollo's temple was like a ferocious menagerie, the names of Lautrec, Seurat, Signac filled the air and shook the windows.

He was soon overjoyed to notice that violet, placed near emerald green, forms a more pleasing harmony than when it adjoins yellow. In a setting sun, one hears shouts of gladness: the ochre of the sand, the orange of the kelp, the red of the rocks, the violet of the shadow fired his enthusiasm. The law of derivatives was about to be created.

Oh! that damned theory that gave me such violent headaches, how often he repeated it to me, analyzed it, commented upon it. It was in 1894, in Pont-Aven; I was treating the wound that he got for saving my life. All day long, and sometimes at night, when his suffering kept him awake, he explained it to me endlessly, in all its subtleties, making me repeat it in all its variants, taking pleasure in submitting problems to me, which made me believe somewhat that he doubted its power: I thought that he wanted to convince himself.

I can still hear his roars when my answers were wrong . . . . [L]ike a Romantic I wanted an abyss to open beneath my feet. My assignment was to undertake a study under his direction, which was severe. The subject I was to treat portended that I would make a thousand mistakes. There, on a napkin, in an earthenware vase, a great bunch of those purple and carmine peonies. As for the flowers, orange, vermilion, lacquer, and violet almost verging, in the shadows, on ultramarine, got me, happily, to the emerald green of my leaves; the dominant being red, my background goes to yellow, and ochre gives it more warmth. A tone that one has muddied harmonizes agreeably with a pure color, and for the white of the pottery, for the fragments of branches, I use a blend of different shades in which blue predominates. All that was right, pleasing to look at, and followed so well the rule of the master, who smiled to see my work, that, unable to contain my joy and pride, I outlined the drapery with a hint of orange and thus relapse into the complementary. A sharp noise made me turn abruptly. Gauguin was leveling his loaded gun at me, threatening to kill me, and so great was his fury that he would have fired ruthlessly for the glory of his theory, had I not taken the wise course of immediately erasing my error.

At Le Pouldu—since I am trying to follow the different stages of his talent, to analyze his researches, as I would like to tell the story of his life—he was slowly able to make the law of derivatives his own; he let it act freely on the various minds around him who understood him; he did not formulate it verbally until his return from Tahiti, because he never wholly obeyed it in his works, or else because he was unable to do so.

* * *

Auti te Pape (Women at the River). 1894. Woodcut, printed in color with stencils. Block: 8¹/₁₆ × 14″ (20.5 × 36 cm). The Museum of Modern Art, New York; Gift of Abby Aldrich Rockefeller.

Julien Leclercq

MERCURE DE FRANCE

"Paul Gauguin Exhibition"

January 1895

Paul Gauguin Exhibition: Just a few days back from Brittany, Paul Gauguin opened his atelier from December 2 to 9 to a small number of sympathetic people who didn't think that his work was as despicable as a few imprudent critics vainly claimed it to be. This great and prolific artist did not complete all the work he'd hoped to do this year; a serious accident left him immobilized in bed for several months at the inn where he was

On this "serious accident" see Maurice's "Concerning Gauguin," in this volume.

Ia Orana Maria (Hail, Mary). 1894.
Monotype. 8¾ × 5½″ (22.2 × 14.2 cm).
Museum of Fine Arts, Boston; Bequest of
W. G. Russell Allen.

staying in Pont-Aven. It was an excellent idea to show these watercolors
and engravings in his own space, right in the midst of the canvases seen
last year at Durand-Ruel's which, here, take on a particular quality of silence—their true character—and near as well to the ceramics and sculptures, where his attention to shapes is so well manifested. Between the
paintings on the yellow walls of the radiant atelier, where color loses
nothing of its quality, there are Japanese prints and photographs of old
works (Cranach, Holbein, Botticelli) and modern ones (Puvis de Chavannes, Manet, Degas) whose company, so dangerous for others, proves
that the master of this house is from the great family, the beautiful family of the strong; of those whose presence inspires him; there are also
sketches by Odilon Redon, paintings by Cézanne and Van Gogh. Gauguin is only happy in this world because it is his.

I spoke of him at great enough length two months ago so as not to

*Leclercq "spoke of him" in his article on
Gauguin in the November 1894 issue of*
Mercure de France.

Arearea No Varua Ino (The Amusement of the Evil Spirit). 1894. Monotype. $9\frac{1}{8} \times 8\frac{3}{4}''$ (23.2 × 22.4 cm). National Gallery of Art, Washington, D.C.; Rosenwald Collection.

need to go back over him in a general fashion. I only wish to point out, therefore, his recent research in matters from which he has taken a highly original standpoint. Through a method of watercolor transfer, he gives a seriousness, a sumptuousness, and a depth to watercolor which, to him, are needs art must meet in whatever subject he depicts. In his sketches as well as in his woodcuts, he doesn't spend his time trying to create new concepts, he simply transposes the motifs of his Tahitian works into another medium. Among the watercolors there are, however, some new landscapes where it seems that this method has worked more lovingly and more completely. Those who find his very decorative paintings to be barbarous will find these watercolors more seductive; for me, it's still Gauguin: simple and rich, courageous and happy in his enterprises. But how does he manage this? It's a mystery!

Of a design his sculpture has already shown us, his woodcuts establish—for people who unfortunately would not otherwise have felt the

Tahitian Girl in a Pink Paréo. 1894.
Monotype. 9 × 5½″ (22.9 × 14 cm). The
Art Institute of Chicago; Gift of Walter
S. Brewster.

link between them—the very personal harmony of the former with his
painting. Between sculpture and painting, it is an intermediary medium
which takes as much from one as the other. Imagine a deep bas-relief
with full figures, thickly printed with a somber touch of red or yellow to
break the monotony of blacks and whites. Powerful effects that are the
secret of the artist's temperament emerge from them.

Showing us such beautiful things, Paul Gauguin has not surprised us.

Letters from Strindberg and Gauguin
On Endorsing a "Savage" Art
February 1895

AUGUST STRINDBERG TO PAUL GAUGUIN, 1 FEBRUARY 1895

You insist upon my writing the preface to your catalogue as a remembrance of the winter of 1894–1895, when we lived here behind the Institute, not far from the Panthéon, and right next to the Montpar-
nasse cemetery.

I would willingly have given you this remembrance to take to that
Oceanian island where you are going to look for some space and for a

*August Strindberg (1849–1912), Swedish
writer and painter who, while living in
Paris in 1894, met Gauguin through the
musician William Molard and his
Swedish wife, Ida Ericson, Gauguin's
neighbors. When Gauguin asked
Strindberg to write the introduction to the
catalogue of his 18 February 1895
exhibition, the writer was stirring
controversy with writings advocating
nonfigurative art and anti-Feminism and
revealing intense hatred for his first wife.*

setting harmonious with your powerful stature, but I feel that I have been in an equivocal situation from the beginning, and I'm immediately responding to your request with an "I cannot" or, more brutally, with an "I don't want to."

At the same time, I owe you an explanation for my refusal, which does not come from a lack of kindness or from a lazy pen, although it would have been easy for me to have placed the blame on the already famous disease of my hands, which, in any event, has not caused my hands to fall into disuse from inactivity.

Here's why: I cannot grasp your art, and I cannot like it. (I cannot get a grip on your art, which is now so exclusively Tahitian.) But I know that this confession will neither surprise nor hurt you, because you rather seem to be strengthened by other people's hatred; anxious to remain intact, your personality delights in the antipathy it provokes. And rightly so, perhaps, because, from the moment that you were appreciated and admired and had followers, you would be grouped and classified, and your art would be given a name which young people would use, not even five years from now, as an epithet to designate an outdated art which they would do anything to make even more obsolete.

As for me, I made serious efforts to categorize you, to see you as a link in the chain, and to bring myself to an understanding of the story of your development—but in vain.

*   *   *

Last night my thoughts turned toward Puvis de Chavannes, to the southern sounds of the mandolin and guitar: I envisioned the confusion of sun-filled paintings on the walls of your studio, an image which pursued me into my sleep. I saw trees no botanist would ever find, animals Cuvier never thought existed, and men only you could create.

A sea that would flow from a volcano, a sky in which no God can live. "Sir," I said in my dream, "you have created a new earth and a new sky, but I don't like being in the midst of your creation. It is too sunny for me, a lover of *chiaroscuro*. And an Eve lives in your paradise who is not my ideal, for I, too, have a feminine ideal or two!"

This morning, I went to visit the Luxembourg museum in order to glance at Chavannes' works, which kept coming back into my mind. With a deep appreciation, I contemplated the *Poor Fisherman,* so attentively awaiting the prey that will bring him the faithful love of both the wife who gathers flowers and his idle child. How beautiful it is! But then my eye is struck with the fisherman's crown of thorns. I hate Christ and crowns of thorns. Monsieur, I hate them, hear me well. I want nothing to do with this pitiful God who accepts being hurt. Rather, my God is Vitsliputsli, who eats the hearts of men under the sun.

No, Gauguin was not created from Chavannes' rib, nor from Manet's, nor Bastien-Lepage's.

What is he, then? He is Gauguin, the savage who hates the restraints of civilization, who has something of the Titan who, jealous of the Creator, makes his own little creation in his spare time, the child who takes his toys apart to make others; the one who renounces and defies, preferring to see the sky red, rather than blue with the crowd.

Upon my word, it seems to me that, now that I've gotten excited writing, I'm starting to have a certain understanding of Gauguin's art.

A modern author has been reproached for not having painted real beings but for having constructed *quite simply* his own characters. *Quite simply!*

Have a good trip, Master; but do come back and find me. Perhaps then I will have learned to understand your Art better, which will allow me to write a sincere preface for a new catalogue in a new Hôtel Drouot, because I, too, am starting to feel an immense need to become a savage and to create a new world.

In an August 1899 letter to Fontainas, Gauguin recalls how depressed Puvis de Chavannes was when critics failed to understand his proto-Symbolist canvas The Poor Fisherman *(1881), bought by the State at an 1887 Galerie Durand-Ruel exhibition. The "crown of thorns" is not literal; Strindberg is referring figuratively to the fisherman's unkempt hair.*

Nave Nave Fenua (Delightful Land). 1894.
Monotype. 15¼ × 9¼" (39 × 23.5 cm).
Museum of Fine Arts, Boston; Bequest of
W. G. Russell Allen.

PAUL GAUGUIN TO AUGUST STRINDBERG, CA. 16 FEBRUARY 1895

I got your letter today, your letter which is a preface for my catalogue.
I had the idea of asking you to do this preface when I saw you playing
the guitar and singing the other day in my studio; your blue Nordic eyes
were looking attentively at the paintings hung on the walls. I felt the
premonition of a revolt: a great shock between your civilization and my
barbarity.

Civilization from which you suffer. Barbarity which is, for me, a rejuvenation.

In front of the Eve of my choosing, whom I painted with forms and harmonies from another world, your precious remembrances perhaps evoked a painful past. The Eve of your civilized conception makes you and makes us almost misogynous; the ancient Eve in my studio who scares you may very well smile less bitterly at you some day. This world, which perhaps neither Cuvier nor a botanist would be able to recognize, could be a Paradise only I could have sketched. While there is a great distance from the sketch to the realization of the dream, it doesn't matter! To envision happiness, isn't this a foretaste of *nirvana*?

The Eve I painted (she alone) can, logically, go naked before our eyes. Yours, in this simple attire, could not walk without shamelessness and, too beautiful (perhaps) would be the evocation of evil and pain.

In order to make you fully understand my thoughts, rather than compare these two women directly, I will compare the Maori or Turanian language my Eve speaks with the language spoken by your woman and chosen amongst all others, the inflected European language.

With basic components of the language conserved in their state of crudeness—isolated or linked without any care for polish—everything is naked, striking, and primordial in the language of Oceania.

In inflected languages, on the other hand, the roots by which they started, as with all other languages, disappear in the daily commerce that has worn away their relief and contours. It is a perfected mosaic in which the joints between the stones (more or less crudely aligned) are no longer seen, and one admires only a beautiful lapidary painting. Only a skilled eye can survey the process of construction.

Forgive me for this long digression on language; I find it necessary to explain the savage drawing I had to use in order to decorate a Turanian country and its people.

All that remains, dear Strindberg, is for me to thank you.

When will we see one another again?

Until then, as today, I am yours truly.

Eugène Tardieu

L'ECHO DE PARIS

"M. Paul Gauguin"

13 May 1895

He is the wildest of all the innovators, and of all the "misunderstood" artists the one least inclined to compromise. A number of his *discoverers* have forsaken him. To the great majority of people he is just a humbug. Yet he calmly goes on painting his orange rivers and red dogs, and for every day which passes adheres more and more to this personal *manner*.

Gauguin is built like a Hercules: his graying hair is curly, his features are energetic, his eyes clear; and when he smiles in his characteristic way he seems alike gentle, shy, and ironical.

"What exactly does it mean, this expression 'to copy nature?'" he asks me, stretching himself defiantly. "Follow the example of the masters," we are advised. "But what for? Why should we follow their example? They are masters for the sole reason that they refused to follow anybody else's example. Bouguereau has talked of women glowing in all the colors of the rainbow and denies the existence of blue shadows. One can just as well deny the existence of brown shadows such as he paints; what cannot be denied is that his canvases are devoid of any glow. He may have glowed himself when he painted his pictures, but it was with sweating to make slavish copies of objects as they appear to be, and striving for success in a field where, in spite of his exertions, he is surpassed by photography. A man who sweats smells, and his tastelessness and incompetence smell a long way off. After all, it matters little whether blue shadows do or do not exist. If a painter tomorrow decides that shadows are pink, or violet, there is no reason why he should have to defend his decision, assuming that his work is harmonious and thought-provoking."

"Then your red dogs and pink skies. . . ."

". . . are deliberate. Absolutely deliberate. They are necessary. Every feature in my paintings is carefully considered and calculated in advance. Just as in a musical composition, if you like. My simple object, which I take from daily life or from nature, is merely a pretext, which helps me by means of a definite arrangement of lines and colors to create symphonies and harmonies. They have no counterparts at all in reality, in the vulgar sense of that word; they do not give direct expression to any idea, their only purpose being to stimulate the imagination—just as music does without the aid of ideas or pictures—simply by that mysterious affinity which exists between certain arrangements of colors and lines and our minds."

"These are rather novel theories!"

"They are not at all novel!" Monsieur Gauguin exclaimed emphatically and with some feeling. "All great artists have always done exactly the same. Raphael, Rembrandt, Velázquez, Botticelli, Cranach, they all distorted nature. Go to the Louvre and look at their pictures and you will see how different they are. According to your theory, one of them must be right and the rest wrong. Unless they have all been deceiving us. If you demand that a work should be true to nature, then neither Rembrandt nor Raphael succeeded, any more than Botticelli or Bouguereau. Shall I tell you what will soon be the most faithful work of art? A photograph, when it can render colors, as it will soon be able to. And you would have an intelligent being sweat away for months to achieve the same illusion of reality as an ingenious little machine? It is the same with sculpture. It is possible already to make perfect casts. A skilled molder can make a Falguière statue for you with ease whenever you like."

"So you do not wish to be called revolutionary?"

"I find the expression ridiculous. Monsieur Roujon has applied it to me. I told him that all artists whose work differs from their predecessors' work have merited it. Indeed, it is for that reason alone that they are masters. Manet is a master, and Delacroix. At first their work was considered atrocious, and people laughed at Delacroix's violet horses—which, incidentally, I have looked for in vain in his pictures. But such is the public. I have become reconciled to the idea that I shall remain misunderstood for a long time to come. If I only did what others have already done before me I should in my own estimation be just a worthless plagiarist. But whenever I strive to conceive something new I am called wretched. In that case, I would rather be a wretch than a plagiarist.

"There are many cultivated people who think that, as the Greeks achieved sculpture of ideal perfection and purity and the Renaissance did the same in painting, nothing now remains but to emulate their works. The same people would even say that the plastic arts have exhausted their potentialities!

"That is an absolute mistake. Beauty is eternal and can have a thousand forms. The Middle Ages had one ideal of beauty, Egypt another. The Greeks strove for complete harmony of the human body, and Raphael had very beautiful models. But you can equally well produce a valid work of art from a model that is as ugly as sin. There are plenty of such works in the Louvre."

"Why did you make your journey to Tahiti?"

Alexandre Falguière (1831–1900), academic sculptor.

Henri Roujon (1853–1934), director of the Ministry of Fine Arts from 1895 to 1899. On the understanding that Roujon's predecessor had promised to buy a Gauguin work for the State, both Gauguin and Morice were embittered when Roujon refused to do so. In an 1899 letter to Monfreid, Gauguin asked: "Do you know some anarchist who could dynamite Roujon?"

Noa Noa (Fragrance). 1894. Woodcut, printed in color with stencils. Block: 14 × 8¹/₁₆″ (36 × 20.5 cm). The Museum of Modern Art, New York; Lillie P. Bliss Collection.

COLORPLATE 80

"I had once been fascinated by this idyllic island and its primitive and simple people. That is why I returned and why I am now going back there again. In order to achieve something new, you have to go back to the sources, to man's childhood. My Eve is almost animal. That is why she is chaste for all her nakedness. But all the Venuses in the Salon are indecent and disgracefully lewd. . . ."

Monsieur Gauguin fell silent, and with a rather ecstatic expression on his face turned to regard a picture on the wall of some Tahitian women in the jungle. A few moments after, he continued:

"Before leaving, I shall publish in collaboration with my friend Charles Morice a book about my life in Tahiti and my views on art. Morice comments in verse on the works I have brought back with me. In short, the book will be a statement about why and how I made the journey."

"What will be its title?"

"*Noanoa*—a Tahitian word meaning 'fragrant.' In other words, the book will be about what Tahiti exhales."

Letter from Gauguin to Armand Séguin

On His Life in Tahiti

15 January 1897

I will send you sometime, as soon as I have taken one, a photograph of my home studio with the polychrome wood bas-reliefs, the statues among the flowers, etc . . . but just to sit here in my doorway, without a single worry, smoking a cigarette and drinking a glass of absinthe, is a pleas-

Te Rerioa (The Dream). 1897. 37½ × 52" (95 × 132 cm). Courtauld Institute Galleries, London; Courtauld Collection.

ure I enjoy every day. And my fifteen-year-old wife prepares my simple meals daily and gets down on her back for me any time I want, all for a 10-franc dress every few months. . . . You can't imagine how far 125 francs a month will go here. I ride a horse or get in my buggy whenever I want. All of it belongs to me, just like my house and the rest. Yes, I will stay until I die if I manage to bring in 1,800 francs a year, that's all I desire and nothing else.

Letters from Gauguin to Daniel de Monfreid

On Life's Mutability

1897

APRIL 1897

Your letter arrives at the same time as a very brief and very terrible letter from my wife. She tells me bluntly of the death of my daughter, who was taken after a few days by a pernicious pneumonia. This news did not

Two Tahitian Women. 1899. 37 × 28½" (94 × 72.4 cm). The Metropolitan Museum of Art, New York; Gift of William Church Osborn, 1949.

Aline, Gauguin's daughter. ca. 1895.
Photo courtesy of Musée Gauguin,
Papeari, Tahiti.

touch me at all, long-schooled as I am in suffering: then each day, as the reflections come, the wound opens deeper and deeper and at this moment I am completely despondent. I surely have some enemy up there who does not give me a minute's rest. Whenever I start to restabilize myself with a little money to work for a few months, some exceptionally bad luck falls on me. The person who rented me a little piece of land on which to set up my hut has just died, leaving his affairs in great disorder, and as a result his land has been sold. So here I am in search of a piece of land, and I will have to build again. Besides a considerable waste of time, I estimate that it will cost me 700 to 1,000 francs; it's enough to drive you crazy. Chaudet only writes me when he has money, and I have not received anything despite what he told me before: my debt-ridden life is thus about to start up again. I received (sent by Schuff) *Les Hommes du Jour* (my absurd portrait by Schuff). That boy wears me out, exasperates me, what an idiot! and what pretense! A cross, flames, wham! there you have symbolism.

I hope that you will be in Paris when my canvases arrive, and I am anxious to know what you think of them; for I myself cannot judge, even though I have a feeling that there is something good at the bottom of it.

I also hope that you will be done with your divorce and that you will have a clear situation from now on. . . .

14 JULY 1897

The canvases that I sent you arrived, and you admired them; I'm glad, I was afraid—for in the state I'm in, I truly do not know just what they're worth. You make serious criticisms: I am not careful with my materials. Oh, to be sure, I am very careful with it as paint—but the preparation falls short. It's true. What do you expect, in the state I was in, so nervous and anxious that the preparation obsessed me, tired me out. After that, the canvases of which you speak were rolled up by a naval officer

(I was in the hospital) who didn't know how, and thus slackly rolled for two months, without air, and in extreme heat, they were enormously at risk. Once stretched and waxed they are less at risk. In case of a great disaster, Portier has an excellent remounter, and that costs about twenty francs. Otherwise, here's what you can do: Right away, you paste some paper with *flour paste* on the painted side; then you turn it over, spread out on a board, and you pour some light, almost cold paste; spread well with a knife and dry in such a way that the paste passes down through the white ground. Once dry, you press it with a warm iron, with as much pressure as possible. When later your canvas is well stretched on stretcher, the paper can easily be taken off with a damp finger—how much work I'm giving you. I repaired this way a Van Gogh that was flaking all over. If there remain any visible cracks, so what? After all, one must do what one can, and Tahiti is a far cry from Paris. . . .

Paul Gauguin

DIVERSE CHOSES

1896–1898

I think that humanity has certain playful moments—childish things are far from being injurious to a serious work, giving it its soft, cheerful, and naive character. Our age has begun to tire of overextended analyses, and simplicity, the gift of a great lord, could not be understood by the bourgeois. Machines came, art went; and I feel far from thinking that photography is suited to us. Since the snapshot, a horse lover said, the painter has understood this animal, so Meissonier, glory of the French, has been able to render all the attitudes of this noble animal. As for me, I went much further back, further than the horses of the Parthenon . . . back to the dada of my childhood, the good old toy wooden horse. I also began to hum the sweet melody from Schumann's children's scenes: *The Wooden Horse.* I also lingered over Corot's nymphs in the woods of Ville-d'Avray. Without sketching dance at the Opéra and, with great naiveté and honesty as well, this delicious Corot knew how to make all these nymphs dance, and how to transform the shacks of the Parisian suburbs in the misty horizons into veritable pagan temples. He loved to dream, and in front of his paintings I dream as well.

Men of science, forgive these poor artists who have forever remained children, if not for pity, at least for the love of flowers and inebriating perfumes, because they often seem like the flowers. They blossom as flowers do and give off their scents at the least ray of sunshine, yet wilt at the impure contact of the hand that soils them. The work of art, for the one who knows how to see, is a mirror that reflects the artist's soul.

*   *   *

THE PAINTING I WANT TO DO

It is six meters long, two meters high. Why this measurement? Because this is the width of my studio, and I can't work without getting extremely tired at greater height. The canvas is already stretched, prepared, and smoothed out with care: not a knot, not a wrinkle, not a spot. Just think, it will be a masterpiece.

With an eye toward geometry, the composition of lines will begin in the middle, at first elliptical, then they will undulate towards the edges.

Around 1881–1882, Meissonier became passionately interested in stop-action photographs of horses in motion taken by E. J. Marey and Eadweard Muybridge.

The Wooden Horse *refers to "Ritter von Steckenpferd" from Robert Schumann's* Kinderszenen, *opus 15 (1838).*

Camille Corot (1796–1875), pioneering landscape painter who elevated the oil sketch to an important art form. Gauguin refers to the fanciful, poetic landscapes that Corot embellished with dancing Arcadian shepherdesses. Corot did make quick pencil sketches of dancers at the Opéra.

COLORPLATE 81. *Nave Nave Moe (Delightful Drowsiness).* 1894. 28¾ × 38½″ (73 × 98 cm).
The Hermitage, Leningrad.

12.

D'eux sont nés les Dieux suivants:
Elle enfanta Teirii et il était Dieu
Téfatou – Rouanoua.
Quand le Dieu Roo, saisissant ce
qu'il y avait dedans, sortit par le côté
du sein de sa mère.
La femme accoucha ensuite de ce qu'elle
contenait encore; il en sortit ce qui
s'y trouvait encore renfermé:
L'irritation ou présage des tempêtes,
la colère (ou l'Orage) la fureur ou
un vent furieux, la colère apaisée
ou la tempête calmée).
Et la source de ces esprits est dans le lieu
d'où sont envoyés les messagers.

Eternité de la Matière -
Dialogue entre Téfatou et Hina (les génies
de la terre - et la lune.

Hina disait à Fatou; "faites revivre (ou
ressusciter, l'homme après sa mort.
Fatou répond; Non je ne le ferai point
revivre. La terre mourra ; la végétation
mourra ; elle mourra, ainsi que les hommes
qui s'en nourrissent; le sol qui les produit
mourra. La terre mourra, la terre finira ;
elle finira, pour ne plus renaître.
Hina répond : Faites comme vous voudrez;
moi je ferai revivre la Lune. Et ce que
possédait Hina continua d'être ; a que
possédait Fatou périt, et l'homme dut mourir.

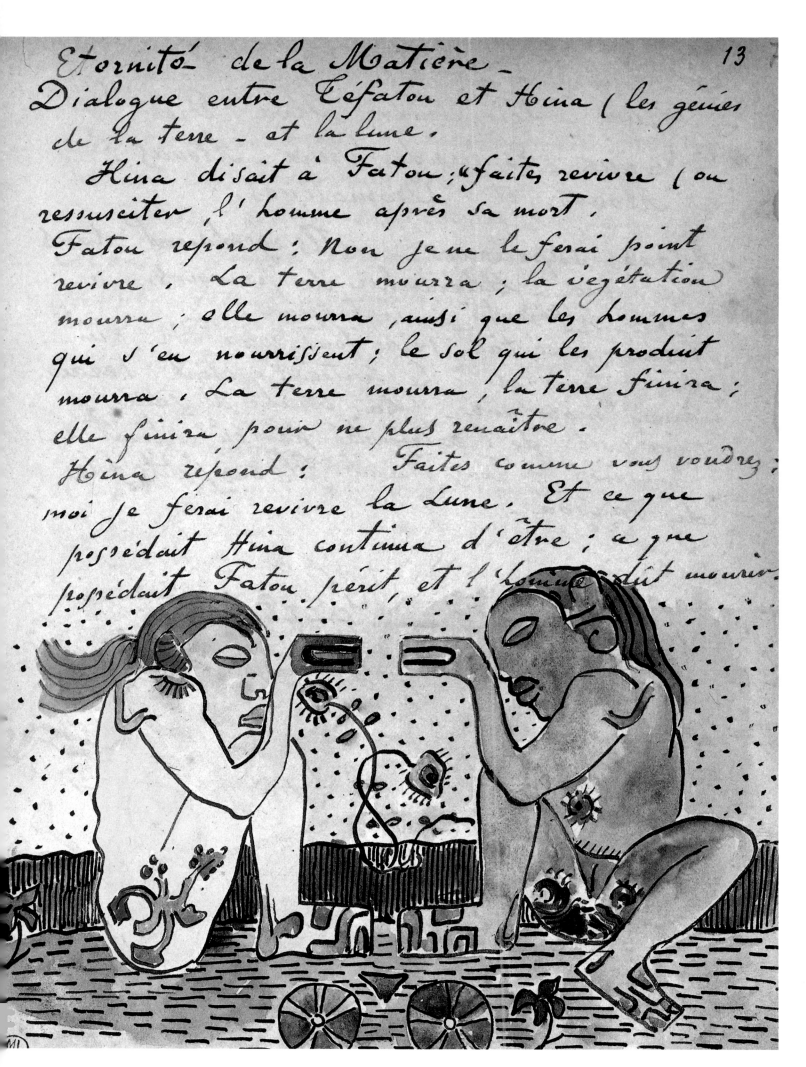

COLORPLATE 82. Illustrated pages from *Ancient Maori Cult.* ca. 1892–1893.
Cabinet des Dessins, Louvre Museum, Paris.

COLORPLATE 83. *Self-Portrait with a Hat.* 1893–1894. 18 × 15″ (46 × 38 cm).
Musée d'Orsay, Paris.

COLORPLATE 84. *Portrait of Fritz Schneklud*. 1894. 36⅜ × 28⅝″ (94 × 72.5 cm).
The Baltimore Museum of Art; Given by Hilda K. Blaustein in memory of her husband, Jacob Blaustein.

COLORPLATE 85. *Nave Nave Fenua (Delightful Land)*. 1894. Woodcut, printed in color with stencils.
Block: 13⁵/₁₆ × 8¹/₁₆″ (35.5 × 20 cm). Museum of Fine Arts, Boston; Bequest of W. G. Russell Allen.

COLORPLATE 86. *Aita Parari te Tamari Vahine Judith (Portrait of Annah the Javanese)*. 1893.
45¾ × 31⅞″ (116 × 81 cm). Private collection. Photo: A. C. Cooper, Ltd.

COLORPLATE 87. *Breton Woman in Prayer*. 1894. 25⅝ × 18⅛″ (65 × 46 cm).
Sterling and Francine Clark Art Institute, Williamstown, Massachusetts.

COLORPLATE 88. *Breton Peasant Women*. 1894. 26 × 36⅜″ (66 × 92.5 cm).
Musée d'Orsay, Paris.

COLORPLATE 89. *Brittany Landscape, "David's Mill."* 1894. 28¾ × 36½″ (73 × 92 cm).
Musée d'Orsay, Paris.

COLORPLATE 90. *Breton Village in the Snow*. 1894–1895. 24⅜ × 34½″ (62 × 87 cm).
Musée d'Orsay, Paris.

COLORPLATE 91. *Portrait of a Girl.* (Vaite Goupil.) 1896. 29½ × 25½" (75 × 65 cm).
Ordrupgaardsamlingen, Copenhagen. Photo: Ole Woldbye.

COLORPLATE 92. *Savage Poems*. 1896. 25½ × 19″ (65 × 48 cm).
The Harvard University Art Museums; Fogg Art Museum; Bequest of Maurice Wertheim, Class of 1906.

COLORPLATE 93. *Te Arii Vahine (The Noble Woman)*. 1896. 39 × 51½″ (97 × 130 cm).
The Pushkin Museum, Moscow.

COLORPLATE 94. *Vairumati*. 1897. 28¾ × 37″ (73 × 94 cm).
Musée d'Orsay, Paris.

COLORPLATE 95. *Portrait of the Artist, Dedicated to his Friend Daniel.* 1896. 16 × 12½″ (40.5 × 32 cm).
Musée d'Orsay, Paris.

The principal figure will be a woman turning into a statue, remaining alive but becoming an idol. The figure will stand out against a group of trees like those that grow in paradise, nowhere on earth. You can see what I mean, can't you? It's not the statue of Pygmalion coming alive and becoming human, but woman becoming idol. Nor is it Lot's daughter changed into a pillar of salt: good Lord, no!

From everywhere, fragrant flowers spring up; children frolic in the garden; young girls gather fruit; fruits pile up in huge baskets; in gracious postures, young and robust men carry them to the foot of the idol. The painting's appearance must be serious, like a religious evocation, melancholy, and exuberant as children. Oh! I forgot, I also want to put in some cute little black pigs who use their snouts to sniff out the good things that they will eat, their snickering tails giving signs of their desire.

My characters will be life-size in the foreground, but, here, rules of perspective will oblige me to have a very high horizon, and my canvas is only 2 meters high. Therefore, I won't be able to develop the wonderful mango trees of my garden.

How difficult painting is! I'll stomp on rules with both my feet and I'll be stoned.

To be serious, colors will be serious. To be cheerful, colors that sing like sheaves of wheat will be light. How can one make a painting dark and light? Certainly there is the "between the two" which satisfied people in general but hardly pleases me.

My God, how difficult painting is when one wants to express one's thought by pictorial means and not literary ones. Obviously the painting that I want to do is far from being done, the desire is larger than my power, my weakness is immense (immensity and weakness, hmm!) Let's sleep. . . .

* * *

At my Tahiti exhibition at Durand-Ruel (in spite of the boredom of having to speak about myself, I do it here to explain my Tahitian art since it's famous for being incomprehensible): at this exhibition the crowds and then the critics howled in front of these paintings, which weren't sufficiently ventilated. No cherished perspective: only narrow alleys, alleys. . . . The air was stifling such as in an impending cataclysm, etc. Probably, the ignorance of perspective, lack of a point of view, especially incomprehension of the laws of nature. Well then, I want to defend myself.

Would they prefer that I present an imaginary Tahiti, similar to the Parisian countryside, in proper lines, raked? And, this product of deep thought and deductive logic, drawn from me and not from materialistic theories made by Parisian bourgeois, in their eyes becomes a serious error, that of not screaming along with the crowd. One of them cries: "Do you understand Symbolism? Personally I don't understand it at all." Another, witty one (my God, how much wit in Paris!) writes; "To amuse your children, send them to the Gauguin exhibition; they will have fun looking at the colored images representing quadrumanous females lying on the cloth of a billiard table, all of it adorned with words of the local language," etc.

These people don't understand anything! Is it too simple for the overly witty and refined Parisians?

The island—a mountain above the horizon of the sea, surrounded by a narrow strip of land on the coral reefs. Geographic information. Thick is the shadow that falls from the large tree backed against the mountain, from the large tree which masks the formidable cave. The depth of the woods, thick as well.

Any receding perspective would be nonsense. Eager to suggest a luxurious and disordered nature, a tropical sun that inflames everything around it, I had to give my characters a suitable environment.

This is truly life outdoors, but it is *intimate*, in the thickets, the shady streams, these women whispering in an immense palace decorated by nature itself with all the richness that Tahiti contains. Whence all these fabulous colors, this enflamed—but softened, silent—air.

"But none of that exists!"

"Yes, it exists, as the equivalent of the grandeur, depth, and mystery of Tahiti when it must be expressed in one square meter of canvas."

This Tahitian Eve is very subtle, very intelligent in her naiveté. Hiding in the depths of their childlike eyes, the enigma remains incommunicable for me.

It is no longer a little, pretty Rarahu listening to a beautiful romance by Pierre Loti while playing the guitar (also by pretty Pierre Loti). It is Eve after the fall, still able to walk naked without being immodest, maintaining all her animal beauty as on the first day. Her loins stay solid—maternity couldn't disfigure her: the feet of quadrumane! Fine. Like Eve, her body has retained an animal grace. But her head has progressed with evolution, thought has developed subtlety, love has imprinted an ironic smile on her lips and, naively, she looks into her memory for the reason for the past, for the present. Enigmatically, she looks at you.

"It's intangible," it has been said.

Fine, I agree.

* * *

I still have to talk about color from the unique point of view of art. Of color alone as a language of the eye that listens, of its suggestive property (says A. Delaroche) well suited to helping the imaginative impulse, decorating our dream, opening a new door into the infinite and the mysterious. Cimabue seemed to have pointed out the gates of this Eden to posterity, but posterity responded that his was dare-devilish. Orientals, Persians, and others have, above all, printed a complete dictionary of this language of the eye that listens; they endowed their carpets with a marvelous eloquence. O, painters who ask for a color technique, study those carpets, you will find in them all that is science but, who knows, the book might be sealed; you can't read it. Then the recollection of bad traditions obstructs you. From color, so determined by its own charm and indetermined as a designation of objects perceived in nature, a "What could that possibly mean?" comes forth, disquieting, and disrupting your capacities for analysis. So what?

Rarahu is the vahiné of the European visitor to Tahiti in Pierre Loti's novel The Marriage of Loti, *which was first entitled* Rarahu.

Letter from Gauguin to Daniel de Monfreid

On Renewed Plans To Work

February 1898

I did not write you last month, I didn't have anything more to tell you that wasn't repetitive, then later I didn't feel up to it. As soon as the mail arrived, having received nothing from Chaudet, suddenly my health was almost restored; that is, with no risk any more of dying naturally, I wanted to kill myself. I went off to hide on the mountain where my corpse would have been devoured by the ants. I didn't have a gun, but I had some arsenic that I had hoarded when I was sick with eczema:

Georges-Alfred Chaudet (d. 1899), painter with whom Gauguin left many of his works when he returned to Tahiti in 1895. Chaudet was able to sell some of them and send the money to Gauguin at intervals until 1898, when he helped to organize the Gauguin exhibition at Vollard's and temporarily consigned some of the unsold works to that dealer. After Chaudet's death, Gauguin, feeling he still had receipts of sales due him, tried unsuccessfully to settle accounts with his brother.

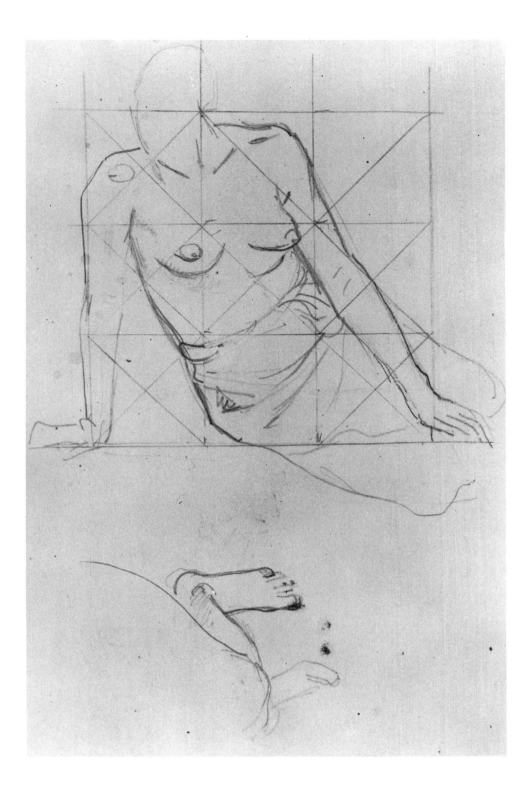

Sketch for *Where Do We Come From? What Are We? Where Are We Going?* On deposit at the Musée Gauguin, Papeari, Tahiti. Although Gauguin told Monfreid that he used no preliminary studies for his large mural *Where Do We Come From?*, this study indicates otherwise.

whether the dose was too strong, or the vomiting nullified the action of the poison by expelling it, I don't know. Finally, after a night of terrible suffering, I went back to my lodgings. All during this month, I have been plagued by a pressure at the temples, then dizziness, and nausea at my tiny meals. This month I receive 700 francs from Chaudet and 150 francs from Mauffra [sic]: with that I pay the most relentless creditors, and continue to live as before, on troubles and shame, until May, when the bank will have seized and sold dirt-cheap my belongings, among other things my paintings. Well, we'll see then about starting over in some other way. I must tell you that my resolution was firmly made for December. At that time I wanted, before dying, to paint a great canvas that I had in mind, and for the whole month I worked day and night in an unprecedented fever. What! it's not a canvas done like a Puvis de Chavannes, with studies from nature, then preliminary cartoon, etc. It is all dashed off with the tip of the brush, on burlap full of knots and wrinkles, so that it's appearance is terribly rough.

Maxime Maufra (1861–1918), painter who met Gauguin in Pont-Aven in the summer of 1890 and reestablished contact after Gauguin returned to Paris in 1893. Evidently Maufra bought art from Gauguin on credit, and here Gauguin refers to receipt of partial payment.

COLORPLATE 105

They will say it's slipshod . . . unfinished. It is true that one cannot judge oneself accurately but, nonetheless, I think that this canvas not only surpasses in merit all the preceding ones, but even that I will never do a better or a similar one. I put into it before dying all my energy, such a sorrowful passion in terrible circumstances, and so clear a vision without corrections, that all that is hasty disappears, and life rises up out of it. It doesn't stink of models, technique, and so-called rules—which I have always shaken off, though sometimes with fear.

It is a canvas 4.5 by 1.7 meters high. The two upper corners are chromium yellow with the inscription on the left and my signature on the right, like a fresco damaged in the corners and applied onto a gold wall. On the lower right, a sleeping baby, then three crouching women. Two figures dressed in purple confide their reflections to one another; an enormous figure crouched deliberately and not in perspective raises its arms in the air and looks, astonished, at the two personages who dare to think about their destiny. A figure in the middle picks a fruit. Two cats near a child. A white goat. The idol, its two arms raised mysteriously and rhythmically, seems to point to the hereafter. A crouching figure seems to listen to the idol; then, lastly, an old woman near death seems to accept, to resign herself to what she thinks and brings the legend to an end; at her feet a strange white bird holding a lizard in its foot represents the uselessness of idle words. Everything takes place on the bank of a stream in the woods. In the background, the sea, then the mountains of the neighboring island. Despite the gradations of color, the appearance of the landscape is consistently blue and Veronese green from end to end. Against that, all the nude figures stand out in bold orange. If one were to tell the students of the Beaux-Arts for the Rome competition, "The painting you are to do will represent: "Where do we come from, what are we, where are we going?"—what would they do? I have finished a philosophical piece of work on this theme comparable to the Gospel: I think it is good: if I have the strength to copy it, I will send it to you. . . .

His "philosophical work" is "L'Eglise Catholique et les temps moderne" ("The Catholic Church and Modern Times"), forty pages of the Diverses Choses *manuscript in which he asked: "Coming to terms with this ever-present problem 'Where do we come from? What are we? Where are we going?' what is our ideal, natural, rational destiny?" He did copy this text, although he never sent it to Monfreid. Entitled* L'Esprit moderne et le Catholicisme, *it is now in the St. Louis Art Museum.*

Henry Lemasson

ENCYCLOPEDIE DE LA FRANCE ET D'OUTRE-MER

"Paul Gauguin as Seen by One of His Contemporaries in Tahiti"

February 1950

Henry Lemasson (1870–1956) was an ethnographic photographer specializing in scenes of Oceania.

I knew the painter Paul Gauguin very well during the last eight years of his life, from 1895 to 1903. Like him, at that time I lived in our Polynesian colony, where I held both the posts of Director of Postal Services for French Oceania and Postmaster for the Postal Bureau in Papeete, the capital of the colony. Because of this double title, I had reason to see Gauguin frequently. He lived in the district of Punaauia, about ten kilometers from Papeete, and whenever the monthly postal courier that linked Tahiti and France through America came or went, Gauguin would come to my office to receive or to mail his personal correspondence.

*   *   *

Colonial house in Tahiti, ca. 1900. Photo by Henry Lemasson. Musée Gauguin, Papeari, Tahiti.

Mask. ca. 1893. Bronze. Height: 9⅞″ (25 cm). Musée d'Orsay, Paris.

Well, in 1898 Gauguin had just finished his large painting . . . *Where do we come from? What are we? Where are we going?* He asked me to photograph it for him so that he could send the photos to his correspondents in Paris.

So, on 2 June 1898, I went to Punaauia by bicycle to take this photo. I was accompanied by my friend M. Vermeesch, the Collector and Director of the Registry Service, the same man who, five years later, acting as trustee, instituted the public sale of Gauguin's furniture and household goods after his death. This is the explanation of the painting's subject that the artist gave us: "On the right, a newborn child; on the left, an old woman with a bird, symbolic portent of approaching death. Between these extremes of life is mankind, loving and active. And in this terrestrial space, a statue symbolizing the Divinity that is inherent in humanity."

* * *

Gauguin, who had just turned 50 in 1898, was 22 years older than I. In Punaauia, the artist lived in a wooden hut in the simple style of most of the local European and even native habitations, a hut summarily fitted out with ill-matched furniture and other objects, where, in the words of the poet, a handsome disorder was an artistic effect! On either side of

COLORPLATE 105

Eve. ca. 1895. India ink and gouache. National Gallery of Art, Washington, D.C.; Rosenwald Collection.

Colonials and native women in front of wooden house. Papeete, Tahiti. ca. 1900. Photo by Charles Spitz. Photo courtesy of Musée Gauguin, Papeari, Tahiti.

the entrance there were statuettes in both wood and clay that he had made himself. Several meters separated his house from the road coming from Papeete, which circled Tahiti by the west coast of the island. In his neighborhood there were several other wooden and straw huts made with leaves of coconut-palm trees spread asymmetrically beneath the foliage of the large trees and shrubs that grew according to Nature's whim. On the other side of the road, facing Gauguin's house, there were small, very fertile, and well-timbered hills forming the foothills of the mountains that made up the whole interior of the island, among which there were very picturesque valleys and a prodigious abundance of vegetation.

Gauguin's neighbors within a few hundred meters were two or three simple French colonists and several native families. His painting studio, perpendicular to the road and a few meters from his hut, was made of unplaned pieces of wood which supported the inner partitions and the roof of coconut-palm leaves. One of the sides was movable and served as a bay window without glass. And there also, even more so than in his hut, reigned the greatest disorder, or rather, it was somehow temporary or unfinished, as can be verified in my photo of his painting. The artist was an imposing figure, blue eyes, somewhat swarthy, ruddy complexion, brown hair and beard that were graying, a sparse goatee. When at home he generally dressed in the manner of the natives, in a simple cotton pullover and a loincloth or *pareu* (pronounced paréou), leaving his legs naked. When he came into Papeete, he dressed like a European: a jacket (with a straight collar) and white linen pants, or more often blue, of a type of Vichy cotton, white linen slippers, and a wide-brimmed straw hat. Ulcerous wounds on his legs, the consequence of his highly unhealthy state, caused him to limp slightly; he was aided by a heavy, rustic cane.

His habitual mode of transportation when he came into Papeete was a light, American horse-drawn carriage. This was certainly no indication of luxury. In Tahiti, where there were not yet any cars, this mode of transportation, because of its inexpensiveness, was attainable by most of the European inhabitants and many of the natives. A small carriage on sale did not cost much more than two or three hundred francs, and a

Title for *Le Sourire*. 1899–1900.
Woodcut. Museum of Fine Arts, Boston;
The William E. Nickerson Fund.

Te Atua (The Gods). 1894. Woodcut,
printed in color. Block: 8¹/₁₆ × 14″ (20.5
× 36 cm). The Museum of Modern Art,
New York; Lillie P. Bliss Collection.

small native horse even less, and it was less expensive and easy to feed
due to the abundance of grazing land.

Embittered by the mediocrity of his material existence and by his
physical suffering, his uncompromising artist's pride wounded, irrever-
ent by temperament, Gauguin was naturally moody and often morose.
Believing, rightly or wrongly, that the authorities of the administration
were responsible for his tribulations, he became involved in local politics
and helped to edit the opposition newspaper, *Les Guêpes*, the title of
which was inspired by the unforgettable newspaper run by Alphonse
Karr half a century earlier. In his articles the painter proved himself to
be very satirical and sharp-tongued. He attacked each one of them, taking them, as they say, by rank, starting with the Governor and continuing with the Secretary General and other persons of distinction who
made up the majority party of the General Council. With an ingratitude
that could not help but turn against him in such a small, closed political
atmosphere as that of this tiny colony . . . he hurt himself with his own
wasp's stinger by putting off certain people who had until then extended to him their sympathetic assistance both materially and morally.

*Alphonse Karr (1808–1890), novelist
and satirical essayist.*

Independent of his role as a writer at the newspaper *Les Guêpes*, he
founded by himself and with his own money a small satirical monthly
review which he called *Le Sourire*, an allusion to the other great Parisian
humoristic review, *Le Rire*. *Le Sourire* was illustrated and mimeographed
by Gauguin himself and he wrote the articles in an apocalyptic style that
forced the readers to reread them to try to understand or interpret their
exact sense.

One of the first issues of *Le Sourire* began with this racy antithesis: "The *Petit Journal* has a circulation of one million, *Le Sourire* has 21!" And the rest of the article continued in the same biting style. This revue only came out for a few months. In the meantime, the position of Secretary Treasurer of the Caisse Agricole became vacant. The Caisse Agricole de Tahiti was a small banking establishment for deposits and mortgages. Gauguin, who worked in banking before he became a painter, made the most of this reference in order to obtain the vacant position. But his impenitent Bohemian attitude, his irreverence, his pamphlets against the local administration did not speak in his favor. Therefore, he was ousted. . . .

Gustave Geffroy

LE JOURNAL

"Gauguin"

20 November 1898

Gustave Geffroy (1855–1926), novelist, journalist, and regular contributor to the liberal review La Justice. *He championed the Impressionists, especially Monet, in the 1880s and 1890s.*

Still in Tahiti, Paul Gauguin sends a series of canvases to Paris of the same grand decorative style as before and, for the most part, softened with a human grace that delicately contrasts with the rebarbarative rudenesses and also with the deformations often willed by the artist. In this manner, Paul Gauguin eases access to his conceptions and removes from discussion not only the pretext of an enigmatic bitterness, but also the assumption of a mystifying thought hidden behind lines and arbitrary colors. I think that a too-strongly held belief in artifice is still evident here, but there is also a very lively and very charming taste for nature returning. This taste is perceptible—what am I saying?—it is asserted by these bathing women in puerile gestures, in the pink countryside with flowering trees, by these gatherings, by this group of girls of a living beauty locked in statuary shapes, and by so many details of this huge beach where beings rest, dream, and pass in slow movement; these young girls, this old woman, these children, and these kittens of such a pretty, true animation.

COLORPLATE 105

More than ever it is regrettable that the powers of Paul Gauguin's decorative creation have not been recognized and that he has not been given complete freedom to express himself in glass and tapestry. While so many jobs are arbitrarily distributed to painters who are content to hang their ordinary paintings on walls that ought to be decorated, this painter, who has in him what so many others lack, is ignored. Stained-glass work especially would make him valued and would illuminate the opaque element of his compositions. Will someone one day want to experiment with giving Paul Gauguin the opportunity for a complete expression of his mind?

Tahitian Woman. 1898. Canvas.
28¼ × 36½″ (72 × 93 cm).
Ordrupgaardsamlingen, Copenhagen.
Photo: Ole Woldbye.

Thadée Natanson

LA REVUE BLANCHE

"On M. Paul Gauguin"

December 1898

M. Vollard is exhibiting in his shops ten or so canvases recently arrived
in France. In reality, aside from a very successful landscape and a small,
particularly pleasing panel that has the charming look of an illumination of olden days—of which it has the pure and brilliant coloration and
naiveté, right up to the gilding—there are eight motifs inspired by the
setting in which the painter lives and a large, mysterious, decorative
panel that groups them together. These motifs could just as well represent studies in counterpoint as discrete studies.

    M. Gauguin's talent has lost none of its delicacy or its pungency: his
color maintains that fine purity, those jewel-like shimmerings, those
depths and transparencies of which he holds the secret. It even seems—
is it only the artist's merit, and has time not played a role?—that one takes
greater pleasure in his riches. What appears more perceptible is the
freedom of his forms, and, for example, the grace of certain nudes; it is
as if the painter, more truly courageous, is less afraid of seducing us; the
fact is that, for example, a canvas like these nude women, bronzed
nymphs frolicking among the branches, is full of seductions, altogether
alluring. It is not that M. Gauguin has given up demonstrating energy,
boldness, or even terrifying us. He can still square the limbs of a Negress and carve in wood as he used to the monstrous and magnificent
hideousness of a fetish. But increasingly seductive backgrounds embellish his canvases with graceful or dazzling fairylands, and more pretty
details mingle therein, like those fleeing nude silhouettes or the animals

COLORPLATE 94
COLORPLATE 105
COLORPLATE 103

Tahitian Bathers. 1897. 28⅞ × 36¼"
(73.3 × 91.8 cm). The Barber Institute
of Fine Arts, Birmingham, England.

he has observed. He has not given up his taste for hieratic ornaments, but not far from some sacred bird two supple little cats play; pretty goats climb along steep rocks; and if he presents for us a sort of altar or bed as being sacerdotal, made of precious metals, the nude female body that stretches out upon it displays a grace to which the painter had disaccustomed us.

Neither has M. Gauguin given up making us think by means of the plastic arts; of painting here. The motto inscribed in the frame of the principal painting invites us to meditate upon the mystery of our destiny. It is the Tahitians who have provided the models, but the motto—written in French, it must be added—is universal.

M. Gauguin's philosophical or, if you will, moral merit can be considered separately, especially if one relishes it less than his plastic gifts. It would lead to examining serious and complex questions and would lead us too far. Moreover, the paintings stand, if not in spite of, at least apart from, him. One can limit oneself to them.

Rendering homage once again to the profound, charming qualities that they evidence, let us yet note that the meaning that ought to emerge from the large canvas is at first difficult to grasp, and that, furthermore, it does not confer sufficient unity upon the painting. The composition, in order to justify itself—since it does not do so materially enough—calls for comment: it remains obscure.

Each of the motifs, on the contrary, needs no comment. One must take into account the modifications that the whole required and the role to which each motif had to adapt, but, taken by itself, each motif fills the frame that encloses it better, stands on its own as a full canvas, a self-sufficient object, and is generally more satisfying, more gratifying, than its counterpart on the whole.

Letters from Gauguin to
Daniel de Monfreid

On His Sufferings

22 February 1899

The future looks very dark to me once more, see for yourself. Still very ill, I don't know when I'll be able to work; in that case, you will receive nothing new before September 1900. From now until then, the odds are against my selling anything and in five months I will have nothing left in my pocket despite everything you have sent me. When one is late, one loses on every side. The time that I was obliged to work at the public works made me lose an enormous amount of time: I went back to find my hut in a deplorable state. The rats destroyed the roofing and as a result the rain damaged many things. A whole series of drawings, very useful records, destroyed by the cockroaches, a large unfinished canvas also destroyed by those dirty insects. I had taken my courage in both hands, and somewhat confident, reassured by your recent successes in selling, I was a little quick in forging ahead—too quick (I see it today). But it was very necessary not to lose everything, to repair the disasters, restore the roofing, and somewhat replenish my wardrobe and linen. I had *nothing* left.

I don't understand the poor condition of my last canvases at all: it must be that they were badly damaged in transit.

A lot of color, you suggest . . . but with what money could I pay for it, if I were lavish with paints. You can see for yourself how many *meters* there are on a large covered canvas. Furthermore, working with a full brush is very dangerous if you go fast, especially in a *hot* country, you must apply the paint carefully and daily, as it dries, otherwise you make *mud*. And in that case, I would attain only a third of my output; at the prices they sell for. . . . Besides I think that time, with wax, will effect great improvements in my canvases. Moreover, on my first trip my canvases were considerably less loaded with paints, and I don't think they were any the worse for that.

Excuse the incoherence of my letter, but I am enormously agitated. This bombshell from Vollard is tormenting my brain and I can't sleep. A new doctor has come to the hospital and has taken, I don't know why, a liking to me and has undertaken to cure me, but he says it will take a long time, for the disease is very complicated and chronic. The eczema is complicated by erysipelas and by the rupture of small varicose veins.

Why didn't I die last year? I'm going to be 51 years old, worn out, tired in all parts; my vision is becoming worse every day; so the energy necessary for this continuous struggle is running out. . . .

André Fontainas

MERCURE DE FRANCE

"Modern Art"

May 1900

André Fontainas (1865–1948), Belgian Symbolist poet and art critic for Mercure de France *with whom Gauguin corresponded during his second Tahitian sojourn.*

I do not like M. Paul Gauguin's art very much. For a long time I turned away from it; I spoke of it in a bantering, somewhat dismissive tone; I hardly knew it. This time, I have carefully studied the handful of recent canvases that are exhibited in M. Vollard's shop in the rue Laffitte, and if my feeling about them has changed very little, I have at least sensed within myself a birth and affirmation of a definite and profound esteem for the painter's grave, deliberate, and sincere work. I sought to understand; I believe I fathomed a few of his motives or goals; I caught myself commenting on them and discussing them, enthusiastic about several, rejecting a few others. In any case, even after that diligent study I was never enraptured or moved as I remember having been by certain other artists; I sought reasons for my coldness, and I believe I have discovered them.

I hold against M. Gauguin neither his drawing, so often criticized, nor his exoticism. I would praise him for them, rather, if there were, in reality, any reason to. Indeed, what other explanation for his drawing can one accept than Balzac's, in the *Unknown Masterpiece*: "The line is the means by which man makes an accounting of the effect of light upon objects. Form is . . . an intermediary for communicating ideas, sensations, a vast poetry among ourselves. Art's mission is not to copy nature, but to express it." Thus, I acknowledge Gauguin's right to express himself as he sees fit, as long as he gives birth in the soul of the observer to sensations, ideas, whatever—a reverie analogous to his own. In this, I admit, M. Gauguin is irreproachable. He has invented his drawing, perhaps, although it is close to Van Gogh's or even Cézanne's; his drawing, willful, with a precise and new arabesque, acts with certainty; one could not, in good faith, find fault with it.

As for the exoticism, it is the same; everyone chooses, as he pleases, a common or a singular domain; of itself, that is of no importance. The essential thing, for I cannot see here an exact reproduction of Tahitian or Marquesan sites, is that the painter's art gives us the idea—false, true, it doesn't matter—of a warm, luxuriant, primitive land, with vast and dense vegetation, deep and clear waters, violent contrasts of light and air, peopled by a grave, somewhat precious, and uncultured race. M. Gauguin forsook Brittany's too-affected simplicity for oceanic mirages; that is one more guarantee of his absolute sincerity: he is over there, on his happy isle, no longer bolstering the universal mania for the pleasures of the Breton lay, the antiquarian resuscitation of that vast chivalric romance—tedious as it is! He no longer cares for the advantages of his glory among cliques; he is alone in the heart of the distant seas, and the few works that he sends to friends now and then still attest to us that he is working.

What, from the outset, strikes whomever wishes to look is the high concern in his canvases for an arrangement that is above all decorative. The landscape that in composing the skillful, calm harmony, is ordered not so much with an eye to a brusquely picturesque effect as with the nearly always realized aim of establishing a hearty yet pensive basis for the emotion that is to spring from it. If the brutal contrasts of rich, full,

In Balzac's Chef d'oeuvre inconnu *(1831, revised 1837) a reclusive, eccentric painter, Frenhofer, is tortured by an inability to realize his most compelling pictorial ideas, which evolve as chaotic, indecipherable skeins of paint. Cézanne identified his own plight with Frenhofer's.*

and vibrant tones, which never blend or glide into one another through intermediary values, compel a momentarily diverted attention, one must certainly recognize as well that, though often musical, bold, and triumphal, at other times they miss their effect through the monotony of repetition, by the clash, irritating in the long run, of a bright red beside a vibrant green, done the same way, to an identical end. And yet, without fail, in M. Gauguin's art, it is the landscape that is satisfying and exalting. He has conceived a broad, new way of executing this, synthetically, and, according to a phrase he himself wrote in the *Mercure,* "by seeking the harmony of human life and animal and plant lives, in compositions in which I left an important part to the great voice of the earth."

There is, at M. Vollard's, conceived in this fashion, and, I believe, quite characteristic of the artist's personality, not far from a most delicate, already old, landscape in which people at the water's edge gaze at reflected sunlight quivering on the waves, an entirely decorative panel: Amid the dark blues and the greens, there intermingle, in pure arabesques, noble plant and animal forms. Nothing more; it is a perfect harmony of forms and colors.

And here, too, is a landscape of various yellows, spread like the delicate curtain of a fine and weightless golden rain. Here and there the green of a single leaf and the multiple detail of berries of a vivid red. A man in burlap raises himself toward the lower branches of a tree. That, the light, the easy effort of the gesture, the grouping of things and colors, make up a simple and exquisite painting.

Ah, if only M. Gauguin were always like that! Or even when he presents us with hieratic dancing women, slow amid the dense landscape, beneath the trees; or nude women bathing in the glory of a strangely irradiated vegetation; but, too often, the lean, colorless, and rigid characters in his dreams imprecisely represent the sickly forms of a clumsily metaphysical imagination, whose meaning is haphazard and whose expression is arbitrary. Nothing resides in such canvases save the evidence of deplorable errors, for abstractions are not communicated by concrete images if, in the artist's very dream, they have not first taken shape in some material allegory that, living, signifies them. That is the value of the lofty example that Puvis de Chavannes gives by his art. In order to represent a philosophical ideal, he conceived harmonious groupings whose attitudes were able to inspire in us a dream analogous to his own. In the large panel that M. Gauguin is exhibiting, nothing, neither the two supple and pensive figures who are passing through it, tranquil and so beautiful, nor the skillful evocation of a mysterious idol would reveal the allegory's meaning to us, had he not taken care to write in a corner at the top of the canvas: "Where do we come from? What are we? Where are we going?"

One's interest, furthermore, is diverted from the crouching nude woman making a gesture in the foreground—despite the bizarreness, to which one becomes accustomed, of these almost savage figures. Again, it is attracted entirely by certain charms of the setting where the scene unfolds.

I do not want, moreover, if I draw attention to the grace of a woman half-reclining out of doors in a magnificent and strange sort of bed, to stress the other panels, where the obstinate innovator's dogged technique appears in all the somewhat brutal fury of his effort.

On the whole, M. Gauguin is unquestionably a rare painter to whom the opportunity to manifest the generous ardor of his temperament in some important decorative composition on the walls of a public building has been too long denied. There, we would know just what he can be, and, were he to guard against his tendency toward the abstract, we would see born from his effort, I am certain, a powerful and naturally harmonious work.

The "phrase in the Mercure*" is from Gauguin's introduction to the catalogue for an exhibition of Séguin's works in February 1895, reprinted that month in* Mercure de France.

COLORPLATE 105

Tahitian Woman with Children. 1901. 38¼ × 29¼" (97.2 × 74.3 cm). The Art Institute of Chicago; Helen Birch Bartlett Memorial Collection.

Paul Gauguin

LES GUÊPES

On the Chinese in Oceania

12 October 1900

Gentlemen:

I must first thank you for having responded to our appeal, for having come to this conference. This is not a common assembly of men like one would find anywhere else that I see here before me, but a united family, a reunion of friends, all far from the motherland, having at heart to secure, through their hard work and courage, their own fortune and that of the colony—thus responding to the desires of the homeland and, above all, feeling the glory of being French.

In Papeete at a protest meeting organized by the Catholic Party on 23 September 1900, Gauguin spoke against the increasing presence of Chinese people in the South Pacific.

It is especially on these grounds, which are particularly dear to me, that I wanted, and that I dared (overcoming my timidity), to speak to you for just a few minutes. My situation as a newcomer and as an artist does not permit me to expand upon details that others more competent than myself will address after me. It is therefore in a general sense that I am going to speak to you about a very grave question (the celebrated Chinese question), a very grave question, in that the vitality of Tahiti is compromised. It is up to you, if there is still time, to remedy the situation at the end of the meeting by passing a thoughtful resolution that is as strong as it is legitimate.

Statistics show the imposing figure of twelve million Chinese in the Pacific progressively seizing all the commerce of Oceania. What is the famous invasion of Attila the Hun, whose terror history hands down to us, next to this onslaught?

Unless we remedy the situation, Tahiti will quickly be lost: Gentlemen, will you wait for death, that you may be buried? No, not when this is in the memory of your glorious ancestors who made you free citizens at the price of their blood.

Along with the Chinese who are invading our beautiful colony, something else is naturally occurring; I mean this new half-Chinese, half-Tahitian generation. Half! do not believe it, because the Chinese leave their indelible mark physically as well as morally. The child is given French citizenship at birth, and later becomes a voter like ourselves. This yellow stain soiling our national flag brings a flush of shame to my face. In the name of morals so precious to certain people for some time now, it is becoming a crime to make such a monstrosity.

I will strive to believe, and you may think completely the opposite, that the administration has the best intentions in the world for the country, for its prosperity today and tomorrow. However, involved as it often is in the political struggles that are always the ruin of a colony, or misled by a surplus of labor, it sometimes preaches in ignorance. Certainly the press, which is made up of people competent in colonial matters, experienced in the affairs of Tahiti, loyal to their duty, without greed, and devoted, all, to the just cause of the working colonists, strives, though in vain, to warn the administration of the danger posed by the Chinese invasion, asking for the protection it feels it has a right to. But one may have believed that this was not the general opinion, that it was only the opinion of a few malcontents who wished to be critical just for the sake of being critical.

Confronted by this absolute and methodical silence, it was our responsibility to appeal to all those who in their hearts love their country; because it is up to you, gentlemen, to take care to save the colony.

Once you have voiced your opinion by putting your signature at the bottom of the petition that will be passed among you, people in France will know that there is a corner of the world far from the capital, a French Colony, where the French take pride in the title they bear, not wishing to become Chinese, and in this way people will not be able to ignore our rights without incurring terrible responsibilities.

COLORPLATE 96. *Vase of Flowers, after Delacroix* (Frontispiece for *Noa Noa*). 1894–1897. Watercolor.
6¾ × 4¾" (17 × 12 cm). Louvre Museum, Paris. Based on a painting by Delacroix, now in the Philadelphia Museum
of Art, which Gauguin knew from a reproduction in the 1878 catalogue of the Arosa collection.

COLORPLATE 97. *Tahitian Landscape.* ca. 1897. Watercolor. 10 × 13¾″ (25.5 × 35 cm).
Private collection.

COLORPLATE 98. *Thatched Hut under Palm Trees* (Folio 181 from *Noa Noa*). ca. 1896–1897.
Watercolor. 11¾ × 8¾″ (30 × 22.5 cm). Cabinet des Dessins, Louvre Museum, Paris.

COLORPLATE 99. *The Bathers.* 1898. 23¾ × 36¾″ (60.4 × 93.4 cm).
National Gallery of Art, Washington, D.C.; Gift of Sam A. Lewisohn.

COLORPLATE 100. *Three Tahitians.* 1898. 28¾ × 36⅜″ (73 × 93 cm).
National Gallery of Scotland, Edinburgh.

COLORPLATE 101. *Nave Nave Mahana (Delightful Day)*. 1896. 37 × 51″ (94 × 130 cm).
Musée des Beaux-Arts, Lyons. Photo: Bernard Lontin.

COLORPLATE 102. *No te aha oe Riri? (Why Are You Angry?)*. 1896. 37½ × 51¼ (95.3 × 130.5 cm).
The Art Institute of Chicago; Mr. and Mrs. Martin A. Ryerson Collection.

COLORPLATE 103. *Tahitian Man with His Arms Raised.* 1897. 36¼ × 28¾″ (92 × 73 cm).
Private collection.

Letter from Gauguin to
Daniel de Monfreid

On Moving to the Marquesas

June 1901

I think that in the Marquesas, with the ease with which one can get models (something that is becoming more and more difficult in Tahiti), and then with landscapes to discover—in short, with entirely new and more primitive elements, I will do some fine things. Here my imagination was starting to cool; then, too, the public is too used to Tahiti. The world is so foolish that, when it is shown canvases containing new and *terrifying* elements, Tahiti will become comprehensible and charming. My canvases of Brittany became rose water because of Tahiti; Tahiti will become *eau de Cologne* because of the Marquesas. . . .

Paul Gauguin

AVANT ET APRES

On Atuona

January–February 1903

There I was, when I told myself it was time to take off for a simpler country, with fewer civil servants. And I intended to pack my trunks to go to the Marquesas. The promised land, more land than one knew what to do with, meat, poultry, and, to take you around here and there, a gendarme gentle as a lamb.

In this fashion, with a carefree heart, confident as a locked-in virgin, I took the boat and arrived serenely in Atuona, county seat of Hiva-Oa.

I had to cut down my excesses particularly. The ant is not a lender, that's his least fault: and I came across like a grasshopper that had sung all summer long.

First of all, the news upon my arrival was that there was no land whatever for sale or for rent, except from the mission, and perhaps not even there. The bishop was away, and I had to wait a month; my trunks and a load of timber remained on the beach.

During that month I attended Mass every Sunday, as you might expect, forced to pay my role of sincere Catholic and polemicist against the Protestants. My reputation was made, and His Eminence, with no inkling of my hypocrisy, was willing (because it was I) to sell me a small lot filled with pebbles and brush, for a price of 650 francs. I set courageously to work, and thanks again to some men recommended by the bishop, I was quickly settled in.

Hypocrisy has its merits.

Once my hut was finished, I had no intention of fighting with the

Hiva-Oa, or Hivaoa, was the Marquesan island where Gauguin was to remain, in the town of Atuona, to the end of his life.

Photo (ca. 1903) of three wooden sculptures by Gauguin. Left to right: *Père Paillard, Cylinder with Two Figures, Thérèse* Photo courtesy of Musée Gauguin, Papeari, Tahiti.

Protestant pastor, who moreover is a well-brought-up and very liberal-minded young man: nor did I intend to go back to church.

A tart came on the scene, and war was declared.

When I say a tart, I am being modest, for all the tarts arrived without even being asked.

His Eminence is a rabbit, whereas I am an old rooster, good and tough and fairly husky. If I were to say that it was the rabbit that started, I would be telling the truth. To seek to condemn me to the vow of chastity! it's a bit much: No, no, Nanette.

It was nothing for me to cut two superb pieces of rosewood and carve them in the Marquesan style. One portrayed a horned devil (Father Paillard). The other, a charming woman, flowers in her hair. It was enough to have called her Thérèse so that everyone, without exception, even the schoolchildren, could see there an allusion to that well-known love affair.

If it is a fib, at any rate it is not I who created it.

* * *

The Marquesan, especially, has an extraordinary sense of decoration.

Give him an object with any geometric shape at all, even a hump-backed geometry, he will manage—all harmoniously—to leave no shocking and jarring empty space. The basis of it is the human body or face. Especially the face. One is amazed to find a face where one thought there was a strange geometric figure. Always the same thing, yet never the same thing.

Today, one could not find, at any price, those beautiful objects of bone, tortoise-shell, or ironwood that they used to make. The police *stole* everything and sold it to amateur collectors, and yet something that would have been easy for it to do never occurred to the Administration for a single instant: To set up a museum in Tahiti of all Oceanian art.

Yet all those people who profess to be so educated had no idea, not for an instant, of the merit of the Marquesan artists.

Not the least civil servant's wife, faced with it, failed to cry out, "But it's horrible! It's barbarity!" Barbarity! That's all they can talk about.

* * *

Let us return to Marquesan art. That art has disappeared thanks to the missionaries. The missionaries considered that to sculpt, to decorate, was fetishism, was to offend the Christian God.

The Call. ca. 1902–1903. Monotype. 17 × 10½″ (43 × 27 cm). Museum of Fine Arts, Boston; Otis Norcross Fund.

Letter from Gauguin to Gustave Fayet

On a New Printing Technique

March 1902

Gustave Fayet (1865–1925), important collector of Post-Impressionist art, a painter, and curator of the museum in his home town of Béziers who, with Monfreid's help, acquired many major Gauguin works. Fayet wrote Gauguin in 1902 proposing a retrospective at the Béziers museum; this show never took place.

I take the liberty of sending you two worthless sketches; this is no gift. At most, a kind thought. But I think they might interest you, as a painter, for the process I used to make them, which is of a childish simplicity. With a roller, you coat a sheet of ordinary paper with printer's ink; then, on another sheet placed over it, you draw whatever you want. The harder and thinner your pencil (as well as your paper), the thinner the line. That goes without saying.

   Coating the sheet of paper with lithographic ink, wouldn't there be

The Spirit Watches
(recto). ca. 1900.
Monotype. 25 × 20⅛″
(63.8 × 51.2 cm).
Städelsches
Kunstinstitut, Frankfurt.

a means of using it to make quick lithography? This is worth looking into.

I've always felt horror at all the skulduggery employed in making prints: the paper that gets dirty, the pencils that are never strong enough, the time that is lost, etc.

I forgot to tell you that if the spots left on the paper bother you, all you have to do is watch until the surface of the ink is dry without being totally so. All this to each one's temperament.

Pardon me: it's probably a secret of Pulcinella's I'm disclosing to you. However, I haven't yet seen it used.

I end my letter in a hurry because, even though our couriers take a long time to arrive, they are, on the other hand, wild to be redispatched immediately.

Accept my assurance of sincerest regards. . . .

Two Tahitians Gathering Fruit (verso). ca. 1900. Graphite pencil and blue crayon pencil. 24¾ × 20¼″ (63 × 51.5 cm). Mr. and Mrs. Paul Mellon, Upperville, Virginia.

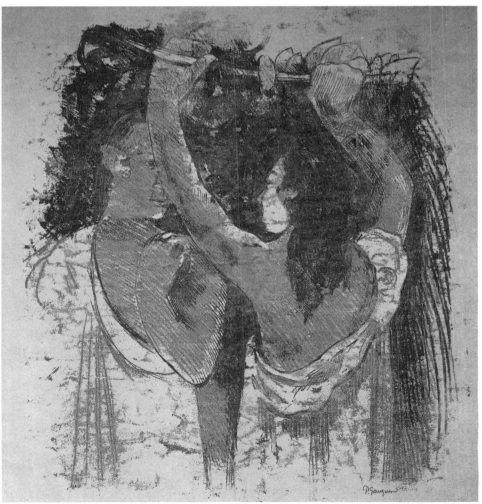

Two Tahitians Gathering Fruit (recto). ca. 1900. Monotype, printed twice, in dark brown and brown. 24¾ × 20¼″ (63 × 51.5 cm). Mr. and Mrs. Paul Mellon, Upperville, Virginia.

Letter of Sgt. Charpillet

On Gauguin's Troubles in Atuona

ca. 1935

As our friend Guillot told you, I knew the master, Paul Gauguin, in Tahiti and particularly in the Marquesas. In Tahiti, where I arrived in the beginning of 1894, I was detached to Mataiea, where, while visiting my district, I was very surprised to see paintings, at the Tahitian Anani's, on the partitions and inside windows of his European hut, that I easily recognized as those of the school of Gauguin. I then learned that this artist had stayed about a year in Mataiea, where he lived with his French vahiné. This period is described to us by Gauguin himself in *Noa-Noa*. In 1896, attached to the hospital in Papeete, I saw Gauguin there for the first time, when he returned from France. He, too, was detached to the aforementioned hospital to care for his foot, ailing as a result of a blow that he had received in a brawl in Pont-Aven [sic]. I later saw him again in Punania, toward the Punaro, where he had had a hut built the way he wanted it; there, ten minutes of conversation, as at the hospital, without becoming better acquainted. At the time, he, his originality, even his unsociability, were already much spoken of. I was then commanding the brigade at Tarapao, where all the tourists, officers, and officials stopped to eat at our headquarters, for lack of a restaurant in the area. Thus I often heard talk of Gauguin from my guests, in terms sometimes good, sometimes bad. But, as I have always liked artists, I was happy to hear the praises.

After that, it was in the Marquesas, in Atuona, that I lived for fifteen months as good neighbors with that man whom, in the course of the relations we maintained, I found extraordinary. One day, when the mail boat arrived from Tahiti, I saw Paul Gauguin enter my office, announcing to me that he wanted to settle in the Marquesas because Tahiti had become unlivable for him, and to ask me how he could obtain a plot of land in Atuona on which to build a hut. I replied that is was very difficult, that as far as I could see only the mission might perhaps let him have a parcel from one of its numerous properties. As always in the thrall of my weakness for artists, I offered to accompany him to the bishop, the Most Reverend Martin, to introduce him, and to state his case. The bishop, in some small part because I was accompanying the petitioner, sold him a plot of land in the heart of the village for 700 francs.

Paul Gauguin then had his famous "House of Pleasure" built, in the style of a lakeside dwelling elevated on piles, where I went many times to see his paintings and to have an aperitif (I reciprocated). At the time, we both went to Mass, sometimes with Dr. Buisson; seats were reserved for us. For the Fourteenth of July, I had asked Paul Gauguin to be so kind as to accept the presidency of the committee in charge of the festivities, which were to last several days, as in Papeete; he seemed to me to be happy to accept. The first small conflict between himself and the mission began from this, because he had given the first prize for singing (*ex aequo*) to the boys from the school of the Brothers of Ploërmel and to the children from the Reverend Pastor Paul Vernier's Protestant school. The director of the Brothers immediately protested the *ex aequo*. For my part, since I could not be on the committee, I could say nothing, but my conviction was that the Brothers' students had, in any case, sung their *Hymn to Joan of Arc* better than those of the opposing school *The Marseillaise*. After that, Paul Gauguin once more took up, with virulence, his gospel of the return to nature, advising the natives to live in their own fashion, and in all ways antagonizing the bishop, who forbade

Père Paillard (Father Lechery). ca. 1901. Wood. 26¾ × 7⅛ × 8⅛″ (67.9 × 18 × 20.7 cm). National Gallery of Art, Washington, D.C.; Chester Dale Collection.

his flock from associating with Gauguin. Things became more bitter. One day, I went to see how our artist was doing; I had not seen him for a few days, and he was said to be ill. When I arrived, I then saw the two effigies on either side of the stairway: one portrayed a head with a great beard, with the carved inscription: "Father Paillard," and the other, a woman's head: "St. Thérèse."

Since the bishop's trusty maid was named Thérèse, I understood. Things became increasingly bitter. With everything going from bad to worse, our poor great artist, growing more and more ill, found himself in the same situation as in Tahiti, aggravated by the state of his health; he had gotten the Catholic mission, all-powerful in the Marquesas, on his back.

Shortly after, when the dispatch boat *Durance* arrived on a tour with the governor, accompanied by M. Edouard Charlier, Chief of the Justice Department (Gauguin's *bête noire*), the governor, Edouard Petit, asked me to accompany him on a horseback ride into the most interesting part of the Atuona valley, As his guide, I showed him, in passing, Paul Gauguin's hut; he replied, to my amazement: "Oh! You know he's a rogue?" Taken aback, I replied: "*Monsieur le Gouverneur*, for my part, I have no reason to find fault with him."

Edouard Charlier (1864–1937), amateur painter, judge, and colonial administrator in Tahiti. Although Charlier befriended Gauguin in 1895, he became impatient when the artist tried to press petty charges against native women; his disfavor caused Gauguin to state his case in a polemical local newspaper, Les Guêpes (The Wasps). *In 1902, Charlier ignored Gauguin's complaints when he visited Atuona on a government fact-finding mission.*

Bernard Villaret

LA REVUE DE PARIS

"Gauguin's Final Years"

February 1953

Dr. Bernard Villaret (b. 1909), author of several travel books on Oceania.

> A mad, but sad and sorry
> adventure was my voyage to Tahiti.
>
> Paul Gauguin

Some time ago, Henri Pambrun, a literary friend, who happens to be the godson of the gendarme Claverie, famous for his quarrels with Gauguin, showed me six yellowed forms that he had discovered in the middle of a bundle of old papers forgotten in a Papeete attic. I leafed through them with growing interest.

Chance had just placed in my hands a document of indisputable authenticity, that shed an entirely new light on the almost unknown period of Gauguin's final years.

Indeed, these papers showed the account opened for M. Paul Gauguin, of Atuona, by the S.C.O., the "Société Commerciale de l'Océanie," a German company whose headquarters were in Hamburg and that had a "trading post" in Hiva-Oa. The account was opened 16 September 1901, that is, the day of Gauguin's arrival in Atuona, and closed 1 May 1903, a week before his death.

In a letter of August 1901, Gauguin was already speaking to Monfreid about the S.C.O., which was to serve him as both banking house and supplier. In its shop, he expected to find "all the objects a European needs, as well as a Tahitian." In practice, for nearly two years, he used them exclusively for his financial affairs and his provisions.

Jean-Pierre Claverie replaced Charpillet at Atuona in December 1902 and soon clashed with Gauguin, who sided with innocent natives against prosecution. Charged by Claverie with defamation of government officials, Gauguin was fined 500 francs and sentenced to three months' imprisonment; he died before his appeal could be heard.

* * *

We know that Gauguin's letters reflect his constant material concerns. Many of them, moreover, contain pressing requests for money. His extreme poverty has been extensively commented upon and still is by art lovers and artists. Furthermore, being able to rely only on that correspondence, the biographers describe the painter as living his final years "with a few dozen francs a month. . . ."

Now, the S.C.O. accounts show him spending, per year, an average of 5,500 *gold* francs, that is, around 1.1 million 1953 francs. And that was living alone, without dependents, in one of the places in the world where temptations and necessities are reduced to the minimum and where the natives manage to subsist almost without money.

The figures are there: from 16 September to 31 December 1901, the painter, who was having his hut built, spent exactly 5,712.90 francs. In the course of the year 1902, the total mounted to 5,421 francs. Although the Louis d'or is currently worth two hundred times more than in 1902, for Oceania one generally calculates the average increase in the cost of living fifty years ago on the basis of a coefficient of 175. In Gauguin's day, potatoes cost 0.50 francs per kilogram; in the Marquesas, they currently go for the equivalent of 125 French francs. Chicken, which the painter said he bought for 0.60 francs in his letters, costs 250 francs. But the prices of wine and rum have only centupled.

* * *

The painter was still in Papeete on 7 August 1901; on that date, he paid back a loan there that he had contracted at the farmers' bank. The S.C.O. records tell us the date of his arrival in the Marquesas: 16 September. On that day, he appears at the trading post, takes out a loan for 200 francs, and orders the materials necessary for the construction of his future hut.

The first letter from Hiva-Oa sent to Monfreid left in November. In it, Gauguin explains that, for him, the month of October was taken up with the chores of construction and moving in. Before building a house, he needed a plot of land, and "here, the mission owns everything." Nevertheless, eleven days after his arrival, he succeeded in buying a half-hectare from the Bishop of the Marquesas.

I found the bill of sale.

Monsignor Martin (Rogatien, Joseph) sells, 27 September 1901, to M. Gauguin (Paul), painter:

1. A parcel of land called *Papanui,* bounded: to the north; the ring road for 54 meters: to the west; Vaïtékea land, 17 meters; to the south; *Tioka*'s Aïtéani land, 54 meters: to the east; Tipa's Aïtéani land, 17 meters.

2. A parcel of land called *Aïtéani,* bounded: to the north; the above-named Papanui land for 21 meters: to the west; *Tioka*'s Aïtéani land, 106 meters: to the south; Hapuku's Téauupoo land, 44 meters: to the east; Tipa's Aïtéani land, 67 then 43 meters.

The bill stipulates the selling price: 650 francs, and Gauguin complains to Monfreid of this sum, which he considers high.

* * *

Thanks to the order for materials, we know that the frame of the house was of squared timber, and not of rough bourao trunks, as the native huts generally are, that there were four windows and a door, closed with a "French lock." He had probably hung on the walls the reproductions of the old masters that previously decorated his dwelling in Tahiti. . . .

* * *

These are the quantities of alcoholic beverages purchased by him at the Société Commerciale's Atuona branch:

In 1901 (three and a half months): red wine, 134 and a half liters; absinthe, 12 liters; rum, 35 liters.

In 1902 (twelve months): red wine, 224 and a half liters; absinthe, 32 liters; rum, 55 liters; whiskey, 3 bottles; beer, 96 bottles (to which must be added 3.4 kilograms of tobacco).

In 1903, finally (four months): red wine, 202 liters; absinthe, 10 liters; rum, 10 liters; unspecified alcohol, 5 liters; beer, 80 bottles.

One is left stunned by this great consumption, which represents: in 1902, a quarter of a liter of *100 percent pure alcohol* a day; in 1903, a third of a liter, that is to say, the equivalent of more than a half-liter daily of cognac. Attacking a strained system, this alcohol abuse must have hastened the artist's end.

* * *

It would be tedious to enumerate the cans of tripe, salmon, sardines, asparagus, beef, and the kilograms of salt provisions that Gauguin bought at the trading post. Their quantities are more than adequate, and therein lies the essential point that explains a state of vitamin deficiency that aggravated the skin infection "to mid-calf" from which Gauguin was increasingly suffering. In short, the eczema was worsened by his diet, and the artist drank more to forget his pain. . . .

* * *

Furthermore, here are his accounts: the anonymous credits correspond probably to two of Vollard's monthly payments sent together—the payments being fixed at 350 francs per month as of January 1901—and transferred to the S.C.O. by the bankers Scharff and Keyser of Hamburg:

1901

27 NOVEMBER 1901:
Without particulars (balance from the sale of his Tahiti house, deposited with the S.C.O.)   Fr 3,200.00
Vollard, Paris   685.18
Vollard, Paris   342.88

23 DECEMBER 1901:
Anonymous   348.88

Total for 1901 (two months) Fr 4,576.94

1902

23 MAY 1902:

Anonymous, the only heading: received 3p.100 (no doubt a purchase by Fayet, of March 1902, transmitted by Monfreid)   Fr 1,530.00
Anonymous (received 3p.100)   651.03
Anonymous (received 3p.100)   1,000.03

2 APRIL 1902:
Received   702.07

21 NOVEMBER 1902:
Received (sent by Vollard, 3 July 1902)   701.40
Received (Monfreid, 12 October 1902)   601.17
Received (Vollard, 22 October 1902)   706.95

Total for 1902 Fr 5,892.65

That year, until his death, nothing came for him in Atuona, but the file of the Gauguin estate indicates:

25 APRIL 1903:
Vollard   Fr   707.83

30 JUNE 1903:
Fayet (a sum that Gauguin asked him for,
as a loan, in his last letter)   1,544.19

13 AUGUST 1903:
Vollard   704.22

Total for 1903 Fr 2,956.24

*   *   *

It was because the painter accused the police of misappropriation of funds that he found himself condemned on 31 March 1903 by the Papeete court, for defamation, to three months in prison and a 500-franc fine. Gauguin is exaggerating when he gives Monfreid the figure as 1,000 francs. . . .

Here is the end. For a few months, he did not withdraw any money and does not know that he will be receiving some from Vollard and Fayet. He writes that he owes the S.C.O. 1,400 francs (that is exact: at his death we find a debit of 1,389 francs), and that he hesitates to make a trip to Tahiti to defend himself. His letter, the last, written in April to Monfreid when he was no longer leaving his bed, is a cry of anguish that ends with these often-quoted words: "All these cares are killing me. . . ."

*   *   *

The administrator of the Marquesas, Piquenot, who would later acknowledge that the painter's allegations against the police were "in part justified," would soon announce to the trustee of vacant estates, in Papeete, the death of M. Gauguin (Eugene, Henry, Paul), who departed this life in Atuona on 8 May, at eleven o'clock in the morning.

Here is the hitherto unpublished text of his report:

François Piquenot (1861–1907) was a government clerk Gauguin befriended on his second Tahiti trip. Piquenot was transferred from Papeete to Atuona to become the colonial administrator.

I have notified the deceased's creditors that they must provide me with their claims in duplicate and I am already convinced that the liabilities will greatly exceed the assets, there being little likelihood that the few paintings of the deceased, a decadent painter, will find a taker.

That was to be, at the time, his only eulogy.

Guillaume Le Bronnec

BULLETIN OF THE OCEANIC STUDIES SOCIETY

"Gauguin's Life in the Marquesas"

March 1954

Guillaume Le Bronnec (b. 1884) arrived in the Marquesas in 1910 and interviewed everyone there who had known Gauguin.

Gauguin passed away in Atuona (Hiva-Oa) on 8 May 1903. It is more than half a century since a few French and Marquesan friends accom-

Natives and Peacock. ca. 1902. Monotype. 9 × 15¼″ (23.1 × 38.6 cm). The Art Institute of Chicago; Gift of Emily Crane Chadbourne.

panied him one morning to the churchyard that overlooks Traitors' Bay. Much has been written about his final years, chiefly inaccuracies. Nearly all the writers who drew on his correspondence with his friend de Montfreid [sic] did their best to weave him a martyr's crown: Gauguin wretchedly poor, suffering from hunger; Gauguin persecuted by the police; Gauguin dying abandoned by all.

There is much exaggeration; we know that in his letters Gauguin could cleverly disguise the truth as he complained incessantly: lack of paints, of canvases; quarrels with police, with priests; and above all requests for money, with which he was, according to him, continually unprovided.

The *Revue de Paris* recently (February 1953) published an article by Dr. Villaret, who found the account books for 1901 to 1903 of the German S.C.O. trading post in the Marquesas. These accounts show that Gauguin was well provided with money, for he was able to spend more than a million francs in our currency per year.

The same accounts revealed to Dr. Villaret that Gauguin made substantial purchases of wine, rum, and absinthe (he gives the breakdown) from the S.C.O.; he concludes that the painter died as the result of alcoholism.

The author of these lines, who has been in the Marquesas for forty-three years, did not know Gauguin, having arrived in Atuona only in 1910, seven years after his passing. At that time, Gauguin's memory was still very much alive, and the author visited all the painter's French and native friends. It is their remarks, gathered over the course of long conversations, that will be reproduced hereafter, but let us first give a few details about the places and the European and native society in which he was living.

Gauguin was already well informed on Hiva-Oa before his departure for Tahiti, as he wrote his friend de Montfreid ("I am not going out there by chance"). He had only had to consult the schooner captains, the supercargoes, the merchants, and the many servicemen discharged in Tahiti, who had stayed there at the time of the occupation nineteen years earlier.

The village of Atuona, where he disembarked, occupied a few hectares of plain at the edge of the sea and dated only from the establishment of the Catholic and Protestant missions some fifty years earlier. Before that, it was the battlefield of the bellicose Naiki, Tiu, and Hamau tribes. That is why one sees none of the large platforms on which the native huts were once built. They lived high in the valley, in order to be safe from nocturnal raids, but after the establishment of the civil administration, the opening of schools for boys and girls, and by virtue of the security afforded by the presence of the French military force, a large part of the valley population came to settle there. In 1901, there were already several Europeans. At the Catholic mission was the Most Reverend Martin and often a visiting missionary; across from the church was the girls' boarding school, which numbered about two hundred students, run by six French nuns. Some 100 meters away, the School of the Brothers of Ploërmel—three brothers and about a hundred students.

On the west side of the village was the Protestant mission—with the pastor, Paul Vernier, Mme. Vernier, and two children—where a few students were also taught.

The administration, situated in the heart of the village, was represented by Dr. Buisson and the gendarme Charpillet. Across from the police headquarters was the shop of Frébault, a former noncommissioned officer. Between the church and the Brothers' school, Varney's shop ("the American, a charming lad": see Gauguin's letter to his friend de Montfreid). Going up into the village, one saw two Chinese shops: baker-restaurateurs. In the same neighborhood lived Nguyen Van Cam, a political deportee from Annam, who was Gauguin's friend from his arrival on and who helped him settle in.

He disembarked on Thursday, 16 September; Van Cam would find him a house in the heart of the village, 1.5 kilometers from the seashore, belonging to a half-Chinese, Matikaua, at a rate of 2 francs a day; his baggage would be transported there.

Gauguin wanted to have a property of his own so that he could build as he pleased. It so happened that there was a vacant lot in the heart of the village, but it belonged to the bishop. In order to dispose that church official favorably towards him, Gauguin went to Mass every morning and played the game so well that, eleven days after his arrival, the bishop sold him the coveted two pieces of land, around a hectare, for the sum of 650 francs. He admitted to his friend de Montfreid: "Having obtained my land, I never appeared in church again."

These two pieces of land were planted in breadfruit trees and some coconut palms and banana trees. Gauguin began by marking out an alley that started at the road, and decided to build, at the other end, on the ocean side, a hut on piles 2.4 meters high. The rafters and tongue-and-groove boards that had come by the schooner *Gauloise* were transported there, and under his direction two native carpenters, Tioka and Kekela, raised the house while other workmen made the bamboo framework and native women wove the coconut-frond roofing. When that work was done, there was dug, at the west end, a shallow well, the water table beneath the village being only one meter down. Three or four meters farther on, a bathtub was built of a lime and pebble mixture raised half a meter from the ground, and as deep.

At the end of October, the work done, Gauguin settled into his house, for Varney's account book for that period shows the payment for the Matikaua rent as thirty days at 2 francs: total 60 francs. He had until then taken his meals at Ayu the cook's, but before he equipped the house, he had hired as his cook a certain Kahui, a young half-Chinese, nephew of

Benjamin Franklin Varney (b. 1867) was an American who owned the best general store in Atuona.

309

his neighbor and friend Tioka. Another young man, Matahava, was already working as gardener.

The house, oriented east–west, was 12 meters long by 5.5 meters wide, built on piles 2.4 meters high. It had two rooms upstairs; one went up by a wooden staircase that ended at the door of a small room that was used as the bedroom; one passed through that to come to a large room, the atelier, lit by six large windows, two on either side, and two at the west end.

The lower part of the house was divided into four parts; below the bedroom, a small sculpture studio was set up, panelled in bamboo and laths; then came the dining room, open on two sides, and another room, also open, that was later to be used as coach house for the cart; the fourth room, the largest, below the studio, was used as the kitchen and was also panelled in bamboo and laths.

He began by placing the easel at the west end of the studio and by hanging in the bedroom a series of paintings of sexual anatomy and physiology, which is impossible to describe other than as the natives did with their crudeness of language.

Then the painter set to work, despite a continuous stream of natives coming to see his paintings—the news having spread quickly through the village (besides, Gauguin already knew everyone). Sometimes it was a white who came to pay a call; for him, he went down to the dining room to offer a glass of rum or a glass of absinthe; if it was morning, the visitor was often hosted with lunch.

His settling in completed, Gauguin began to show himself in quite a different light; he was, certainly, a great artist, but in truth it must be said that by moral standards he was not a fine character. Of an anarchistic turn of mind, he detested all authority civil and, especially, religious, whose teaching ran counter to the passions of this aging man.

Since he did not lack for money, he had at his disposal five or six girls from the valley, not shy in their ways, whom his servants fetched to serve as models by turns and who stayed all night. Nevertheless, these girls, being of changeable mood, wearied of these summonses, and the painter soon knew nights of solitude. What to do? True, at the nuns' boarding school thirty-odd girls were kept until the age of fifteen, in order to preserve them from precocious licentiousness, whom Gauguin used to see filing by on walking days.

The administration had put moral pressure on the parents to send their little girls to the nuns. It did not take Gauguin long to discover that parents who resided farther than 3 kilometers away were under no obligation to send their children to the school. He summoned the parents and explained to them that they need not fear any penalty if they withdrew their children from the nuns' school.

The result was immediate; many parents left with their daughters. A chief from Moka, in the district of Hekeani, withdrew his daughter Vaeoho Marie Rose, and Gauguin took her as his companion. She was fourteen years old. This was certainly in November, for in the American merchant Varney's sales register we see the painter buying 31 meters of chintz, muslin, and calico, plus a 200-franc sewing machine to make his new conquest's clothes.

He kept her until the middle of the following year, when, pregnant by the painter, she returned to her parents to give birth, on 14 September 1902, to a girl who was registered under the name of Tahiatikaomata Vaeoho. She is, according to the natives who knew Gauguin, his living image. She still lives in Hekeani. Married to a native of her village, a certain Hapa, she had only one daughter, Tohohina, today about thirty years old; she, too, has Gauguin's marked features.

Tohohina, in turn, married a certain Timau and had three daughters; they are, therefore, the third generation of Marquesan Gauguins. Two of the little girls are being educated at the Sisters of Atuona school, and it is a touching sight to see them, every All Saints' Day, lay flowers at the painting of their illustrious great-grandfather.

After the mission, Gauguin took on the civil authority, especially the police, who, from his point of view, harassed the natives. Well before Gerbault, he wanted to bring them back to the primitive ways they had barely abandoned. They used to visit him frequently, and he strongly advised them to stop paying the 12-franc personal tax, and he and his cook practiced what he preached; the police had to seize some of his belongings and auction them in order for him to pay his tax, as we will see shortly.

Upon settling into his home, he no longer had any relations with any civil or religious notable, yet he very generously received several colonists who had been living in the country for several years. They shared his hostility toward the police, whom the painter could not bear. We will cite below those who were his intimates.

NGUYEN VAN CAM

The one he knew longest was Nguyen Van Cam, whose acquaintance he made the very day of his arrival on 16 September 1901. Because Van Cam was from Annam and of good family, the French authorities of Indochina sent him as a scholarship student to the lycée of Algiers, which he left with a baccalaureate. Back in his own country, he told us, he was appointed administrator of a province, but soon, soured by the favoritism enjoyed by those born in the mother country, he began writing under a false name in the Annam newspapers that were hostile toward France. What was worse, he was seriously implicated in a matter of terrorism. Claude Farrère mentions his name in his book *Hoang Tam, Pirate*. He escaped court-martial, but was deported to Oceania for life. By the time of Gauguin's arrival, he already spoke the Marquesan language very well, and he immediately found the painter lodgings in the heart of the valley, by the river. Let us hand the story over to Van Cam:

His lodgings secured, I accompanied him to Ayu's, who ran a restaurant and with whom he would be taking his meals for a few weeks. The Chinese man also sold tea and cakes. The painter was soon concerned with finding a native companion, and, as it happened, while walking we ran into five or six young Marquesan women of easy virtue, whom he invited to take tea and cakes with him. Since the painter seemed very generous, they all agreed to live with him. It was our traveler's turn to be embarrassed. Which one to choose? It was Fetuhonu (turtles' star) who carried the day. She was a large and beautiful girl of twenty, though she was club-footed. The rejected ones, out of spite, heaped taunts on the new couple in Marquesan, which Gauguin could not understand.

I rendered this scene into a little comedy, in mock-heroic verses, which I showed Gauguin a few days later; he was heartily amused. From that day on, I remained very close to him, and if the requirements of my nursing services did not detain me, I went to see him every morning, and took an aperitif with him in the evening. In 1902, he did my portrait and gave it to me as a present, a token of his friendship. It was, moreover, the only portrait I saw him do here. After the painter's death, there arrived from Fatuhiva a friend, Grelet, who had an appointment with him for a portrait.

Grelet was very upset not to have something to remember him by and offered to buy my portrait. I gave it to him as a gift, for Grelet had always received me very handsomely every time my service had called me to his island.

F____

Adjoining the Gauguin property on the west side was F____'s property. He kept a shop across from the barracks. A former ship's corporal in the Marine Light Infantry who was discharged in Atuona in 1882, he was married and the father of three children. He had been educated in a seminary. Before the painter's arrival, he had a license to sell spirits. There must have been abuses, for the license was revoked as a result of the police reports; F____ from that point on detested them, which earned him Gauguin's liking, and F____ became a frequent visitor. F____ told us:

"F" refers to Emile Frébault (b. 1861), one of Gauguin's closest friends in the Marquesas.

> Often the painter would come to the edge of his property at around 11 o'clock to call me: "Oh, hey, F____, come on over, it's time for a drink!" We would have one or more absinthes and long conversations. Gauguin often told me about his Peruvian background, his months of sailing as an apprentice seaman on windjammers, his marriage to his Danish wife, his life in the artistic world. I saw him receive many letters from Parisian celebrities; at least two were from Georges Clemenceau.

Having read in various accounts that Gauguin died abandoned by all, I asked F____ what happened. "All that is inaccurate," he replied:

> When I learned of his sudden death, I went, along with a few natives, to dress him and lay him out on his bed, and we took turns at his bedside all day. That night, the bishop, forgetting all the insults that Gauguin had heaped upon him, sent a catechist and many natives to keep vigil with me all night. Before daybreak, we noticed that the body was in an advanced state of decomposition; I went to see the gendarme and the bishop, and we decided to hold the funeral very early. At sunrise, a young priest came to say the prayers, and we accompanied Gauguin to his final resting-place, which the bishop had had prepared the day before. No doubt, because of that the legend arose that the bishop had had him buried surreptitiously.

P. GUILLETOUE

Another intimate of Gauguin's was P. Guilletoue, of Basque origin. In his youth, he had been a schoolteacher in the environs of Orthez, then he enlisted in the Marine Light Infantry and was discharged with the rank of sergeant, at the same time as F____. He went into business as a merchant in Hekeani, but with little success, for he had two serious passions, gambling and drinking. He was, nevertheless, a very intelligent man. One of his obsessions was interfering in native affairs; he knew by heart a large part of the civil code, which he owned in several editions. The natives had just found themselves suddenly under the jurisdiction of the French laws, of which they knew absolutely nothing; the apportioning of an inheritance among legitimate, natural, and adoptive children was incomprehensible to them, and the administration officials often made mistakes.

So Guilletoue urged court actions in Papeete, which irritated the officials. They claimed that Guilletoue was asking for money for this purpose and keeping part of it. There was, no doubt, some truth to these accusations, for Guilletoue served some time in prison. From that time on, he conceived a fierce hatred for the police.

He was tending a herd of wild cattle in Hanaiapa at the time of Gauguin's arrival. Every week, one would see him arrive with quarters of beef that he cut up at the house of his friend, the native Tioka, Gauguin's neighbor and friend. From there, it was a few paces to the painter's to tell him of their mutual enemies' abuses. All the old-time colonists agreed

COLORPLATE 104.
Mahana No Atua (Day of the Gods).
1894. 27 × 36″
(68.3 × 91.5 cm).
The Art Institute of Chicago;
Helen Birch Bartlett
Memorial Collection.

COLORPLATE 105.
Where Do We Come From?
What Are We? Where Are We Going?
1897. 54¾ × 147½"
(130.1 × 374.6 cm).
Museum of Fine Arts, Boston;
Tompkins Collection.

COLORPLATE 106.
Te Tamari no Atua (Son of God).
1896. 37¾ × 50½"
(96 × 128 cm).
Bayerische
Staatsgemaldesammlungen,
Munich. Photo: Artothek.

COLORPLATE 107. *O. Taiti (Nevermore)*. 1897. 23¾ × 45¾" (60.5 × 116 cm).
Courtauld Institute Galleries, London, Courtauld Collection.

COLORPLATE 108. *Faa Iheihe (Tahitian Pastoral)*. 1898. 21¼ × 66½″ (54 × 169 cm).
Tate Gallery, London.

COLORPLATE 109. *The White Horse*. 1898. 55 × 36″ (140 × 91.5 cm).
Musée d'Orsay, Paris.

that Guilletoue played a large part in reawakening the painter's fighting spirit. One would see them, mugs in hand, in long discussions every time Guilletoue passed through.

REINER

This retired gendarme retreated to the Marquesas, where his wife had acquired some large coconut-palm plantations. He claimed that his successors lacked the integrity of their elders and, through the natives, stayed informed about their doings, which he reported to Gauguin when he came for an aperitif. It was he, it is claimed, who set off Gauguin's quarrels with the gendarme Guichenay. Had the latter bought some provisions aboard a whaler? It is quite probable, for in the remote posts, supplies often failed to arrive, and the officers then lacked bread and all foodstuffs. Under those conditions, could one object to their having bought, from a passing whaler, a sack of flour, a little sugar, etc., etc.?

Such was the European milieu that visited Gauguin. We have shown their frame of mind. We will add that all these old colonists that we have met were hearty drinkers and that in their gatherings a few bottles of rum were quickly drained.

We will now introduce a few of his native friends. The one that was his intimate friend was certainly Tioka, his neighbor.

TIOKA

Below the F___ property came Tioka's. This Marquesan, who was about Gauguin's age, lived there with his wife and two nephews, whom they had raised; the elder, Kahui, Gauguin's cook, was the wife's nephew; the second, Timo, was the husband's nephew. Tioka, from the first days following the painter's arrival, exchanged names with him, which means, according to Marquesan custom, that Tioka became Gauguin, while Gauguin became Tioka. This native was devotion itself; he was a good carpenter and helped build Gauguin's hut, refusing to accept the least remuneration. An excellent fisherman as well, he frequently supplied fish for his adoptive relation's table.

Sister of Charity. 1902. 25¾ × 30" (65.5 × 76 cm). McNay Art Museum, San Antonio; Bequest of Marion Koogler McNay.

He had one small fault: despite his being a Protestant deacon, he had a weakness for strong spirits, and it so happened that Gauguin was amply provided with them. He was the only Marquesan that the painter allowed into his house to tipple with his European friends. Tioka was the first to discover that Gauguin had died. We will hear about that in the reminiscences of his nephew Timo.

HAPUANI

Hapuani, when I met him in 1910, was about thirty years old, pure Marquesan, powerfully built; he was magnificently lazy. I never saw him do any hard work: his wife, a beautiful blonde native, took care of the housework alone. From birth, Hapuani was intended to become *Taua*, a sort of priest of the ancient Marquesan customs. In his childhood, he had been educated toward that end; no one knew as well as he the ancient native customs. The arrival of the Protestant and Catholic missionaries, and the French occupation of Hiva-Oa, came to halt that career, so he became the organizer and master of ceremonies of festivals in Hiva-Oa.

A great drinker of coconut juice and all alcoholic beverages, a good storyteller, very influential among the natives (whose spokesman he was), and something of a procurer, it was not long before he became one of the painter's frequent visitors.

Hapuani told me:

Gauguin was the Marquesans' friend, he championed them against the police. He was very generous. At every hour of the day, one saw natives going into his house bearing fruit, poultry, eggs, or fish, all of it for free, but Gauguin paid all those people with well-discounted glasses of rum; without interrupting his work, he would call his cook through the window: "Hey, Kahui, give So-and-So a glass of rum."

But it was mainly the native women one saw filing through his house from morning to night. Gauguin loved women very much; he would sit among them in order to caress them.

One could go into his house, sit, smoke, chat as long as one wanted; he never appeared bad-tempered, and often he took part in the conversation; when the women, showing the obscene paintings around, said to him, "Gauguin mea faufau" ("That's dirty"), he laughed long.

Gauguin detested the police, and he advised the natives not to pay the personal tax any longer; he told us that his cook, Kahui, and himself were going to set the example. For the cook, who owned nothing, no trouble was made, but Gauguin one day found himself seized by the gendarme. There was a judgment and, a few days later, an auction.

The objects seized were the two statuettes and the gun. The day of the sale, the very popular Gauguin saw his compound overrun by his native friends, who had come to see how things would go.

When the gendarme arrived, he was at the table, laughing and talking loudly with his friends F——, Guilletoue, Reiner, and Van Cam, drinking champagne; when he noticed me, he poured me a glass of rum and did the same for several other natives. The gendarme arrived and called on him to pay his taxes and costs, which amounted to 65 francs. No reply. Then the gendarme declared the sale open: one gun and two tikis for 65 francs; no bids. After a moment, without leaving the table, Gauguin announced 65 francs and called his cook: "Listen, Kahui, give these 65 francs to that man and tell him to go away." And he went on drinking without paying the gendarme any further mind.

When Gauguin, in the afternoon, went for his usual drive, he always wore a green beret, and on his body he wore a shirt that was also green; his hips were wrapped in a blue *paréo*. He sat in the front seat, the *paréo* raised fairly high, perhaps because of the sores on his legs. He never stopped, merely greeting with a "Kaoha" the natives he passed.

ZACHARIE TOUAHAAFEU

This native was Gauguin's age; he had been educated at the Puamau Brothers' school and spoke French very correctly. At the time of Gauguin's arrival, he had a business in Hanaiapa on the north coast; he often came to Atuona for business and never failed to go see the painter.
Zacharie told this story:

I ran into him at Varney's shop one day, and I told him that a few days earlier, with about thirty other Marquesans, we had drunk some coconut juice, up at the top of the valley; someone complained about us, and the gendarme drew up a report. He took me to his house to have a glass of rum and tell him about the matter in detail. "They can't sentence you," he told me. "You will deny everything, and I'll go to court with you."

When that day arrived, Gauguin came with us and went in first. He was in a *paréo*. Since there were no chairs, he sat on the floor. The judge ordered him to get up and leave, under the pretext that his clothing was indecent to the court. Gauguin, furious, replied that he would go dress and requested that the court wait. He returned a few minutes later, having put on a pair of trousers. They read the gendarme's report, and the judge pronounced sentence: we were all sentenced to five days in prison and a 100-franc fine.

Then Gauguin asked the judge: "By what text do you sentence these people? Don't you know that in a simple police matter there must be *flagrante delicto*, which was not the case?" A violent quarrel began between Gauguin and the judge. The latter angrily told the two gendarmes who were present: "Throw this man out." Gauguin, seated until then, rose and, brandishing his cudgel at the judge, replied: "Listen, the gendarmes are not to lay a hand on me," and he calmly went out.

Addressing us in the courtyard, he said to us: "Come, we'll appeal in Papeete," which we did. A few months later, Gauguin announced to us that we had all been acquitted.

TIMO

Timo was the nephew of Tioka, Gauguin's friend and neighbor. Contrary to what Dr. Villaret claims, who confused him with someone else, he had no tattoos on his body. A very handsome man, undoubtedly a mestizo, intelligent, and speaking very pure French, he acted as chef and interpreter.
Said Timo:

I knew Gauguin very well, since the house of my uncle who raised me was in the vicinity of his own. Tioka and Gauguin were great friends, and when, in 1903, our land was ravaged by flooding, Gauguin gave us half his property for nothing.

He arrived in Atuona at the end of 1901; I was already about fifteen years old, and I remember him very well. He was a man around fifty years old, big and powerfully built, slightly round-shouldered and pot-bellied.

At first he took lodgings in the village itself, then he bought

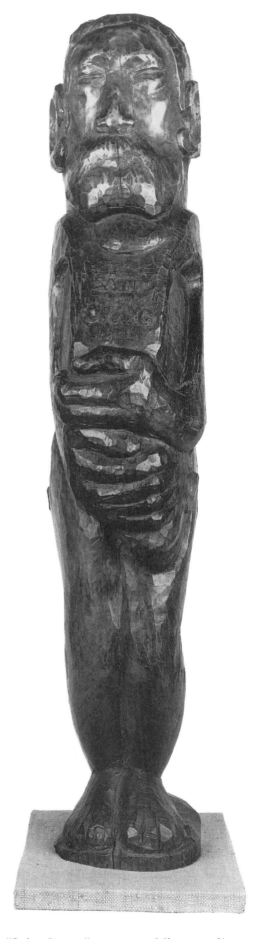

"Saint Orang." ca. 1902. Miro wood? Height: 37″ (94 cm). Musée d'Orsay, Paris.

Carved door frame from Gauguin's "House of Pleasure" in the Marquesas. Lintel. 1901. Redwood, carved and painted. 94 × 15¼" (242.5 × 39 cm). Musée d'Orsay, Paris.

from the bishop, a few days later, two lots of land adjacent to our own, on which my uncle and I built him a large, tall hut, the second floor of which was made up of a small room where the painter slept and a large room that was used as a painting studio.

One went up to the second floor by a staircase placed at the east end and came out into the painter's bedroom; his plank bed was there; on one side one of the panels was carved, a lewd scene. Paintings of sexual anatomy were hung almost everywhere. Unfinished paintings everywhere against the partitions.

At the foot of the staircase, on the right, there were two wooden statuettes around 0.4 meters high, portraying a man and a woman, carved down to the navel; the man bore, in an engraving at his feet, Father Paillard's name, the woman, Thérèse's. Below, on a small board was engraved: "Be in love: You will be happy." Above the doorway into the bedroom, there was a panel engraved with the words: "House of Pleasure."

The downstairs of the house was divided into four parts, the sculpture studio, the dining room, the coach house, and the kitchen.

Gauguin had a cook in his service, my cousin Kahui, and two young men who ate there and were paid 20 Chilean francs a month. They did not tire in Gauguin's service; one saw them strolling through the valley at all hours of the day. Gauguin never scolded them; they were only punctual at mealtime and in the afternoon to harness the horse when it was time for his drive.

Kahui cooked; in the mornings, Gauguin detailed the dishes he was to prepare. When the meal was ready, at around eleven o'clock, Kahui would call Gauguin, who would come down to the dining room. Kahui brought all the food to the table, and Gauguin divided it into three parts: one for himself, one for the servants, and the third for his dog, Pegau (diminutive of Paul Gauguin), and the cat.

Gauguin, the dog, and the cat ate in the dining room; the servants, in the kitchen. With his meals Gauguin drank wine, but moderately, unlike the absinthe of which he was a great drinker. From the studio, by means of a long bamboo pole and a fishing line through the window, Gauguin put the absinthe bottle and the water cooler to chill in the well without interrupting his work; from time to time, one saw him appear in the window frame, take hold of the bamboo pole, fish up the bottle and the cooler, and let them back down a moment later.

He rarely went out during the day, but around four o'clock in the afternoon, he took his walking stick, the handle of which was carved into a virile phallus, and left for a walk. Sometimes he took his double-barreled shotgun and went to the beach to shoot a few sea birds. Around the middle of the year in 1902, he bought a horse and cart, and from then on the outings were in the cart, always along the same route: once around the

By 1888, Gauguin had begun to sign some of his letters and works of art with the initials P Go *or* Pegau, *pronounced "pay-go." According to Wayne Anderson in* Gauguin's Paradise Lost *(1971), Gauguin thus invoked a play on the slang term "pego" for "prick."*

beach, he then went up into the village, to return a little before nightfall.

He never went to see anyone, except, sometimes, Varney's shop, which was 50 meters away, but nearly every day he received visits from a few colonists, Van Cam, Frébault, Guilletoue, and Reiner, who drank absinthe with him.

He always painted at home, I never saw him paint outdoors; besides, walking was painful for him because of the sores on his legs, which were often bandaged. Sometimes the sores healed, but then soon reappeared.

To ease his sufferings, he injected himself with morphine; his buttocks were speckled with black spots, the marks of the injections. In his final months, he was often ill, and when my uncle found him dead one morning, he had a vial of morphine beside him. All the Europeans here thought that he had taken too strong a dose that morning.

After Gauguin's death, the administration sent the carved bed, the paintings, and the cart to Papeete.

Everything else, a few small objects and the kitchen utensils, was sold on the spot. The day of the sale, there was a crowd in Gauguin's compound, natives and several Europeans. The gendarme Claverie directed the sale. I remember that when he saw Gauguin's walking stick he said: "What is this filth?" And taking a hammer, he smashed it. Then Pastor Vernier told him: "You have no right to break this walking stick, you do not know that it is a work of art and not the piece of filth you have just called it."

Two liters of absinthe were found in the bedroom. Louis Otto, a mestizo from Hanaiapa, bought them and opened them, then called to the Europeans: "We will drink to Gauguin's memory right now."

The land and the house were bought, for 1,500 francs in Chilean money, by Varney, the American. He had the house torn down and sold the materials to the natives. There remained of Gauguin's passage only the well and the bath, which were filled in, in their turn, a few years later.

Letter from Gauguin to Daniel de Monfreid

On Living and Working

February 1903

I received two of your letters very late due to a cyclone the likes of which we have never seen before, as it seems it came from the north. We think that it rose up from beneath the sea.

All the low islands, right in the middle of the diving season, were inundated by a horrible tidal wave and nearly the whole population perished. The rest of us, we were less harshly afflicted. During 48 hours of rain, the thunder was deafening, until one night the cyclone became terrible. Despite the fact that I am well protected by trees, I expected my hut to be swept away or demolished by wind at any minute. At ten o'clock, I heard a continual, muffled noise that was very unusual. It was the river, which had destroyed everything in its path while searching for new outlets. I left my bedroom to have a look and to my great surprise found myself up to my waist in water. Impossible to see anything at all. Useless to think of fleeing for even a second. I went back up into my bedroom and spent the night dreading that the water would rise up to the level of my poor hut. Fortunately, I had built it two meters off the ground on twice the number of piles than was necessary. In the morning I was able to see the horrible situation that Atuona was in. No more bridges. No more roads. Enormous trees upended everywhere, these tropical trees that have such shallow roots, houses turned over, and so on.

In the end, all's well that ends well, and I have everything back to normal for the price of a few francs' worth of expenses for repairs.

I do not quite agree with you about the importance of my return to France, in the sense that I will only just pass through Paris on my way to Spain to work for a few years. Except for friends, no one would be the wiser.

No, it is not homesickness but this horrible eczema that does not allow me to work soundly. For almost three months I have not touched a paintbrush. My outlook seriously worries me, and I say to myself: what would I have become if Vollard had just given up? A man like myself, always struggling, even without wanting to, for the sake of his art, is surrounded by people who would be happy to trample him, while in France one can hide one's misery, and also find some pity. To avoid that, I would have to have four or five thousand francs always at the ready, so that in case of an accident I could return.

Otherwise, I am fine here in my solitude.

I received a letter from Fontainas that said the *Mercure* did not wish to run the piece I wrote. I did not think they would. They are all the same; they so want to criticize the painters, but they do not like the painters to demonstrate their imbecility. There is no harm done, and here is why: all this time recently, during my long nights of insomnia, I set myself to write a miscellany of what I have seen, heard, and thought during my lifetime. There are some things in there that are *terrible* for some people, regarding the conduct of my wife and especially of the Danes. If the article did not appear, it will be inserted into my book, which can only make it better. Fontainas is not Morice, he's a serious man who's on the up and up. I'm sending him my book with a plea to have it *printed at any cost* and am telling him that he is in agreement with you. All my paintings from the first trip to Tahiti are for sale. *Sell the lot at any price*. I anxiously await this publication since it will make me better known and understood at the same time that it brings me revenge.

"The piece I wrote" refers to Racontars de Rapin.

The book Gauguin eagerly seeks to publish is Avant et Après, *which, when published, did not include* Racontars de Rapin.

Pierre Borel

PRO ARTE ET LIBRIS

"The Final Days and Mysterious Death of Paul Gauguin"

September 1942

Pierre Borel published studies on Gustave Courbet and Edgar Degas in the 1940s.

This letter was recently sent to me by M. Grelet, a Swiss industrialist who lived for a long time in the Marquesas, where he produced copra and raised cattle. Besides being a businessman, M. Grelet was a man of taste,

Savage Tales. 1902. 51 × 35″ (130 × 89 cm). Museum Folkwang, Essen.

a man of letters. He was always interested in painting. At the Tour de Peilz, his family was very attached to Gustave Courbet.

M. Grelet often saw Gauguin on his island. He told me:

I first met the painter at the house of an American settler, Mr. Varney, who was his next-door neighbor. Although he paid little attention to his diet, Gauguin liked to drink wine and sometimes absinthe. The first time I met him, he was dressed like the natives. I was immediately impressed by his height, his magnificent and proud head, his large blue eyes, and his athletic torso. He was having a great deal of trouble holding himself upright. I noticed that his right leg was literally gnawed through by a horrible sore that was buzzing with green flies.

This sore must have dated back to when he had been injured by sailors at Le Pouldu. Several years after this brawl,

333

Gauguin complained of the wound that would disturb him the rest of his life. To one of his friends, he wrote, "I only wish for one thing: to return to Oceania (he was then in Brittany), my leg is getting better. I don't know if it's the effect of the morphine or the constant rain, but I suffer horribly in all my bones, and I don't sleep until about three in the morning from the effect of the narcotics. Naturally, it is impossible for me to do any work at all and you know how impatient I am. To remain inactive for days is an enormous punishment. Decidedly, the only possibility I can see is to spend two years down there."

In the end, it was as if I were hypnotized by Gauguin's atrocious sore, and he must have noticed. He became quite vexed. He always hated it whenever anyone took any notice of his illnesses because by that time he was already suffering frequent heart attacks.

Paul Gauguin saw few people. At this time, the opinion of the inhabitants of Atuona, the island where he lived, was the following: To the natives, the painter was a good man; to the Europeans, he was deranged.

M. Grelet must have made an excellent impression on Gauguin. Not

Young Girl with Fan. 1902. 36¼ × 28¾" (92 × 73 cm). Museum Folkwang, Essen.

only did the painter speak amiably of him, but he once allowed him to come visit him in his "House of Pleasure," which was fronted by the two wooden sculptures the artist had done himself. They were burned the day after he died, "because they were obscene."

The studio was the largest room, virtually filled with bric-a-brac. There were many canvases on the floor, turned against the wall. On the easel was a composition barely sketched in. Paul Gauguin did not even seem to be concerned with it. He worked by whim, following his fantasies. He complained that the 300 francs that the dealer in Paris sent him every month was late! To relax, the artist sometimes played the harmonium—he played very well—Schubert, Johann Sebastian Bach, Mozart, or he leafed through a large album of licentious prints by Utamaro. Gauguin had a veritable cult for the Japanese artists: "Here are our masters of everything," he would often say. Distrusting his "corrupt morals" the Bishop of the Marquesas had forbidden the women of the Catholic mission to go to the painter's house. Despite that order, several of the native women did visit him out of curiosity and, struck by the good manners of the solitary man, they would return there.

*　　*　　*

One night, Varney, the American, found his neighbor more depressed than usual. Gauguin was tired, in pain, his nerves were frazzled, the leg was torn with atrocious pain. Taking stock of his long-tormented existence, his disappointments and struggles, he suddenly let slip this thought: "Perhaps I loved painting too much."

It was just that, despite his suffering and his run-ins with the colonial administration and the police, Gauguin had done an enormous amount of work. In Atuona, he discovered a magnificent model, a native girl of royal lineage, who posed for several important works. This woman was one of those creatures of whom one could say that she was directly descended from the Acropolis. In her presence sailors stopped like mad men and murmured ecstatic oaths under their breath. When she passed by, she left behind her a wake of delight. She lived intimately with the painter, always caring for him except during his attacks; then she turned him over to an old native woman named Tioka or to Ky-Dong, the student from Annam who was deported for political reasons and to whom he gave his last portrait: a portrait done with a trembling hand only a few days before his death. In it the artist is hard to recognize, his face wasted, ravaged, his eyes blinking behind crude, metal-rimmed glasses.

We are now left only to clarify one important point in this sad existence. How and of what did Paul Gauguin die? There are several more or less acceptable hypotheses, but nobody saw anything. Until his death the painter was alone. There was no autopsy. Here is our opinion, based on an inquest undertaken by individuals very close to our sources. To lessen his intolerable suffering, Gauguin used morphine. He had numerous ampules in a box. One day, a month before his death, he called his friend Varney, and said to him, "Keep my morphine for me and don't let me have it under any circumstances, even if I threaten you!" When the American then attempted to explain that under those conditions it would be simpler just to throw it in the ocean, Gauguin replied, "Oh, not that! It might turn out, in the end, that I need it, if I suffer too much!" Varney took the box, and on 8 May 1903, the painter was found dead in his hut. At the foot of the couch was the box of morphine.

The two wood sculptures, Père Paillard *and* Thérèse *were in fact not burned.*

Kitigawa Utamaro (1753–1806), master Japanese printmaker who created several albums of shunga, woodblock prints of erotic subjects, and greatly influenced nineteenth-century French painting.

Self-Portrait. 1903. 16¼ × 9½" (41.5 × 24 cm). Kunstmuseum, Basel.

Letter from Paul-Louis Vernier to
Jean de Rotonchamp

On Gauguin's Life and Death
in Atuona

8 March 1904

I would be happy to give you a few details on the last period of M. Paul Gauguin's life and of his death, all the more since it was I who cared for him until the morning of his death, which came unexpectedly on 8 May 1903, a Friday, at about eleven o'clock in the morning. And if I was not his friend—really knowing him very little, since Gauguin was unsociable—I was at least his neighbor and, consequently, fairly up-to-date on his life. Several times he came to see me; three times he called me to come to him for a consultation, since I am something of a doctor.

I always knew M. Paul Gauguin to be ill and almost crippled. He rarely left his house, and the few times when one would run into him in the valley of Atuona he cut a pathetic figure, dragging himself along with difficulty, his legs wrapped in strips of cloth and dressed, moreover, in the very original costume of the Maori: the colored loincloth and the Tahitian blouse, barefoot, almost always wearing a green beret with a silver buckle on the side. A very likable man, perfectly sweet and natural with the Marquesans. They were certainly that way with him. And when your friend died, I can remember hearing several of the natives cry something like: *"Ua maté Gauguin, ua pété énata!"*—"Gauguin is dead, we are lost!" alluding to the help Gauguin had often given them, delivering them from the hands of the police, who were often hard and unjust where the natives were concerned. Gauguin, who was very generous and chivalrous, defended the natives. There are numerous examples of his goodness and his consideration.

He had very little rapport with the Europeans in Atuona. I believe he cordially detested them, with a few rare exceptions. He was, above all, horrified by the gendarme and by the constabulary in general. He had resounding quarrels with them. One day, about three months before his death, he was sentenced to fifteen days in jail and fined 500 francs for supposedly insulting the police. But Gauguin was sure he would be acquitted on appeal. He was, in fact, preparing to go to Tahiti when death surprised him. Gauguin appeared to be in the right and to have justice on his side, but, in truth, he was above all that.

As for the country, he had the highest ideals, a true worship for this nature, so beautiful in itself and so savage, where his soul naturally found its niche. He could immediately discover the special poetry of this region that is bathed in sunlight and still untainted in places. You must have perceived this in the paintings he sent you from down there. The Maori soul no longer held any mystery for him. Meanwhile, Gauguin found that our islands lost some of their originality every day.

> The Gods are dead and Atuona is dying from their death.

he wrote somewhere. . . .

One morning near the beginning of April 1903, I received the following note from Gauguin:

Dear Monsieur Vernier,

May I be so bold as to ask you for a consultation, since my powers have become wholly insufficient? I am very sick. I can no longer walk.

P.G.

I went immediately to the artist's home. He suffered horribly in his legs, which were red and swollen and covered with eczema. I recommended the proper medication, offering to rub it on for him if he wished. He thanked me very kindly, saying he could do it himself. We talked. Forgetting his pain, he spoke to me of his art in very admirable terms, portraying himself as an undiscovered genius. He made a few allusions to his troubles with the police, named a few of his friends, although, to tell the truth, I do not remember hearing your name; he loaned me several of Dolent's and Aurier's books and *L'Après-midi d'une faune*, which he had from Mallarmé himself. He gave me a sketch of the latter, with the following words: *To Monsieur Vernier*, a piece of art. **P.G.**

I left him and did not see him for ten days. Old Tioka, a friend of Gauguin's, said to me, "You know, things are not well at the white man's, he is very sick!" I went back to your friend's house and found him, very low indeed, in bed and moaning. Once again, he forgot his illness when speaking of art. I admired this obsession.

The morning of 8 May, he had this same Tioka call me. I went. Gauguin, still in bed, complained of sharp pains in his body. He asked me if it was morning or evening, day or night. He told me that he had had two fainting fits and he worried about them. He spoke to me of *Salammbô*. I left him on his back, calm and resting, after this short conversation. Around eleven o'clock that same morning, the young Ka Hui, a servant (unfortunately too irregular, in the sense that he often deserted his master's house during his illness) came and called me with all haste: "Come quick, the white man is dead!"

I flew. I found Gauguin lifeless, one leg hanging out of the bed, but still warm. Tioka was there, he was beside himself; he said to me: "I came to see how he was, I called him from below, '*Ko Ké*' (the native name for Gauguin). Not hearing anything, I came up to see. Aie! Aie! Gauguin did not stir. He was dead." And, having said this, he began to chew hard on his friend's scalp, a particularly Marquesan way of bringing someone back to life. I myself tried rhythmic pulling of the tongue and artificial respiration, but nothing would work. Paul Gauguin really was dead, and everything leads to the conclusion that he died of a sudden heart attack.

I am the only European to have seen Gauguin before he died. I must say, he never spoke to me of his family in Europe, nor did he make any suggestions or express any last wishes. Did he leave a will? I do not think so. The authorities went through all his papers, and I do not believe anything was found. The word was that he had a family in Europe, a wife and five children. There was a photograph of a family group that, people said, was them. I saw that photograph. Moreover, people said a lot of things. We did not know what to believe. Naturally, I never asked Gauguin anything about that subject. Now I must tell you several things of the circumstances of his burial and the circumstances in which these were produced.

When I arrived at Gauguin's hut on the famous Friday when I was told of his death, I found that the Catholic bishop and several brothers of the Christian faith were already there. I was immensely surprised to see them. Everyone knew what Gauguin's sentiments toward *these gentlemen* were, and *these gentlemen* knew them as well. My astonishment turned to indignation when I saw that the bishop decided to bury Gauguin with a full Catholic ceremony, which is what was done on Saturday, 9 May. The corpse was to be moved at two o'clock. I wanted at least to assist at

Vernier refers to Gauguin's only etching, his portrait of Mallarmé from 1891.

Salammbô is Flaubert's decadent and violent historical novel about Carthage, based on the writings of Polybius.

the removal of the body, and to that end I went to Gauguin's residence at the appointed hour. His body had been transported to the church by one-thirty! A real sleight-of-hand trick, as you can well see. And Gauguin now rests in the Catholic Calvary, sacred ground par excellence! In my opinion, Gauguin should have had a civil burial.

Some of the things that were left by Gauguin were sold at two auctions. The first sale, at Atuona, took care of the things that the natives and the few local Europeans would buy; his clothes, his trunks, his carpentry and woodworking tools, his kitchen utensils, his saddle, his horse, his preserves, his wine, his house and his land (all in one lot), assessed by an American at 1,050 francs, I think. The green beret went to Tioka, who wears it day and night; and that was given to him by the auctioneer. Poor Gauguin!

The second sale took place in Tahiti and dealt only with the valuable things, the paintings in particular, and the rare objects. Doctor Ségalen told you everything on that subject. . . .

Victor Ségalen

LETTRES DE PAUL GAUGUIN A GEORGES-DANIEL DE MONFREID

"Homage to Paul Gauguin"

1918

Victor Ségalen (1878–1919), physician, novelist, and archaeologist who came to Tahiti aboard the naval transport La Durance *in 1903 and went to the Marquesas in August of that year. Although he never knew Gauguin, he purchased several items from the sale of Gauguin's possessions in September 1903. In December, Daniel de Monfreid received a letter about Gauguin from Ségalen that Monfreid published in the June 1904* Mercure de France.

Neither whites, nor yellows, nor blacks, the Maoris, if one is to paint them, even with words, must be compared to no other kind of men. They do not have, beneath the sun, the washed-out appearance of the European nude. They do not have false eyelids, the "Mongolian crease," nor pronounced cheekbones, nor do the women have that oval moon face. They have nothing in common with the woolly Negro. Therefore one must—and the painter has magnificently resolved to do so—contemplate them under their savage enigma, the one they will carry with them into their foreseen death, the totally human question:

"Where do we come from? Who are we? Where are we going?"

We will read in the letters with what desperate fury Gauguin painted then day and night; and we will see in his work how he put himself into the hands of the only ones who could deliver judgment: the ancestor-gods of the race. Thus he dreamed of a Maori genesis. He must have felt,

Carved door frame from Gauguin's "House of Pleasure" in the Marquesas. Right horizontal panel. 1901. Redwood, carved and painted. 80½ × 15¾" (205 × 40 cm). Musée d'Orsay, Paris.

Carved door frame from
Gauguin's "House of Pleasure"
in the Marquesas. 1901.
Redwood, carved and painted.
Left vertical panel. 78½ × 15½"
(200 × 39.5 cm). Right vertical
panel. 1901. 62½ × 15¾" (159 ×
40 cm). Musée d'Orsay, Paris.

swelling in his arms, the primordial gesture of the creator Mahui, catching the still unfathomable islands like fish, hauling them in, hoisting them up, bringing them out all young and pearly.

It is beside the point here to explain the Polynesian theogony. Every god becomes a living god, a god that acts, only in the moment he takes shape, becomes incarnate or encrusted. Before Gauguin in Tahiti, no Maori embodiments existed. Taaroa the Creator had plunged once more—weary, no doubt after the work was finished—into the dream. Oro inhabited the sun; Hina, the moon; without revealing any features but those of light. This lack of presence on the part of the great native gods has certainly led to the destruction of the Polynesians, who are dying . . . of all diseases, but chiefly of the contagion of the Christian god, god made man, incarnated in a Jewish skin.

As for the demigods, the native sculptor had delivered wooden statuettes of him, man-dolls, nothing more—or, if he was a lava-carver on Easter Island, great cylindrical standing beasts with angular and wicked chins, broad flat eyes, brows crushed beneath millstones worn as hats. . . . The idol is ridiculous and lock-jawed. One meets it without respect, standing upright or recumbent. They were post-gods, boundary stones between the sea and the mountain. They have for names nothing but common and collective words.

* * *

I did not know Gauguin when he was alive; and yet we were contemporaries in Polynesia. But between Gauguin and myself there were more than 400 miles of ocean; no direct relationship; no echo through the "whites" of Tahiti. One person would say: "Gauguin? A madman. He paints pink horses!" Another, a shopkeeper: "Things are going much better for him, he's even beginning to sell. There's one born every minute." A magistrate: "Gauguin gives us a lot of trouble." A pious person: "Every day he prostrates himself before a terracotta monster and they claim he's worshiping the sun." We were in the first months of the year 1903. It wasn't until June or July that they announced to me: "Oh! Gauguin passed away." I had to wait some time longer before I could reach the Marquesas and, among those islands, the one he had chosen. His house, which he built practically with his own hands, was still standing. It had held up under the cyclone's great wind—but emptied by the official liquidators like the bulb of a coconut palm by land crabs. It was a better-made Marquesan hut, raised off the ground, with its great roof laced with pandanus leaves. No trace, save of being stripped. It was up above, over the lintel of the door, that was fixed the entrance motto, House of Pleasure, so full in the substantive form of its verb, so explicit that it is almost indecent to emblazon any other home with it—but one can set it up within oneself as a motto. And to the left and right, long sculpted panels rubbed with colors. "Be in love," said one, "and you will be happy," and one saw two secret, cloaked figures going, as if fleeing toward love; another, rearing in a leap of fear or horror or joy. The second panel instructed "Be mysterious, and you will be happy," and other visions penetrating the wood like larvae flowed from the other side of space, toward the land beyond all evil, all good, all manifest existence.

Across from it, a few steps away, another house, tiny, a little kiosk, but sheltering a god. That clay statuette, so cracked by the daily firing, despite the roof, so crackled, so fragile that I dared not carry it away to sea, by rolling it, so as not to have to commit the sacrilege of gluing it back together again, or the indecent act of keeping the crumbled pieces; it seemed to me an act of devotion to let it split in its place, beneath the same daily weather that had seen its maker die.

One hesitated to give it a name. One could boorishly, as I did at the time, describe it as: "A Buddha born in the land of the Maoris." That is not true. Beneath the mantle of a heavy, blunt, obese shape, that idol was full of teaching. It is the massive realization of the divine ascension, the emergence of the creator as perhaps he thundered in Gauguin. The skull is high and dominates the face to that point that it takes in, in a single line—far better than the Greek!—the bridge of the nose, the fall of the nape. The entire head is a protuberance, a thrust, a summit. The shoulders are sloping; the back is perfectly straight; the hands, formless, useless, rest on the knees; and the aborted seat is sitting on a low plane. From the top of the head to the toenails falls a single gesture, a single gathered will, scarcely formed, as though this being rose out of the womb of matter. Not the god past, present, or awaited . . . the other, immanent, a genius of the life-giving kind, who lifts a crust of lava, of flesh, or of membranes, puts it over his thought like a helmet, with it masks his face, sticky with primordial meconium and gives birth to himself, painfully, despite his reduced backside: a sort of unclean and powerful fetus-god.

This clay statue, a foot high, this was perhaps Gauguin's savage genius. So in Tahiti they used to say that he prostrated himself before it. That is unlikely. But if the voyage remained to be made again to bring it back, save it—I would make it and bring it back.

* * *

The next day, the Bishop and the mission, ridiculed by Gauguin when he was alive, had their revenge on his corpse, and "forcing entry," smuggled his body away well ahead of time, in order to bury him with a Catholic ceremony, in the Catholic cemetery, private property of the bishopric.

Then there was the sale by order of the court, following the most legal, most sordid procedures. The "useful" things—clothes, kitchen utensils, preserved foods, and wines—were sold off on the spot. Another auction took place in Papeete, and included a few canvases, two albums, the statue of Satan and the concubine Thérèse, the pediment and the panels of the House of Pleasure, the painter's walking stick, his palette.

The buyers: shopkeepers and civil servants; a few naval officers; the reigning governor at the time; some idlers; and a painting professor without students, become a public letter-writer. The governor had an album purchased discreetly then repurchased it for the same price. A shopkeeper made himself the owner of the walking stick (the handle had set in it a huge baroque pearl) and the two wood sculptures, "Thérèse" and "Father Paillard." An ensign refused to relinquish an extremely beautiful canvas: three women, one of them nursing, seated at the feet of the others, posed in a yellow sky. The painting professor, with a knowledgeable air, tested the suppleness of the brushes; bristles against his left thumbnail and acquired an entire lot for three francs. The palette fell to me for 40 sous. I purchased everything I could catch on the fly as it came up for auction. A canvas shown upside-down by the appraiser, who called it "Niagara Falls," succeeded in drawing great laughter. It became my property for the sum of seven francs. As for the wood carvings—pediment and metopes of the House of Pleasure, no one went higher than my bid of . . . 100 sous. And they stayed with me.

Returned alone, with a great dazed sorrow, to my Tahitian *faré*, whose walls were bare, I hung these trophies, sacrilegiously wrested by chance from tossed words and a gavel that nothing could ever raise again. The wood carvings of the House of Pleasure I intended from that moment for the other end of the world, for the Breton country house that Saint-Pol-Roux was building himself, he, too, as an irrevocable home, overlooking the Bay of Toulinguet on the Atlantic peninsula. The palette I could not decently offer better homage than to give it to the only one worthy of holding it—not with his fingers, like a relic whose origin one appraises along with its authenticity—but rather placing through the

double-beveled oval the thumb that bears and displays the field of colors, . . . to Georges-Daniel de Monfreid.

Looking at that palette closely, with its pearly-bluish pinks, its whites of 10,000 shades, its mountains of still-soft emerald or Veronese green, and other tones kneaded by the brush whose bristles had left their marks—that palette was the mirror in relief of the canvas that, in my hut, hung on the wall, the "number" put up for auction under the label "Niagara Falls." Brought back, set in place, and contemplated with neither blasphemies nor bargaining, that canvas became a Breton landscape, a winter village beneath the snow; a few thatched houses shoulder the horizon line and crowd around the exactly central church tower. (The top of the frame cuts off the too-steep point of the spire.) On the left, a violet cliff falls toward a sky at dusk. On the right run thin trees. All the ground is made of snow, streaming with melted lights, a magnificent pelt of blue and pink, a fur on the cold ground. Was that, then, what the painter, as he was dying, nostalgically recreated? Beneath the daily suns, the one who called forth the warm gods saw a *Breton Village under the snow*!

I have kept that canvas. The very giving it away would be insulting. Gauguin died painting it, it is a legacy. Alone among so many others, it is signed by the absence of the name.

COLORPLATE 90

Charles Morice

MERCURE DE FRANCE

"Paul Gauguin"

October 1903

The sorrow that Paul Gauguin's death leaves in his friends' hearts belongs to them. I will not break into futile tears. The great artist, after a brief, full, and troubled life, has gone to his rest. We number him now,

COLORPLATE 110. *Tahitian Woman and Boy.* 1899. 37¼ × 24½″ (93 × 58.5 cm).
Norton Simon Art Foundation, Pasadena.

COLORPLATE 111. *Crouching Marquesan Woman Seen from the Back.* ca. 1902. Monotype. 21 × 11¼″ (53.2 × 28.3 cm).
Mr. and Mrs. Eugune V. Thaw, New York.

COLORPLATE 112. *Two Marquesans* (recto). ca. 1902. Monotype. 18 × 13⅝″ (45.9 × 34.6 cm).
National Gallery of Art, Washington, D.C.; Rosenwald Collection.

COLORPLATE 113. *The Call.* 1902. 51¼ × 35½" (130 × 90 cm).
The Cleveland Museum of Art; Gift of the Hanna Fund.

COLORPLATE 114. *The Ford,* or *The Flight.* 1901. 30 × 37½″ (76 × 95 cm).
The Pushkin Museum, Moscow.

COLORPLATE 115. *Sunflowers*. 1901. 28⅜ × 36″ (72 × 91 cm).
The Hermitage, Leningrad.

COLORPLATE 116. *Still Life with Parrots.* 1902. 24½ × 30″ (62 × 76 cm).
The Pushkin Museum, Moscow.

COLORPLATE 117. *And the Gold of Their Bodies.* 1901. 27⅜ × 29⅞″ (67 × 76 cm).
Musée d'Orsay, Paris.

in our heaven, among the lights that will not be extinguished, among Manet and Mallarmé, Puvis de Chavannes, Paul Verlaine, Rimbaud, Van Gogh: There, there is no longer any distinction between the arts, that heaven is the heaven of Art.

Of an existence made up of struggles, of rebellions, of works, only these last remain, and our homage will be only to say, with these as testimony, what sort of man their author was, despite the disputes, what sort of man he is; lines dedicated to the simple truth.

A succinct and discreet biography.

He was born in Paris on 7 June 1848. He died in Dominica on 9 May 1903.

Dominica (Dominique), a sixteenth-century Spanish term for Hivaoa, the main island of the Marquesas.

A wandering destiny, as if condemned by his double and distant origin to seek everywhere, without finding anywhere, the place where his two homelands met. His father was Breton, his family on his mother's side was Peruvian. It is probably logical to attribute to this mixed heritage the seemingly contradictory tastes that tyrannized since childhood this son of two worlds. A desire to possess the earth in space, to enjoy by turns nature's joyous and somber beauties; the temperament of a conqueror who wanted to take hold of things with his hands; the spirit of a dreamer who only attained true pleasure through his imaginative and recreative powers. And there was in him as well a bit of the soul of a man of property, of the landowner attached to the soil, home-loving, simple, and not without ostentation, who would have delighted in walking his own property in sabots. This is perceptible in certain of the painter's works, and especially in those many "Bonjour, M. Gauguin!"—revived from Courbet and so different from his own, wherein, at times, the Breton peasant, at times the colonist of Martinique or Tahiti receives, with a small nod, the humble civilities of the local natives. To be the Master: he, too, was susceptible to all the tyrannies. A dream that he only realized in art; but that is the most solid of realities.

Gauguin's father was not Breton; he was born in Orléans.

COLORPLATE 38

Gauguin would have seen Courbet's Bonjour, Monsieur Courbet *(1854) in the Musée Fabre in Montpellier during his 1888 visit there with Van Gogh.*

The only superior personality in his ancestry with whom he claimed kinship is his maternal grandmother, Flora Tristan, a friend of Proudhon.

"Proudhon used to say that she had genius," Gauguin would state. "I trust Proudhon," he would add with a smile.

She was a Socialist. She wrote. She began the Trade Union. The grateful workers dedicated a monument to her in the Bordeaux cemetery. In collaboration with Père Enfantin, she founded a certain religion, the *Mapa* religion, according to which Enfantin was the god Ma, and she was the goddess Pa.

Clovis Gauguin, the artist's father, was, in 1848, a political columnist for *Le National*. He left, some time before the coup d'état, for Lima, where he planned to found a newspaper. He died of a burst blood vessel on the way, in Port-Famine, in the Strait of Magellan.

After a four-year sojourn in Lima, Mme. Clovis Gauguin returned to France, summoned by financial interests. Paul's paternal grandfather had just died, and it was a question of settling his estate. The next year, in 1856, Don Pio de Tristan de Moscoso, a Peruvian great-uncle, died in Lima. He had reached the prodigious age of 113. He left a considerable fortune that was squandered before the future artist reached the age of reason.

At fourteen, he signed on as a cabin boy. He had, at the time, a very weak constitution; the sea air expanded his chest and made him the colossus we knew and loved.

These details of his origins and childhood will not, perhaps, be useless to anyone who wishes to account for Gauguin's talent. It follows, with fateful logic, from his hereditary antecedents and the circumstances of his own life.

"There are, in me, many mixtures," he wrote. "A vulgar sailor, agreed: But there is some culture, or, to put it better, two cultures."

And he merged their not easily reconcilable qualities: the Breton's harsh, obstinate energy, the Peruvian's need for sumptuousness, for material brilliance; and from both he inherited that dangerous and delightful, delusive and consoling capacity for imagining, which had attracted his grandmother to humanitarian enterprises, his father to politics. He was a painter, a sculptor, yet, how important was the part abstraction played in his plastic invention! Physically and spiritually, even up to the accidents of his health, heredity betrayed itself: it was to a burst blood vessel that he, too, succumbed, after numerous warning signals of the terrible disease.

"My heart hurts, my heart is affected," he wrote me as early as 1899. . . .

His life as a cabin boy, then as a sailor for an import-export firm, cast him here and there onto all the famous shores of the two continents. When he saw before him the natural splendors of all humanity, and all the flora, there wakened in him the desire to express beauty as he saw it. Thus, one can truly say that he was a student of nature. But it was awkward, in the brief stopovers or on the wave-tossed decks, to spread his colors and carve his wood. Was it in the hope of working more peacefully, more steadily, that he finally landed—never, he believed, to depart again?

The first time, the results thwarted his plans.

He got married; he wed a young woman, beautiful and charming but without means. He deferred his own fulfillment, his work as an artist, to do a man's work and start a family. A position found for him by his parents-in-law in the Spanish bank of the Calgados [sic]—who became his friends—took up his week. On Sunday, he painted. That went on for a few years, during which Gauguin met artists who, on the contrary, gave their whole lives to their work: Degas, Cézanne, Renoir, Pissarro, Monet, Guillaumin. . . . Was it their example, was it the imperious inner command of the genius that prevailed one day over his scruples as a husband and a father? Yet his "situation" was a good one; the teachings of his American ancestors, powerful money managers, did not remain unfruitful in the memory of the apprentice banker, the outside broker; he earned a great deal of money, and astonishment greeted his sudden announcement to his wife, to his friends: "From now on, I paint every day."

At that hour began the loneliness, the poverty—and the work.

At this point, biography merges with the study of the artist's works, doctrine, evolution, influence. Gauguin no longer has any history other than that of his works. Between the man and the artist, he made the choice: He believed he had to choose. Let him who dares judge him.

I will therefore pass over—to come back to them shortly and explain their meaning—the successive trips to Brittany, several times, to Provence, to Martinique, and to the Marquesas. He came back to Paris from every expedition, to show what he had done. There were commotions, terrors in the art press. He watched people grimace, smiled his disdainful and sly Indian's smile, left again, returned, left again.

A sale upon his return from Martinique—that is when I had the honor of meeting him—was profitable and allowed him to implement a long-cherished plan: Tahiti! A sojourn of long months in the Happy Island. He stayed there nearly three years; then Paris was invited, at Durand-Ruel's, to the exhibition of the Tahitian harvest: abundant, brilliant, marvelous, the revelation of genius in its proud maturity. Paris was amazed; chattered; and passed on, blind.

It was a material disaster for the artist and, to all intents and purposes, proof positive that he could not count on the understanding he had hoped for, the admiration due him.

After long bitternesses, etched into the increasingly enigmatic smile, into the increasingly sad and haughty gaze, into the few and deep creases

Calgados, actually Calzado, the son-in-law of Gustave Arosa who may have helped Gauguin find employment at the firm of Paul Bertin.

of the gaunt cheeks and the low, hard brow—he went away again, with almost nothing, forever; he made his way back out there where he had tasted the only happiness that was granted him, that of serene creation in a free life, among simple beings with neither criticism nor prejudices.

"I have nothing to hope for here," Gauguin would conclude in long conversations with his friends; "the administration of the Beaux-Arts, the Ecole, the dealers. . . . It is only left for me to carve my tombstone, over there, in the sun and flowers. . . . They'll bring it back here one day, at great expense, when I am dead!"

And he would add, rising as if already about to leave: "Let's go to work."

That was in 1895. The last departure.

Already ill, Gauguin no longer had that resistance, that energy that up until then had allowed him to brave the perils of a life that had to be invented, so to speak, every day. He worked, regardless; he worked until the end. But joy abandoned him, and his painting felt the effects of the insuperable sadness that overwhelmed his soul. Furthermore, somewhat embittered, instead of trying to ensure himself peaceful conditions of existence, he continued, in the heart of Oceania, his struggle against Western civilization, which he saw, over there, assuming the innocent and brutal shape of the surveyor or the gendarme. To attempt to rally the colonists settled in Papeete and the educated natives to liberal opinions, he published a short-lived newspaper. As controversial there as here, he adopted somewhat violent behavior in order to startle his detractors, and, having witnessed the injustices of which the Marquesans were victims, he took their side. Who could have the heart to blame him for that? Those poor people loved him, implored him, begged him to defend them, and his pride forbade him to believe that he could do nothing for them. It cost him dearly. He was prosecuted and fined heavily. He wrote me in April 1903, a few days before his death:

I am down, but not yet defeated. Is the Indian who smiles while being tortured defeated? You were mistaken one day when you said that I was wrong to believe that I was a savage. I am a savage. And the civilized ones sense it: for the only thing that could confuse in my work is that savageness-in-spite-of-myself. That is why it is inimitable. The work of a man is the explanation of a man. Whence, two kinds of beauties: one that arises from instinct, and another that comes from studying. Doubtless, the combination of the two, with the modifications this entails, produces a great, very complex richness. Art criticism must apply itself to discovering it. . . . Raphael's great learning does not disconcert me, nor does it prevent me, for a single instant, from feeling, seeing, and understanding its prime element, which is the *instinct* of the beautiful. Raphael was born beautiful. Everything else in him is but modification. We have just undergone, in art, a very long period of losing our way, caused by physics, chemistry, mechanics, and the study of nature. The artists, having lost all their savagery, no longer having instinct—one could say imagination—have strayed into every path to find productive elements that they did not have the strength to create. They only act like a disordered crowd, feeling fearful, as if lost, when they are alone. That is why one must not advise solitude for everyone, for one must be strong enough to endure it, to act alone. Everything I learned from others hindered me. I can therefore say: No one taught me anything. It is true that I know so little! But I prefer that little bit that is my own. And who knows if that little bit, cultivated by others, may not become a great deal? How many centuries, to create a semblance of movement!"

These are the thoughts with which Paul Gauguin died. His generous gestures on behalf of the weak, the oppressed, merged with his ideal of beauty and proceeded from him. He saw himself in those gentle savages who (at least *they* did) understood his goodness, if not his genius. The last beats of that twice-wounded heart were for humanity and for art. This is the man presented to us in the official press, still today, as an egoist and a madman.

But his situation had become difficult, impossible. He lived in a state of siege with the civil and religious authorities. I am reliably informed that the Bishop of Papeete has people seek out Paul Gauguin's paintings and woodcarvings, buys them for a few coppers, and burns them: nudes, obscenities, idols . . I resist believing, but I am afraid.

I would like to preserve that great figure exactly as it appeared to me just now; heroic because of fine endeavors and high hopes.

The first characteristic that commanded one's attention, in that angular face, with its massive and rugged features, in those expressions powerful at rest, in that heavy, well-balanced, and tranquil gait—was a particular strength, particularly lofty, or rather, perhaps, a sort of visible despotism, which scorned justification and simply stated itself. The general appearance was coarse. The square, large head and shoulders; the prominent cheekbones and eyes; the heavy eyelids; the blunt forehead, more developed in width than in height; the nose, not aquiline, but almost round, as if broken, with very delicate and constantly quivering nostrils; the small chin; the mouth, of a simplified design: a virtually straight line—his least attractive feature, destined more, alas! to the expression of bitterness than to broaden with the effusions of tenderness. And yet, the gaze that escaped those strong pupils was often veiled with a strange gentleness and when he smiled Gauguin astonished one with the unexpected revelation of a naive and almost childlike soul. The smile is a glimpse of the soul, and that Gauguin, I am sure, was the real one. But he rarely smiled. They were involuntary slips. Master of himself, the artist showed only the outward appearance of a great, exotic lord—or else of an authentic aristocrat raised in the heart of lower Brittany by no less authentic peasants—or else of some tribal chieftain, miraculously spared tattooing, but surprised, himself, at his European disguise.

He had a taste for jewels, rings, brilliant fabrics. He always wore a Breton vest, embroidered in blue and yellow. And he loved to have around him the song of light colors: on his walls, which he painted in bright chrome yellow; on his windows, which he transformed into stained glass; on his furniture, which he carved and painted. It was there, in his studio in the rue Vercingétorix, for example, in that environment attuned to himself by himself, that one had to see him to understand him: Though he still astonished, he did not disconcert, and, if I may believe my personal experience, it was difficult then to avoid the truly supreme charm of that illustrious nature, an exceptional representation of truly *complete humanity*.

These words call for a few remarks. Gauguin himself felt that he was, in effect, a complete man, a total realization of the species, victorious in all spheres open to his activity, and it was in that regard that he meant to justify his claims to royalty in all domains. It was not entirely in that respect that I consented to acknowledge his supreme rights. Without saying it in so many words, he wanted to make it appear that all the gifts had been bestowed upon him: the sense of truth, as well as the sense of beauty; practical wisdom, as well as imaginative power; skill, as well as strength; accuracy and precision of observation and action, as well as mental agility and verbal eloquence. . . . A man, a real man, according to him, had to be, if he deigned to paint, the master of masters; if he rode horseback, first among riders; if he took up the sword, the undefeatable fencer; and even if he played billiards, it was to exhaustion only that he had to concede. Pride! Those who have approached Gauguin will recognize here his pride—a very great pride, to his own measure, and a bit childish, as he was. One could not, if one thinks about it carefully, blame him for his need to be first everywhere, in everything, always. It was a harmonic and logical consequence of the truly superhuman nature of his general conception, and also of the small deficiencies of his education, especially of his schooling. The cabin boy had not had the time to pursue very regular studies. Even in painting, Gauguin was an autodidact, and if, in the empire that was his own, he made up in genius the teaching he lacked, if he was able, in the end—in that painful letter we have just read—to boast sincerely of having learned nothing from anyone, if he was, there, the miner and the smith of his gold, he could only be so there, he could only practice his divination there, and only there did genius make him the complete man, the superior being he believed himself to be everywhere—whom only there I admired and loved. This is not to say that everything in his naive bragging was untrue, or even that apart from his art he did not prove to be a rare spirit, quite often curiously intuitive and eminently sensible. The great

L'Esprit Moderne et Le Catholicisme (The Modern Spirit of Catholicism). 1902. Book cover: 12½ × 7½" (31.8 × 19.2 cm); pages: 13⅞ × 6½" (35.2 × 16.5 cm). The Saint Louis Art Museum; Gift of Vincent Price in memory of his parents, Marguerite and Vincent L. Price.

painter could wield a sword marvelously and he truly was a very skillful billiards player. The general mastery he had over matter, the infallible instinct that guided him in adapting the material means of expression to the plastic end, the keenness of his vision, his constant presence of mind, the instantaneous awakening of his intelligence, and his ability to collect immediately all his energies at his will's command—these qualities and still others of an active and robust artist accompanied him into spheres inferior to his proper one, but close to it every time he set out to triumph in them. But, brush in hand, he was a philosopher, a poet. His eloquence was the sum of his figures.

I attribute to no other cause than to this desire to rule—by divine right—the care that he took to try to make himself a legend, to stand back from his contemporaries in an immemorial perspective. When he writes, his style readily borrows a Biblical, Oriental, proverbial color. It is sometimes in questionable taste, but it almost never lacks a certain, somewhat heavy majesty.

The naiveté that underlies that pride gives him a charm that you will also find, albeit within the glory of a true and definitive grandeur, in the artist's work.

And if we reject, with, so to speak, a smile of respectful indulgence, the legendary behaviors into which he tried to escape, all things considered, as well, perhaps, from this age whose uniformity, conformity, and deformity he despised, it will not be, at least, to allow a different sort of legend to gain credence, one which shameless journalists, upon learning the distressing news, threw to the winds of publicity. "Wreck, drunkard"; this, if it were necessary to believe one of the two, was the sort of man and artist whom we worshipped. And the malicious joker whom I will not name, finding an opportunity to insult two dead men at once, surrenders to the pleasure it promises. He portrays, in the studio of which I spoke to you just now, the demigod—it is Gauguin—on a sofa perched on a dais, while at his feet the poet Julien Leclercq improvises occasional couplets, or else the frizzy-haired acolyte hails, at the top of his voice, the regenerator of painting. . . . The deviser of these indecent scenes was never, and for good reason, received at Gauguin's. As for the departed poet, whose sickly but sincere and delicate talent we liked, we have never seen him in the ridiculous character attributed to him, and he is not, he cannot be wounded in his memory, which is dear to us, by the insulting remarks of that incompetent critic.

No; Gauguin was a domineering, ambitious, proud intelligence, but a very sound and steady one. In no one more than in him was the clarity of purpose more intense. He did not realize his dream in its entirety; the obstacle was not in himself. But what he did, he meant to do, for reasons that he understood, that were logical; and logical, too, was the development of his thought—logical and constant. No accident came to trouble or to interrupt him, and when one knows what an enormous body of work, in painting and drawing, in etching and in drypoint, in sculpture and in ceramics, this artist's brief career produced, one asks oneself which of his hours or of his minutes he could have sacrificed to demon alcohol!

What one does not need to ask oneself—though at first glance one might be amazed by it, if one were not warned beforehand—is the cause of the orthodox and highly paid critics' hatred of Gauguin. One knows too well with what they reproach him—and that for having been, in this flattened world, an upright man, a proud artist, infatuated with everything those people, so well personified in the critic mentioned above, detest or fear: unsubmissiveness, sincerity, conscience. That hatred, which takes the form of contempt—it is a phenomenon of this age: contempt comes from below—is a protest against the condemnation, living and without appeal, that those great savages, those great exiles, the true poets, the true artists, are to this society without beauty and without

Morice refers to Thiébault-Sisson's description of Gauguin's studio, published in Le Temps *on 2 September 1903.*

honor, our own. Rich in infamy, it hurls it at them by the handful, and after making them poor and pariahs, it accuses them of lacking dignity, propriety, and honesty as well; they are hard-hearts, egoists—and wasn't Gauguin, one of those in the highest degree? Odious and gratuitous calumnies.

* * *

Gauguin's attitude, I here appeal to all the witnesses of his life, was one of perfect dignity. And he was not an egoist, no—I know it and I declare joyfully that I know it.

If the effort of the intellectual and the visionary sometimes side-tracked the artist's sensibility, if the pride and the bitterness of the man were taken as evidence of his heart's aridity, the illusion soon dissipates when one looks a little more closely at his work, inquiries about his life. Will the very solitude that he willed be held against him? Well, I—and I hesitate to say it because I do not know if he would approve—I have seen him cry when speaking to me of his family. Those who knew him *see* those terrible tears. And he wrote me: "My children have never said to me: 'Dear father,'" And in his manuscript I note this:

> I have just lost my daughter. I no longer love God. Her name was Aline, like my mother. Everyone loves in his own way: for some, love ignites at the coffin. For others . . . I do not know. Her grave, over there? Flowers? Illusion. Her grave is here beside me. My tears are flowers; only living ones.

* * *

Many years ago, the painter Maurice Denis wrote that the school [of Pont-Aven] would one day surpass the renown of the more ostentatious school of Fontainebleau. That day has come. The school of Pont-Aven! Very small, in truth, the school: an ordinary inn. But, as one of Gauguin's dearest students—Armand Séguin—very well put it, the master and the pupils made the inn into a temple of Apollo: "Its walls were covered with decorations that astonished the rare traveler, and no surface was spared: noble maxims framed fine drawings, the windows of the tavern became dazzling stained glass windows, and the whole village of le Pouldu resembled Plato's garden.

In those days, Gauguin, back from Martinique, already possessed all his mastery and still had the ardor of hope and faith that compelled him to elucidate his convictions, to seek adherents to his doctrines, to the idea of great common enterprises in which his hands and spirit would multiply. His was not, therefore, a purely objective and disinterested teaching. Certainly, one could develop in the luminous shadow of such a master, but I can well imagine that one had to resist it somewhat, so as not to let oneself be crushed by it. And it is noteworthy that, although all were more or less profoundly imbued with his influence, none of those who heeded him imitated him slavishly, copied him directly. His despotism signaled danger and would have driven them away, had not the nobleness of his systems and the splendor of his examples profoundly conquered and held them. They tried to proceed from him "from the core," and not from externals. That is more valuable to Gauguin's glory than mere repetitions of his formula—more valuable to the general interest of art, as well, and it is thus that the little school of Pont-Aven expands, that it comes to border on Paris and radiates there. I believe I have found that more than one of our contemporary artists, still young, were at Pont-Aven; their presence there was never pointed out. Spiritually, very numerous, materially, a smaller group—their presence was quite real. . . . Together, and to name but a few: Séguin, who became the "movement's" historiographer, Bernard, Maurice Denis, Filiger, Sérusier, Bonnard, Vuillard, Chamaillard, Verkade, O'Conor,

Durio [sic] the sculptor, Maufra, Ranson, Mayol [sic], Roy, and others; and how many others! All of them understood that "loving synthesis of line," that "harmony through derivatives, in the arabesque's overall envelopment," painting's necessary and natural orientation toward decoration that calls for the symbol, and that consequently demands an inner and individual effort, on the one hand, that is, something to symbolize; and on the other hand, places pictorial art in relation to all the other arts, and to the crowd, and to life, but in order to dominate it. They all understood that the great revolutionary was, in reality, the most strictly *traditionalist* of painters, but also that the tradition, true and austere, with which he claimed kinship had nothing in common with the Academy's; that it went beyond even the Renaissance, far back toward primitive times; that it was, in reality, a new opening onto the infinite, through which all talents, all temperaments, and even several varieties of aesthetics could comfortably pass.

So one can say that Gauguin's actions were principally general instruction, of general benefit. As for the details of his system, without of course failing to respect them, one must circumscribe their value within the pure domain of technique and not forget that every artist invents his own. Gauguin himself, after having, in theory—with the intractable Jacobinism that was peculiar to him—stated, defined, codified, and promulgated laws and rules, especially restrictions and, or nearly, penalties. When he set to work on his own, when he gave himself up to that joy of creating that was his life's natural occupation, he was the first to forget his precepts—and I quite believe that, very truly, he never applied them.

What remains—beside the work—is the example, that is, as with all the great masters, impulse, guidance, revelation. Even if we could give this study all its breadth, we would still not be led, in revealing Gauguin, into excursions beyond art, and the following elucidates it. On the subject of Puvis de Chavannes, for example, historical criticism is inevitably conjured up; with a Carrière, we cannot help entering without the power to defend ourselves, an atmosphere of tender and rational spirituality, where philosophical, and, above all, moral considerations arise, as if of themselves: There is, there, guidance for life. With Gauguin, there is guidance for art; his revelation is aesthetic and, in its broader sense, his impulse touches on the other arts, all of them, only them. What abounds in him, what radiates from him, is not tenderness, it is strength, and it is so rich that it goes beyond the boundaries of a specific art: at once instinctive and subject to a very detailed conception, which is superhuman or inhuman, it disturbs and mingles all the elements of expression of the beautiful and incites architecture, poetry, and music to the effective synthesis that seems to be the express desire of art.

But this is a consequence that we ourselves infer from Gauguin's doctrine. For his part, he wisely limited his teaching to decorative painting, to sculpture, and to ceramics, and if we find that every one of his works seems to call for poetic commentary, he leaves us to do so, lavishing the excessive energy that was in him on the embellishment of the objects of everyday life, with a decorator's endless inventions, thereby leaving, by every means possible, a luminous and beautiful trace of his passage through time and space. "He invented everything," said Séguin; "he had invented his easel; he had invented a process for reproducing watercolors." Following his example, his students used to invent their paintboxes, their outfits, their hats, and their sabots, that is, they transformed everything they touched into art objects. But the master, despite his generous efforts to make it public, kept the secret, the gift of his style.

In Pont-Aven (1888), between the Martinique and the Provence stages, Gauguin, already a master, as I said, reaches the last period of his evolution. But he had nonetheless not yet forgotten any of the little that he was able to learn from others in the course of an always adventurous life; he did not know himself until this time; it only remains for him to

"Idol with a Pearl." ca. 1892–93
Tamanu wood. Height: 9⅞″ (25 cm).
Musée d'Orsay, Paris.

penetrate further into the personal mysteries of his thought. The teaching that he himself teaches is, in this respect, very beneficial. His glory gained by it as well, and lo! Paris is roused by the clamor being made around a new aesthetic, a man who could endow the objects of street and home, of ordinary life, with style.

Is it necessary to point out what his part was in the alleged Art Nouveau movement? It is quite certain that, even as they deny it, the humbugs, so perfectly ignorant of any style, who differ agreeably on the tiresome theme of modern fashion, have studied the sculptures and the ceramics originating in Pont-Aven very closely indeed. Except that they have not understood them. It would no doubt have been desirable for Gauguin himself to have presided over that embellishment of life, that union of beauty and life, the justification or pretext for the so-called Art Nouveau. For a thousand reasons, the sculptor's assistants would have been unable to accept his authority—and the movement miscarried, as we see. . . .

It would be better if we stopped and inferred the path by which Gauguin had arrived at his Pont-Aven theories, at *Synthetism,* at *the characteristic,* at *Cloisonnism*—and let us speak more clearly by one word—at *Symbolism.* I must content myself with recalling that he had behind him at the time, besides his background in two worlds, his life as a sailor and, toward the end of his very earliest studies, the Impressionists' ateliers in Paris, where he did technical research, followed by his Martinique campaign, where he took counsel with nature in order to express himself.

The four artists he loved best, among his contemporaries and his elders, are certainly Puvis de Chavannes, Degas, Odilon Redon, and Cézanne. A few family ties, not direct descent; noble cousinship. He admired Rodin, Carrière, Renoir—the heads of other families.

* * *

And also these brief notes, on a few other contemporaries:

> Harmless criticisms. On converging paths, rustic figures, without ideas, seek they know not what.
>
> That could have been by Pissarro.
>
> At the seaside, a well: a few Parisian figures, dressed and motley in stripes, thirsty, with ambition no doubt, seeking in this dried-up well the water that could quench their thirst. All of it, confetti.
>
> That could be by Signac.
>
> Beautiful colors, though one is unaware of them, exist and can be guessed at behind the veil that modesty has drawn. Conceived out of love, the little girls evoke tenderness, their hands grasp and caress.
>
> Without hesitation, I say that it is by Carrière.
>
> Cézanne. The woman cleaning the cesspool, the two-bit wine, the hanged man's house.
>
> Impossible to describe. Do better; go see them.
>
> Ripe grapes overhang the rim of a fruit dish; on the linen, the apple-green apples and the plum-red ones harmonize. The whites are blue, and the blues are white.
>
> One hell of a painter, that Cézanne.
>
> Crossing the Pont des Arts, he meets a pal who has become famous.
>
> "Well, Cézanne! Where are you going?"
>
> "As you see, I'm going to Montmartre, and you, to the Institute."
>
> Carolus-Duran complains about the Impressionists, about their palette: "It is so simple," he says. "Look at Velázquez: a white, a black. . . ."
>
> So simple as that, Velázquez's whites and blacks?
>
> I like to hear those people. On those terrible days when one thinks one is good for nothing, when one throws away one's brush—one remembers them, and hope is born anew.

Though he was long counted as one of their group, and though he never became entirely a stranger to them, all things considered, Gauguin only trained briefly with the Impressionists. The most important piece that he gave us in their formula dates from 1881, it is the *Nude Woman,* which aroused the censure of all the critics. Naturally, on that path, with his natural boldness, Gauguin had gone to all extremes; but he was already showing his strength as well. Young at the time, Impressionism still claimed kinship with Delacroix and kept itself within Manet's sober lines—Manet, the painter Gauguin looked at most—after Corot, Ingres, and Raphael. There exists (where is it?) a copy of *The Beautiful Olympia* signed by Paul Gauguin—a masterpiece arising from a masterpiece.

It was Martinique that liberated the future Symbolist master. He found there once more the aspirations and inspirations of his first dreams, an exuberance sister to his own, a richness of colors that awakened his palette. There, too, he figured out that to portray matter, or rather, to master it, to couple oneself victoriously with it, one must not compose in front of it. A great general truth, at least for the artist-decorator; once he understood it, Gauguin suddenly felt himself near his own goal, as to the general truth. He could, from then on, create "a personal beauty, the only human one," as he was fond of saying.

It is therefore with a wealth of observations, meditations, well-founded aesthetic convictions, that he came to Brittany; he established himself there, seeking, within the limits of the West, where he was held back by the attractions of atavism or preexistence, the motifs of the decorative syntheses that he planned.

The Impressionists were, at the time, moving toward scientism, chemical art, and the production of the infallible masterpiece, according to a certain mechanical mathematics, a very ingenious process that allows one to seize the vibration of light, to cause the figures to tremble within the atmosphere of the canvas, which is, perhaps, unfavorable to the plastic expression of thought and feeling. Gauguin broke with the Impressionists. Resolutely, he was on his way toward the past, and that Brittany, full of immemorial monuments to an art so naive and so knowing, was to serve him perfectly. In the face of those old wayside crosses where the suffering of Christian artists, once and still barbarians, was so simply, so instinctively expressed; in the face of that evidence of a primitive and fervent humanity, grave, reflective, but not without the gift of childhood, Gauguin shivered: it was the last warning. Martinique had revived in him the intoxication with matter, even as it taught him to mistrust it; Brittany reminded him that the spirit of man can express itself most movingly by forbidding itself detail, the overfinished, by sacrificing everything to subjective unity through a daring synthesis, which humanity, in its innocence, spontaneously improvised everywhere on earth. Primitive Egypt, at the same time as India and Mexico: the Hindu, Aztec, Mexican arts—a single art. It had made a discreet reappearance in ancient Brittany, as if from outside history into the very heart of history, and it manifested itself there with that very soberness that is true wealth, with that disdain for grace that does not exclude true beauties. The sum of the figures, in their massive fullness, triumphed over angular thinness, grotesque attitudes, and affirmed that one can create beauty, not contrary to ugliness, but with ugliness, as long as the synthesis of simple lines is reduced, so as to be significant, and, fully alive, is subordinated to the unpolished envelopment of a rigorously harmonic arabesque.

I have told how, by his very origins, Gauguin was to be inevitably attracted to that primitive ideal of open-air and popular art, mystical and massive. He was, therefore, obeying his own law. How could they accuse him of having impoverished and immobilized the feeling of life? We have seen that Professor Mani advises his students not to render their models in motion, to bring them back to the static state—and how can a synthesis fidget and move around? But if you understand immobility to be the absence of life, then you are not speaking of Gauguin; not of those figures in which it is impossible not to feel that life is coiled, has withdrawn into itself, and that it borrows a prodigious intensity from the subtraction of those details in which real life does not multiply, but rather dissipates. As for impoverishment, the criticisms are even more incomprehensible. Do they mean that the sadness ordinarily stamped upon such creations rules out any idea of luxury, of abundance, of joy? But if that sadness is, once again, intense—and I intentionally repeat the word that cannot be substituted—if it is expressed even in the grieving pleats of the least drapery, if it impresses itself upon every sensibility through the very contours—jarring, broken—of the total line, that sadness is *rich*, in the only sense of the word that art can accept.

All that one can admit on this point, only on the subject of the Brittany paintings, and not of all of them—except principally the *Yellow Christ*, the *Garden of Olives*, the *Jacob Wrestling with the Angel*—is that the dark beauty of the lines was missing for Gauguin's work to be definitively his own, that splendor of colors, for which, moreover, he yearned. Here, at that time, there occurred, in the artist's life, that episode that bears the name of Vincent van Gogh—Van Gogh, drunk with the great explosions of light, devoted to yellow and to the sunflower! He worked then in the environs of Arles, the old Provençal city. He summoned Gauguin there, toward the sun. . . . We know how sadly the friendship of the two artists was interrupted by the death of one of them.

* * *

Vincent van Gogh's death and the miscarriage of the undertaking dreamed by his diseased brain led to the ruin of the great little school of Pont-Aven. But Gauguin was thenceforth well and truly, wholly Gauguin. In Tahiti, which he first visited in 1891 and 1892, he achieved his most incontestable masterpieces—yes, exactly, the very ones whose Paris sale was an absurd disaster. In the childlike and sculptural humanity of that place he found his true models, and, in the charming flora of the Happy Island, their necessary setting: the matter, above all others, of which his mind was to be the womb. It is not of the artworks dating from Tahiti, notably from that first trip, that one could say: immobility, impoverishment. Musical painting, with a full orchestra, with beautiful, vast harmonies, in which theme and variations are so closely, so magnificently united! Straightforward colors, boldly settled side by side and harmonizing, despite their audacity, in singing gradations, in which the air, lord of tones, vibrates. In the gigantic statues of the Maori idols, which he perhaps invented, Gauguin once again found the beautiful masses of rock, naively and finely hewn, that he had loved in Brittany; from them he took the pretext for the contrasts essential to the expression of his thought.

Still, it must be said, to the shame of the masters of the moment and to our sorrow: Gauguin will not have given, could not have given, the great, total, unified proof that the decoration of vast walls would have allowed him. We have only some sublime pieces.

In an exemplary fashion, the destiny of this artist is representative of the abominable lot imposed by this society upon the lovers of the beautiful who dedicate their lives to it. Just as there are cursed poets, Gauguin was a cursed painter. "In art," he used to say, "there are only revolutionaries or plagiarists." But the only happy ones, in the immediate meaning of the word, are the plagiarists. Gauguin suffered a great deal. He was constantly in exile, and his final retreat to the island where he had fled from us—to the island whence he himself but lately brought me a little, cursed book, his memories, his regrets, so that I could use it for *Noa Noa*—was but a last image of his entire life.

Will justice be rendered him, today? Or will hatred and incomprehension, even in the face of death, refuse to lay down their arms? Will they still dispute us that real glory, pure and grave, rings in those dear syllables: Paul Gauguin?

He is not in the Luxembourg yet. . . . I have been told that the man harmed the artist. Well, the man is no longer there. . . .

There are several of Gauguin's students in the Luxembourg. Could they not manage to make a little room for their master?

Let us speak more frankly: it is shameful, it is scandalous that in a museum of modern artists, which is accountable to the public—without the latter having to be subjected to the preferences or whims, the learning or the ignorance of the Administration of the Beaux-Arts—for "outstanding" demonstrations of contemporary painting and sculpture, it is hard to believe that we find nothing by the great painter and great sculptor Paul Gauguin. And we demand that no time be lost in rectifying, at least in the rather modest form of the installation of two of his works among those (of his peers? let us say:) of his contemporaries, a long-standing injustice.

Charles Morice

MERCURE DE FRANCE

"A Few Opinions about Paul Gauguin"

November 1903

A human ceremony (unavoidably reduced to a written form by the conditions of our social life): In front of everyone, by selected witnesses conscious of his efforts and by his peers, the day immediately following the burial, the judgment of an artist who was ardently admired, violently scoffed at; sanctioned affirmations or negations, in numbers large enough to ascertain glory or reduce to silence—with this thought we sent the following letter to a number of people:

Paris, 30 September 1903

Sir,

The death of Paul Gauguin, who had been somewhat forgotten these last few years in the faraway exile where he'd fled from our civilization, brings his name and work back to everyone's attention.

It is in the nature of our journal to offer for opinion the means to appreciate properly and definitively an artist discussed with passion, as was this one.

Of a small number of people qualified to respond to us we are asking for elements of this certitude.

Would you have the kindness to review, in at most one page, what you think of Paul Gauguin: his talent, his doctrine, his work, his influence, his attitude?

Some of our correspondents understood us.

M. EUGÈNE CARRIÈRE

Gauguin was a decorative expression. His enthusiasm for exalted color would have passed for wonderful flames on the stained glass windows and decorated the walls of life with powerful and fruitful harmonies.

His origin, so primitive, kept him close to the great spectacles of nature. He remained completely penetrated by the power of the elements. Sky, water, and fire played a continuous drama in his rough and delicate soul, as fascinating for him as for wild animals, the scenery of their flamboyant solitudes.

His was a faraway mysticism, stirred-up and troubled by an instinct he couldn't conquer and by a modern education from which, in vain, he believed he could escape.

This subtle, richly nuanced personality, so fresh in spirit, supple and violent but impatient in its philosophy, despaired too quickly.

We certainly didn't know how to benefit from his genius. Talents rarely find their proper outlet; this must be said with the pain of feeling how so many beautiful constitutions are denied—rather more from indifference than from true hostility—the means of development, so productive for society.

But humanity lives less from complete realizations, impossible in any event, than from strong directions.

These must have been Gauguin's thoughts. He found his approval and joy within himself.

His work, as we know it, suffices for the admiration and grateful emotion of his friends.

M. ALIDOR DELZANT

About M. Gauguin I have nothing in particular to say. I am one of those backward people who prefer talent without genius to genius without talent!

Alidor Delzant was a French printmaker.

M. JEAN DOLENT

I owe my having known Gauguin to M. Charles Morice.

Before this man of persistent will I was a bit taken aback, being one of those people able to receive an appointment from the Immortal which a woman made them miss (that's how they excuse themselves) . . . and thus they were unadmirable, which has the advantage of sparing the reader the unpleasant sensation, the humiliation, of feeling inferior to them. They only make small talk.

Paul Gauguin spoke of everything with assurance. He spoke softly about that which he didn't understand well, saying that he didn't have "letters," perhaps expecting an objection from us for which, because of our imperfect education and also our malice, he was sometimes left waiting a rather long time.

I remember one glorious day: I had Paul Gauguin, Albert Trachsel, and Odilon Redon together at my table. I said, "No one is stupid; that which is stupid in us is borrowed." That is all I had to say. I listened.

Albert Trachsel (1863–1929), Swiss architect, painter, and writer who exhibited with the mystico-Catholic group Rose + Croix.

One liked Gauguin, eyes opened. There were two people in Gauguin and when I was with one of them, I agreed with Gauguin sometimes in disagreement with the other. The theoretician was effusive and imprecise but the artist at his easel was silent. He defended himself. He defends himself better dead than alive.

Toulouse-Lautrec (said in front of a painting of Paul Gauguin): "A foot is prettier than that!"

He also said: "Gauguin can't be swallowed like a pill."

Rodin (in front of a wood sculpture of Gauguin's): "It's a curiosity piece."

Carrière, affirmative and authoritarian, which he'd acquired the right to be: "Gauguin is above Burne-Jones."

I like the portrait Gauguin did of himself, given to Carrière, and the portrait of Gauguin by Carrière, given to Gauguin. That means something, I think.

There is no "known" history; there is absolutely no "new" history. Gauguin is a creator in the sense of differences. Some of the group,

Eugène Carrière. *Portrait of Paul Gauguin.*
1891. 21½ × 25¾″ (55 × 65.5 cm). Yale
University Art Gallery; Bequest of Fred
T. Murphy, B.A., 1897.

among those who analyze all week long and synthesize on Sundays, tell
themselves (unduly) reassured: "Gauguin doesn't bother me in the least.
He doesn't know how to draw."

And so everybody is happy.

He came in between.

M. F. DURIO [sic]

My affection for the man was profound, my admiration for the artist, absolute.

His very pure feeling for the decorative destination of plastic art, the
exceptional importance of his personal contribution, the necessary reaction he instituted against the official decadence of all the arts, and his
extraordinary production all made him, in my eyes, the equal of the
greatest of the old masters.

As for his doctrine, I read it in his works rather than in his words,
and in his means of execution, which were so free and independent of
any predetermined position. I don't know if he was scientifically or the-
oretically right against Chevreul and the latest Impressionists; I don't
know if his precepts were impeccable; but I can testify to the beauty of
his example and to the splendor of his creation.

His influence hardly reached more than a restricted group of people, at least directly. There is, however, more or less something of him
in all of the young people of this period, and I'm convinced that more
and more artists worthy of the name will take interest in a man and an
oeuvre that were an unmerited honor bestowed upon this miserable period.

As for his attitude, I will sincerely express what I think by saying that
it was that of a martyr and a hero.

M. FAGUS

This accursed descendant of the old, extinguished races exhausted
his strength struggling against our civilization to extricate himself from

*Paco Francesco Durrio (1876–1940),
Spanish sculptor and ceramicist influenced
by Gauguin when they met in Paris in the
1890s. Durrio's collection of Gauguin's
work, formed before 1895, was exhibited
at the Leicester Gallery in London in
1931.*

*Eugène Chevreul (1786–1889), chemist
whose books on color theory were a
foundation for Neo-Impressionist
aesthetics.*

*Fagus was the pseudonym of the poet
Georges Faillet (1872–1933).*

it and, struggling against himself to try to feel at home within it, used up his entire life searching in darkness, in nature and in *his* nature. He found at last the path to his authentic gods: he still had the time—just enough—to build a temple for them and himself, and then, tired-out, he expired on its threshold. We refer to his last known works: a serenity, as though virginal, and an angelic ease inhabits them. They are truly the Elysian marriage of Hercules with Hébé.

So inexpressibly sad, all of his previous work represents the same Hercules laboring and bleeding, if Puvis de Chavannes is Apollo. The two names invincibly summon one another by a similarly sublime harmony attained by means of the most astonishingly and the most providentially contradictory gestures. Puvis sums up twenty centuries of culture. Gauguin emanates from no one, no more from Cézanne than from anyone else. Gauguin is an antediluvian brought to light. Gauguin is the sumptuous, vehement, tumultuous, and deaf barbarian with a bit of the savage and the child and all the incurable despair of condemned races. Stubborn, proud, worried, and obstinate rather than dominating, he made the primitive and native element bloom in all its coarse beauty. But isolated—undoubtedly the reason for his influence: Through his work and his life he was an example and a lesson. His painting conjures up in the individual human an animated architecture which finds its motive in some obscurely superhuman conscience and its decorative aspect in a torrentially virginal nature. It makes the eye, worn out by art, turn back toward primary harmony: this is truly Hercules, the one who displaced mountains which stood in the way of another world. Let's not speak of doctrine, let's not say, "He instigated a school," when, of the artists who kept company with him, not a single one (at least of those who show talent) has kept absolutely anything of his manner. He didn't make disciples; directly, if not as a consequence, he was the precursor, revealer, and liberator for an entire generation; he formed artistic temperaments.

M. GUSTAVE GEFFROY

With understanding and explanatory admiration, Charles Morice spoke of the charm, force, and significance of the work of Paul Gauguin. Besides, all the scrutiny and all the critics could not prevent this work from having its eternal existence, now that the craftsman is dead. In the austere figures and the violent and subtle colors, one distinctly perceives the battle that took place within Gauguin to forget acquired art in order to find nature again. As all artists, he was often the tributary of the past, but he was also, with his direct vision, the victorious one who seized his prey. It must be hoped that an exhibition of his works will once again permit study and attempts at definition of them. We will then see what great decorative effects Gauguin was capable of producing through stained glass, tapestry, sculpture—and painting. It matters little that this effort had not been fully realized. The incomplete can have the supreme beauty of life.

M. CHARLES GUÉRIN (*painter*)

If, as Nicolas Poussin said in his reflections and advice, painting has as its sole objective the delight and joy of the eyes—and for me, I don't think it has any other—Paul Gauguin, who just died, is a very great painter.

Those who hypnotize themselves with the word "Life" without, moreover, understanding its true meaning, as well as those who want our paintings to tell stories, to teach or to moralize, will never know the art of Gauguin, who is only a maker of images and a decorator of walls.

Paul Gauguin was an artist of tradition, "throwing form into the crucible of forms," composing and coloring to his whim, following precon-

Charles Guérin (1875–1939), painter who studied with Gustave Moreau and later became a friend of Matisse.

COLORPLATE 118. *The Magician of Hivaoa.* 1902. 36¼ × 28¾″ (92 × 73 cm).
Musée d'Art Moderne, Liège.

COLORPLATE 119. *Landscape with Three Figures*. 1901. 26½ × 30½″ (67.3 × 77.5 cm).
The Carnegie Museum of Art, Pittsburgh; Acquired through the generosity of Mrs. Alan M. Scaife.

COLORPLATE 121.
Riders on the Beach.
1902.
28¾ × 36¼"
(73 × 92 cm).
Private collection.

371

COLORPLATE 120.
Women and White Horse.
1903.
28⅞ × 36⅛″ (72 × 91.5 cm).
Museum of Fine Arts, Boston;
Bequest of John T. Spaulding.

370

ceived laws created by him for his own use, as is always and in every country practiced by those we nowadays call Masters, and whom we no longer know how to understand.

M. ANTOINE DE LA ROCHEFOUCAULD

I consider Paul Gauguin a noble and courageous artist, one of those whose work will "survive" and will fully assert itself, to the admiration of our descendants. In our time of universal counterfeiting and, especially, of artificial science, he was the artist Providence designated to express some of the immutable truths. In a pictorial language, sometimes rude but always free of dissimulation, he knew how to say that Art is very closely linked to Idea and that a work is beautiful only if it reflects the soul of the painter who conceived it and the soul of that Nature that served simply as a pretext. Through his paintings, essentially those of a decorative arrangement and executed without any care for imitation, he showed the inanity of all objective research. We should be thankful to Paul Gauguin for having begun the good fight in a period when many fine minds were still bemired in the last turpitudes of Naturalism. We should be grateful to him both for his beginning gropings and for the deliberate exaggerations of that period when his talent reached its apogee. The former as well as the latter brought us back onto the correct path and taught us what to detest and fight against and what, on the other hand, to admire, without reservation.

Here are the principal reasons for which I appreciate the great value of Paul Gauguin and his work:

1. The latter taught me, definitively, to be interested no longer in the stupidities and cunning tricks of the "officials," those game birds of the Institute who encumber jury salons and reign therein.

2. As a forerunner, Gauguin braved "distortion" and scorned the science of anatomy and the very debatable axioms of perspective; in the boldness of his drawings, he somewhat discredited the illusory "canons" professed in the academies or the sinister headquarters in the rue Bonaparte.

3. His decorations made me further understand the genius of the Masters who had preceded him. Descendant of our great ornamental painters and sculptors of the twelfth and thirteenth centuries, he attempted to bring our national art back to its sources in ridding it of the baneful contributions of the Italian Renaissance. Thus he remains an artist of the purest tradition, and, on this ground, he has in the manifestations of his thinking a right to the gratitude of those who above all love the fatherland.

I will refrain from analyzing Paul Gauguin's doctrine here. Men of letters in art, friends who shared the life of the Master in Brittany, have expressed themselves on this subject with all the competence one could desire. It is therefore useless to make a pastiche of the perfectly documented lines written by an Aurier, an Octave Mirbeau, a Charles Morice, and, lastly, by M. Armand Séguin.

Gauguin's influence exerted itself, it seems to me, only on the very few artists who had the intelligence to unite their efforts with his, instead of giving in, as did so many others, to the contemporary sentiment, *par excellence,* of jealousy. In order for his authority to spread abroad, first it would have been indispensable for modern man's mentality to undergo a complete transformation that would teach him to distinguish beauty from ugliness, the noble from the vulgar, and, especially, to reject the whole lot of insane elucabrations of an across-the-Channel, bric-a-brac, flea-market "modern style." But who will the art critic be who, gifted with enough clairvoyance and sufficiently independent, will

Count Antoine de la Rochefoucauld (1862–1960), Symbolist painter, writer, and collector who was associated with Péladan's Rose + Croix movement.

perfect the education of a certain general public to the point that it will no longer take the Grand and Petit Palais for admirable masonry, the Metro stations for elegant masterpieces of originality, Rodin for a sculptor of statues, Messieurs de la Gandara and Zuloaga for painters, M. Besnard for a colorist, Lévy-Dhurmer and Cottet for stylists, and Henri Martin for the continuation of the lamented Seurat and the chosen successor of Puvis de Chavannes?

In Gauguin's work, the paintings which appear to me the most bounteously instructive and the most radiant in beauty are those that he executed in Martinique and in Brittany: *Belle Angèle, Mystical Vision (Struggle with the Angel), The Calvaries, Bonjour, M. Gauguin* remain unforgettable, and also a certain effigy of Emile Schuffenecker surrounded by his family.

Gauguin the man could equal the artist; the former never lowered himself to degrading transactions. He had the great merit of following to its completion the path of Symbolism he had discovered, and he never abandoned—as some others did, either because of discouragement or on simply material grounds—the artistic cause to which he had so generously sacrificed his skills. His voluntary exile to a bit of an island situated at the antipodes of the "civilized world" shows the disdain in which he held a society having no other ideals than those of gain, vainglory, and imbecilic or murderous sports.

I like to believe that certain works of Gauguin will not take long to find a good position in the galleries of the Luxembourg, not far from those of Claude Monet, Pissarro, Renoir, and Edouard Manet, whose sublime *Olympia* he formerly was able to interpret . . . this is while waiting for the Louvre, some ten years from now, to deem it an honor to offer its walls. But what a revolution and what a row are necessary to arrive at such a result!

With all my prayers I name him the Man of pure race, the Avenger of jeered-at talents, the intellectual Dictator who will rid us of the paintbrush profiteers and of the false celebrities, who will have the noble audacity to liquidate the Institutes, to padlock the Academies, to abolish the malevolent juries and, finally, to put an end to the ignorant routines and disastrous stupidities of the paper-scribblers under the direction of the Beaux-Arts.

M. CAMILLE LEMONNIER

I didn't have the opportunity to follow Gauguin's work closely. I don't know his starting points or curves of evolution. His works were rarely seen in Belgium, and perhaps I was far from Paris when I could have been able to study them there.

What I knew of him left me with the impression of a homogeneous, violent, rigid personality expressing itself by means of art that sometimes seemed a rebirth of the sensation of life in a tree that had lived in an indeterminate time. His art seemed nevertheless to correspond to the period of the great Breton calvaries.

This seemed to be his filiation, unless it would be better to say that he belonged to all of the masters of excess: Greco, Grünewald, Daumier, etc. He had the skill, the scorn of common beauty, and the cheerful gift of excess to the point of caricature. He must not have been unaware of classic style to have scoffed at it so magnificently: He used an agile and decisive science to alter the nature of human ability. He himself, taking his example from the old image-carvers, sculpted subjects which had characteristics of icons, kermis dolls, and naked figures on ships' prows. Is that enough to call him a Creator who refers back to a sense of primitiveness? In any event, he was a native who released an element of savory barbarism and, as a master, knew how to cultivate his differences with the art and artists of his time.

Antonio de La Gandara (1862–1917); Ignacio Zuloaga (1870–1945); Lucien Lévy-Dhurmer (1865–1953); Charles Cottet (1863–1925); Henri Martin (1860–1943): painters associated with Symbolist circles in France.

Camille Lemonnier (1844–1913), Belgian novelist and critic.

M. LUCE

Not having seen the works of Gauguin for a long time, I can't fulfill your request; the remembrance I have is too vague to permit me to give you my appreciation.

Please accept my apology and kindly accept my sincerest regards.

M. ADRIEN MITHOUARD

Nothing so beautiful as a barbarian's gesture putting an end to a civilization. His brusqueness is efficient; his anger is useful. He simplifies.

In works of art, in fact, as intelligence becomes refined and notions multiply, expression becomes proportionately duller and unity of conception becomes obsolete. If he is strong enough to eliminate in one sweep all the excess baggage from his mind and to free it from all obstacles, the primitive who then appears, prophetic and prompt, will be a man of genius. His proper worth is to be an energetic being at a moment of intelligence. That is what Gauguin was. The Peruvian blood he had in him awakened the blood of the original Celt. Preserved in whole,

Maximilien Luce (1858–1941), anarchist and Neo-Impressionist painter.

Adrien Mithouard (1864–1929), poet.

L'Esprit Moderne et Le Catholicisme (The Modern Spirit of Catholicism). 1902. Inside covers, front and back: 13⅞ × 6½″ (35.2 × 16.5 cm). The Saint Louis Art Museum; Gift of Vincent Price in memory of his parents, Marguerite and Vincent L. Price.

the pure man of beginnings rose up in him, powerful in his exacting instinct and strong in what Charles Morice so properly calls "the gift of childhood." Leaping beyond our sullied visions, with a savage's anger he understood in one glance that painting was beautiful only in purity of color. He said, "This tree is green; therefore, put your most beautiful green on your canvas." He accentuated the import of each line, asserted each color to its own effect, pushed each object into its proper meaning—wanting each thing to be itself as best it could, so that man would proclaim himself the highest of all. He was lyrical. Thus he gave to the painted work all its brilliance in all its homogeneity. He loved nature so profoundly that he wanted to attain its most tremulous harmonies. He translated the world with all his might. Gauguin's work is an act; profoundly healthy, it is purifying as fire. He was a violent redeemer.

M. GASTON PRUNIER

I didn't know Gauguin personally, and I have seen only a small fragment of his works in exhibitions, all of which I was prevented from seeing because of an absence of several years from Paris.

I look forward to the promised exhibition to make a definitive judgment.

At this time I can already say that I have the greatest admiration for Gauguin's artistic will, for his proud and honest attitude and, if I cannot very well discern the scope of his influence (which, over some people, was complete), I believe that his art and his life are a fine example and an uncommon lesson.

Please accept my regrets in not being able to expand further upon such an interesting subject; besides, it seems to me that Charles Morice's fine article leaves little left to say for someone who did not know Gauguin personally.

M. ODILON REDON

I don't know if it is possible to appreciate accurately the work of a contemporary when one is oneself a craftsman of the time in the same art—incompletely, without a doubt. And, incredibly gifted, Paul Gauguin expressed himself capriciously in diverse materials; in the course of time one will be able to say better than today what he made of wood or terracotta or put on canvas.

I especially like the sumptuous and princely ceramicist in him; this is where he created new forms. I compare them to flowers of a primeval region where each flower would be the prototype of a species, leaving the trouble of providing varieties through affiliation to the artists who follow. The wood sculptor was a refined savage, grandiose or delicate, and especially free from any formal school. The painter was a willful seeker, very conscious of his potential; he found that powerful originality whose repercussions can be traced in others. Everything he touched has his visible stamp; he was a master and I mean this in the most energetic sense of the word, if, at least, mastery consists of commanding through influence and of transmitting new rudiments of knowledge. Art's Scope is wide. His is visible: In this harsh painting, acidic in flavor and stamped with a maritime, faraway, non-European spirit, it's difficult not to perceive the ever-foreign mark as well as the new. Although derived from that of another, his color is truly his own: young eyes unaccustomed to so-called Impressionist art will see therein, more easily than we, a simplifying and open mode of coloration objectively taken from reality as much as from thought, and organized according to laws which were personal to him: no gray, three or five generic tones, repeated in strokes juxtaposed or attenuated according to rhythms, an analogy with the fugue.

We cannot look for excellence, seduction, perfection, affectation in

Gaston Prunier (1863–1927), landscape painter.

Odilon Redon (1840–1916), visionary artist and coexhibitor at the final Impressionist show of 1886. When in 1890 Gauguin was deciding on a tropical island for his exile, he sought advice from Redon's wife, who came from La Réunion in the Indian Ocean. In Tahiti, Gauguin hung a Redon work in his hut for inspiration. In memoriam, Redon later created several imaginary Gauguin portraits.

A pair of wooden shoes. Left shoe: 11⅜ × 6⅜ × 4¾″ (29 × 16.3 × 12 cm). Right shoe: 11¼ × 4 × 4¾″ (28.5 × 10 × 12 cm). Private collection. Photo: Musées Nationaux, Paris.

Gauguin, no; the continuous and powerful stream of his varied production prevent him from attaining this; rather, we look for decoration, pomp, airy and sovereign fantasy, all the proud expansiveness of autonomy.

It has been said that the psychology of the beings he represented was perverse. Oh! not a single seraphic angel finds its place in Gauguin; and yet, as with the image of the Tahitian women, an inexplicable and exceptional emotion of attraction, pure sweetness, and innocent tenderness was at times revealed to me.

I wouldn't be able to say anything of his attitude because, frankly, in the presence of the universe, I find it vain to adopt any attitude.

His life? It was, through its disappointment, poverty, and pain, always subordinate to the blossoming of his potential: what could be more grand and noble? Let us pass judgment on nothing and move on. Our gauge of measurement would not be his. Beyond bad and good, straight to the heart of the great mystery, let us try to see his beautiful works by themselves, removed from and unscathed by the necessary and fatal tests of judgment.

M. HENRI DE RÉGNIER

Henri de Régnier (1864–1938), poet.

I encountered Paul Gauguin a number of times. He had a rough and curious look about him and gave the impression of a powerful and obstinate person; but I have seen very few of his works: a few paintings and some wood sculptures . . . too few to be able to give any sort of judgment on the value and the scope of his talent, for one should speak only with precaution of an artist who, like him, gave his entire life to his art. That is why I prefer to leave to those more competent the task of saying what they think of him. I remember that Mallarmé had a great respect for him.

That alone is already something.

M. LOUIS ROY

To deliver painting from every *literary explanation,* to want it to live only by its harmonies of lines and colors, that was his doctrine. Like his contemporaries, he studied the decomposition of light, then launched out boldly into the synthesis of the great division, as understood in the Japanese manner—bearing in mind only the equivalent of colored surfaces. He then put into practice his theory of the derivation of colors, accurately maintaining that it is easier to obtain harmony with two secondary colors than with two complementary colors. Generally, Gauguin pre-

377

tended to be ignorant of the trade of art he practiced. Sly as a savage and sometimes more ingenuous than a child, he composed a new technique for himself which appeared to be the very reverse of that habitually used by patented specialists.

His continual preoccupation was to look for the expression of beauty, thwarted at times by the arrogant desire to astonish, to surprise by novelty or by the strange boldness of his conceptions. Everyone knows the importance—the artistic and numeric value—of his output: painting, sculpture and woodcuts, lithography, etching, ceramics—everything tempted him. He tried everything and in everything he excelled. He was a master whose talent, at times disconcerting to his friends, is incontestable to his very enemies.

M. ARMAND SÉGUIN

In Turner, England had a genius whose influence in France can be noticed in the works of Monticelli, Van Gogh, Monet, and Renoir. One century later, Paul Gauguin has given us new formulas; the perfect decorator, his teaching is healthier and more widespread than that of Turner. Springs of Beauty, these two geniuses are truly painters. Boecklin in Germany and the Pre-Raphaelites are nothing but literary illustrators.

French artists still don't understand the importance of the loss they've just had of Paul Gauguin; foreigners have an inkling of it. Those who plagiarized his considerable work aren't in the least aware of it. In analyzing his work with love and respect, one will find the wise laws that commanded his various pursuits. Paul Gauguin's death in exile spared him the terrible suffering of seeing his imitators become famous and seeing with what poor means they plagiarized his art; this death also enables us to judge the critics who dared scoff at one of the greatest masters of these times.

Future generations will know how to recognize this truth.

M. PAUL SIGNAC

My, but how atrocious these funereal interviews are! Under such circumstances—and to stand apart from the slanders of the art reporters—I can only address a respectfully tender homage to the life and to the labor of the proud rebel and fine painter that Gauguin was.

He was a master.

Such is, very clearly—yet not without the few dissonances essential to such a modern concert, sweet in the way they make known each soul by the emitted sound—the conclusion of this type of an inquiry.

He was a creative, touching, and imperious force; a final result and a new beginning. Very old and pure traditions found, through prolific transformations, the necessary agent for their renaissance in his very sensitive, enlightened, and active will. Turning the vessel from the sea of a lying civilization, this adventurous sailor will not have attempted in vain the great voyage—further than Tahiti!—the "Return to Principles." From this Odyssey which had the tragic look of a bloody Iliad, the world will now benefit, now that death has made the gesture of life. For men will always have the custom of waiting for the mournful lightning bolt in order to collect their thoughts, to understand, to look, and to see,

> Tel qu'en lui-même enfin l'éternité le change
> [Such as unto himself eternity finally changes him]

(and this immortal line of Stéphane Mallarmé who loved him is in complete harmony with the destiny of this great artist). Gauguin appears to us forever, yes, the master that he remains: with the prodigious sense of huge decorations particular to him, with his inexhaustible ingenuity, with the valor that made a hero of him in his struggle—of *Jacob with the Angel* (isn't this the subject of one of his most beautiful works?)—of Mind against Nature.

The homeland ignored him, and there is shame for many in his glory, now that it is assured. No matter. Except only for those who, having everything at their disposition, denied the genius everything (whereby I straightforwardly intend to designate the men ridiculously placed in "management" of fine arts, and as museum curators), while from almost nothing he made eternity—bounty for all! even for the ungrateful mother, even for the brother enemies, the bounty of sublime thought and work!

At this time, it is impossible to describe precisely the depth of the impact Paul Gauguin's accomplishments made upon art and in the souls of artists by his example and influence. This will be the study for a long time to come. But, without waiting, we want here the honor of having brought to light the affirmations of some who count, and of having left the former deniers and detractors with nothing to say in response. . . .

One more permanent star shines in the sky of French art.

W. Somerset Maugham

PURELY FOR MY PLEASURE

1962

Time passed. I had long had it in mind to write a novel founded on the life of Paul Gauguin, and I went to Tahiti in the hope of finding people who had known him and whom I could induce to give me some useful information. I discovered presently that somewhere in the bush there was a hut where Gauguin, being ill, had spent some time, and during his convalescence had painted. I hired a car, and with a companion, drove about till my driver sighted the hut. I got out and walked along a narrow path till I came to it. Half a dozen children were playing on the stoop. A man, presumably their father, strolled out and when I told him what I wanted to see, asked me to come in. There were three doors; the lower part of each was of wooden panels and the upper of panes of glass held together by strips of wood. The man told me that Gauguin had painted three pictures on the glass panes. The children had scratched away the painting on two of the doors and were just starting on the third. It represented Eve, nude, with the apple in her hand. . . . I asked the man if he would sell it. "I should have to buy a new door," he said. "How much would that cost?" I asked him. "Two hundred francs," he answered. I said I would give him that and he took it with pleasure. We unscrewed the door and with my companion carried it to the car and drove back to Papeete. In the evening another man came to see me and said the door was half his. He asked me for two hundred francs more, which I gladly gave him. I had the wooden panel sawn off the frame and, taking all possible precautions, brought the panelled glass panes to New York and finally to France.

I have it in my writing-room.

Ambroise Vollard

RECOLLECTIONS OF A
PICTURE DEALER

On Gauguin

1936

Redon was very much struck by the diversity of Gauguin's gifts. One day when some workmen had been repairing a stove, he said, showing me a piece of sheet-iron:

"Give it to Gauguin, he will make a jewel of it."

It was a fact that Gauguin turned everything that fell into his hands—clay, wood, metal and so forth—into little marvels.

The dilapidated exterior of the house where he had his studio reminded one of a barn; but once inside, one might have been in a palace. The miracle was achieved by the paintings with which the artist had covered the walls. He had given the place of honor to the two painters he liked best: Cézanne and Van Gogh. Three Van Goghs hung above his bed: in the middle a landscape in a mauve tonality; to right and left, *Sunflowers*—the same, I believe, that were so much admired at the Degas sale—and opposite these, a still life by Cézanne, the very one that led Huysmans to talk of "lopsided fruit in drunken pottery."

Toward 1898, when Gauguin, then in Tahiti, was in such pressing need of money, his friend Chaudet offered this picture to all the collectors at six hundred francs. Nobody would have it. At last somebody decided to buy it, but demanded the frame, which was of carved wood, into the bargain. This painting passed later into the hands of Prince Wagram. At present it belongs to the Pellerin collection, and when an amateur who does not mind what price he pays, wants a still life of Cézanne's, he never fails to add, "It must be as good as the one which belonged to Gauguin."

Degas ranked Gauguin very high. He only reproached him for having gone to the ends of the earth to paint.

"Cannot one paint just as well in the Batignolles," he would say, "as in Tahiti?" But Gauguin was so little appreciated that one can understand the need he felt to escape from his contemporaries. Like Cézanne, Gauguin had at first imagined he would conquer their hostility if he could succeed in being admitted to the official *Salons*. Like Cézanne too he met with refusal after refusal at the hands of the juries. It was only through a trick on the part of a friend, the master-ceramist Chaplet, that he was enabled at last to see one of his works in the *Salon*. But under what conditions! Chaplet, who had fired one of Gauguin's earthenware pieces, the *Oviri*, in his kiln, exhibited it in his own showcase. But of course the artist's name was visible on the terracotta. This was still too much for the *officiels*. It was only upon Chaplet threatening to withdraw his own work that the *Oviri* was allowed to remain.

One can imagine the sort of reception Gauguin was likely to get from the curator of the Musée du Luxembourg, M. Bénédite, who considered his professional duty forbade him the faintest indulgence toward an art that had not obtained the hall-mark of the Institute. Gauguin was the victim on two occasions of M. Bénédite's scruples: at his return from Tahiti, when he offered him the finest of his paintings from his exhibition at Durand-Ruel's for his museum; and when, backed by Degas, he

Alexandre Berthier (1883–1918), Prince of Wagram, formed a celebrated collection of Impressionist and Post-Impressionist paintings. Auguste Pellerin (d. 1929), French industrialist who formed an important collection of modern art especially strong in works by Cézanne.

Ernest Chaplet (1835–1909), master ceramicist with whom Gauguin worked around 1886. According to Morice's 1919 biography, Gauguin's sculpture was refused altogether or removed from the exhibition after the opening.

COLORPLATE 80

In his position at the Musée Luxembourg, which was devoted to contemporary art, Léonce Bénédite (1859–1925) often found himself caught between the conservative faction, lead by Gérôme, and those who pressured him to include Impressionist works.

came to ask him for a commission for a fresco. Bénédite started up in amazement:

"But fresco-painting is done on a wall!"

Which in Bénédite's mind evidently signified that a wall cannot be stored away in the attic like a mere painting, when the artist's patron has disappeared.

Gauguin was to have his revenge—thirty years after his death, it is true. When a plaque commemorating the centenary of his birth was placed on the house where he was born, there were gathered together in his honor the Curator of the Museum of Fontainebleau, the President of the Municipal Council, on behalf of the City of Paris, M. Maurice Denis representing the Académie des Beaux-Arts; and lastly the Minister of National Education, M. de Monzie, who spoke in the name of the Government. Recalling the saying of a critic that Gauguin's art had everything against it—women, collectors, museums—M. de Monzie pointed out that to-day museums and collectors were proud to possess even the smallest of Gauguin's works, and that the women had begun to powder their faces with the ocher with which Gauguin painted the flesh of his Tahitians.

It is curious, in this connection, to note the difference of the reactions provoked in France and in other countries by anything connected with art. I remember that when a picture of Manet's was to be bought by the Mannheim Museum, even the workmen esteemed it a point of honor to contribute. With us an occasion of that sort leaves factory hands indifferent.

Alongside the birthplace of the painter of Tahiti, there was a milliner's shop, of which the two saleswomen, from the doorstep, seemed to be following the ceremony with lively curiosity. A customer, coming up, asked what was happening. The milliners looked at one another, and one

Gauguin's Birthplace, 52 Rue Notre-Dame-de-Lorette, Paris.

said, "We don't know . . . apparently it's a Minister speaking." Soon after, I listened to two peaceable *bourgeois*:

"Who was this Gauguin, exactly?"

"Didn't you hear? He was a sailor."

"Didn't they say he was a stockbroker too?"

"I don't know, that must have been a brother; they talked of another Gauguin too, who was a painter."

A comic incident marked the beginning of the ceremony. Among the people who had gathered round the little platform on which the orators spoke in succession, was a hawker, carrying a parcel of braces and suspenders on his shoulder. As he could see little of what was happening and could not hear the speeches, he thought there must be another hawker there, puffing his wares like himself. He inquired of his neighbors, "What's the mate gassing about? What's he trying to fob off on them?" and then, catching sight of the police, he made off himself without waiting to be told.

INDEX

385